MISSION
IN ACTION

There has been much discussion in recent years about being missional – about missional church, missional identity, missional living. In *Mission in Action*, Martin Salter provides a rich exploration of this theme by examining key biblical texts. The result is not only a robust exegetical foundation for missional ethics, but also a sharper definition of the missional task of God's people. Plus, en route, *Mission in Action* brims with exegetical insights. I warmly commend it to anyone interested in the theological underpinnings of missional church.
Dr Tim Chester, Crosslands faculty member

Martin Salter's *Mission in Action* makes an important contribution to the exciting developments in how we as church read the Bible in the light of God's mission. As the discussion around missional readings of the Bible continues to emerge, books such as this are essential for pushing the conversation deeper and in new ways. This thoughtful study will certainly stimulate the mind but, taken to heart, its message will also inspire the local church to action.
Tim Davy, Research Fellow, Redcliffe College, UK, and Co-director, Centre for the Study of Bible and Mission

'There is no biblical mission without biblical ethics.' That is a mantra I have repeated for many years in many countries. I am delighted to welcome Martin Salter's book, which expands and demonstrates my conviction from a wide swathe of the biblical canon itself. It should go without saying (for individuals and communities who profess Jesus as Lord) that God's people must live in ways that reflect God's character and obey God's commands, if they are to participate with any effectiveness in God's mission. But sometimes what goes without saying needs to be said – emphatically and clearly and with comprehensive biblical support. That is what this book does with persuasive thoroughness.
Christopher J. H. Wright, Langham Partnership; author of The Mission of God

MISSION
IN ACTION

A Biblical Description
of Missional Ethics

MARTIN C. SALTER

APOLLOS (an imprint of Inter-Varsity Press)
36 Causton Street, London SW1P 4ST, England
Email: ivp@ivpbooks.com
Website: www.ivpbooks.com

First published 2019

British Library Cataloguing in Publication Data
A catalogue record for this book is available from the British Library.

ISBN: 978-1-78359-780-2
eBook ISBN: 978-1-78359-781-9

Set in Monotype Garamond 11/13pt
Typeset in Great Britain by CRB Associates, Potterhanworth, Lincolnshire
Printed and bound in Great Britain by Ashford Colour Press Ltd, Gosport, Hampshire

To Grace Community Church,
who graciously gave me the time and space to study and write

CONTENTS

PREFACE

This book arose out of doctoral research into a relatively new area of missiological thinking called 'missional ethics'. Missional ethics is concerned with the ways in which the believing community's ethic is missional. Debates have raged about the relationship between mission and action for decades, and this research provided an opportunity to try to bring greater clarity to the debate.

In tackling the question I wanted to engage carefully with the primary sources – the Holy Scriptures – which are the formative authority for every generation of God's covenant people. Michael Barram describes an unfortunate 'rift between missiologists, on the one hand, and biblical scholars, on the other'.[1] He states:

> Generally speaking, missiologists have tended to disdain both the academic sterility
> of biblical scholarship and a perceived lack of pragmatic evangelical engagement
> by many of its practitioners. One senses a deep frustration among some missiological
> writers toward a discipline that is seen as having drained much of the life out of the
> gospel message. Not surprisingly, missiological research until relatively recently has
> tended either to ignore or to interact only superficially with serious biblical
> scholarship.[2]

---

1. Michael Barram, 'The Bible, Mission, and Social Location: Toward a Missional Hermeneutic', *Int* 61.1 (2007), p. 47.
2. Ibid.

Therefore in this book the majority of space is given to careful exegesis of key texts that pertain to the definition and description of 'missional ethics': Deuteronomy, the Major Prophets and Luke–Acts. The justification for choosing these texts is given in the methodology of chapter 1. Having examined these texts the final chapter seeks to provide some more practical conclusions and a definition of missional ethics – something which has thus far been assumed.

The scope and aims of this work are limited. Other texts could be examined, and other conclusions might be drawn. In the light of this I offer this as an initiatory word, rather than a final word, concerning the definition and description of missional ethics. It will remain for others to continue the conversation.

I would like to express my gratitude to a number of people who have made this book possible. First, I am thankful to my church family who permitted me the time to research and paid the financial costs involved. Second, I am hugely grateful to my doctoral supervisor, Dr Jamie Grant, whose patient guidance and supervision made the process a pleasure. I am also grateful for the advice and guidance of Hector Morrison and Dr Timothy Davy, who encouraged me to seek publication. Third, I am thankful to my family, whose constant support and encouragement has made my research and writing possible and enjoyable. Fourth, I am grateful to the friends who read and commented on various drafts of this work. Fifth, I am thankful for the gracious support, encouragement and patience of Phil Duce and the editorial team who have enabled the publishing of this work to become a reality. Finally I am thankful to God whose own *missio Dei* reached me in grace and mercy, and impassioned and equipped me to play a small part in furthering the kingdom.

ABBREVIATIONS

1 En.	*1 Enoch*
2 En.	*2 Enoch*
1QS	*Serek hayyaḥad* (Rule of the Community) from Qumran Cave 1
11Q19	*Temple Scroll* from Qumran Cave 11
11QMelch	*Melchizedek Scroll*
AARSR	American Academy of Religion Studies in Religion
AASFDHL	Annales Academiae Scientiarum Fennicae. Dissertationes Humanarum Litterarum
AB	Anchor Bible
ABD	David Noel Freedman (ed.), *The Anchor Bible Dictionary*, 6 vols. (New York: Doubleday, 1992)
AnBib	Analecta biblica
ANE	ancient Near East(ern)
ANET	James B. Pritchard, *Ancient Near Eastern Texts Relating to the Old Testament* (Princeton: Princeton University Press, 1950)
ANTC	Abingdon New Testament Commentaries
AOAT	Alter Orient und Altes Testament
AOTC	Apollos Old Testament Commentary
ArBib	The Aramaic Bible
ATR	*Anglican Theological Review*
AUS	American University Studies
b. Šabb.	Babylonian Talmud, *Šabbat*
b. Sanh.	Babylonian Talmud, *Sanhedrin*

BBR	*Bulletin for Biblical Research*
BBRSup	Bulletin for Biblical Research Supplements
BDAG	Walter Bauer, Frederick W. Danker, W. F. Arndt and F. W. Gingrich, *Greek–English Lexicon of the New Testament and Other Early Christian Literature*, 3rd edn (Chicago: University of Chicago Press, 2000)
BECNT	Baker Exegetical Commentary on the New Testament
BETL	Bibliotheca ephemeridum theologicarum lovaniensium
BI	*Biblical Interpretation*
Bib	*Biblica*
BIS	Biblical Interpretation Series
BJS	Brown Judaic Studies
BLS	Bible and Literature Studies
BMSEC	Baylor-Mohr Siebeck Studies in Early Christianity
BNTC	Black's New Testament Commentaries
BSac	*Bibliotheca sacra*
BST	The Bible Speaks Today
BTB	*Biblical Theology Bulletin*
BTCB	Brazos Theological Commentary on the Bible
BZAW	Beihefte zur Zeitschrift für die alttestamentliche Wissenschaft
BZNW	Beihefte zur Zeitschrift für die neutestamentliche Wissenschaft
CBOTS	Coniectanea Biblical Old Testament Series
CBQ	*Catholic Biblical Quarterly*
CCT	Contours of Christian Theology Series
CD	Cairo Damascus (Document)
CE	The Laws of Eshnunna
CH	The Code of Hammurabi
CL	Lipit-Ishtar Lawcode
COQG	Christian Origins and the Question of God
CoS	William W. Hallo (ed.), *The Context of Scripture* (Leiden: Brill, 2003)
CTJ	*Calvin Theological Journal*
CU	The Laws of Ur-Nammu
DC	The Deuteronomic Code
Dtr/Dtn	The Deuteronomistic History/Deuteronomist
EBC	Expositor's Bible Commentary
ECL	Early Christianity and its Literature
ECNT	Exegetical Commentary on the New Testament
EKK	Evangelisch-katholischer Kommentar zum Neuen Testament
EQ	*Evangelical Quarterly*

ET	*Expository Times*
FRLANT	Forschungen zur Religion und Literatur des Alten und Neuen Testaments
FZAT	Forschungen zum Alten Testament
GKC	E. Kautzsch (ed.), A. E. Cowley (tr.), *Gesenius' Hebrew Grammar* (Mineola: Dover, 2006)
HALOT	L. Koehler and W. Baumgartner, *The Hebrew and Aramaic Lexicon of the Old Testament*, 5 vols. (Leiden: Brill, 1994–2000)
HAR	*Hebrew Annual Review*
HBM	Hebrew Bible Monographs
HL	The Hittite Laws
HSMS	Harvard Semitic Monograph Series
HSS	Harvard Semitic Studies
HTKAT	Herders Theologischer Kommentar zum Alten Testament
HTR	*Harvard Theological Review*
HUCA	*Hebrew Union College Annual*
IBS	*Irish Biblical Studies*
ICC	International Critical Commentary
IJFM	*International Journal of Frontier Missiology*
Int	Interpretation
Int	*Interpretation: A Journal of Bible and Theology*
IRM	*International Review of Mission*
ITC	International Theological Commentary
JAAR	*Journal of the American Academy of Religion*
JAS	*Journal of Anglican Studies*
JBL	*Journal of Biblical Literature*
JDDS	Jian Dao Dissertation Series
JETS	*Journal of the Evangelical Theological Society*
JJS	*Journal of Jewish Studies*
JM	P. Joüon and T. Muraoka, *A Grammar of Biblical Hebrew* (Rome: Editrice Pontifico Istituto Biblico, 2006)
JNES	*Journal of Near Eastern Studies*
JNSL	*Journal of Northwest Semitic Languages*
JPT	*Journal of Pentecostal Theology*
JPTSup	Journal of Pentecostal Theology: Supplement Series
JSJSup	Journal for the Study of Judaism: Supplement Series
JSNT	*Journal for the Study of the New Testament*
JSNTSup	Journal for the Study of the New Testament: Supplement Series
JSOT	*Journal for the Study of the Old Testament*

JSOTSup	Journal for the Study of the Old Testament: Supplement Series
JSS	*Journal of Semitic Studies*
JTISup	Journal of Theological Interpretation Supplements
JTS	*Journal of Theological Studies*
Jub.	*Jubilees*
LBT	Library of Biblical Theology
LCBI	Literary Currents in Biblical Interpretation
LCC	Library of Christian Classics
LCL	Loeb Classical Library
LHB/OTS	Library of Hebrew Bible/Old Testament Studies
LICC	London Institute for Contemporary Christianity
LNTS	Library of New Testament Studies
LXX	Septuagint
m. Bab. Qam.	Mishnah, *Baba Qamma*
m. Šeb.	Mishnah, *Šebi'it*
MAL	The Middle-Assyrian Laws
MT	Masoretic Text
NAC	New American Commentary
NBBC	New Beacon Bible Commentary
NBD	I. H. Marshall, A. R. Millard, J. I. Packer and D. J. Wiseman (eds.), *Bible Dictionary* (Leicester: Inter-Varsity Press, 1996)
NBL	The Neo-Babylonian Laws
NCB	New Century Bible
NIB	New Interpreter's Bible
NIBC	New International Biblical Commentary
NICNT	New International Commentary on the New Testament
NICOT	New International Commentary on the Old Testament
NIDOTTE	Willem A. Van Gemeren (ed.), *New International Dictionary of Old Testament Theology and Exegesis*, 5 vols. (Grand Rapids: Zondervan, 2008)
NIGTC	New International Greek Testament Commentary
NIVAC	New International Version Application Commentary
NovTSup	Supplements to Novum Testamentum
NSBT	New Studies in Biblical Theology
NT	New Testament
NTC	New Testament Commentaries
NTL	New Testament Library
NTM	New Testament Monographs
NTS	*New Testament Studies*
OBT	Overtures to Biblical Theology

OT	Old Testament
OTE	*Old Testament Essays*
OTL	Old Testament Library
OTM	Oxford Theological Monographs
OTT	Old Testament Theology
PBC	The People's Bible Commentary
PCNT	Paideia Commentaries on the New Testament
PNTC	Pillar New Testament Commentary
PRSt	*Perspectives in Religious Studies*
QR	*Quarterly Review*
RB	*Revue biblique*
RQ	*Restoration Quarterly*
SABH	Studies in American Biblical Hermeneutics
SBAB	Stuttgarter biblische Aufsatzbände
SBB	Stuttgarter biblische Beiträge
SBG	Studies in Biblical Greek
SBLDS	Society of Biblical Literature Dissertation Series
SBLMS	Society of Biblical Literature Monograph Series
SBLSS	Society of Biblical Literature Semeia Studies
SBT	Studies in Biblical Theology
SHBC	Smyth & Helwys Bible Commentary
SJLA	Studies in Judaism in Late Antiquity
SNTSMS	Society for New Testament Studies Monograph Series
SNTU	Studien zum Neuen Testament und seiner Umwelt
SP	Sacra pagina
ST	*Studia theologica*
SubBi	Subsidia biblica
SWJT	*Southwestern Journal of Theology*
T. Ben.	*Testament of Benjamin*
T. Dan	*Testament of Dan*
T. Iss.	*Testament of Issachar*
T. Mos.	*Testament of Moses*
TDNT	Gerhard Kittel and Gerhard Friedrich (eds.), Geoffrey W. Bromiley (tr.), *Theological Dictionary of the New Testament*, 10 vols. (Grand Rapids: Eerdmans, 1964–76)
Them	*Themelios*
TDOT	Johannes Botterweck, Helmer Ringgren and Heinz-Josef Fabry (eds.), *Theological Dictionary of the Old Testament*, 15 vols. (Grand Rapids: Eerdmans, 1974–2006)
ThLZ	*Theologische Literaturzeitung*

TNTC	Tyndale New Testament Commentaries
TOTC	Tyndale Old Testament Commentaries
TynB	*Tyndale Bulletin*
VE	*Vox evangelica*
VT	*Vetus Testamentum*
VTSup	Supplements to *Vetus Testamentum*
WBC	Word Biblical Commentary
WTJ	*Westminster Theological Journal*
WUNT	Wissenschaftliche Untersuchungen zum Neuen Testament
WW	*Word and World*
ZAR	*Zeitschrift für altorientalische und biblische Rechtsgeschichte*
ZAW	*Zeitschrift für die alttestamentliche Wissenschaft*
ZNW	*Zeitschrift für die neuetestamentliche Wissenschaft*

INTRODUCTION

Missional ethics is concerned with the ways in which the believing community's behaviour – their ethic – is missional. The term 'missional ethics' is relatively recent, first appearing in an article by M. Douglas Meeks in 2001.[1] Subsequently the term has been used by a number of scholars, missiologists in particular.[2] Although the term 'missional ethics' is relatively recent, the concept has been evolving steadily over the course of the last century. Following the first World Missionary Conference (WMC) in Edinburgh, 1910, discussion has developed in considering the missional roles that the church and social engagement play. As Stephen Neill observed, 'The WMC at Edinburgh in 1910 marked the beginning of the modern ecumenical

---

1. 'Being Human in the Market Society', *QR* 21.3 (2001), pp. 254–265. The phrase 'missional ethics' appears in a footnote to denote the life and ethos of the church.

2. Christopher J. H. Wright, *The Mission of God: Unlocking the Bible's Grand Narrative* (Downers Grove: InterVarsity Press, 2006); Darrell L. Guder, *Called to Witness: Doing Missional Theology* (Grand Rapids: Eerdmans, 2015); C. J. P Niemandt, 'Trends in Missional Ecclesiology', *HTS Theological Studies/Teologiese Studies* 68.1 (2012), <www.hts.org.za/index.php/HTS/article/viewFile/1198/2353>, accessed 10 December 2012; Andy Draycott and Jonathan Rowe (eds.), *Living Witness: Explorations in Missional Ethics* (Nottingham: Apollos, 2012).

movement.'[3] This was an attempt to redress the previous separation of missions and the church.[4]

Renewed zeal led to the formation of a number of councils and movements. Following Edinburgh 1910 the International Missionary Council (IMC) was formed in 1921, and two other movements grew out of Edinburgh 1910 (Faith and Order and Life and Work). These two latter movements combined in 1948 to form the World Council of Churches (WCC). Out of these groups a host of missionary gatherings occurred in the following years.[5] Two World Wars and the rise of atheistic communism meant that optimism and zeal gave way to a quieter, humbler, more modest expression of mission.[6] There was a growing consensus that church and mission should not be separated, but belonged together. By the WCC assembly in New Delhi, 1961, the IMC had been incorporated into the WCC. The point being made was clear – unity, church and mission belong together.[7]

This new direction in missional theology recognized the prevenient work of God such that the church is taken up into the *missio Dei*. As missiologist David Bosch would later affirm, 'the *missio Dei* institutes the *missio ecclesiae*'.[8] The church was not the sender, but the sent. There was recognition that the whole life of the church, not just the message of the church, was a central part of the church's mission at home and abroad. The ecumenical movement grew in number and influence with the newfound sense of the importance of unity for mission. Goheen notes the development of thought that was occurring throughout the twentieth century as old dualisms were being rejected: mission versus church;

---

3. Stephen Neill, *A History of Christian Missions*, rev. edn (Harmondsworth: Penguin, 1986), p. 410.

4. Ibid., p. 381.

5. After Edinburgh 1910 World Missionary Conferences were held in Jerusalem (1928) and Tambaram (1938). IMC gatherings occurred in Whitby (1947) and Willingen (1952). The first World Council of Churches assembly occurred in 1948, and the IMC and WCC merged at the subsequent assembly in New Delhi, 1961. See Willem Adolf Visser t'Hooft, 'The Genesis of the World Council of Churches', in *A History of the Ecumenical Movement 1517–1968*, 2 vols. (London: SPCK, 1993), vol. 1, pp. 695–724.

6. Scott W. Sunquist, *Understanding Christian Mission: Participation in Suffering and Glory* (Grand Rapids: Baker Academic, 2013), p. 120.

7. David J. Bosch, *Transforming Mission: Paradigm Shifts in Theology of Mission* (Maryknoll: Orbis, 1991), p. 470.

8. Ibid., p. 379.

mission as preaching versus social action; and salvation as spiritual versus total. In their place more 'holistic', 'integral' or 'comprehensive' approaches were advocated. The result was profitable in that the old dualisms were unscriptural, but there was also confusion as to the roles and relationships in these new marriages.[9] Additionally, with the formation and growth of the WCC, ecumenicals and evangelicals became increasingly divided, particularly over the nature of mission, and the relationship between evangelism and action.[10]

The first International Congress on World Evangelization met in Lausanne, Switzerland, in July, 1974. Lausanne was in large measure a reaction against the perceived drift seen in the IMC and WCC away from the priority of evangelism in favour of an ecumenical project.[11] In the light of such concerns Lausanne sought to redress the perceived errors and reassert the primacy of evangelism over social action and ecumenical projects. Lausanne did not reject holistic mission, but rather sought to redress the perceived imbalance of WCC ecumenism.[12] Lausanne was seen as a 'rallying point for those who feared that the WCC was failing to deliver an explicit and convincing commitment to evangelism'.[13]

In Billy Graham's opening address he expressed the feeling that since Edinburgh 1910 the church had become distracted and lost its zeal for the primary task of world evangelization. Another key contributor to the conference was John Stott who, like Graham, recognized the importance of social action but viewed evangelism as primary.[14] While Lausanne affirmed the importance of ethics to mission, the committee also held to the primacy of proclamation, and made little progress on the missional role or function of ethics.

The Second Lausanne Congress occurred in Manila in 1989. Manila gave more space to the social implications of mission. For example, 'The biblical gospel has inescapable social implications. True mission should always be incarnational.'[15]

---

9. Michael W. Goheen, *Introducing Christian Mission Today: Scripture, History and Issues* (Downers Grove: InterVarsity Press, 2014), p. 160.

10. Ibid., p. 165.

11. Ibid., p. 168.

12. Kenneth R. Ross and David A. Kerr, 'The Commissions After a Century', in *Edinburgh 2010: Missions Then and Now* (Oxford: Regnum, 2009), p. 313.

13. Ibid., p. 315.

14. John Stott and Christopher J. H. Wright, *Christian Mission in the Modern World* (Nottingham: Inter-Varsity Press, 2015), pp. 27, 58.

15. 'The Manila Manifesto', 1989, para. 4, <www.lausanne.org/content/manifesto/the-manila-manifesto>, accessed 4 July 2016.

Nothing commends the gospel more eloquently than a transformed life, and nothing brings it into disrepute so much as personal inconsistency. We are charged to behave in a manner that is worthy of the gospel of Christ, and even to 'adorn' it, enhancing its beauty by holy lives . . . Our inconsistency deprives our witness of credibility.[16]

'The Manila Manifesto' displays a subtle movement towards greater recognition of the missional importance of the life of the believing community.

The Third Lausanne Congress met in Cape Town in 2010. The resulting 'Cape Town Commitment' represented a further shift in modern missiological thinking. Social responsibility was no longer seen as a necessary preliminary or distinct partner, but the language of integral mission was used to describe the relationship between evangelism and sociopolitical involvement.[17] 'The Cape Town Commitment' states:

All our mission must therefore reflect the integration of evangelism and committed engagement in the world . . . evangelism and socio-political involvement are both part of our Christian duty. For both are necessary expressions of our doctrines of God and humankind, our love for our neighbour and our obedience to Jesus Christ . . . Integral mission is the proclamation and demonstration of the gospel . . . in integral mission our proclamation has social consequences as we call people to love and repentance in all areas of life. And our social involvement has evangelistic consequences as we bear witness to the transforming grace of Jesus Christ.[18]

Later in the same document we find the following:

Our calling is to live and serve among people of other faiths in a way that is so saturated with the fragrance of God's grace that they smell Christ, that they come to taste and see that God is good. By such embodied love, we are to make the gospel attractive in every cultural and religious setting. When Christians love people of other faiths through lives of love and acts of service, they embody the transforming grace of God.[19]

---

16. Ibid., para. 7.

17. The language of integral mission had appeared previously in 'The Micah Declaration' of 2001, <www.micahnetwork.org/sites/default/files/doc/page/mn_integral_mission_declaration_en.pdf>, accessed 4 July 2016.

18. 'The Cape Town Commitment', 2010, I.10.B, <www.lausanne.org/content/ctc/ctcommitment>, accessed 4 July 2016.

19. Ibid., IIC. 3.

Here is a description which is drawing nearer to subsequent notions of missional ethics. Ethics is not the partner or pathway to evangelism, but itself can 'bear witness to the transforming grace of Jesus Christ'.[20] A missional ethic is still couched in terms of attraction and embodiment, and as something with 'evangelistic consequences', but the two things (word and deed) are being brought together into an ever-closer union. The missiological development through Lausanne (1974), Manila (1989) and Cape Town (2010) demonstrates an increasing sensitivity to the importance of ethics and mission as an integrated whole.

A number of scholars from the 1960s onwards have made significant contributions to the construction of a more holistic missiology. Many of these have sought to bring together the best insights of both the ecumenical and evangelical tradition in a synthesis of mission as both word and deed.

A writer whose work has proved foundational in twentieth-century missiology is Lesslie Newbigin. He, like others who have followed him, roots mission in the *missio Dei* – the idea that the Father sends the Son, the Father and Son send the Spirit, and the Son and the Spirit send the church. The church does not have a mission: it is rather taken up into the wider mission of God.

Newbigin is critical of the earlier views of mission which separated the mission from the church. In an essay for the IMC he advocated a more ecclesiocentric view of mission. He states, 'it has become customary to speak of fellowship, service and witness as the three dimensions of the church's mission. I believe that careful reflection will show that this is a mistake.'[21] He continues:

> The basic reality is the creation of a new being through the presence of the Holy Spirit. This new being is the common life (koinonia) in the Church. It is out of this new creation that both evangelism and service spring . . . This new reality – namely the active presence of the Holy Spirit among men – is the primary witness.[22]

In later work Newbigin describes the importance of the church's *being* to the church's witness. In *Truth to Tell* he says, 'the most important contribution which the Church can make to a new social order is to be itself a new social order'.[23]

---

20. Ibid.

21. Lesslie Newbigin, *One Body, One Gospel, One World: The Christian Mission Today* (London: IMC, 1958), p. 20.

22. Ibid.

23. Lesslie Newbigin, *Truth to Tell: The Gospel as Public Truth* (Grand Rapids: Eerdmans, 1991), p. 85.

The surrounding culture has a missional encounter when it observes 'the spontaneous overflow of a community of praise ... [and] the radiance of a supernatural reality'.[24]

Newbigin argued that the church in the power of the Spirit is not so much the *agent* of mission as the *locus* of mission:

> The Church is not the source of the witness; rather it is the locus of witness. The light cast by the first rays of the morning sun shining on the face of a company of travellers will be evidence that a new day is coming. The travellers are not the source of that witness but only the locus of it.[25]

Following Newbigin, David Bosch's work *Transforming Mission* has also proved to be influential in shaping the missiological conversation. Bosch argues that Christianity is by its very nature missionary or else it denies its *raison d'être*.[26] He, like Newbigin, is therefore nervous about defining mission too narrowly. He goes so far as to say, 'Ultimately, mission remains undefinable ... The most we can hope for is to formulate some *approximations* of what mission is all about.'[27] He distinguishes, like others, between the mission of God and 'missions', with the latter referring to particular contexts and needs as a subset of, and participation in, the wider *missio Dei*.[28] Mission for Bosch is 'as coherent, broad, and deep as the need and exigencies of human life'.[29] Bosch, following Newbigin, situates missiology primarily in the Trinity, and secondarily within the disciplines of ecclesiology and soteriology:

> The classical doctrine of the *missio Dei* as God the Father sending the Son, and God the Father and Son sending the Spirit [is] expanded to include yet another 'movement': Father, Son and Holy Spirit sending the church into the world.[30]

Bosch traces the history of various missionary paradigms including the medieval, the Reformation, the Enlightenment, the postmodern and the ecumenical. Having

---

24. Lesslie Newbigin, *Foolishness to the Greeks: The Gospel and Western Culture* (London: SPCK, 1986), p. 149.

25. Lesslie Newbigin, *The Gospel in a Pluralist Society* (London: SPCK, 1989), p. 120.

26. Bosch, *Transforming Mission*, p. 9.

27. Ibid. Emphasis original.

28. Ibid., p. 10.

29. Ibid.

30. Ibid., p. 390.

traced the development in thought through the paradigms, he offers his own conclusions regarding contemporary mission that include an emphasis on what I am terming 'missional ethics'. Bosch states, 'Mission is a multifaceted ministry, in respect of witness, service, justice, healing, reconciliation, liberation, peace, evangelism, fellowship, church planting, contextualization, and much more.'[31]

Perhaps the most influential recent contributor to the missio-ethical conversation is Christopher Wright. Building on the work of Newbigin and Bosch he defines mission as 'our committed participation as God's people, at God's invitation and command, in God's own mission within the history of God's world for the redemption of God's creation'.[32] Wright argues that, since God is a missionary God, the Bible is a product and agent of God's mission.[33] The existence of Scripture itself is evidence that God is a missionary. He uses this theocentric world view to demonstrate that God has a mission, which leads to humanity with a mission, Israel with a mission, Jesus with a mission and the church with a mission.[34] For Wright, election is for the purpose of bringing blessing to the nations, and since election, in his view, is transformative, there can be 'no biblical mission without biblical ethics'.[35] Wright locates missional ethics in the doctrines of election, redemption, covenant and church.[36] Thus, while Wright utilizes Newbigin's Trinitarian framework, he also develops the narratival approach in his biblical exposition of mission.

Thus far the only book-length treatment devoted to 'missional ethics' is *Living Witness: Explorations in Missional Ethics*, edited by Draycott and Rowe. Released in 2012, the book contains a number of chapters exploring the theme of missional ethics in relation to the Trinity, creation, church, preaching, friendship, politics, servanthood, economics and immigration. Many of the chapters are, as the subtitle suggests, exploratory in nature. So far the meaning of missional ethics has been assumed rather than defined. The most explicit attempt to define missional ethics is in Rowe's opening chapter, 'What Is Missional Ethics?' The opening lines state:

> Because God calls his people to be a living witness to him, morality is mission.
> Conversely, immorality is 'anti-mission', a failure to give true testimony or witness . . .

---

31. Ibid., p. 524.
32. Wright, *Mission of God*, p. 23.
33. Ibid., pp. 48–49.
34. Ibid., pp. 62–68.
35. Ibid., p. 358.
36. Ibid., pp. 358–392.

the whole life of the people of God, not only verbal proclamation, testifies to the church's faith – or lack of faith – in her Lord.[37]

Rowe summarizes the scope of missional ethics as being 'as wide as human life itself'.[38] He argues that it can only ever be shaped in outline: 'we cannot completely describe the form of missional ethics. In a fundamental sense, missional ethics is only an outline that needs to be filled in by believers in their own time and place.'[39] He continues, missional ethics 'never "arrives," is never definitive, but is always in some sense provisional even though we know the direction in which we wish to travel'.[40] In Rowe's outline of missional ethics he concludes:

> It is not possible, therefore, to prescribe particular shapes to the moral or missional life applicable to all. We may only say that the idea of missional ethics encourages Christian believers to take seriously their specific calling and their place in the moral community called to witness to our Lord.[41]

The problem *in nuce* is a lack of definition with regard to missional ethics, a problem that is also present in missiology more broadly. Bosch describes mission as being 'as coherent, broad, and deep as the need and exigencies of human life'.[42] Rowe follows Bosch in adopting a deliberately broad and provisional outline of missional ethics.[43] Wright, responding to the accusation 'if everything is mission, nothing is mission', states, 'It would seem more biblical to say "If everything is mission . . . everything is mission."'[44] Neill's famous statement regarding mission could be applied to missional ethics – if everything is missional ethics, nothing is missional ethics.[45]

---

37. Jonathan Rowe, 'What Is Missional Ethics?', in Andy Draycott and Jonathan Rowe (eds.), *Living Witness: Explorations in Missional Ethics* (Nottingham: Apollos, 2012), p. 13.
38. Ibid., p. 17.
39. Ibid., p. 24.
40. Ibid., p. 25.
41. Ibid., p. 26.
42. Bosch, *Transforming Mission*, p. 10.
43. Rowe, 'What Is Missional Ethics?', pp. 13–31.
44. Christopher J. H. Wright, *The Mission of God's People: A Biblical Theology of the Church's Mission* (Grand Rapids: Zondervan, 2010), p. 26.
45. Neill's original statement was, 'if everything is mission, nothing is mission'. Stephen Neill, *Creative Tension* (London: Edinburgh House, 1959), p. 81.

A broad definition, it will be argued, is biblically defensible, yet greater definitional precision is both desirable and possible. This book will seek to provide a definition of missional ethics arising from the exegesis of key biblical texts. Such a definition will generate further discussion and fresh insights into this important missiological theme.

The following chapter will outline the methodological approach and the justification for the approach taken. In essence, this book will adopt a canonical approach tracing the development of the theme through significant biblical texts. Exegetical chapters will then work through pertinent texts, namely Deuteronomy, the Major Prophets and Luke–Acts. The methodology in chapter 1 will provide the justification for the choice of these particular texts. Chapter 2 will explore Deuteronomy in its ANE context and note the way in which missional ethics is a central theme. Deuteronomy will also provide the fundamental components for the definition of missional ethics. Chapter 3 will examine the Major Prophets, noting both the failure of and hope for Israel's missio-ethical vocation. Chapter 4 will examine Luke–Acts and note the fulfilment of the narrative trajectory begun in Deuteronomy, as the missio-ethical ideals are taught and embodied in the life of Jesus and the early church. Finally, conclusions will be drawn situating the findings of the investigation in the contemporary missiological debates, before offering an exegetical definition of missional ethics. The hope is that this work will enable others to continue the dialogue regarding the nature, form and situational application of missional ethics. Mission lies at the heart of many confessional Christian expressions and identities. It is therefore of both theoretical and practical importance to further the ongoing dialogue regarding the nature and form of missional engagement.

1. A METHODOLOGY FOR THE STUDY OF MISSIONAL ETHICS

Introduction

In a recent study of missional ethics Rowe summarizes the scope of missional ethics as being 'as wide as human life itself'.[1] Such a broad summary invites further enquiry in an effort to bring increased precision to the concept. This book is an attempt to move the discussion forward by offering an exegetical definition of missional ethics. A crucial question in any thematic enquiry concerns the most appropriate methodology for such an exploration.

The hermeneutical method

The method of exploration will work from four proposals which will be developed below. In sum they are as follows: First, the canonical text, as the authoritative text for the faith community, is the appropriate foundation for the study of missional ethics. Second, an appreciation of the narrative trajectory

---

1. Jonathan Rowe, 'What Is Missional Ethics?', in Andy Draycott and Jonathan Rowe (eds.), *Living Witness: Explorations in Missional Ethics* (Nottingham: Apollos, 2012), p. 17.

of that text can lead to a profitable understanding of the theme. Third, a missional hermeneutic reveals the centrality of 'mission' as it runs through the canon. Fourth, an appreciation of performative hermeneutics discloses how texts serve to shape the community. In short, an approach that utilizes, and is sensitive to, the authority, shape, emphases and intent of the canon is well placed to investigate the theme. Each of these four proposals will now be developed.

A canonical approach

The first element in this methodology proposes that the final form of the canon is the best context for enquiry. This is not to say that questions of historical criticism are unimportant, but rather, as will be argued here, the final form is more suited to this investigation.

Thiselton notes that the area of canonical approach is controversial.[2] He cites Barr as saying, 'In biblical times the books were separate individual scrolls. A "Bible" was not a volume one could hold in the hand . . . The boundary [of] . . . what was Scripture . . . was thus more difficult to indicate.'[3] Thus for Barr it is unreasonable to expect to find a united witness across different texts in the exploration of any given theme. However, an increasing number of contemporary scholars are advocating a canonical approach as the context for sound theological method.[4] Two influential scholars in this area are James Sanders and Brevard Childs.

Sanders advocates the discipline he terms 'canonical criticism'. He does not deny the value of the traditional higher and lower criticisms, but argues that the texts can only be fully understood when we consider not just their origin and structure, but also their *function* and *authority* in the believing communities that shaped them.[5] Sanders contends that all scholarship approaches the text with

---

2. Anthony C. Thiselton, 'Canon, Community and Theological Construction', in *Canon and Biblical Interpretation*, Scripture and Hermeneutics 7 (Milton Keynes: Paternoster, 2006), p. 2.

3. James Barr, *Holy Scripture: Canon, Authority, Criticism* (Oxford: Oxford University Press, 1983), p. 57.

4. For example, see Charles J. Scalise, *Hermeneutics as Theological Prolegomena: A Canonical Approach*, SABH 8 (Macon: Mercer University Press, 1994); Christopher R. Seitz, 'The Canonical Approach and Theological Interpretation', in *Canon and Biblical Interpretation* (Milton Keynes: Paternoster, 2006), pp. 58–110; Robert W. Wall, 'The Canonical View', in *Biblical Hermeneutics: Five Views* (Downers Grove: InterVarsity Press, 2012), pp. 111–130.

5. James A. Sanders, *Torah and Canon* (Philadelphia: Fortress, 1972), p. xx.

certain values and presuppositions. For some of the higher critics the notion of the text's authority lies outside the realm of proper enquiry, since it is concerned with matters of faith. Sanders replies that 'the sociology of knowledge, however, has now brought us to recognise that scholars themselves have systems of values of which they should be fully conscious'.[6] The enquirer needs to be aware of these values and place them alongside the text. The problem of presuppositions affects all enquiry, and the solution is to be clear about the presuppositions present.

Sanders offers three observations regarding the 'sacred text'. First, the canon of Scripture emerged out of the faith communities of Israel, early Judaism and the early church seeking to answer the questions 'Who are we?' and 'What are we to do?' Second, the community shaped the texts in their common cultic and cultural life. Third, the canon's proper function is continued dialogue with the heirs of those early communities as they continue to try to answer those first two questions: 'Who are we?' and 'What are we to do?'[7] For Sanders an appreciation of the communities' shaping of the texts is critical to the hermeneutical approach of modern exegetes. The enquirer cannot isolate the texts from the communities of faith that canonized them. Canonical criticism is important because it 'focuses on the *function* of authoritative traditions in the believing communities, early or late'.[8] A dynamic dialectic is operative in the shaping of texts, traditions and communities. To focus piecemeal on the parts is to miss the significance of the whole.[9] The task of hermeneutics is to span the gap between the historical-critical method, and the ongoing communal reception and application of the texts.[10] To focus on the former alone is to miss something of the *telos* of the text; canonical criticism appreciates the value of these disciplines but proceeds to consider the *function* of the texts within and upon the communities that received and shaped them.[11]

While Sanders's interest is in the *function* of the text for the community, Childs's interest is primarily in the *place* from which the text is read. Childs suggests that although Sanders argues for a theocentric approach, he permits too much influence to the needs of each successive community. Too much

---

6. James A. Sanders, *Canon and Community: A Guide to Canonical Criticism*, repr. (Eugene: Wipf & Stock, 2000), p. 21.

7. James A. Sanders, *From Sacred Story to Sacred Text* (Philadelphia: Fortress, 1987), p. 63.

8. Sanders, *Canon and Community*, p. 24. Emphasis original.

9. Thiselton, 'Canon', p. 5.

10. Sanders, *From Sacred Story*, p. 65.

11. Sanders, *Canon and Community*, p. 45.

power is attributed to the believing community in adapting the texts for their own current needs. In discussing Sanders's approach Childs states:

> It is an anthropocentric, sociological interpretation of canon . . . [a] history-of-religions reading of its role. In contrast, according to the Old Testament pattern (Deut. 31:9–13) the formation of a written authoritative corpus was theocentric in orientation. It identified the will of God for successive generations so that they might live in accordance with the enduring commands of God expressed in Torah. It is not simply a flexible paradigm without an established content.[12]

Childs also declares his unhappiness with Sanders's term 'canonical-criticism', as it conveys the notion of another technique that takes its place alongside the other 'criticisms'. Instead he suggests a canonical 'approach' that establishes a *place* from which the Bible is read as sacred scripture.[13] Childs's canonical approach challenges the exegete to 'look closely at the biblical text in its received form and then critically discern its function for a community of faith'.[14]

Childs, like Sanders, argues that the 'practice of dividing the biblical passages into their various historical stages (a "diachronic approach") and developments often destroyed the "synchronic" dimensions of the text in which it was viewed altogether as a whole'.[15] In response Childs, like Sanders, suggests that 'the canon of the Christian church is the most appropriate context from which to do Biblical Theology'.[16] He continues, 'The status of canonicity is not an objectively demonstrable claim but a statement of Christian belief.'[17] Childs recognizes that value systems are universal and is unembarrassed about his own faith-based approach to the question of methodology.[18] Childs, like

---

12. Brevard S. Childs, 'The Canon in Recent Biblical Studies: Reflections on an Era', in *Canon and Biblical Interpretation* (Milton Keynes: Paternoster, 2006), p. 39.

13. Brevard S. Childs, *Introduction to the Old Testament as Scripture* (London: SCM, 1979), p. 82.

14. Ibid., p. 83.

15. Lee M. McDonald, *The Formation of the Christian Biblical Canon* (Peabody: Hendrickson, 1995), p. 301.

16. Brevard S. Childs, *Biblical Theology in Crisis* (Philadelphia: Westminster, 1970), p. 99.

17. Ibid.

18. Schröter, commenting on the historical-critical method, says, 'If, however, reference is made to the dependence of every construction upon the understanding of reality that is guiding in each case and the always-necessary constructive element of

Sanders, is demonstrating an awareness of the forces at work in the reception of the text by the ancient community. And Childs, like Sanders, is aware that interpretation needs to consider *function*. Childs's interest is in the formative and transformative impact of the texts on the communities that received them. The theological task 'has as its proper context the canonical scriptures of the Christian church, not because only this literature influenced its history, but because of the peculiar reception of this corpus by a community of faith and practise'.[19] He argues that canonical consciousness lies deep within the formation of the corpus.[20] As Thiselton notes, the church 'did not *"make"* the canon, but through its life and identity *recognized* the formative impact of divine revelation through the call of the "prophets and apostles" as a whole'.[21] Similarly Hahn states, 'The Scriptures themselves are regarded by the biblical authors as the divinely inspired testament to the divine economy as it has unfolded throughout history.'[22]

Any theological exploration, including the exploration of missional ethics, must engage with the peculiarly authoritative corpus of Scripture in its received form. To ignore this crucial feature of the biblical texts would be to miss the meaning and significance of them. Childs does not deny the significance of the canonical process which formed the text, but the primary interest of the canonical approach is the theological reflection on 'the text as it has been received and shaped'.[23] He goes on to state, 'At the heart of the canonical proposal is the conviction that the divine revelation of the Old

---

(note 18 *cont.*) historical work is brought into play, then through this the research of historical criticism is itself restricted epistemologically.' Jens Schröter, *From Jesus to the New Testament: Early Christian Theology and the Origin of the New Testament Canon*, tr. Wayne Coppins, BMSEC (Waco: Baylor University Press, 2013), p. 31. He thus argues for a Christian hermeneutics on the basis that such an approach 'cannot prove that the view of history that is thereby brought to light is true; it can, however, express the fact that there have been and still are human beings for whom it represents the foundation of their life and actions' (p. 48).

19. Brevard S. Childs, *Biblical Theology: A Proposal* (Minneapolis: Fortress, 2002), p. 11.

20. Ibid., p. 39.

21. Thiselton, 'Canon', p. 13. Emphases original.

22. Scott W. Hahn, 'Canon, Cult and Covenant: The Promise of Liturgical Hermeneutics', in *Canon and Biblical Interpretation*, Scripture and Hermeneutics 7 (Milton Keynes: Paternoster, 2006), p. 226.

23. Brevard S. Childs, *Old Testament Theology in a Canonical Context* (London: SCM, 1985), p. 11.

Testament cannot be abstracted or removed from the form of the witness which the historical community of Israel gave it.'[24] Childs concludes, 'there is no one hermeneutical key for unlocking the biblical message, but the canon provides the arena in which the struggle for understanding takes place'.[25]

As a consequence of Childs's approach his interest is not just in individual texts, but in the shape and function of the entire canon. His desire is that theologians approach the text as a whole, rather than as a collection of isolated texts. The text comes to us not from individuals but from 'ancient communities of faith'.[26] As McConville notes, the consequence of this is that 'Canon thus takes on a *hermeneutical* quality, since texts must always be read with alertness to other texts.'[27] In canonical terms, 'no text is an island'.[28] Each text has a web of interactions with other texts, utilizing, interpreting and developing motifs in dependence and interaction. Therefore, while a limited investigation into missional ethics in just one text (e.g. Deuteronomy) would be valuable, it is also worthwhile (perhaps of greater importance) to consider the theme in the context of the wider canon.

A modern disciple of Childs and advocate of the canonical approach, Christopher Seitz, states, 'a canonical approach will acknowledge the Holy Spirit's activity in both Hebrew and Greek canons, which guide and constrain the church's reflection and confession'.[29] The benefits of such an approach are helpfully summarized by Seitz as follows:

> A canonical approach is an effort to read texts in a fresh way, to engage in questions of historical, theological, practical, and conceptual significance, and to keep the lines of communication between the testaments, between the Bible and theology, and between them both and the church, open and responsive.[30]

---

24. Ibid., p. 12.

25. Ibid., p. 15.

26. McDonald, *Formation*, p. 301.

27. Gordon McConville, 'Old Testament Laws and Canonical Intentionality', in *Canon and Biblical Interpretation*, Scripture and Hermeneutics 7 (Milton Keynes: Paternoster, 2006), p. 267. Emphasis original.

28. Peter D. Miscall, 'Isaiah: New Heavens, New Earth, New Book', in *Reading Between Texts: Intertextuality and the Hebrew Bible*, LCBI (Louisville: Westminster John Knox, 1992), p. 45.

29. Seitz, 'Canonical Approach', p. 96.

30. Ibid., p. 101.

The canonical approach provides a useful methodological context for the hermeneutical approach outlined in the next three sections.

A narratival hermeneutic

The canonical approach values the *function* of the text and the *place* from which it is read. Additionally, it is concerned with the relationship between the texts, specifically the overall *shape* of the text. The canonical collection recounts historical events as the story of God's deliverance and commission. Various genres are present – narrative, poetry, wisdom, prophetic and apocalyptic – and uniting them all is one overarching narrative tracing the story of creation, fall, redemption and new creation. The canon is not a random collection of texts: it is a narrative.[31] Recognizing the overarching story and trajectory of the canonical texts utilizes a narratival hermeneutic. A narratival hermeneutic acknowledges the 'organic unfolding of the divine plan in its execution through the word (announcement), act (accomplishment), and word (interpretation). Revelation is a servant of redemption'.[32] Two scholars from different theological traditions have both noted the importance of narratival sensitivity: Geerhardus Vos and Gerhard von Rad.

On 8 May 1894 Vos delivered his inaugural address as Professor of Biblical Theology at Princeton Theological Seminary. In his lecture he outlines his own approach to theology, an approach that informs his subsequent writings, and has influenced many of his followers. He proposes that 'biblical theology' approaches Scripture as 'the revealing act of God himself . . . and tries to understand and trace and describe this act . . . [it is concerned with] the economy of revelation itself'.[33] Vos is concerned not just with the form of the canon, but with the economy of the unfolding revelation. He later states that 'Biblical theology, rightly defined, is nothing else than *the exhibition of the organic progress of supernatural revelation in its historic continuity and multiformity.*'[34] For Vos the progress of the wider story affects the interpretation of any place within that story. Vos

---

31. N. T. Wright, 'Narrative Theology: The Evangelists' Use of the Old Testament as an Implicit Overarching Narrative', in *Biblical Interpretation and Method: Essays in Honour of John Barton* (Oxford: Oxford University Press, 2013), pp. 189–200.

32. Michael S. Horton, *Covenant and Eschatology: The Divine Drama* (Louisville: Westminster John Knox, 2002), p. 5.

33. Geerhardus Vos, 'The Idea of Biblical Theology as a Science and as a Theological Discipline', in *Redemptive History and Biblical Interpretation* (Phillipsburg: P&R, 1980), p. 7.

34. Ibid., p. 15. Emphasis original.

suggests that such an approach to biblical theology must be characterized by three things: a commitment to the objective character of revelation (as the oracles of God); the historical character as having 'been employed by God for the very purpose of revealing the truth';[35] and the truthfulness of Scripture as a whole. It is the second of these which is distinctive – the desire to take seriously the historical nature of the revelation, and God's purpose in such self-revelation. Vos's plea is for the theologian to take seriously 'the form of the historical organism of the inspired Scriptures'.[36] He concludes, 'Our Theology will be Biblical in the full sense, only when it not merely derives its material from the Bible, but also accepts at the hands of the Bible the order in which this material is to be grouped and located.'[37] Vos argues that for those who approach Scripture as God's revelation the consideration of its shape, order and redemptive-historical narrative is the most fruitful path to understanding.[38]

In the early 1940s, in a different context, another new movement in biblical theology sought to redress the weaknesses perceived in the modern approach. Gerhard von Rad argued that the category of history, for Israel, was entirely theological.[39] It was the 'story' that was the vehicle carrying theological content. Attempts at systemization and theological abstraction which failed to take seriously the unifying and organizing principles that gave shape to Israel's Scriptures were inadequate in von Rad's view.[40] The interpreter must recognize both the wider story and the theological message being conveyed; the two cannot be divorced. Von Rad's *Heilsgeschichte* (salvation history) embraced the unity of the Old and New Testaments in the light of the promise and fulfilment motif, embracing typology while rejecting allegory. There is, in the unfolding of salvation history, a divine pedagogy which functions through the whole narrative.[41] Therefore the exegete must consider not just the content but its shaping in Israel's history. In von Rad's second volume on Old Testament theology he argues:

---

35. Ibid., p. 19.
36. Ibid., p. 20.
37. Ibid.
38. Ibid., pp. 21–24.
39. Gerhard von Rad, 'Grundprobleme einer biblischen Theologie des Alten Testaments', *ThLZ* 68.9/10 (1943), p. 227.
40. Gerhard von Rad, *Old Testament Theology*, 2 vols., tr. D. M. G. Stalker, repr. (London: SCM, 1975), vol. 1, pp. 115–121.
41. Ibid., p. 233.

> The chief consideration in the correspondence between the two Testaments does not lie primarily in the field of religious terminology, but in that of saving history, for in Jesus Christ we meet once again – and in a more intensified form – with that same interconnexion between divine word and historical act with which we are so familiar in the Old Testament.[42]

Von Rad states emphatically, 'The coming of Jesus Christ as a historical reality leaves the exegete no choice at all; he must interpret the Old Testament as pointing to Christ, whom he must understand in its light.'[43] In von Rad's view the only appropriate approach towards theology is to consider the relationships of multiple texts and voices as a historical reality and unity pointing towards Christ. Von Rad's hermeneutic has important implications for this work. His insight demonstrates that the enquirer must consider not just the theme of missional ethics in the abstract, but in the narrative. The theme becomes 'storied' through the canon, flowing into, and out from, the Christ event.

A number of modern interpreters utilize the insights of von Rad (and Childs). Wall observes that a canonical approach recognizes Scripture as both a 'single text' and a 'shaped text'. Regarding the latter he states:

> The canonization process involved a gathering of collections of individual writings, which were formed into coherent units in a purposeful way . . . each collection was designed to perform certain roles within Scripture, typically in relationship to other collections.[44]

This ordering is termed the 'aesthetic principle' by which the collection is shaped for a purpose.[45] The canon is not a piecemeal collection of fragments, but rather is shaped into the narrative of the redemption of mankind in history.[46] The texts exist in relationship to one another. As Fewell notes, 'no text exists in a vacuum. All texts are embedded in a larger web of related texts, bounded only by human culture and language itself. Intertextual reading is therefore inevitable.'[47] This

---

42. Ibid., vol. 2, p. 382.

43. Ibid., p. 374.

44. Wall, 'Canonical View', p. 117.

45. Ibid.

46. Richard B. Gaffin, 'The Redemptive-Historical View', in *Biblical Hermeneutics: Five Views* (Downers Grove: InterVarsity Press, 2012), pp. 89–110.

47. Danna Nolan Fewell, 'Introduction', in *Reading Between Texts: Intertextuality and the Hebrew Bible*, LCBI (Louisville: Westminster John Knox, 1992), p. 17.

observation is important for the approach of this work. It is insufficient to consider one text's contribution to the theological theme under consideration. The intertexts also need to be identified and interpreted. This will be important in considering our interpretation of both Old and New Testament texts. As Childs observes, 'The Old is understood by its relation to the New, but the New is incomprehensible apart from the Old.'[48]

Hays's work in this area is particularly helpful. He notes that a figural reading of the New Testament recognizes the ways in which early Christians were 'embedded in a symbolic world shaped by the Old Testament . . . that their "encyclopedia of production" is constituted in large measure by Israel's Scripture'.[49] Hays recognizes the impact of Graeco-Roman culture, but argues it is secondary, with the Old Testament being the primary source of influence. Hays's thesis goes further. It is not simply that we understand the New Testament with reference only to the Old Testament. Hays suggests that we can only understand the Old Testament fully with reference to the New Testament. Hays's contention regarding a properly theological and narratival hermeneutic is as follows:

The Gospels teach us how to read the OT, and – at the same time – the OT teaches us how to read the Gospels. Or to put it a little differently, we learn to read the OT by *reading backwards* from the Gospels, and – at the same time – we learn how to read the Gospels by *reading forwards* from the OT.[50]

In other words, to explore our motif of missional ethics properly we need to examine the motif as a storied theology with an origin and terminus. Hays would argue we need to understand something of the end of the story if we are to approach and interpret the beginning properly. Francis Watson, in a similar vein, says, 'Understood as a Christian theological enterprise, Old Testament theology rejects the view that the Old Testament can and should be interpreted in abstraction from its context within the Christian Bible.'[51] A thorough appreciation of canon as context requires an appreciation of the overarching shape of the text. Therefore, a narratival approach will enable

---

48. Childs, *Proposal*, p. 51.
49. Richard B. Hays, *Reading Backwards: Figural Christology and the Fourfold Gospel Witness* (London: SPCK, 2015), p. xii.
50. Ibid., p. 4. Emphases original.
51. Francis Watson, *Text and Truth: Redefining Biblical Theology* (Grand Rapids: Eerdmans, 1997), p. 185.

the theologian to appreciate how motifs, such as the one under consideration in this work, develop and function. As such the exegesis of each major text will inevitably give some consideration to the intertexts. Köstenberger and O'Brien helpfully outline various benefits to a narratival hermeneutic: it permits each part of Scripture to make its own contribution; it enables the interpreter to trace developments; and finally, it does not claim to be the final word, but seeks to make a useful contribution to other disciplines including systematics and missiology.[52]

A missional hermeneutic

Our next important hermeneutical strategy is to take note of the missional thread that runs through the canon. The narratival approach enables the interpreter to discern the story of redemption. This narrative is both divine and human. Ultimately it is a story of God's redemption, and yet throughout the canonical text the human side of that narrative is evident. A missional hermeneutic considers that mission is 'not simply one of many themes the Bible touches upon but, rather, is constitutive of the very nature of the Bible'.[53] Davy's discussion of missional hermeneutics provides a helpful sumary: '"Missional", it could be suggested, characterises the emergence, content, and purpose of the biblical writings.'[54]

Hengel described the history of early Christianity as 'mission history' and 'mission theology'.[55] He argues the New Testament emerged from communities with a mission facing new situations. This is undoubtedly true, but missional hermeneutics is more fundamental than just a situational requirement. It is generally agreed that the term 'missional hermeneutic' was first used by James Brownson.[56] His basis for this term is that the 'early Christian movement that produced and canonized the New Testament was a movement with a specifically *missionary* character'.[57] More recently, in response to the ongoing

---

52. Andreas J. Köstenberger and Peter T. O'Brien, *Salvation to the Ends of the Earth: A Biblical Theology of Mission*, NSBT 11 (Leicester: Apollos, 2001), pp. 19–20.

53. Timothy James Davy, 'The Book of Job and the Mission of God: An Application of a Missional Hermeneutic to the Book of Job', PhD diss., University of Gloucestershire, 2014, p. 30.

54. Ibid.

55. Martin Hengel, *Between Jesus and Paul: Studies in the Earliest History of Christianity* (London: SCM, 1983), pp. 48–64, 166–179.

56. James V. Brownson, *Speaking the Truth in Love* (Harrisburg: Trinity, 1998), p. 14.

57. Ibid. Emphasis original.

conversation surrounding missional hermeneutics, George Hunsberger has attempted to identify four facets of a missional hermeneutic as follows: (1) the *missio Dei* as the narrative theme of Scripture; (2) the purpose of Scripture to equip the church for witness; (3) the social 'locatedness' of the missional community; and (4) the application of the gospel to contemporary culture.[58] Hunsberger argues that the various ways in which the term 'missional hermeneutic' has been used are valid but have the potential for confusion. For the sake of clarity it is the first two aspects of missional hermeneutics that Hunsberger outlines that are of greatest interest to this work. The latter two are important but go beyond the scope of this work into the exploration of contextualization.

Richard Bauckham, in a series of lectures delivered in 2001, asks what sort of hermeneutic is necessary to take proper account of the missionary direction of Scripture – in particular Scripture's movement from the particular to the universal.[59] He suggests that such a hermeneutic must first of all be canonical, recognizing the unity of Scripture. Second, he says:

> It will be a narrative hermeneutic, one which recognizes how the bible as a whole tells a story, in some sense a single story, an overall narrative encompassing, of course, many other stories and including many forms of non-narrative literature within it, but constituting in its overall direction a metanarrative, a narrative about the whole of reality that elucidates the meaning of the whole of reality. A narrative hermeneutic recognizes the way narrative creates its own world in front of the text and so interprets our world for us.[60]

Bauckham's proposals fit with what has been argued above. A missional hermeneutic is part of an approach that will include the canonical and the narratival.

Christopher Wright is one of the most significant contributors to the development of a missional hermeneutic. He deduces a missional hermeneutic from Jesus' own words in Luke 24:45–47:

---

58. George R. Hunsberger, 'Proposals for a Missional Hermeneutic: Mapping a Conversation', *Missiology* 39.3 (2011), pp. 309–321; and more recently, 'Mapping the Missional Hermeneutics Conversation', in Michael W. Goheen (ed.), *Reading the Bible Missionally* (Grand Rapids: Eerdmans, 2016), pp. 45–67.

59. Richard Bauckham, *Bible and Mission: Christian Witness in a Postmodern World* (Carlisle: Paternoster, 2003), p. 11.

60. Ibid., p. 12.

Then he opened their minds so they could understand the Scriptures. He told them,
'This is what is written: The Messiah will suffer and rise from the dead on the third
day, and repentance for the forgiveness of sins will be preached in his name to all
nations, beginning at Jerusalem.'

With these words Jesus claims himself to be 'the focus of the whole canon of
the Hebrew Scriptures'.[61] This fits with the comments already made above in
discussing the canonical approach and a narratival hermeneutic. Wright helpfully
continues, 'Jesus went on, however, beyond his *messianic* centering of the Old
Testament Scriptures to their *missional* thrust as well.'[62] That which is written,
referred to in Luke 24:46, includes repentance and forgiveness being preached
to all nations. The Old Testament has an inherent missional thrust and *telos*.
Therefore, continues Wright, 'the proper way for disciples of the crucified and
risen Jesus to read their Scriptures is *messianically* and *missionally*'.[63] The Scriptures
are about mission as well as Messiah. Wright goes on to note that this 'does not
mean that we try to find something relevant to evangelism in every verse. We
are referring to something deeper and wider in relation to the Bible as a whole.'[64]
A missional hermeneutic suggests that it is possible and profitable to read the
whole Bible with a missional perspective that is more than mere proof-texting.
Wright argues for the need to take note of the wider narrative, and, crucially,
to engage with the phenomena of Scripture itself:

> A missional hermeneutic of the Bible begins with the Bible's very existence. For
> those who affirm some relationship between these texts and the self-revelation of our
> Creator God, the whole canon of Scripture is a missional phenomenon in the sense
> that it witnesses to the self-giving movement of this God toward his creation.[65]

Goheen concurs with this view: 'Both in the case of the Old Testament and
the New Testament, the books arose as products of the ongoing mission of
God in and through his people.'[66] Mission is not only the mother of theology,

---

61. Christopher J. H. Wright, *The Mission of God: Unlocking the Bible's Grand Narrative*
    (Downers Grove: InterVarsity Press, 2006), p. 29.
62. Ibid. Emphases original.
63. Ibid., p. 30. Emphases original.
64. Ibid., p. 31.
65. Ibid., p. 48.
66. Michael W. Goheen, *A Light to the Nations: The Missional Church and the Biblical Story*
    (Grand Rapids: Baker Academic, 2011), p. 98.

but also the mother of revelation. Wright helpfully summarizes his argument as follows:

> A missional hermeneutic, then, is not content simply to call for obedience to the Great *Commission* (though it will assuredly include that as a matter of non-negotiable importance), nor even to reflect on the missional implications of the Great *Commandment*. For behind both it will find the Great *Communication* – the revelation of the identity of God, of God's action in the world, and God's saving purpose for all creation. And for the fullness of this communication we need the whole Bible in all its parts and genres, for God has given us no less.[67]

A missional hermeneutic begins with the *missio Dei*, and all other aspects of mission flow out of this source.[68] Wright is aware of the limitations of any one framework for the interpretation of Scripture, and he compares a hermeneutical framework to a map. A map cannot fully represent the reality, but it offers the significant landmarks and features. Wright suggests that a missional hermeneutic, while not exhaustive, is nonetheless profitable in mapping the terrain of the canon.[69] Here is another reason why the study of missional ethics must be broader than the contents of a single book. It is the whole Bible in all parts and genres that will provide the most profitable avenue for exploration of the theme.

To explore the motif of missional ethics is, as Poythress notes, not an attempt to minimize or relativize other Scripture motifs, but rather to enrich our view of the whole by focusing on a particular perspective: 'we do not aim at relativising truth, which would be tantamount to making truth disappear. Rather, we aim to gain more truth and to set truths in more and more complex relationships to other truths. There is harmony, not contradiction, in truth.'[70] The narrative is multivocal, but, taken as a canonical whole, the Bible narrates the story of God's mission to and for the world.[71] This book will utilize a missional hermeneutic to explore the more specific theme of missional ethics.

---

67. Wright, *Mission of God*, pp. 60–61. Emphases original.

68. Ibid., p. 62.

69. Ibid., pp. 68–69.

70. Vern S. Poythress, *Symphonic Theology: The Validity of Multiple Perspectives in Theology* (Grand Rapids: Academie, 1987), p. 88.

71. Hunsberger, 'Proposals for a Missional Hermeneutic', p. 311.

A performative hermeneutic

So far I have argued for a canonical approach as the context for enquiry, employing a narratival and missional hermeneutic. Further, in my exploration of the canonical approach, I have already considered the importance of the *function* of texts on communities. Considering the way in which texts serve to shape communities is a key part of interpretation and theological reflection, and therefore warrants further reflection here. There is a two-way dialectic between the community that shapes the text and the text that shapes the community. The canonical approach must reckon with both ends of this dialogue.

The development of speech-act theory has provided a tool for linguists to describe the content and function of communication. One of the first major contributors to the performative nature of speech, J. L. Austin, observed three main parts to communication. These are the locution (the thing said or written), the illocution (the meaning intended) and the perlocution (the intended effect).[72] An often-used example is the sentence 'Is the door open?' That is the locution. The illocution (meaning) could convey a genuine request for information or, more likely, the illocution contains a request for action (i.e. 'Shut the door!'). The perlocution (intended effect) in this case may be that another closes the door. The example illustrates the power of language, not just to convey information, but to effect action. The biblical text, similarly, conveys information; it serves to provoke action, to form a people for a purpose. This is the text's perlocutionary function. The text is concerned not just with information but transformation, and therefore part of the interpreter's approach must be to consider not just the locution and illocution but also the perlocution.

In Adams's introductory discussion of performative hermeneutics he states, 'certain utterances include an illocutionary force or forces that personally involve a speaker and/or hearer in extra-linguistic actions prescribed in the propositional content that brings about a state of affairs in the world'.[73] Similarly to Austin, Adams notes the personal response required and initiated by the locution of the text. As Vanhoozer states, 'All narratives project "worlds" and possible ways for humans to live in the world.'[74] The text presents a vision of life that is meaningful and significant. Such a vision demands an enacted

---

72. J. L. Austin, *How to Do Things with Words* (Oxford: Clarendon, 1962), pp. 108–119.

73. Jim W. Adams, *The Performative Nature and Function of Isaiah 40–55* (New York: T&T Clark, 2006), p. 1.

74. Kevin J. Vanhoozer, *Biblical Narrative in the Philosophy of Paul Ricoeur: A Study in Hermeneutics and Theology* (Cambridge: Cambridge University Press, 1990), p. 120.

response from the audience. Therefore the text needs to be considered not just as a description, or a 'history of religion', but a communication for a purpose. Anthony Thiselton states:

> The biblical writings, it may be argued, embody an institutional framework of covenant in which commitments and effects become operative in acts of promise, acts of blessing, acts of forgiveness, acts of pronouncing judgment, acts of repentance, acts of worship, acts of authorization, acts of communion, and acts of love.[75]

The reader is not merely a passive recipient but is engaged in reader-response. Moreover, this is always the intent of the text.[76] Thiselton continues:

> [T]here is more than a merely textual or intralinguistic *claim* to perform acts in speech-utterances like those of actors on a stage; *the acts are effectively performed. They bring about a transformation in the extra-linguistic relationship between the speaker and the audience, and invite the reader to participate in that extra-linguistic transformation and relationship.*[77]

In other words, forgiveness, repentance, blessing, curse and worship are not simply pronounced, but performed in the speech-act. Texts, particularly sacred texts, function as a 'self-involving illocutionary act, which carries practical consequences for the life and behaviour of the reader'.[78] Because the reader believes the text to have its origin in the divine, the importance of response is heightened for the reading community. The implication is that the missio-ethical locution carries missio-ethical perlocution.

Kevin Vanhoozer has been a leading contributor in developing a performative hermeneutic. He argues, 'speakers, and authors as well, are both perlocutionary and illocutionary agents. Interpreting texts is thus a matter of understanding purposive action – communicative and strategic.'[79] Scripture, as an authoritative script, calls for 'appropriation on the part of the believing community – in a word, *performance*'.[80] Vanhoozer notes, 'The text can become more than a

---

75. Anthony C. Thiselton, *New Horizons in Hermeneutics* (London: HarperCollins, 1992), p. 18.

76. Ibid., p. 50.

77. Ibid., p. 291. Emphases original.

78. Ibid., p. 599.

79. Kevin J. Vanhoozer, *Is There a Meaning in This Text?* (Leicester: Apollos, 1998), p. 224.

80. Kevin J. Vanhoozer, *The Drama of Doctrine: A Canonical Linguistic Approach to Christian Theology* (Louisville: Westminster John Knox, 2005), p. 101. Emphasis original.

dialogue partner; it can become a pedagogue that illumines one's existence and opens up new ways of living in the world.'[81] The text is not truly understood until the appropriate response is performed:

> Scripture is intended to 'actualize' what is proclaimed – to bring the believer into living contact with the *mirabilia Dei*, the mighty saving works of God . . . [this is] the performative power of the Word of God as a 'divine speech act.'[82]

As Vanhoozer notes, 'Dramas are not devised primarily to convey information but to move us, to persuade us, to delight us, to purge us.'[83] He continues, 'The biblical script asks not to be admired but *performed*.'[84] The covenant people of God are invited and called to perform a role – a role which takes on a missio-ethical form – before a global audience.

Theological endeavour, within a canonical approach, comes to the text not as a neutral observer, but as an actor seeking a script. The study of missional ethics requires us not only to describe the content but to consider the function of the text on the first hearers and, inevitably, on ourselves. Vanhoozer neatly encapsulates this: 'Theology is less a matter of *in*doctrination than it is of *ex*doctrination: the living out of Christian teaching.'[85] Theology seeks to 'continue the way of truth and life, not by admiring it from afar but by following and embodying it'.[86] The encounter with the past is 'rendered through a plot, which in turn renders a proposition: a possible way of viewing and living in the world. The reader, thus propositioned, becomes a player in the ongoing drama of creation and redemption.'[87] Goheen has written helpfully on this shaping power of Scripture as follows: 'The Bible does not simply give us true information about or provide a reliable commentary on the work of God but takes an active part to actualise and bring about that ongoing purpose of God.'[88] He continues, 'To understand the authority of Scripture, then, is to understand its formative role, how it powerfully works

---

81. Vanhoozer, *Is There a Meaning?*, p. 375.

82. Hahn, 'Canon, Cult and Covenant', p. 228.

83. Vanhoozer, *Drama*, p, 182.

84. Ibid., p. 253. Emphasis original.

85. Ibid., p. 400. Emphases original.

86. Ibid., p. 15.

87. Ibid., p. 18.

88. Michael W. Goheen, 'Continuing Steps Toward a Missional Hermeneutic', *Fideles* 3 (2008), p. 90.

to shape a missional people. To miss this role and purpose of Scripture is to misunderstand it.'[89]

To explore the theme properly, that of missional ethics, the student needs to be aware of the design, intent and function of the texts. Further, a proper hermeneutic of 'self-involvement' necessitates a sensitivity to various ways in which the text speaks to the research community. Adams concludes his study by stating the following:

> By understanding the language of the Bible as performative and not solely as descriptive, readers of every generation have the opportunity of being exhorted, promised, confronted, and commissioned by God as well as to confess, promise, pray, lament, and offer praise to him.[90]

As has been argued throughout this chapter, an appreciation of the intended function of the text is crucial to the hermeneutical process.

The texts for consideration

This book aims to offer some further exploration and definition of missional ethics in scriptural terms, thereby furthering the ongoing conversation. This raises the question of which texts should be considered given the limits of this book. It is here proposed that Deuteronomy, the Major Prophets and Luke–Acts constitute fertile ground for further exploration of missional ethics. Others have noted the theme of missional ethics in Genesis and Exodus, as well as the Sermon on the Mount and 1 Peter.[91] Further work may legitimately be undertaken in those texts. For the following reasons Deuteronomy, the Major Prophets and Luke–Acts are worthy of detailed consideration.

Deuteronomy is widely considered a foundational and constitutive text for Israel's history, identity and vocation.[92] Block describes Deuteronomy as a 'theological manifesto', the product of four decades of reflection on God's

89. Ibid., p. 91.

90. Adams, *Performative Nature*, p. 216.

91. See for example Goheen, *Light to the Nations*, pp. 173–189; David J. Bosch, *Transforming Mission: Paradigm Shifts in Theology of Mission* (Maryknoll: Orbis, 1991), pp. 70–71; Wright, *Mission of God*, pp. 357–375.

92. S. Dean McBride Jr, 'Polity of the Covenant People: The Book of Deuteronomy', *Int* 41.3 (1987), pp. 229–244.

covenant with Israel.[93] Glanville describes Deuteronomy as a 'Charter for a Contrast Community'.[94] Walter Brueggemann has said it is 'impossible to overstate the importance of the book of Deuteronomy for the shape and substance of Israel's faith'.[95] Robson regards it as the centre of the Old Testament and Old Testament theology.[96] It is a text intended for religious formation and transmission through the generations – a constitutive covenant document.[97] Millar argues that Deuteronomy, more than any other book in the Old Testament, can be considered pivotal for its affinity with both preceding pentateuchal material and with prophetic and wisdom traditions.[98] The stamp of Deuteronomy is prominent throughout the Old and New Testaments – particularly in the Deuteronomistic History, the Psalms, the Prophets, the rabbinic writings, and in the teachings of Jesus and Paul.[99] It serves to shape a people commissioned to witness to the nations (Deut. 4:5–8).[100] Consisting primarily of Moses' speeches the text charges the covenant community to live in the light of redemptive history and possession of the land. The repetition of themes, particularly synonyms for the words 'learn', 'keep', 'teach', 'observe' and 'do', all serve, along with the impending death of Moses, to heighten the impact and importance of his programmatic speeches for the present and subsequent generations as they live in the land.[101] As Robson notes, regardless of the

---

93. Daniel I. Block, *Deuteronomy*, NIVAC (Grand Rapids: Zondervan, 2012), p. 25.

94. Mark Glanville, 'A Missional Reading of Deuteronomy', in *Reading the Bible Missionally* (Grand Rapids: Eerdmans, 2016), p. 127.

95. Walter Brueggemann, *Deuteronomy*, Abingdon Old Testament Commentaries (Nashville: Abingdon, 2001), p. 17.

96. James Robson, *Honey from the Rock: Deuteronomy for the People of God* (Nottingham: Apollos, 2013), pp. 18–19.

97. Duane L. Christensen, *Deuteronomy 1:1–21:9*, WBC 6A (Nashville: Thomas Nelson, 2001), p. lvii.

98. J. Gary Millar, *Now Choose Life: Theology and Ethics in Deuteronomy*, NSBT 6 (Leicester: Apollos, 1998), p. 36.

99. Block presents the evidence for this in *Deuteronomy*, pp. 25–35. Olson describes Deuteronomy as the capstone of the Pentateuch: Dennis T. Olson, *Deuteronomy and the Death of Moses* (Minneapolis: Fortress, 1994), p. 1.

100. J. G. McConville, *Deuteronomy*, AOTC 5 (Leicester: Apollos, 2002), p. 43; Moshe Weinfeld, *Deuteronomy 1–11*, AB 5 (New York: Doubleday, 1991), p. 5; Richard D. Nelson, *Deuteronomy*, OTL (Louisville: Westminster John Knox, 2002), p. 1; John H. Sailhamer, *The Pentateuch as Narrative* (Grand Rapids: Zondervan, 1992), p. 423.

101. Weinfeld, *Deuteronomy 1–11*, p. 5.

date of the final form of Deuteronomy it is undoubtedly a crucial text in forming the people Israel into the way they were supposed to be.[102] Deuter-onomy is the culmination of the Torah and is in some respects *the* text that shapes and governs the lives of the old-covenant people of God. The book is of particular interest because it is 'avowedly a recasting of old ethical material for a new situation'.[103] The text transcends one particular generation as it addresses multiple generations of YHWH's covenant people. The attempt to understand missional ethics can profit from the consideration of this foundational text.

The Major Prophets are also worthy of attention since they provide detailed reflection upon Israel's calling, plight and future in Deuteronomic terms.[104] As Brueggemann notes, they contain some of the 'boldest and most eloquent theological probing' in the Old Testament.[105] All three appeal to Deuteronomic tradition in their condemnation of Israel's sin, and in their eschatological hope of renewal.[106] Prophets were covenant mediators concerned with covenant breach and its ramifications.[107] As such their reflection on the legal and coven-antal traditions as understood and applied is of interest in the consideration of Israel's plight, call and eschatology. Their pronouncement and call is rooted in covenant tradition.

The book of Isaiah has been described as the 'prince of the prophets' in part because of its length and its position at the head of the prophetic corpus, but primarily due to its 'unparalleled sweep of theology'.[108] Oswalt describes Isaiah as 'the Bible in miniature'.[109] Isaiah's importance for the community of faith is

---

102. Robson, *Honey from the Rock*, p. 64.

103. Millar, *Now Choose Life*, p. 36.

104. R. E. Clements, *Prophecy and Covenant* (London: SCM, 1965), p. 18; Jack R. Lundbom, *The Hebrew Prophets: An Introduction* (Minneapolis: Fortress, 2010), pp. 33–34; Willem A. VanGemeren, *Interpreting the Prophetic Word: An Introduction to the Prophetic Literature of the Old Testament* (Grand Rapids: Zondervan, 1990), p. 68.

105. Walter Brueggemann, *Hopeful Imagination: Prophetic Voices in Exile* (Philadelphia: Fortress, 1986), p. 1.

106. Barton describes the prophets as primarily teachers of Moses' words. John Barton, *Oracles of God: Perceptions of Ancient Prophecy in Israel After the Exile* (London: Darton, Longman & Todd, 1986), p. 21.

107. William J. Dumbrell, *The Faith of Israel: A Theological Survey of the Old Testament*, 2nd edn (Grand Rapids: Baker Academic, 2002), p. 107.

108. John N. Oswalt, *Isaiah*, NIVAC (Grand Rapids: Zondervan, 2003), p. 17.

109. Ibid.

evident from its prominence at Qumran and in the New Testament, which cites Isaiah more than any other book in the Old Testament.[110] Seitz notes the importance of Isaiah in the history of Christianity: 'the church fathers (Eusebius, Theodoret, Jerome, Augustine) regarded Isaiah not just as the first and greatest prophet but as the first apostle and evangelist'.[111] As Firth and Williamson conclude in their introduction to Isaiah, 'it is a text to be weighed, on which to meditate and pray, and through which to explore the ways in which God works. It is a text that has been understood as formative to the identity of the people of God.'[112]

Jeremiah, like Isaiah, is noted for its 'strong Deuteronomistic flavour and echoes of Deuteronomy'.[113] Brueggemann argues that

> the governing paradigm for the tradition of Jeremiah is *Israel's covenant with Yahweh, rooted in the memories and mandates of the Sinai tradition.* That covenant taught that the sovereign God of Israel required obedience to covenant stipulations about social practice and power.[114]

Specifically that paradigm is 'related to and derived from the traditions of Deuteronomy'.[115] Elsewhere Brueggemann notes the centrality of Jeremiah in terms of its use of antecedent material and its generative power for the continued reflection by the community of faith.[116] Jeremiah is a 'lively force' for the early church and is cited a number of times in the New Testament, most significantly in the infancy narratives and new-covenant passages of Hebrews.[117] Jeremiah's rich theology intersects with themes and texts from Genesis to

---

110. David G. Firth and H. G. M. Williamson, 'Introduction', in *Interpreting Isaiah: Issues and Approaches* (Nottingham: Apollos, 2009), p. 15; Steve Moyise and Maarten J. J. Menken, 'Introduction', in *Isaiah in the New Testament* (London: T&T Clark, 2005), p. 1.

111. Christopher R. Seitz, *Isaiah 1–39*, Int (Louisville: John Knox, 1993), p. 1.

112. Firth and Williamson, 'Introduction', p. 15.

113. Leslie C. Allen, *Jeremiah: A Commentary*, OTL (Louisville: Westminster John Knox, 2008), p. 1.

114. Walter Brueggemann, *A Commentary on Jeremiah: Exile & Homecoming* (Grand Rapids: Eerdmans, 1998), p. 3. Emphases original.

115. Ibid., p. 4.

116. Walter Brueggemann, *The Theology of the Book of Jeremiah*, OTT (Cambridge: Cambridge University Press, 2007), p. 184.

117. Ibid., pp. 188–192.

Revelation.[118] Fretheim notes that Jeremiah's 'depth of reflection on divine action and human response, as well as the range and rigor of its rhetoric, has kept the book very much alive in the religious communities that recognize its canonical stature'.[119]

Ezekiel also draws heavily on the covenantal traditions of Deuteronomy.[120] Much of the first half of Ezekiel's prophecy rebukes Israel for their failure to live out the ethical requirements of the Torah. Ezekiel, like Isaiah and Jeremiah, also contains themes of eschatological hope – a day of restoration in which Israel will be cleansed and enabled to live out the ethical ideals of the Torah in a way that will bring blessing to the nations. The influence of the prophecy that bears Ezekiel's name can also be seen in later Jewish, and early Christian, communities, not least in the eschatological and apocalyptic literature.[121]

The Major Prophets stand at the head of the prophetic corpus, providing the longest and most complex theological reflection on the crisis facing the community. Their judgment is grounded in the covenantal traditions of Deuteronomy, as is their hopeful vision of restoration and universal mission. As such the Major Prophets provide an important window into Israel's failure to live out a missional ethic. Additionally the Major Prophets provide a bridge towards a realized missional ethic as they devote considerable space to the hope of a future in which Israel *will* live out their high calling to bring blessing to the nations in fulfilment of the Deuteronomic vision.[122]

The canonical narrative does not, however, end in exile. Moving into the New Testament, Luke views the events of Jesus' birth, life, death, resurrection

---

118. Alex Varughese, *Jeremiah 1–25: A Commentary in the Wesleyan Tradition*, NBBC (Kansas: Beacon Hill, 2008), pp. 17–18.

119. Terence E. Fretheim, *Jeremiah*, SHBC (Macon: Smyth & Helwys, 2002), p. 1.

120. Daniel I. Block, *The Book of Ezekiel: Chapters 1–24*, NICOT (Grand Rapids: Eerdmans, 1998), p. 40.

121. Ibid., pp. 42–43. Manning also notes Ezekiel imagery in John's Gospel. See Gary T. Manning, 'Shepherd, Vine, and Bones: The Use of Ezekiel in the Gospel of John', in *After Ezekiel: Essays on the Reception of a Difficult Prophet*, LHB/OTS 535 (New York: T&T Clark International, 2011), pp. 25–44.

122. Walter Brueggemann, *Old Testament Theology: An Introduction*, LBT (Nashville: Abingdon, 2008), pp. 295–296; Gerhard von Rad, *Old Testament Theology*, 2 vols., tr. D. M. G. Stalker, repr. (London: SCM, 1975), vol. 2, pp. 112–119.

and ascension as the fulfilment of Israel's Scriptures.[123] Luke's narrative world is 'thick with scriptural memory'.[124] Hays goes on to say of Luke:

> His vision allows for a comprehensive appropriation of the things about Jesus 'in all the scriptures' . . . He shows Jesus to be precisely the Lord of Israel who passionately seeks the redemption of the poor and downtrodden. And he also shows how the mission to the Gentiles is the outworking of God's longstanding plan for Israel as a light to the nations.[125]

Hays's quote illustrates three reasons why Luke's two-volume work is significant for this study. First, a distinctive emphasis of Luke's two-volume project is his concern with the plan of God.[126] The opening chapters of Luke's Gospel contain hymns which look back to God's promise in the Old Testament to restore and redeem Israel (Luke 1:68–79; 2:29–32, 38). Jesus' sermon in the synagogue at Nazareth concludes with his claim to fulfil the promise of Isaiah 61:1–2 (Luke 4:16–21). Throughout Luke's Gospel Jesus fulfils Old Testament types and prophecies, and at the end of the Gospel, in his post-resurrection appearances, he says to his disciples, 'everything must be fulfilled that is written about me in the Law of Moses, the Prophets and the Psalms' (Luke 24:44). Missional ethics is not the 'new' in New Testament; it stands in continuity with that which has gone before, fulfilling the Old Testament vision in Old Testament terms.

The second Lukan emphasis to which Hays draws attention is God's plan of salvation to extend beyond the borders of Israel. Jesus is to be a 'light for revelation to the Gentiles' (Luke 2:32), 'all people will see God's salvation' (Luke 3:6)

---

123. Hays, *Reading Backwards*, p. 59; D. A. Carson and Douglas J. Moo, *An Introduction to the New Testament* (Leicester: Apollos, 2005), p. 47; I. Howard Marshall, *Luke: Historian and Theologian* (Grand Rapids: Zondervan, 1971), p. 116. For the purposes of this book Luke–Acts will be considered as a unity given the literary and theological connections, and the intended narrative continuity between Jesus, the Spirit and the early church. See Darrell L. Bock, *A Theology of Luke and Acts* (Grand Rapids: Zondervan, 2012), pp. 28–29, 58–61.

124. Hays, *Reading Backwards*, p. 59.

125. Ibid., p. 100.

126. Carson and Moo, *Introduction to the New Testament*, p. 219; Joel B. Green, *The Theology of the Gospel of Luke*, New Testament Theology (Cambridge: Cambridge University Press, 1995), p. 47.

and he has come to seek and save the lost (Luke 19:10).[127] Further, his disciples are to be witnesses to the ends of the earth (Acts 1:8). Mission is at the heart of Luke's narrative, in fulfilment of Israel's call to be a light to the nations.[128]

The third distinctive Hays alludes to is Luke's ethical emphasis, again rooted in the Old Testament, for the poor and the marginalized. It appears repeatedly, and in strategic locations within Luke's work (Luke 4:18; 6:20; Acts 2:42–47; 4:32–35).[129] The character of the Christian community is integral to the mission in fulfilment of Israel's story.

These three reasons taken together provide a strong case for the consideration of Luke–Acts in the canonical narrative trajectory of the theme of missional ethics. And these texts – Deuteronomy, the Major Prophets and Luke–Acts – provide important building blocks for the exploration of the biblical data as it relates to the theme of missional ethics.

Conclusion

The examination of missional ethics is part of a broader missiological dialogue. As noted, all research proceeds within the constraints of presupposed ideologies. Integrity in the process does not presume neutrality, but rather an awareness and openness regarding those presuppositions. The methodology outlined above is a defence of the approach taken.

As Childs says, the challenge in theological endeavour is to 'engage in the continual activity of theological reflection that studies the canonical text in detailed exegesis, and seeks to do justice to the witness of both testaments in light of its subject matter'.[130] Theological enquiry needs biblical studies. Without this, Childs argues, 'it lapses into a mere *ad hoc* use of the Bible, finding bits and pieces to fit into a scheme derived from elsewhere'.[131] Missional ethics is no different in this respect. Progress requires careful anchoring to the biblical texts, an exercise still in its infancy where missional ethics is concerned.

---

127. Marshall describes Jesus' statement ('For the Son of Man came to seek and to save the lost') in Luke 19:10 as the summary of Luke's Gospel. Marshall, *Luke*, p. 116.

128. Bosch, *Transforming Mission*, p. 85; Bock, *Theology of Luke and Acts*, p. 448.

129. I. Howard Marshall, 'Luke's "Social" Gospel: The Social Theology of Luke–Acts', in *Transforming the World? The Gospel and Social Responsibility* (Nottingham: Apollos, 2009), p. 113.

130. Childs, *Proposal*, p. 55.

131. Ibid., p. 138.

The methodological approach employed in this work will attempt careful and detailed exegesis of the texts proposed. In order to do this I have suggested an overarching approach (canonical) with three subservient hermeneutical strategies. The overarching approach is canonical. This is more than a hermeneutical strategy; it is the *place* from which one engages with the text, acknowledging the unique function of the biblical text for the community of faith. The canonical approach considers not just the form but the function of the text for the community. This, I have argued, is a crucial part of the interpretative process. Within this approach three hermeneutical lenses will underpin the investigation. First, a narratival hermeneutic appreciates the form of Scripture and pays attention to the economy of the organic unfolding of the revelation. This book will consider the 'story', not just the concept, of missional ethics, as Scripture portrays the theme within its narrative structure. Second, a missional hermeneutic considers the existence and purpose of the canon. The *fact* of Scripture suggests a *missio Dei* that the community of faith is called to live out. Missional readings also note that the main theme of the redemptive-historical story is the story of mission to the ends of the earth. A missional hermeneutic is not an eisegetical enterprise, but the recognition of Scripture's central theme. Finally, a performative hermeneutic is sensitive to the force and intent of Scripture as a 'speech act'. It approaches the text by considering not just the bare information but the intended perlocution. This is a crucial part of the process if the interpreter is to understand and interpret the text properly.

In summary, the Bible is received by the community of faith as divine revelation. It is given as a story. It is a story about mission. It is a story intended to *do* something in the hearers. These four truths provide the framework and foundation for the exegetical exploration of missional ethics in Deuteronomy, the Major Prophets and Luke–Acts. If the canonical approach provides the appropriate context, our three strategies provide the methodology required to explore, describe and rightly define missional ethics in Scripture's own terms.

2. MISSIONAL ETHICS IN DEUTERONOMY

Introduction

Walter Brueggemann has argued that it is 'impossible to overstate the importance of the book of Deuteronomy for the shape and substance of Israel's faith'.[1] Deuteronomy has been described as a constitutive document intended for religious instruction and transmission.[2] Comprised largely of Moses' speeches, Deuteronomy forms a charge to Israel to be all that YHWH has called them to be, in the light of redemptive history and an inheritance.[3] As we have seen, regardless of the final-form dating of Deuteronomy, it is undoubtedly a crucial text in shaping the people of Israel.[4] Much of that comes through the teaching of the Torah. Olson observes, 'synonyms for the word *teach* occur at least

---

1. Walter Brueggemann, *Deuteronomy*, Abingdon Old Testament Commentaries (Nashville: Abingdon, 2001), p. 17.
2. Duane L. Christensen, *Deuteronomy 1:1–21:9*, WBC 6A (Nashville: Thomas Nelson, 2001), p. lvii.
3. For the purposes of this discussion canonical form is of primary interest; therefore questions of historical composition and source analysis will not be addressed.
4. James Robson, *Honey from the Rock* (Nottingham: Apollos, 2013), p. 64.

seventeen times in Deuteronomy'.[5] Weinfeld similarly notes the didactic element, and that the imminent death of Moses heightens the impact of his programmatic speeches.[6] Deuteronomy is more than a repetition of the law: it is an exposition of the law and a call to live it out in their new situation as a 'landed' people.[7] The goal of this instruction is 'to create a righteous community'.[8] This prompts a question central to this book: 'To what end?' For whose sake is a righteous covenant community desirable? The contention of this work is that one aspect of Israel's vocation is their witness to the nations. The purpose of this chapter is to consider Deuteronomy's vision of a missional ethic. Additionally, we shall consider the extent to which Deuteronomy's vision is distinctive within its ANE context. This chapter will proceed in three stages. First, a consideration of Deuteronomy 1 – 11 will demonstrate the basic call on Israel to be a distinctive community among the nations. These chapters reveal the fundamental shape of Torah obedience as love for God and love for neighbour. Second, the first of these forms (love for God) will be explored by considering relevant passages in Deuteronomy 12 – 26. Third, also employing passages in Deuteronomy 12 – 26, the second fundamental form (love for neighbour) will be further explored. The second and third stages of the argument will take account of comparative ANE texts in considering Deuteronomy's claim to be distinctive.

Deuteronomic identity and vocation of Israel

The opening eleven chapters of Deuteronomy provide the foundation for the vocation of YHWH's covenant people. The purpose and shape of Israel's existence will be outlined in examining these chapters.

Deuteronomy 1 – 3
Structurally Deuteronomy 1 – 3 and 31 – 34 provide the outer frame of the book.[9] The inner frame is given in chapters 4 and 30. Chapter 5 restates the Decalogue

---

5. Dennis T. Olson, *Deuteronomy and the Death of Moses* (Minneapolis: Fortress, 1994), p. 11. See Deut. 1:5; 4:1, 5, 10, 14; 5:31; 6:1, 7; 11:19; 17:11; 20:18; 24:8; 31:19, 22; 33:10. Emphasis original.

6. Moshe Weinfeld, *Deuteronomy 1–11*, AB 5 (New York: Doubleday, 1991), p. 5.

7. John H. Sailhamer, *The Pentateuch as Narrative* (Grand Rapids: Zondervan, 1992), p. 423.

8. J. G. McConville, *Deuteronomy*, AOTC 5 (Leicester: Apollos, 2002), p. 43.

9. Prologues in ANE law codes can be found in Ur-Nammu (CU), Lipit-Ishtar (CL) and Hammurabi (CH). See *ANET*; William Hallo (ed.), *The Context of Scripture*

and chapters 6–11 expound the first commandment. Chapters 12 – 26 expound commandments two through ten.[10] Chapters 28–29 stipulate various covenant blessings or curses depending upon the people's obedience or disobedience.

As the opening frame, Deuteronomy 1 – 3 gives the people both warning and encouragement through the recounting of failures and victories.[11] Israel are called to think upon their past in order that they may be, in the present, 'more fully, obediently, and responsibly the people of YHWH'.[12] The opening scene (1:1–5) sets the stage for the instruction to follow. The people, on the east of the Jordan, are ready to cross over and take the Promised Land. Wright describes Deuteronomy as 'a book on the boundary'.[13] He picks up the missiological significance of the text as an instruction to people crossing cultural, linguistic, geographical and religious boundaries. The challenges the people would face

---

(Leiden: Brill, 2003). Prologues serve to introduce and offer an apologia for the lawgiver. In his prologue Ur-Nammu claims to have established justice in the land, liberation for the subjugated, security and equity. Hammurabi likewise claims, in his lengthy prologue, to have caused 'justice to prevail in the land . . . that the strong might not oppress the weak'. At the end of his prologue he states, 'I established law and justice in the language of the land, thereby promoting the welfare of the people.' *ANET*, p. 164. The establishment of justice is a major theme in the prologues, as is the greatness of the lawgiver. In Hammurabi's case the law is received from the god Shamash. The king is almost a demi-god, one who has access to the wisdom of the gods; therefore his justice is to be followed by all. Deuteronomy, similarly, has the tripartite structure of prologue, laws and epilogue. Deuteronomy's prologue has an apologia of sorts for the divine lawgiver. However, in Deuteronomy the apologia takes the form of a storied theodicy as the first three chapters retell the story of YHWH's deliverance and the people's rebellion. As the weakness of the people is thrown into stark relief against the greatness of YHWH, the instruction is clear: listen, observe YHWH's instruction. While Deuteronomy, like other ANE codes, has a prologue, the form is different, and YHWH, not the lawgiver, is the king.

10. Braulik has argued that Deut. 12 – 26 follows the order of the Decalogue. The thesis is persuasive as far as commandments two to ten go, but my view is that the first commandment is expanded upon in Deut. 6 – 11. See Georg Braulik, 'Die Abfolge der Gesetze in Dtn 12–26 und der Dekalog', in *Studien zur Theologie des Deuteronomiums* (Stuttgart: Katholisches Bibelwerk, 1988), pp. 240–241.

11. Christopher J. H. Wright, *Deuteronomy*, NIBC 4 (Peabody: Hendrickson, 1996), p. 34.

12. Brueggemann, *Deuteronomy*, p. 25.

13. Wright, *Deuteronomy*, p. 9.

relate to their call to bless the nations.[14] In verses 5–6 of chapter 1 Moses begins his explanation of the instruction (*tôrâ*) by recounting the story of Israel's past: 'The LORD our God said *to us* at Horeb' (Deut. 1:6). These opening words are determinative for the identity and, by implication, vocation of this generation. The words 'to us' place the new generation in continuity with the Horeb generation, on the verge of taking the Promised Land. The Horeb generation was instructed to be a kingdom of priests and a holy nation (Exod. 19:5–6): 'As holy and priestly, Israel is the means by which God will, as his plan unfolds more and more, *bring the nations to have knowledge of him*.'[15] The same expectation falls on the Deuteronomy generation. Another important echo from Israel's past comes a few verses later (v. 10): 'The LORD your God has increased your numbers so that today you are as numerous as the stars in the sky.' God promised Abraham in Genesis 15:5 that his seed would be as numerous as the stars of the sky – a promise repeated in Genesis 22:17; 26:4, and recalled in Exodus 32:13.[16] In the restatement of the promise to Isaac in Genesis 26:4 the connection is made between the prosperity of Isaac's seed and the blessing of the nations. In Deuteronomy 1:10 Moses' words suggest that the promise has been partially fulfilled, at least regarding the number of Abraham's descendants.[17] The intertextual echoes are suggestive in linking their present instruction with their mandate to bless the nations.

The remainder of Deuteronomy 1 recounts the mission to spy out the Promised Land, the positive report and subsequent fear regarding the people of the land, and God's judgment upon the people for their fear and rebellion. Just as the first person plural pronoun is used in 1:6, so the use of second person plural pronouns continues through the historical survey of 1:26–46. The rhetorical effect of this device will be commented upon when we have surveyed the remainder of Deuteronomy 1 – 3.

In Deuteronomy 2 the historical report continues chronicling Israel's journey through the Transjordanian territories and their encounters with Edom, Moab, Ammon and Sihon. Moran has observed that the verb *'ābar* (cross over, pass through) is the *Leitwort* (leading word) of Deuteronomy 2, occurring twelve times.[18] Boundary crossing is an important part of their journey as is their

---

14. Ibid., pp. 8–17.

15. Peter Enns, *Exodus*, NIVAC (Grand Rapids: Zondervan, 2000), p. 389. Emphasis original.

16. A. D. H. Mayes, *Deuteronomy*, NCB (London: Oliphants, 1979), p. 121.

17. Jeffrey H. Tigay, *Deuteronomy* (Philadelphia: Jewish Publication Society, 1996), p. 10.

18. W. L. Moran, 'The End of the Unholy War and the Anti-Exodus', *Bib* 44 (1963), p. 341.

relationship with the surrounding nations. Of interest is the instruction not to provoke or harass the Edomites, Moabites or Ammonites. Twice the Edomites are referred to as 'brothers' (2:4, 8), which reminded Israel of their familial connection. Moabites and Ammonites also share history in the promises of YHWH as descendants of Lot (Gen. 19:37–38). The explicit reason in the text as to why Israel should not provoke or harass the Edomites, Moabites or Ammonites is that God has promised them their land and he will not grant Israel success against them (Deut. 2:5, 9, 19). Olson argues that this theme in Deuteronomy 2 serves a number of purposes in Israel's instruction. First, it demonstrates that God is concerned for other nations beyond Israel. Second, it encourages Israel that, just as God is committed to his promises regarding other nations, so he can be trusted regarding his promises to Israel. Third, it reminds Israel that they exist for the sake of the larger community.[19] As Wright notes, YHWH's 'multi-national sovereignty' demonstrates his deeper concern for Israel's destiny.[20] All of these themes recur in later chapters. Israel's election carries with it responsibilities to their neighbours.

Moran notes two intertextual allusions to the exodus present in Deuteronomy 2.[21] First, in Deuteronomy 2:15 we learn that the 'LORD's hand' was against Israel. That same 'hand of the LORD' had previously been against Egypt (Exod. 6:1; 7:4; 9:3). Israel's rebellious generation experienced a thirty-eight-year 'anti-exodus' at God's hand. Second, in Deuteronomy 2:25 God promises that the nations will 'hear reports of you and will tremble and be in anguish'. That promise echoes Exodus 15:14:

> The nations will hear and tremble;
>   anguish will grip the people of Philistia.

The four decades condensed into Deuteronomy 2 provide a narrative of reversed exodus followed by renewed exodus. By implication if the present generation wish to take the Promised Land they must not repeat the mistakes of their parents.[22] The end of Deuteronomy 2 records Israel's first victory against Sihon and Heshbon. This episode raises important questions for the consideration of Israel's 'mission' towards the nations. The concern expressed for Edom, Moab and Ammon seems radically at odds with the violent

---

19. Olson, *Deuteronomy*, pp. 27–28.

20. Wright, *Deuteronomy*, p. 36.

21. Moran, 'End of the Unholy War', pp. 333–342.

22. Olson, *Deuteronomy*, p. 27.

destruction exacted upon enemies. Terms of peace are offered (Deut. 2:26), but when refused destruction and plunder ensue (Deut. 2:34–35). If any real notion of 'mission' or missionary consciousness is to be argued for in Deuteronomy the concept of *ḥērem* (a devoted thing) will have to be examined more fully. McConville suggestively begins to connect the *ḥērem* with the concepts of election, ethics and holiness.[23] A fuller exploration of these themes in relation to the *ḥērem* will be undertaken when we examine Deuteronomy 7.

Deuteronomy 3 completes the historical introduction to the book. The Og narrative, though somewhat briefer, echoes the report of Sihon; though this time it is Israel who are the aggressor, as they conquer, capture and destroy. The report of successful conquests on the eastern side of the Jordan should steel the resolve for the challenge that waits on the west. As McConville says, 'Faith in Yahweh's future deliverance is possible because of what he has so far done.'[24] And although two-and-a-half tribes have already received their allotment, they are instructed to help their brothers in taking the land on the other side of the Jordan. It is crucial to national identity and unity that they help in the conquest to come.[25] Relationships with those over the boundary are a core component of chapters 2–3. First, there is the command not to provoke those with whom they share ancestral heritage. Second, there is the command to destroy the hostile enemies, Sihon and Og. Third, there is the instruction aimed at Israelite unity. There are, in this introduction to the book, hints at what is to come in terms of the distinctive identity of the people of YHWH evidenced by their ethical conduct.

Deuteronomy 1 – 3 has recounted Israel's past from the time of their exodus from Egypt up until they stand on the verge of the Jordan ready to cross and take the Promised Land. In the opening frame the narrator introduces key themes that recur throughout the book. First, Israel must learn from the past and heed the call to full obedience and covenant loyalty 'today'. Second, the narrator has shown God's sovereign rule and concern for the nations. Third, Israel's election to possession of the land brings with it ethical obligations with regard to both God and neighbour. Fourth, instructions regarding the *ḥērem* and the call not to provoke Edom, Moab or Ammon speak of Israel's holiness among the nations. The division of land is a process of crossing and creating boundaries, but those boundaries, as the rest of the book demonstrates, are porous as Israel relates to the nations. The opening section emphasizes the high

---

23. McConville, *Deuteronomy*, pp. 87–88.

24. Ibid., p. 95.

25. Brueggemann, *Deuteronomy*, p. 48.

call to be a distinct and obedient covenant community. Slater sums up the rhetorical force of Deuteronomy 1 – 3:

> The rhetoric of these chapters [Deut. 1 – 3] is not so much propositional as experiential. Deut. 30:19–20 *says* 'I set before you this day life and death, blessing and curse, therefore choose life that you may prosper in the land.' Deuteronomy 1–3 does not *say* this. Rather, it brings readers through the experience of disobedience and death, fidelity and prosperous life, and sets before them the moment of decision to enter the land in obedience to the LORD's command. It offers the identity required to hear the law and understand the urgency of its imperative, while at the same time reminding readers that this imperative is addressed to them in their own present circumstances, and not in some far off long ago. Identification with the people positions readers to hear the law addressed to Israel in Deuteronomy, while awareness of their own context positions readers to respond faithfully in their own time and place.[26]

Deuteronomy 4

Deuteronomy 4 is the bridge between the historical survey of Deuteronomy 1 – 3 and the restatement of the law in Deuteronomy 5. As Nelson observes, 'It makes a sharp transition from history to paraenesis and from a retrospective horizon to the "now" of Moses' act of speaking.'[27]

Deuteronomy 4:1–40 may be seen as having a chiastic structure as follows:

A: A call for Israel to obey in the sight of the nations (vv. 1–8)
   B: A warning against disobedience (vv. 9–14)
      C: Recollection of the encounter at Horeb and the commandment against idolatry (vv. 15–24)
   B': A further warning against disobedience (vv. 25–31)
A': A final call for Israel to obey before the nations (vv. 32–40)

The frame (A, A') demonstrates the importance of Israel's obedience in the sight of the nations. Deuteronomy 4:1 says: 'Now, Israel, hear the decrees and laws I am about to teach you. Follow them so that you may live and may go in and take possession of the land the LORD, the God of your ancestors, is giving you.'

---

26. Susan Slater, 'Imagining Arrival: Rhetoric, Reader and Word of God in Deuteronomy 1–3', in *The Labour of Reading: Desire, Alienation and Biblical Interpretation* (Atlanta: SBL, 1999), p. 114. Emphases original.

27. Richard D. Nelson, *Deuteronomy* (Louisville: Westminster John Knox, 2002), p. 61.

This forms an inclusio with Deuteronomy 4:40 that reads, 'Keep his decrees and commands, which I am giving you today, so that it may go well with you and your children after you and that you may live long in the land the LORD your God gives you for all time.'

The introductory 'and now' (wĕ'attâ) marks the beginning of a discourse that is in transition from historical recounting to the deduction to be drawn.[28] Immediately following is the 'Israel, listen' (yiśrā'ēl šĕma'), which is characteristic of didactic address. The text indicates that the reader has arrived at a crucial moment in the narrative. This is supported by Moses' explanation that he is to teach (mĕlammēd) the people something to which they must not add or from which they must not subtract. The use of the 'promulgation formula' ('the commands which I am giving/teaching you') is repeated throughout Deuteronomy as an insistent and urgent call for obedient action and decision.[29]

The reason for the strength of Moses' command is rooted in the source of these laws and statutes: they are from YHWH and are to be observed and performed. The use of the verb 'āśâ (to do) occurs five times in the first fourteen verses of the chapter, emphasizing the practical performance of Torah required of the people.[30] The verb šāmar (to keep) similarly refers to obedience. The recollection of the events of Numbers 25, given in verses 3–4, when Israel worshipped Baal of Peor, reiterates the call to purity of worship.

The imperative 'see' (rĕ'ēh) of verse 5 stands parallel to the 'hear' (šĕma') of verse 1. These introductory imperatives serve to capture attention, alerting the reader to the importance of what is to follow.[31] As Weinfeld argues, this pericope 'serves as a kind of motivation for observing the law'.[32]

Deuteronomy 4:6 reiterates the call and gives a positive reason for obedience: 'Observe them carefully, for this will show your wisdom and understanding to the nations, who will hear about all these decrees and say, "Surely this great nation is a wise and understanding people."'

Crucially, the purpose of Israel's obedience is that it constitutes 'wisdom and understanding' in the eyes of the surrounding nations. When those nations

---

28. Weinfeld, *Deuteronomy 1–11*, p. 199. See also Deut. 10:12, following 9:7 – 10:11.

29. S. J. de Vries, 'The Development of the Deuteronomic Promulgation Formula', *Bib* 55 (1974), pp. 301–316.

30. Deut. 4:1, 5, 6, 13, 14. Nelson, *Deuteronomy*, p. 63.

31. Nelson calls these 'foregrounded imperatives'. *Deuteronomy*, p. 63. McConville suggests that the use of the imperative in the singular is for 'arresting effect, as in 1:8'. *Deuteronomy*, p. 99.

32. Weinfeld, *Deuteronomy 1–11*, p. 201.

learn of Torah they will declare Israel to be a wise, discerning and great nation. As Israel embodies Torah the nations recognize something admirable and praiseworthy.[33] The life of the community bears witness to the wisdom of their law, and by implication the wisdom of their lawgiver. Brueggemann describes Israel's call to be a 'contrast society, quite unlike the other nations, a contrast that is lived out in ways that are inimical to the watching nations'.[34] While obedience to YHWH does not *cause* others to enter into covenant relationship with him, it promotes the nearness, wisdom and righteousness of YHWH to others. It is a missional ethic offering a glimpse of something good, which they may choose to investigate or appropriate for themselves.[35] Wright notes the inseparability of mission and ethics:

> [T]he ethical quality of life of the people of God (their obedience to the law, in this context) is a vital factor in the attraction of the nations to the living God . . . There is a vital link between the religious claims of the people of God (that God is near them) and their practical social ethic.[36]

Moses' commission to the people is to obey Torah, for it is through the keeping of the commandments that God may be known and found in the community.[37] The interplay between particularism and universalism – election for mission – comes together here in Deuteronomy 4:5–8. With Moriah and Horeb in the background, Deuteronomy 4:5–8 gives a more specific form to the call to bless the nations, and be a kingdom of priests and a holy nation.[38] There is a threefold repetition of the phrase 'great nation' (*gôy gādôl*) in verses 6–8, a promise first issued to Abraham in Genesis 12:2. In addition to the centripetal nature of Israel's witness there is an implicit centrifugality to their vocation, and it is

---

33. Christopher J. H. Wright, *Old Testament Ethics for the People of God* (Leicester: Inter-Varsity Press, 2004), p. 64.

34. Brueggemann, *Deuteronomy*, p. 52.

35. Tigay notes that 'according to Exodus Rabba, "Akilas the Proselyte" converted to Judaism because of the Torah, while Tatian, a Syrian of the second century, lists "the excellence of the precepts" of the Torah among the factors that induced him to become a Christian'. *Deuteronomy*, p. 45.

36. Wright, *Deuteronomy*, p. 49.

37. Patrick D. Miller, *Deuteronomy*, Int (Louisville: John Knox, 1990), p. 57.

38. Eugene H. Merrill, *Deuteronomy*, NAC 4 (Nashville: Broadman & Holman, 1992), p. 117. Wright considers that Israel's call to be a blessing to the nations was 'in their "genetic code" from the very loins of Abraham'. *Deuteronomy*, pp. 48–49.

enacted through living out YHWH's Torah. Israel's missio-ethical vocation is Torah-morphic.

In Verses 7–8 YHWH is described as being near to his people, and that is evidenced by the righteous decrees in their midst. The nearness of YHWH and the righteousness of his decrees belong together. As Brueggemann notes, 'All through the book of Deuteronomy, the tradition is at pains to hold together *holy presence* and *social practice*, for either alone is inadequate and will not grasp the attention of the nations.'[39] The adjective 'righteous' (*ṣaddîq*) is used to describe the laws and decrees, and has a social and relational dimension.[40] As the laws and decrees are expounded in the rest of the book it can be seen that righteous decrees uphold justice for slaves, widows, orphans and aliens.[41]

In verses 9–14 the people are instructed to 'watch yourselves closely so that you do not forget the things your eyes have seen'. McConville suggests that the noun translated as 'yourselves' (*nepeš*) conveys something of Deuteronomy's holistic ethic. YHWH requires not merely external observance, but whole-life worship and obedience as a response to his redemption.[42] They are to pass on the faith to their children, and remember that constitutive day they stood at Horeb while God addressed them. That formative encounter unites the generations of Israel as one people. It was and remains a unique event decisive for their life as the people of God.[43]

Verses 15–24 recall Israel's encounter with YHWH at Horeb. They are reminded that they saw no form of the divine, and therefore the people are warned against any sort of idolatry.[44] The word for 'image' (*tĕmûnâ*) appears five times in the chapter.[45] It is the same word used in Exodus 20:4 – the second commandment prohibition of making idols. The repeated use of the word emphasizes the seriousness with which YHWH takes idolatry. The repeated

---

39. Brueggemann, *Deuteronomy*, p. 53. Emphasis original.

40. Merrill, *Deuteronomy*, p. 118.

41. Nelson, *Deuteronomy*, p. 65.

42. McConville, *Deuteronomy*, p. 105.

43. Ibid., p. 107.

44. A number of scholars note in Deut. 4:15–20 an allusion to Gen. 1. This order of creation, albeit reversed, reminds them of the distinction between the created and the transcendent Creator. Fishbane describes this passage as an 'explicit aggadic adaptation of Gen. 1 for the purposes of an exhortation against idolatry'. Michael Fishbane, *Biblical Interpretation in Ancient Israel* (Oxford: Oxford University Press, 1985), p. 321.

45. Deut. 4:12, 15, 16, 23, 25.

emphasis on fleeing idolatry is suggestive of the content of the ethical life that displays God's wisdom to the nations. As Wright observes, 'the negative warnings of this central section . . . [are] for the sake of the positive "missionary" potential of verses 6–8'.[46] Purity and singularity of worship is the sum total of what covenant obedience looks like for Israel. It is this sort of obedience that will either commend or blaspheme God's name before the nations. As the people embody Torah they bear witness to the true God.[47] Olson, commenting on Deuteronomy 4:20, suggests that 'the closest one can get to the image of God in the world is to look at the people of Israel'.[48]

In verses 25–31 the consequences of any future idolatry are spelled out. The *rîb* (dispute) pattern is utilized to demonstrate the formality and seriousness of covenant violation.[49] They will suffer divine judgment in the form of exile, and will be few in number – a stark contrast with the promise to Abraham alluded to in Deuteronomy 1:10. However, YHWH promises, on the basis of his compassion and covenant, to restore them so that they will obey him. As Weinfeld notes, the people may forget their covenant with YHWH (v. 23), but YHWH will not forget his covenant with his people (v. 31).[50] This ties in with the later promise of Deuteronomy 30:6, which points to a work of God that will enable the people to live the lives to which YHWH calls them. For Israel this could be described as a life, death and resurrection life pattern.[51] Deuteronomy suggests that a new birth will enable Israel to fulfil their commission vis-à-vis the nations.

Finally, in verses 32–40 Moses' speech is summarized and concluded. The uniqueness of YHWH is stressed as is Israel's status as his chosen people with special privilege and responsibility.[52] Verses 39–40 close the inclusio begun in verses 1–2 with a final call to hear and obey. The repetition through the chapter of the verb *lāmad* (to learn/teach) along with the mention of 'children' and 'children's children' emphasizes the intergenerational dimension of this catechetical enterprise with Israel, and the nations as intended beneficiaries.[53] The missional and ethical are brought together and displayed primarily in the purity of Israel's worship. The position and structure of the chapter communicate

---

46. Wright, *Deuteronomy*, p. 49.
47. Ibid., p. 50.
48. Olson, *Deuteronomy*, p. 34.
49. Merrill, *Deuteronomy*, p. 126.
50. Weinfeld, *Deuteronomy 1–11*, p. 207.
51. See Olson, *Deuteronomy*, p. 37.
52. Brueggemann, *Deuteronomy*, p. 58.
53. Olson, *Deuteronomy*, p. 37.

something of the vision of Deuteronomy. The canonical position of Deuteronomy 4 is crucial in the flow of the book. Coming as it does, immediately after the historical survey, and immediately before the reiteration of the Decalogue, Deuteronomy 4 expresses the overarching message of the book.[54] The chapter opens and closes with reference to the wider world to which Israel stands as witness and example. There is the call for obedience and warnings against disobedience in the inner panels of the chapter. The central section of the chapter further defines what obedience and disobedience look like. The life of obedience is one of whole-hearted devotion to YHWH alone; the life of disobedience is one of idolatry.[55] The repeated call through the chapter is to 'watch yourselves' (vv. 9, 15) and 'do not forget' (vv. 9, 23) lest they turn to idols (vv. 16, 23, 25). Purity and singularity of worship are the essence of obedience, and it is just such an obedience that will impact the surrounding nations.

It is noteworthy here, in our attempt to define missional ethics exegetically, that a core component of a missional ethic is purity of worship. Lives of obedience, shunning idolatry, are lives that bear witness to God to those around. Weinfeld describes the whole of Deuteronomy as a witness *against* Israel in the case of disobedience, yet it seems to offer much more than that. It offers hope of renewal upon repentance, the promise of restoration at God's hand, and a manifesto for a missional ethic.[56]

McConville notes that with Deuteronomy 4 a trajectory is begun in which the righteousness of Israel will bring salvation to the nations: 'For the setting of "righteousness" as the standard for God's people embeds a condition in their being chosen, and postulates a people of God that Israel in the event will not be.'[57] Yet the trajectory points forward to a time when righteousness will appear and begin to spread beyond Israel and to the nations. This is the hope that later prophets anticipate. Wright concludes his survey of Deuteronomy 4 by noting that the ultimate rhetorical thrust of the entire chapter is ethical. He states:

> Unless Israel would live in accordance with God's law, what value would their incredible historical and religious experience retain? And furthermore, how would the nations come to know the uniqueness of Yahweh as the living God and of his saving action in history unless they are drawn by the ethical distinctiveness of God's people?[58]

---

54. Daniel I. Block, *Deuteronomy*, NIVAC (Grand Rapids: Zondervan, 2012), p. 115.

55. Robson, *Honey from the Rock*, pp. 127–135.

56. Weinfeld, *Deuteronomy 1–11*, p. 216.

57. McConville, *Deuteronomy*, p. 116.

58. Wright, *Deuteronomy*, p. 58.

Again mission and ethics coalesce in response to the uniqueness of Israel's God and his dealings with them in history. The stage is set for the reiteration of the Decalogue, and the fuller exposition to follow.

Deuteronomy 5

The recitation of the Decalogue opens Moses' second speech and the second major section of Deuteronomy.[59] The Decalogue brings together, in Miller's words, 'all that is important for Israel's life – the religious, familial, and social'.[60] Brueggemann describes the 'ten words' as 'the most elemental self-announcement of YHWH'.[61] The structure of the Decalogue addresses two areas: relationship to God in commandments 1–3, and relationship to others in commandments 5–10.[62] The fourth commandment serves as a bridge joining the two. The opening verse summons Israel to 'hear' (šĕma'), 'learn' (ûlĕmadtem) and 'do' (la'ăśōtām) 'the statutes and laws' ('et-haḥuqqîm wĕ'et hammišpāṭîm) in terms reminiscent of Deuteronomy 1:1 and 4:1. This introduction alerts the hearer to the importance of that which is to follow. Once again, practical performance is the necessary corollary to cognitive assent.[63]

The Decalogue reveals not only the will but also the character of God. McConville notes the way in which the Decalogue combines precept with explanation and motivation clauses. He argues that 'law' in Deuteronomy 5 is closely linked with wisdom and righteousness. It is more than simply a statute book: it is instruction for right living and ordering of things.[64]

Wright highlights the contrast between life lived under the rule of YHWH and life lived under the rule of Pharaoh. In Egypt there was no worship of YHWH permitted; no Sabbath rest for slaves; no protection from state-sponsored killing; no family to be honoured and cared for; no property of their own to cherish. The commandments thus protect and preserve the blessings of liberation.[65] As Wright observes, 'Liberation is no advantage in itself unless consolidated into social structures that maintain its objectives for the whole community. The Decalogue is the foundation for such consolidation.'[66]

---

59. McConville, *Deuteronomy*, p. 119.
60. Miller, *Deuteronomy*, p. 72.
61. Brueggemann, *Deuteronomy*, p. 65.
62. Tigay, *Deuteronomy*, p. 62.
63. Merrill, *Deuteronomy*, p. 141.
64. McConville, *Deuteronomy*, pp. 120–121.
65. Wright, *Deuteronomy*, pp. 64–65.
66. Ibid., p. 65.

The Decalogue is the fruit of a physical exodus and a social and legal exodus, a piece of anti-Egypt and anti-Pharaoh legislation. Positively the Decalogue is a reflection of YHWH's character. Therefore obedience communicates something of YHWH's character before the surrounding nations. As such the Decalogue could legitimately be described as the missio-ethical foundation for the people of God. Prefacing the imperative with the indicative of redemption frames the Decalogue in terms of the responsibilities that accompany redemption. Wright likens the Ten Commandments to a kind of 'Bill of Rights' for a free people in covenant with YHWH.[67] Similarly, McBride, picking up on Josephus' classification of Deuteronomy as *politeia* in *Jewish Antiquities*,[68] argues that Deuteronomy (as a whole, but with special reference to ch. 5) is a polity, constitution or social charter – a model of 'theocentric humanism'.[69] Recent scholarship has done much to demonstrate that the Decalogue is about far more than simply rules: it is a vision for a contrast society in the midst of the nations.

The first commandment could be viewed as the primary governing principle, with subsequent commandments applying that initial governing principle to various spheres of life. As Christensen says:

> The relationship to the one God must dominate every sphere of life, whether that
> of action, of thought, or of emotion. There can be no areas of life in which a person
> or thing comes before our commitment to the one true God.[70]

For example, murder, theft or adultery are all forms of worshipping something other than YHWH – often worship of self and its desires. This may be made more evident when we come to examine Deuteronomy 6 – 11, which is an extended exposition of the first commandment. The ethical primacy of pure worship is a constituent part of missional ethics for YHWH's people.

Building upon the first commandment, and flowing from it, the second commandment forbids representing the Creator with anything created. The associated blessings/curses for obedience/disobedience demonstrate the importance of right worship and the uniqueness of YHWH. As Merrill notes,

---

67. Ibid., p. 64.

68. Josephus, *Jewish Antiquities* 4.184, 193, 198.

69. S. Dean McBride Jr, 'Polity of the Covenant People: The Book of Deuteronomy', *Int* 41.3 (1987), pp. 229–244.

70. Christensen, *Deuteronomy 1:1–21:9*, p. 115.

'to serve other gods, then, was to reverse the exodus and go back under bondage, thus betraying the grace and favour of Yahweh'.[71]

The third commandment prohibiting 'misuse' of the name of YHWH refers to more than inappropriate use of language. Christensen suggests that the commandment refers to swearing falsely in YHWH's name, reflecting a parallel with Leviticus 19:12.[72] Tigay suggests that it may refer to lying on oath in legal settings.[73] Still others suggest misuse in a cultic (or occult) setting.[74] It could therefore incorporate both corrupt worship and corrupt judicial practices.[75] Furthermore, it seems later Jewish writers understood the commandment in broader scope. We see later within Scripture that other writers interpret this commandment to refer to conduct and actions (Ezek. 36:16–23; Rom. 2:17–24). Ezekiel connects idolatry and injustice with profaning God's name in the sight of the nations. Misuse of the name is an 'anti-witness' to YHWH before the watching world. In this sense the commandment would include actions as well as speech.

The fourth commandment is in some ways central to the law, bridging the responsibility to honour God and the responsibility to honour one's neighbour. The Sabbath is described as holy or set apart for God and carries religious as well as socio-ethical implications. Sabbath keeping is explicitly linked to the remembrance of redemption from slavery in Egypt. As well as having religious significance for Israel, it is an act of protection and care for family, servants, animals and outsiders. As McConville notes, 'The heart of the Sabbath is to acknowledge a profound relationship between religion and the social order; there can be no Sabbath keeping that endures any kind of oppression of the poor and weak (cf. Amos 8:5–6).'[76] Later prophets condemn Sabbath breaking precisely because, motivated by greed, it was linked with exploitation of the weak and vulnerable.[77]

The second table of the Decalogue continues the movement in the commandments from God to society to family. The fifth commandment is concerned with more than simply respect towards parents. In the ANE the extended family was the primary unit of judicial governance; it was the primary economic unit

---

71. Merrill, *Deuteronomy*, p. 148.

72. Christensen, *Deuteronomy 1:1–21:9*, p. 114.

73. Tigay, *Deuteronomy*, p. 67.

74. See Mayes, *Deuteronomy*, p. 168; Merrill, *Deuteronomy*, p. 149.

75. Wright, *Deuteronomy*, p. 73.

76. McConville, *Deuteronomy*, p. 135.

77. Wright, *Deuteronomy*, p. 76.

as possessor of land and producer of crops; and it was the primary spiritual unit in which the covenant was preserved and passed on. Therefore to dishonour parents was to threaten the social, economic and spiritual fabric of society.[78]

Similarly, commandments related to the unlawful taking of life, adultery and theft are also concerned with the wider social implications of breaking such commandments. In a society of extended families, clans and tribes, all living and working in close proximity, the sort of relational breakdown caused by murder, adultery or theft would be devastating and far reaching not just for the individuals concerned, but for the wider society. Nelson notes the social importance of paternity and inheritance, which makes adultery a public concern.[79] Tigay suggests that the sixth commandment is rooted in humanity's intrinsic value as image bearers; therefore unlawful taking of life is prohibited.[80]

The final commandment is concerned not only with appropriation or scheming to obtain but concerns the desires of the heart.[81] This is not something that can be tried by a magistrate, thus demonstrating that the Decalogue is concerned with more than 'law' in a narrow sense. The heart in Deuteronomy is the seat of worship and the source of any true obedience. To break the final commandment is to break the first. Ultimately it is God himself who will have to perform a work on the hearts of his people if they are to live out this new society before the nations (Deut. 30:6).

McConville argues that in the Decalogue we have a 'concern to bring the people of God into genuine liberty, by a full commitment to the good of the other and of all; and in doing so to offer the world an example of the nature of the divine will for ordering the whole creation'.[82] To live out this way of life will require what Brueggemann describes as 'intentionality in the ordering of an alternative community that daily lives differently in the world'.[83] It is the sort of community that reflects its love for God in its love for others; it is the sort of community that causes the surrounding nations to observe, 'surely this great nation is a wise and understanding people' (Deut. 4:6).

The closing of Deuteronomy 5, when paired with the opening, reminds Israel of the larger narrative they inhabit. The closing scene (vv. 22–32) resumes the narrative of the opening scene (vv. 1–5) and expands upon it. Lohfink suggests

---

78. Ibid., p. 77.

79. Nelson, *Deuteronomy*, p. 83.

80. Tigay, *Deuteronomy*, p. 71.

81. McConville, *Deuteronomy*, pp. 130–131.

82. Ibid., p. 136.

83. Brueggemann, *Deuteronomy*, p. 72.

that the language and imagery of theophany serve to intensify the moment and heighten the sense of importance and urgency.[84] It is up to them 'today' to choose to obey, but they are part of a story stretching back to Abraham. It is Abraham's offspring God intends to bless, and through them to bless the nations. If they obey it will go well with them, and if it goes well with them it will go well with the nations.

Deuteronomy 6

Brueggemann has described Deuteronomy 6 – 11 as being 'the richest instructional, homiletical, and theological materials in the book … for they articulate the historical memories and motivations that frame and give context to the commandments to follow'.[85] A number of scholars have noted that Deuteronomy 6 – 11 expounds the first commandment to have no other gods before YHWH, with chapters 12–26 expounding the remaining commandments.[86] Within Deuteronomy 6 – 11 chapters 6–8 form one unit framed by the call to 'Hear, O Israel' (*wĕšāmaʿtā yiśrāʾēl*) introduced in 6:3–4 and then again in 9:1.

The introductory verses of chapter 6 refer back to the Decalogue just given in 5:1–21. The laws of the Decalogue are now applied to the daily life of the people in the present and future generations.[87] It is these commandments that are to be observed and passed on through the generations if the land is to be possessed and enjoyed. The Shema then reiterates, expounds and applies the essence of the first commandment.[88]

There is, however, a lack of consensus regarding the interpretation of the Shema.[89] Deuteronomy 6:4 reads as follows: 'Hear, O Israel: the LORD our God, the LORD is one.' The interpretative challenge arises with the verbless clause in verse 6b (*yhwh ʾĕlōhênû yhwh ʾeḥād*). The clause allows a range of possible translations depending on the placement of the copula. The interpretative issues are twofold. First, is this a statement about God's relationship to Israel

---

84. N. Lohfink, 'Reading Deuteronomy 5 as Narrative', in *A God So Near: Essays on Old Testament Theology in Honour of Patrick Miller* (Winona Lake: Eisenbrauns, 2003), pp. 261–281.

85. Brueggemann, *Deuteronomy*, p. 82.

86. Weinfeld, *Deuteronomy 1–11*, p. 328; Tigay, *Deuteronomy*, p. 75.

87. McConville, *Deuteronomy*, p. 138.

88. Miller, *Deuteronomy*, p. 98.

89. S. Dean McBride, Jr, 'The Yoke of the Kingdom: An Exposition of Deuteronomy 6:4–5', *Int* 27 (1973), p. 291.

(YHWH *our* God; YHWH alone), or a statement about God himself (YHWH our God; YHWH *is* [the only] one)? Second, what does it mean to say YHWH is 'one' (*'eḥād*)?

Moberly, among others, considers it to be a statement primarily about the uniqueness and incomparability of YHWH based on the only Old Testament citation of Deuteronomy 6:4 in Zechariah 14:9.[90] However, this need not mean that 'oneness' refers *only* to ontological uniqueness. Janzen has argued that God's 'oneness' refers to his moral unity, and therefore his dependability.[91] Janzen begins by noting the co-text of the Shema as the Decalogue, with the Shema mirroring the first part.[92] The wider context for the Decalogue, introduced in its opening verses, is the Exodus narrative, which emphasizes God's fidelity to the patriarchs through redemption and the covenant at Sinai. That fidelity is even demonstrated in spite of various rebellions (e.g. Exod. 32; Num. 14). Janzen then moves on to another text in the Deuteronomistic tradition, Jeremiah 32:38–41, and the way in which 'oneness' is used to emphasize YHWH's loyalty to Israel. Janzen finally picks up on Zechariah 14:9–11 as a promise of restoration for Jerusalem, which manifests the oneness or integrity of YHWH.[93] Based upon these wider co-texts and contexts Janzen concludes:

> It is this consistency which is of the essence of the divine faithfulness . . . The divine faithfulness to Israel is what it is because of an even deeper internal divine faithfulness. The fidelity of the divine relation to Israel is rooted in the divine self-relation that I have been calling the integrity and that the Shema calls *'eḥād*.[94]

Perhaps the ambiguity of Deuteronomy 6:4b is deliberate, maintaining both the ontological uniqueness of YHWH and the unique relationship of YHWH with

---

90. R. W. L. Moberly, '"Yahweh Is One": The Translation of the Shema', in J. A. Emerton (ed.), *Studies in the Pentateuch*, VTSup 41 (Leiden: Brill, 1990), pp. 211–215. See also Judah Kraut, 'Deciphering the Shema: Staircase Parallelism and the Syntax of Deuteronomy 6:4', *VT* 61.4 (2011), p. 602.

91. J. Gerald Janzen, 'On the Most Important Word in the Shema (Deuteronomy VI 4–5)', *VT* 37.3 (1987), pp. 280–300.

92. Ibid., p. 281.

93. Ibid., p. 298.

94. Ibid., p. 300. For supporting arguments see Miller, *Deuteronomy*, pp. 99–101; McConville, *Deuteronomy*, p. 141.

his people, Israel.[95] Part of the uniqueness of YHWH, when compared to the fickle deities of the surrounding nations, is his fidelity to his chosen people, Israel.

As noted earlier the Shema is the headline for the rest of the story to follow. Miller argues that structurally the Shema summarizes the Ten Commandments, and the Ten Commandments are signposts for the statutes to follow in chapters 12–26.[96] The Shema is the most compact summary of the law and the heart of the Torah from which the rest flows.[97] The command 'Love the LORD your God with all your heart and with all your soul and with all your strength' (Deut. 6:5) encompasses more than privatized religion.[98] The threefold repetition of 'all' (*bĕkol-lĕbabĕkā ûbĕkol-napšĕkā ûbĕkol-mĕʾōdekā*) emphasizes the holistic and total nature of love for YHWH.[99] These are commands for the individual and the community, and they are to be practised holistically, individually and collectively. The call to love the Lord with heart, soul and strength, in verse 5, is not to divide the human life into three distinct spheres but rather has a cumulative effect 'to accent the superlative degree of total commitment to YHWH'.[100] That call, in the verses which follow (vv. 6–9), extends beyond the realm of the personal and private to become a family, community and public affair.[101]

MacDonald observes six instructions that come from the Shema: the laws are to be upon hearts (v. 6), impressed upon children (v. 7), recited often (v. 7), bound to the hands (v. 8), bound to the forehead (v. 8) and on the door posts and gates (v. 9). Observing these instructions is a way of securing the constant attention of the Israelites upon them.[102] The 'gates' referred to here are the

---

95. Justin M. Fuhrmann, 'Deuteronomy 6–8 and the History of Interpretation: An Exposition on the First Two Commandments', *JETS* 53.1 (2010), p. 50.

96. Patrick D. Miller, 'The Way of Torah', in *Israelite Religion and Biblical Theology: Collected Essays*, JSOTSup 267 (Sheffield: Sheffield Academic Press, 2000), pp. 497–507.

97. Peter J. Gentry and Stephen J. Wellum, *Kingdom Through Covenant* (Wheaton: Crossway, 2012), p. 365.

98. Daniel I. Block, 'How Many Is God? An Investigation into the Meaning of Deuteronomy 6:4–5', *JETS* 47.2 (2004), pp. 193–212.

99. Wright, *Deuteronomy*, p. 99.

100. McBride, 'Yoke of the Kingdom', p. 304.

101. Block, 'How Many Is God?', p. 204.

102. Nathan MacDonald, *Deuteronomy and the Meaning of 'Monotheism'* (Tübingen: Mohr Siebeck, 2012), pp. 128–133.

gates of the city. Here YHWH's instruction would have had 'constant public exposure . . . because the city gate was the centre of public activity'.[103] Residents and visitors alike would have been aware of Israel's laws and statutes. Given that the city gates also functioned as the courts, the wisdom of YHWH's law was publicly evidenced in fulfilment of Deuteronomy 4:6.[104] Israel's life under the law, their devotion to YHWH, and the justice sought under his law for all in every sphere of life testified to the wisdom of his law. Tigay notes that rabbinic exegesis observed that the command to love YHWH with heart, soul and strength required action, not only emotion.[105] Israel's singular devotion to YHWH was not to be a matter of privatized religion, but an all-encompassing way of life reaching every frontier. It was to become part of the 'fabric of life and conversation'.[106]

The great danger facing the believing community is amnesia, particularly in the face of great affluence (vv. 10–11); that they forget who YHWH is and what he has done, and so in time fail to be the distinctive society they are called out to be. Verses 10–19 look forward to the possession of the land, and warn against forgetting YHWH, going after other gods, and the terrible consequences of such behaviour. The warning is, 'do not put the LORD your God to the test' (v. 16), but rather, 'Do what is right and good in the LORD's sight' (v. 18). Arnold has demonstrated the way in which the calls to 'love' (v. 5) and to 'fear' (v. 13) are not antinomies but rather contiguous.[107] Love, like fear, is concerned with daily practical obedience in all the varied spheres of life – a covenant loyalty and fidelity exhibited in action.[108] The way to 'be careful that you do not forget' (v. 12) is to worship and serve YHWH alone.[109]

Verses 20–25 return to the theme of instructing children and provide something akin to a creed or catechism which is to be taught and passed on to the next generation.[110] In response to the child's question about the law, the parent is to answer with the story of redemption. This mirrors the shape of the early chapters of Deuteronomy. The history of redemption is recounted before

---

103. Tigay, *Deuteronomy*, p. 79.

104. Block, *Deuteronomy*, p. 186.

105. Tigay, *Deuteronomy*, p. 77.

106. McConville, *Deuteronomy*, p. 142.

107. Bill T. Arnold, 'The Love–Fear Antinomy in Deuteronomy 5–11', *VT* 61.4 (2011), pp. 567–569.

108. Brueggemann, *Deuteronomy*, p. 84.

109. McConville, *Deuteronomy*, p. 143.

110. Nelson, *Deuteronomy*, p. 94.

the law is reiterated. Election and redemption are for a missional ethic. The righteousness referred to in verse 25 is connected to an observance of Torah. Those who practise Torah will find that it goes well with them in the land. The text presents a serious call to the community to live out singular loyalty to YHWH in both word and deed. The community's obedience must consist of watching themselves so they do not forget who YHWH is and all that he has done, and passing these truths on to the next generation. Deuteronomy 4:6 will come about only as Deuteronomy 6:4 is lived out.

Deuteronomy 7

One of the most difficult questions to address in understanding how a 'missional ethic' might be at work in Deuteronomy is how the promise of Deuteronomy 4:6 sits alongside the command of Deuteronomy 7:2: 'when the LORD your God has delivered them over to you . . . then you must destroy them totally . . . show them no mercy'. Again, in Deuteronomy 7:16: 'destroy all the peoples the LORD your God gives over to you'.

These abrupt and harsh instructions have provoked much debate. For modern readers they trouble the conscience that God might prescribe genocide. For those engaging with the text there appears to be a contradiction between the humane instructions of Deuteronomy 10:18–19 and the brutal imperative of Deuteronomy 7:2. Indeed a number of scholars have noted that one of the distinctive features of Deuteronomy is its humanitarian qualities.[111] Additionally, there are historical and archaeological questions regarding the lack of evidence that such a widespread destruction ever occurred. There is no consensus as to how to resolve these problems, just a plethora of proposed solutions.

The majority of scholars suggest that the *ḥērem* of Deuteronomy 7 and 20 is a later idealized vision, employed for rhetorical purposes, and aiming at religious reform. Stern suggests it has an early northern provenance in the time of Jeroboam II when the nation might have had significant military power.[112] Most think it is later, stemming from the time of Josiah's reform in the south. Weinfeld describes it as a 'wish originating in the 8th–7th century B.C.E', and Nelson considers the *ḥērem* to speak to those tempted to

---

111. Moshe Weinfeld, 'The Origin of the Humanism in Deuteronomy', *JBL* 80 (1961), pp. 241–247; Georg Braulik, *The Theology of Deuteronomy: Collected Essays of Georg Braulik, O.S.B.*, tr. Ulrika Lindblad (Richland Hills, Tex.: BIBAL, 1994), pp. 131–150.

112. Philip D. Stern, *The Biblical Ḥērem: A Window on Israel's Religious Experience*, BJS 211 (Atlanta: Scholars Press, 1991), pp. 89–121.

compromise with the Assyrians – it is a 'rhetorical alarm' in the war for religious reform.[113]

While these views may be correct, the meaning of *ḥērem* is better understood by examining its literary context. Many commentators have observed that Deuteronomy 7 has a concentric structure.[114] The mandate to exercise *ḥērem* upon the inhabitants of the land brackets the chapter (vv. 1–6, 17–26), while the central section is occupied with themes of election, holiness and obedience. This structure illuminates the main emphases of the chapter. As Block has noted, the focus of the chapter is not primarily on *ḥērem*, but rather on the unique status of Israel in relationship to YHWH. Moses' primary concern is 'not ethnic elimination, but ethical scrupulosity'.[115] Moses' primary concern is YHWH's covenant love expressed in election and redemption that calls for a response of holiness, obedience and non-compromise. The brutality of the mandate is proportionate to the love, faithfulness and holiness of YHWH. The chapter therefore deals with the implications of election.[116] Israel's identity as a counter-culture must be preserved: 'election and holiness must be protected by rejection and separation'.[117] As Miller notes, the instructions of Deuteronomy 7 are still related to the first and second commandments regarding the purity of Israel's worship.[118] The commands are rhetorically forceful because of how seductive the alternatives might appear, a fact borne out in Israel's subsequent history.[119]

The instructions of verses 2–5 are holistic in scope. They cover the political, social and religious aspects of Israel's life. They are not to make treaties with the nations, nor intermarry, nor be seduced by religious syncretism. These would be fatal to Israel's distinctive identity and witness. As Nelson notes, any covenant with these people groups would be a counter-covenant or rival covenant to the covenant with YHWH.[120] Both Nelson and Lilley argue that the sense

---

113. Moshe Weinfeld, 'The Ban on the Canaanites in the Biblical Codes and Its Historical Development', in *History and Traditions of Early Israel: Studies Presented to Eduard Nielsen*, VTSup 50 (Leiden: Brill, 1993), pp. 154–155; Nelson, *Deuteronomy*, p. 99.

114. McConville, *Deuteronomy*, p. 151; Nelson, *Deuteronomy*, p. 97; Wright, *Deuteronomy*, p. 108.

115. Block, *Deuteronomy*, p. 206.

116. Wright, *Deuteronomy*, p. 108.

117. Nelson, *Deuteronomy*, p. 94.

118. Miller, *Deuteronomy*, p. 111; contra Mayes, who sees the Canaanite destruction and instructions regarding idolatry as two distinct subjects. Mayes, *Deuteronomy*, p. 181.

119. Brueggemann, *Deuteronomy*, p. 100.

120. Nelson, *Deuteronomy*, p. 99.

of *ḥērem* is perhaps not 'destruction' but something more akin to 'devotion' or 'renunciation'.[121] Both however concede that practically what is meant here is overwhelming military conquest including putting to death that which is 'devoted'.[122] Deuteronomy 20:16 makes clear that what is in view is the putting to death of anything related to or connected with idolatry.

Nelson's work is insightful in proposing that the 'devotion/destruction' is related to culture map categories. That which is *ḥērem* is in a similar category to the holy/profane or clean/unclean.[123] The *ḥērem* is not primarily about military victory, but about religious purity. Nevertheless as Nelson recognizes, that which is 'devoted' to God must not be kept back for human use, and must therefore be destroyed.[124] Wright questions whether large-scale destruction of people was in view given the instructions in verse 3 addressing intermarriage. Further the prime focus is on destroying religious paraphernalia (vv. 5–6, 25–26). It must also be noted that the conquest of Canaan was a historically unique event. The long-term vision is Deuteronomy 4:6; the immediate necessity is Deuteronomy 7:2. There is something unique about the events of the conquest that was not to be repeated by subsequent generations. Once established in the land the wider mission can continue. The uniqueness of the conquest can be seen in the instructions governing subsequent warfare in Deuteronomy 20. When going to war in the future, terms of peace are first offered, and plunder may be taken as spoils of the battle (Deut. 20:10–15). But for the cities to be taken as part of the conquest, total destruction is necessary so that they do not learn to follow the idols of the nations (Deut. 20:16–18).[125]

Deuteronomy 7 is concerned with preserving the identity of YHWH's chosen, holy and treasured people for the sake of the larger historical narrative of which they are a part. Key to understanding Deuteronomy 7 is situating it within the wider historical story. The promise to the patriarchs (and Abraham in particular) was that the nations would be blessed. For that plan to come to fruition the uniqueness of Israel must be preserved. Understanding this makes sense of

121. Richard D. Nelson, 'Ḥerem and the Deuteronomy Social Conscience', in
      Deuteronomy and Deuteronomic Literature: Festschrift C. H. W. Brekelmans (Leuven:
      Leuven University Press, 1997), p. 44; J. P. U. Lilley, 'Understanding the Herem',
      TynB 44.1 (1993), p. 177.

122. See also *HALOT* 1, pp. 353–354.

123. Nelson, 'Ḥerem', p. 42.

124. Ibid., p. 44.

125. Michael G. Hasel, *Military Practice and Polemic: Israel's Laws of Warfare in Near Eastern
      Perspective* (Berrien Springs: Andrews University Press, 2005), p. 28.

the universal and particular elements of YHWH's promise and dealings with Israel and the nations. For the sake of that longer-term universal picture, the immediate practicalities of Deuteronomy 7 were necessary to be administered as part of the one-time establishment of Israel as a holy nation in the midst of other nations.

The reason for such decisive action in the *ḥērem* is given in Deuteronomy 7:6: the people are holy, chosen and a treasured possession. It is YHWH's faithfulness that should motivate the people to uncompromising obedience to YHWH and separation from anything to do with false worship (vv. 7–11). If the people follow YHWH's decrees then they will experience blessing on the land and their flocks (vv. 12–16). Moreover in verses 17–24 the promise of YHWH, in faithfulness to the covenant, is that he himself will fight for his people. This judgment on the Canaanites is not merely human barbarity but the judgment of YHWH.[126] O'Connell observes that in verses 17–24 there is a sevenfold repetition of 'the LORD your God' in contrast with the sevenfold enumeration of nations in verses 1–2.[127] O'Connell suggests that this repetition emphasizes the need to eradicate foreign gods and those who worship them in order to maintain covenant loyalty to YHWH.[128]

The closing instruction to destroy their images emphasizes the repugnance of idolatry. It is described in verses 25–26 as an 'abomination' (*tôʿēbâ*) to be utterly abhorred and detested. It must be set apart and destroyed for it is contagious and could render Israel unholy.[129] As Block says, 'There is only one solution for anything or anyone declared to be *tôʿēbâ*: the rigorous application of the policy of *ḥērem*.'[130] McConville describes false religion as a false way of life, with a false rule; a sort of chaos.[131] Israel's war on idolatry is an abolition of chaos in favour of true order and rule for the whole cosmos. McConville summarizes: '[T]he divine war against the idolatrous nations . . . [is] an act of salvation, in the sense of establishing the possibility of the divine rule in the world, which alone could offer it hope'.[132]

---

126. Olson, *Deuteronomy*, p. 54.

127. Robert H. O'Connell, 'Deuteronomy VII 1–26: Asymmetrical Concentricity and the Rhetoric of Conquest', *VT* 42.2 (1992), p. 260.

128. Ibid., p. 262.

129. Susan Niditch, *War in the Hebrew Bible: A Study in the Ethics of Violence* (Oxford: Oxford University Press, 1993), p. 65.

130. Block, *Deuteronomy*, p. 218.

131. McConville, *Deuteronomy*, p. 164.

132. Ibid.

Here mission and ethics overlap because at stake is 'the preservation of the truth of the revelation of God entrusted to [Israel]'.[133] If Israel fail to remain distinct then they, along with the revelation of truth entrusted to them, will cease to exist. And if Israel cease to exist so too does their mission to bring blessing to the nations. It is for the sake of mission that the people must rid their new geographical, social, political and religious space of anything related to idolatry.

Deuteronomy 8

Deuteronomy 8 consists of further warnings pertaining to the first commandment. A number of scholars note the chiastic structure of Deuteronomy 8 as follows:

A: The promise to their forefathers (v. 1)
    B: Humbling and provision in the wilderness (vv. 2–6)
        C: The goodness of the land (vv. 7–9)
            D: Do not forget the Lord (vv. 10–11)
        C': The goodness of the land (vv. 12–14)
    B': Humbling and provision in the wilderness (vv. 15–16)
A': The promise to their forefathers (vv. 17–18)[134]

Interspersed throughout the chapter are repeated imperatives to be careful to follow the commandments, to remember God's past dealings with Israel, and the central imperative not to forget the Lord.

Deuteronomy 8 seeks to prepare Israel to inherit the Promised Land by addressing two dangers to their faithfulness: adversity and prosperity.[135] The people must remember that God provided and delivered in the midst of their wilderness hardships. Israel's eventual passage through drought, snakes and scorpions (v. 15) was not their own doing but part of the deliberate nurture, discipline and provision of YHWH (v. 5). When they settle in the land and experience blessing and prosperity at YHWH's hand they must not forget that it is God who gives the ability to produce wealth (v. 18). As Nelson notes, 'Remembering and forgetting are not merely mental activities. One remembers by obeying (vv. 2 and 6) and disobeys out of forgetfulness

---

133. Wright, *Deuteronomy*, p. 113.

134. For similar constructions see Tigay, *Deuteronomy*, p. 92; Weinfeld, *Deuteronomy 1–11*, p. 397; Wright, *Deuteronomy*, p. 121.

135. Ian Cairns, *Deuteronomy: Word and Presence*, ITC (Grand Rapids: Eerdmans, 1992), p. 95.

(v. 11).'[136] Thus remembering is not simply an intellectual but also an ethical activity.

In verse 1 the purpose of the instruction is given – that the people might live, increase and possess the land that YHWH promised on oath to their forefathers. References to increasing in the earth are reminiscent of Genesis 1:22, 28. Brueggemann notes, 'Deuteronomy anticipates that a land rightly ordered by *torah* will become fruitful, blessed by the *shalom* anticipated already in the doxologies of creation.'[137] This observation is important in situating the vision of Deuteronomy not only in the promise to the patriarchs but also in the creation narratives of Genesis 1 – 2. A Torah-shaped community fulfils the promise to the patriarchs by, in some measure, renewing creation.

In verse 3 the narrator recounts how YHWH taught the people that they are dependent on him for life itself. There is no sense that the spiritual is more important than the physical, but rather that man is dependent upon God for everything. In the realm of history, creation, salvation and revelation YHWH's works and words are the only source of true sustenance. As O'Dowd states, 'just as Yahweh supplies food and water (past), land and victory (future), he supplies the life-giving commands that will sustain Israel as a nation'.[138] Therefore the people must remember, obey and never forget.

The correct response to the blessing of YHWH (vv. 7–9) is to bless his name (v. 10); the wrong response will be to forget YHWH (v. 11), exalt their own hearts (v. 14) and fall into idolatry (v. 19).[139] Merrill notes the greatest threat facing the people is amnesia.[140] As Mann summarizes, 'material contentment leads easily to spiritual atrophy'.[141]

In verses 12–20 the order of apostasy is satisfaction, which leads to pride, which leads to idolatry, which leads to destruction. The warning of verses 19–20 makes clear that Israel will suffer the same fate as the nations they were told to dispossess and destroy in Deuteronomy 7 if they fall into the same idolatry.

Repeatedly in these early chapters of Deuteronomy the writer has made clear that ethical living before YHWH is concerned with obedience to YHWH's words.

---

136. Nelson, *Deuteronomy*, p. 109.

137. Brueggemann, *Deuteronomy*, p. 104.

138. Ryan O'Dowd, *The Wisdom of Torah: Epistemology in Deuteronomy and the Wisdom Literature*, FRLANT 225 (Göttingen: Vandenhoeck & Ruprecht, 2009), p. 50.

139. Block, *Deuteronomy*, p. 232.

140. Merrill, *Deuteronomy*, p. 187.

141. Thomas W. Mann, *Deuteronomy*, WBC (Louisville: Westminster John Knox, 1995), p. 93.

As Woods notes, all of this is framed in Deuteronomy 8 with God's promise to the forefathers.[142] Israel must remember not only their exodus history but also their patriarchal history. God's purpose in their redemption was to bless the nations, and their obedience to YHWH is a necessary part of that process.

Deuteronomy 9:1 – 10:11

In Deuteronomy 9 Moses expands on why 'forgetfulness' may prove to be such a great danger for the people. Their record is essentially a record of rebellion and apostasy, with the golden calf as the 'paradigm of provocation'.[143] As Hayes states, 'Moses' goal in retelling the golden calf story is . . . [to paint] a portrait of Israel as perpetually rebellious and incorrigibly disloyal, sustained only by Moses' strenuous intercession and God's grace.'[144]

The chapter opens with the fourth Shema (šĕma' yiśrā'ēl; cf. 4:1; 5:1; 6:4) of the book, summoning the people to listen carefully to what is to follow. Moses assures the people that YHWH will deliver the nations and land across the Jordan into their hands, despite Israel's inferior size and strength. The people are warned not to attribute victory to their own righteousness. Rather, it is the wickedness of the nations that determines their fate. Wright notes the important perspective these verses shed on the ethical problem of the conquest raised in Deuteronomy 7. In Deuteronomy 9:4 we learn that one reason for the destruction of the Canaanites was related to their idolatrous and immoral religious practices.[145]

Three times in verses 4–6 the people are told that it is not because of their righteousness that they will take the land. The Israelites do not inherit the land because of their righteousness but because of God's grace and faithfulness to his own promise and character.[146] The call to righteousness in Deuteronomy is not a means to grace, but a witness to grace.

Moses' speech explains why possession of the land could never be due to Israel's righteousness, as five historical examples of rebellion are cited, with the

---

142. Edward J. Woods, *Deuteronomy*, TOTC 5 (Nottingham: Inter-Varsity Press, 2011), p. 157.

143. Merrill, *Deuteronomy*, p. 191.

144. Christine E. Hayes, 'Golden Calf Stories: The Relationship of Exodus 32 and Deuteronomy 9–10', in *The Idea of Biblical Interpretation: Essays in Honor of James L. Kugel* (Leiden: Brill, 2004), p. 73.

145. Wright, *Deuteronomy*, p. 132.

146. Georg Braulik, 'Law as Gospel: Justification and Pardon According to the Deuteronomic Torah', *Int* 38 (1984), p. 10.

golden calf incident occupying centre stage. Moses' recollection of the events of Exodus 32 – 34 occupies verses 11–21; then, in verses 22–23 the rebellions at Taberah (Num. 11:1–3), Massah (Exod. 17:1–7), Kibroth Hattaavah (Num. 11:4–34) and Kadesh Barnea (Num. 14) are recalled. Four times the verb 'provoke' (*qāsap*, vv. 7, 8, 19, 22) is used to demonstrate the repeated ways Israel provoked YHWH. Four times Moses reiterates the fact that YHWH could have annihilated Israel for their rebellion (vv. 8, 14, 19, 25). The gravity of their apostasy is further highlighted as Moses recounts the lengths gone to in providing forgiveness. YHWH threatened to abandon his covenant with Abraham altogether and start again with Moses (v. 14). This was averted only because Moses interceded for forty days and forty nights (v. 18). The golden calf had to be utterly destroyed, and new stone tablets were required (v. 21; 10:1–2). For Moses' hearers it was of utmost importance to underline the message that breaking the first commandment was no trivial sin. The piling up of their sins, and verbs speaking of God's anger, have the cumulative effect of demonstrating that possession of the land is not founded on Israel's righteousness, but on God's faithfulness to his covenant with the patriarchs. The tragedy of the golden calf incident was that it occurred almost immediately after the people had affirmed their commitment to keep the commandments given at Sinai (Exod. 24:3).[147] Brueggemann observes, 'The narrative, moreover, is deeply ironic, for Sinai as *the place of covenant* becomes *the place of rebellion.*'[148] The relevance and poignancy of this account is not to be lost by the Deuteronomy generation. It is the first commandment that they are to keep, and key to this is the act of remembrance.[149] Ethical boundaries are marked by remembering the character and action of YHWH.

The close of the chapter (vv. 25–29) recounts Moses' prayer for the people and appeals to three truths. First, Israel is God's own inheritance that he redeemed with his great power (v. 26). Second, Moses urged YHWH to remember the patriarchs and his promise to them (v. 27). Third, by destroying his own people, his reputation will be damaged among the nations (v. 28). Moses repeats the first argument to close (v. 29).[150] Throughout the chapter Israel are called by way of recollection to uphold the first commandment, and not forget YHWH's grace and mercy.

Wright notes the missiological implications of the chapter's emphasis on Israel's record: 'dwelling overmuch on the wickedness and idolatries of "the

---

147. Weinfeld, *Deuteronomy 1–11*, pp. 423–424.

148. Brueggemann, *Deuteronomy*, p. 116. Emphases original.

149. Ibid., p. 126.

150. Tigay, *Deuteronomy*, p. 103.

pagans" (so-called) can induce precisely the kind of national, ecclesiastical, or cultural superiority complex that Israel's self-righteousness illustrates here'.[151] Israel's awareness of undeserved grace should motivate a gracious spirit towards outsiders.

The first half of Deuteronomy 10 assures the people of forgiveness and reconciliation as it recounts the renewal of the covenant with the new stone tablets, the onward journey, the ongoing ministry of the priesthood and a final reminder of Moses' intercession. Deuteronomy 10:11 'reassures that God's ancient promises stand firm in spite of the people's apostasy'.[152] The repetition throughout the section of 'forty days and forty nights' heightens what Weinfeld terms the 'liturgical-intercessory' nature of this section.[153] As a rhetorical device it serves to reinforce the mercy of YHWH and the seriousness of the responsibility that comes with election.

Deuteronomy 10:12–22

Brueggemann says of Deuteronomy 10:12–22, 'This unit articulates one of the loveliest, most powerful, most freighted summations of covenantal theology offered in the book of Deuteronomy.'[154] Structurally it begins and ends with imperatives that frame motivational clauses related to the identity of YHWH and Israel.

The transition from historical recollection to moral imperative is marked by the introductory 'and now' (we'attâ) of Deuteronomy 10:12.[155] The summons that immediately follows is, like the Shema, formative for the Torah people. Like the Shema it calls Israel to love with all their soul and heart (běkol-lěbāběkā ûběkol-napšekā). The four verbs of verses 12–13, 'walk', 'love', 'serve' and 'observe', are epexegetical of the lead verb, 'fear'.[156]

YHWH is depicted in almost hymnic form as the God of heaven, earth and everything in it. Yet he set his affection on Israel's forefathers and chose them. This motivation leads to the next imperative in the following verse. Verse 16 employs two metaphors to exhort the people towards obedience. Circumcision was given to Abraham as a sign of God's covenant pledge, but Moses employs the image to convey the notion that outward ritual without inward

151. Wright, *Deuteronomy*, p. 134.
152. Cairns, *Deuteronomy*, p. 110.
153. Weinfeld, *Deuteronomy 1–11*, p. 427.
154. Brueggemann, *Deuteronomy*, p. 128.
155. Weinfeld, *Deuteronomy 1–11*, p. 435.
156. Christensen, *Deuteronomy 1:1–21:9*, p. 204.

transformation is inadequate. The ethical life to which YHWH calls Israel necessitates a cutting off of the foreskin of their hearts. This image reappears later in Deuteronomy 30:6 as a promise of something that YHWH himself will perform when Israel has rebelled, suffered exile and is in process of being restored. Lemke notes that 'circumcision of the heart' is a metaphor that is part of a larger trajectory in the Old Testament concerned with spiritual renewal (Jer. 4:4; 9:24–26; Ezek. 44:9).[157]

The next verse (v. 17) depicts God as a mighty warrior, who shows no partiality. This theme continues into verses 18–19, where God is the one who 'does justice' ('ōśeh mišpaṭ) for the 'orphan, widow and stranger' (yātôm wĕ'almānâ wĕ'ōhēb gēr). This triplet recurs throughout Deuteronomy (Deut. 14:29; 16:11, 14; 24:17, 19, 20–21; 27:19) and forms the basis for the character of Israel's social ethic. YHWH seeks the well-being of those most prone to injustice.[158] The end of verse 18 describes 'doing justice' in terms of provision of food and clothing. Israel in turn execute the *missio Dei* by way of the *imitatio Dei* as they love and care for the vulnerable. Love, first for God and then for neighbour, is the corollary of a circumcised heart.[159] As they remember that they too were strangers in a foreign land they are to be the antithesis of Pharaoh and Egypt, and instead offer love, not in the abstract but in the concrete provision of material needs. The mention of the 'alien' (gēr) is significant. The alien does not refer to the nations whom God will dispossess, but rather speaks of a future moment when someone outside the covenant community wishes to join the community. Such people are to be welcomed and looked after. This is a specific example of a centripetal missional ethic. As Wright comments:

> the response required of Israel in this whole section would not be merely for its own good (v. 13b), but would be an integral part of God's ongoing redemptive purpose in the world through the people of Abraham. It is yet another indication of the fundamental link in the OT between ethics and mission.[160]

The description, in verse 22, of Israel as being as numerous as the stars of heaven is not literal but rather forms an inclusio with Deuteronomy 1:10, which

---

157. Werner E. Lemke, 'Circumcision of the Heart: The Journey of a Biblical Metaphor', in Brent A. Strawn and Nancy R. Bowen (eds.), *A God So Near: Essays on Old Testament Theology in Honor of Patrick D. Miller* (Winona Lake: Eisenbrauns, 2003), pp. 317–318.

158. Weinfeld, *Deuteronomy 1–11*, p. 439.

159. Miller, *Deuteronomy*, p. 127.

160. Wright, *Deuteronomy*, p. 151.

itself echoes the promise to Abraham given in Genesis 15:5 and 22:17. Israel are reminded that God is working out his universal purpose. Israel are part of that plan, and the responsibility that accompanies their election is ethical in character. Thus their ethic is missional in God's wider purpose. The weaving together of descriptions of the mighty God, along with his calling of Israel, roots the imperatives of the section in the indicatives of who YHWH is, and what he has done for his people, Israel. As Israel are reminded of their true identity and calling it should motivate a missional consciousness. Brueggemann notes the way in which the book of Acts fulfils the Deuteronomic ideal:

> The tale of the book of Acts is an account of the ways in which this little community became a great assembly. It is, moreover, no stretch to see that it is precisely its practice of a missional ethic – to execute justice, provide food and clothing, love the stranger – that has been the occasion for its growth to be as 'numerous as the stars'.[161]

This striking quote encapsulates the argument of this book. YHWH's call on his people is to be, in fulfilment of the Abrahamic covenant, a blessing to the nations. It is as they live out a life of obedience to YHWH that this becomes a reality, but to do so will require a circumcised heart. As the covenant community finds spiritual renewal they will be empowered to care for the orphan, widow and alien, and when they do they will win the favour of the nations. God's universal purpose will be fulfilled through the missional ethic of his chosen people.

Deuteronomy 11

Deuteronomy 11 summarizes the argument of Deuteronomy 1 – 10 before moving on to the laws of chapters 12–26. It begins with a call to love YHWH, and keep his requirements, decrees, laws and commands perpetually. In verse 2 the speech moves to give a summary of Israel's experience of deliverance. Again Moses is at pains to emphasize that the current generation of Israelites was in some sense present at those constitutive events. Each generation stands in solidarity with others, yet at the same time must make its own stand for covenant loyalty.[162] Remembrance of who YHWH is and what he has done for Israel is crucial for effective obedience. Coupled with the recollection of God's mighty acts of deliverance is recollection of God's acts of judgment on the disobedient and rebellious (vv. 6–7).

---

161. Brueggemann, *Deuteronomy*, p. 134.
162. Wright, *Deuteronomy*, p. 153.

In the light of YHWH's acts of salvation and judgment the people are called again to keep all the commands, that it may go well with them in the land (vv. 8–9). If the imperative of verse 2 is motivated by remembrance, the imperative of verse 8 is motivated by anticipation.[163] The goodness of the land is reiterated, as is YHWH's omnipresent eye over the land he cares for (vv. 10–12). The conditionality of prosperity in the land is again spelled out in verses 13–15, followed by further warnings against idolatry. In words reminiscent of Deuteronomy 6 the Israelites are encouraged to fix these words on their hearts, bind them on their heads and fasten them to their hands. They are to teach these things to children in the everyday opportunity and circumstances of life. If Israel prove faithful in the task then YHWH will go before them to drive out larger and stronger nations so that they may possess the fullness of the promised inheritance.

In a precursor of words that will be repeated in Deuteronomy 30 Moses calls the people to decision – a choice between life and death, blessing and curse. These blessings and curses are to be proclaimed publicly when the people cross over into the land. Moses finishes the speech and the first section of the book with a final call to the people to be sure to obey all the laws set before them. Miller summarizes:

> Again, Israel, whenever it hears this word, is placed on the boundary between land and landlessness, life and death . . . In the manner of their life before God in the sphere of divine blessing, God's people will shape their future as they decide between obedience and disobedience.[164]

The truth of Deuteronomy 1 – 11 is that the people will shape not only their own future with their obedience, but the future of the surrounding nations.

Summary
Throughout these eleven chapters we have observed considerable repetition: YHWH's mighty acts of deliverance, the call to live a life of singular covenantal loyalty to YHWH, the necessity of intergenerational catechism, and the election of Israel for the sake of the nations. Mission always involves some sort of 'boundary crossing', be it geographical, social or cultural.[165] Deuteronomy is a

---

163. Brueggemann, *Deuteronomy*, p. 137.

164. Miller, *Deuteronomy*, p. 128.

165. Johannes Blauw, *The Missionary Nature of the Church: A Survey of the Biblical Theology of Mission* (London: Lutterworth, 1974), p. 111.

book on the boundary. Israel are about to cross a geographical boundary to take possession of the Promised Land, and as they do so their community will be defined by boundaries, both geographical and ethical. The boundaries erected are designed to protect the spiritual integrity of Israel as YHWH's covenant people, but they are also meant to be porous such that an ethic lived out may be seen by outsiders, who may in turn cross the 'boundary-line' to join the covenant people. Israel's ethic is thus a missional ethic and is defined by the Torah: specifically in Deuteronomy 1 – 11 the emphasis is on covenant loyalty to YHWH in obedience to the first commandment. This is what an attractive missional ethic looks like. In summary, from Deuteronomy 1 – 11 the following things may be gleaned with respect to this book.

First, Weinfeld notes the emphasis throughout Deuteronomy 1 – 11 on the universal dominion of YHWH.[166] Besides him there is no other (4:35; 6:4); he is the God of gods and Lord of lords (10:17). Second, alongside the universal dominion of YHWH the particular election of Israel is repeatedly stressed. Israel's particularity is for a universal purpose. Third, obedience is crucial to living out their identity as the people of God, particularly obedience to the first commandment. Repeatedly idolatry is denounced and warned against in the strongest terms. Fourth, obedience and loyalty to YHWH issue derivatively in attentiveness to one's neighbour.[167] Concern for those on the other side of the boundary, whether they be other nations, or the alien in their midst, is repeated multiple times in the opening chapters of Deuteronomy. Israel's own experience as strangers and aliens should motivate them to care for others who are aliens in their land. Love for YHWH issues in love for one's neighbour. Such love for YHWH, displayed through obedience to Torah, causes the surrounding nations to take notice (Deut. 4:5–8). Missional ethics is fundamentally concerned with loving YHWH, and loving neighbour. It is the first of these, love for God, that will now be further examined.

Deuteronomy and love for God

The argument so far may be summarized as follows. Deuteronomy presents a vision of YHWH's covenant people who are called to live distinctive lives in the sight of the surrounding nations. The form of such distinctiveness (their missional ethic) may be summed up as love for God and love for neighbour. In

---

166. Weinfeld, *Deuteronomy 1–11*, pp. 454–455.
167. Brueggemann, *Deuteronomy*, p. 139.

this section the former of those is under investigation. This will involve considering both the form of Israel's love for God, as outlined in the instructions concerning worship in Deuteronomy 12 – 26, and the way in which that provides a distinctive witness to the nations.

Of particular interest is the way in which an internal practice (worship) can have a missional effect on those outside the covenant community. It will be argued that Israel's worship has a direct effect on outsiders present (i.e. resident aliens) and an indirect effect in shaping Israel's community identity. First, we need to attend to a significant question regarding Israel's worship.

Was Israel monotheistic?

Positing the theory of a qualitatively distinctive monolatry begs the question regarding the reality of early Israelite monolatry. The majority of scholars consider Israel's monotheism to have been a late development, coming to maturation in the time of Josiah's reforms or in exile.[168] The distinctiveness of Israel in terms of monotheism and ethics came with the creation of biblical literature in post-exilic Judaism.[169] Gnuse argues that a process of evolution through revolution (a sort of punctuated equilibrium) led Israel to move from being polytheistic during their early days in the land, to becoming monotheistic in the time of the prophets.[170] The changing social and political situation, it is argued, necessitated monotheistic rhetoric in the face of the Babylonian conquest and exile as a matter of national identity.[171] Noth argued that Israel's settlement in, and possession of, the land occurred gradually over a long period.[172] Stories of great battles and conquests were later elaborations bearing little resemblance to reality. Gottwald argued that Israel ultimately came to possess most of the land through some kind of social revolution or peasants' revolt – something more dramatic than Noth's peaceful infiltration, but still later and less dramatic than the account of the biblical texts.[173]

---

168. Robert Karl Gnuse, *No Other Gods: Emergent Monotheism in Israel*, JSOTSup 241 (Sheffield: Sheffield Academic Press, 1997), p. 12.

169. Ibid., p. 21.

170. Ibid., pp. 128–141.

171. Mark S. Smith, *The Origins of Biblical Monotheism: Israel's Polytheistic Background and the Ugaritic Texts* (Oxford: Oxford University Press, 2001), pp. 153–166.

172. Martin Noth, *The History of Israel*, tr. P. M. Ackroyd, 2nd edn (London: Adam and Charles, 1959), pp. 141–153.

173. Norman K. Gottwald, 'Two Models for the Origins of Ancient Israel: Social Revolution or Frontier Development', in H. B. Huffmon, F. A. Spina and

Following Noth and Gottwald, the majority view has been of a religious syncretism in which Israel worshipped the gods of those with whom they dwelt in the land of Canaan.[174] There is some archaeological evidence supporting the claim. Inscriptions found at Kuntillet 'Arjûd and Khirbet el-Qôm, dated to the eighth century BC, speak of Yahweh and his Asherah.[175] However, not all scholars agree. Kitchen argues for the assumption of the basic reliability of the accounts unless there is compelling evidence to the contrary.[176] He cites evidence from the Merneptah Stele (c. twelfth century BC) and the Mesha Stele (c. ninth century BC) that suggests Israel had significant occupation early in their history.[177] Kitchen argues that the form and content of Deuteronomy more closely resembles that of second-millennium treaties than first-millennium treaties; therefore dating the core elements of Deuteronomy earlier than Gnuse, Gottwald and Noth.[178] Additionally De Moor has conducted research into theophoric names and argues, 'the number of Yahwistic names is too high to be dismissed. These names testify that Yahwism must have started as a popular religion long before David.'[179]

In considering Deuteronomy in an ANE context, the breadth of time covered by the texts and their apparently pervasive influence across cultures,

---

A. R. W. Green (eds.), *The Quest for the Kingdom of God: Studies in Honor of George E. Mendenhall* (Winona Lake: Eisenbrauns, 1983), pp. 5–24.

174. Jan Assmann, *Of God and Gods: Egypt, Israel, and the Rise of Monotheism* (Madison: University of Wisconsin Press, 2008), p. 64.

175. See Robert North, 'Yahweh's Asherah', in *To Touch the Text: Biblical and Related Studies in Honor of Joseph A. Fitzmyer* (New York: Crossroad, 1989), pp. 118–137. However, note Ramsey's cautions regarding the ambiguity of archaeological evidence. George W. Ramsey, *The Quest for the Historical Israel: Reconstructing Israel's Early History* (London: SCM, 1981), p. 69.

176. Kenneth A. Kitchen, *Ancient Orient and Old Testament* (London: Tyndale, 1966), p. 29.

177. Ibid., pp. 59–60. So too the Mesha Stele mentions YHWH, therefore placing Yahwism before Josiah's reform. See Andre Lemaire, *The Birth of Monotheism: The Rise and Disappearance of Yahwism* (Washington, D.C.: Biblical Archaeological Society, 2007), pp. 19–28.

178. Kenneth A. Kitchen and Paul J. N. Lawrence, *Treaty, Law and Covenant in the Ancient Near East*, 3 vols. (Wiesbaden: Harrassowitz, 2012), vol. 3, pp. 201–259. Kitchen argues that Deuteronomy bears most similarity to thirteenth- to fourteenth-century treaties.

179. Johannes C. de Moor, *The Rise of Yahwism: The Roots of Israelite Monotheism*, rev. and enlarged edn, BETL 41 (Leuven: Leuven University Press, 1997), p. 33.

the precise dating of the final form of Deuteronomy is not crucial to the argument. The final form of the book presents and exhorts Israel as a community to a qualitatively distinctive monolatry.

Monotheism, henotheism or monolatry?

Crucial to any discussion of Israel's religious life is a consideration of terminology. Much discussion has occurred over terms like monotheism, polytheism, henotheism and monolatry, and which, if any, adequately describes Israel's religious experience.[180] MacDonald suggests that modern discussions are overly concerned with ontology, and proposes 'monolatry' as the term that best captures Israel's confession and practice.[181] Having conducted a survey of historical approaches MacDonald suggests a canonical approach concerned with the intentionality of the texts themselves.[182] He lists the key texts as Deuteronomy 4:35–39, 5:7, 6:4, 7:9, 10:17, 32:39 and 33:26, and works through them in an attempt to elucidate the meaning and shape of monolatry for an ancient Israelite context. In discussing the first commandment (Deut. 5:7) he argues that the phrase 'but/before me' ('al-pānāya) suggests the notion of 'in opposition'. Thus the meaning of the first commandment is 'you shall have no other gods alongside or in opposition to me'. Critically, he says, 'the existence of other deities is not denied, rather the assumption of Deuteronomy's rhetoric is that other deities do exist and are a real temptation for the affections of the Israelites ... the issue at stake is devotion'.[183] His examination of the other texts brings him to the same conclusion: 'The absolute terms are confessional, not ontological.'[184] For MacDonald monolatry is a relational commitment of love expressed through internal obedience, and corporate cultic worship. As Wright states, 'there is no suggestion that "monotheism", or praying the *Shema*, had anything to do with the numerical analysis of the inner being of Israel's god himself'.[185] It was rather the expression of devotion in practice.

---

180. Michael S. Heiser, 'Monotheism, Polytheism, Monolatry, or Henotheism? Toward an Assessment of Divine Plurality in the Hebrew Bible', *BBR* 18.1 (2008), pp. 1–30.

181. MacDonald, *Meaning of 'Monotheism'*, pp. 23–48.

182. Ibid., p. 58.

183. Ibid., p. 77.

184. Ibid., p. 96.

185. N. T. Wright, *The New Testament and the People of God*, COQG 1 (London: SPCK, 1992), p. 259.

In a similar vein Heiser argues against the idea that monotheism signifies God as the only 'god'. He notes that in Psalm 82:1 God stands among the 'gods' (*'ĕlōhîm*) to judge, and proceeds to argue that the strongly monotheistic statements in Deuteronomy 4:35–39 and 32:12, 39 must be viewed against the backdrop of Deuteronomy 4:19–20 and 32:8–9. Deuteronomy 4:19 affirms that the sun, moon and stars – the heavenly host – have been allotted to the other nations. The LXX of Deuteronomy 32:8 speaks of national boundaries being established according to the number of the angels (*kata arithmon angelōn*), which suggests the existence of other heavenly beings.[186] In Deuteronomy it is not the case that YHWH is the only 'god' but rather that he is unique among the 'gods', and the only one worthy of worship.[187] YHWH is the 'grand vizier of the imperial court'.[188] The other gods of the nations around Israel are not ontological nothings. It is precisely because they are real somethings that they pose a danger to Israel's worship of YHWH alone. As Garr notes, 'Israel's very election precludes non-Yahwistic service, and God's own jealousy (see Ex 34:14) virtually defines these other gods as potential rivals. Gods exist, but Israel must worship only Yahweh.'[189]

For the purposes of this work we will follow MacDonald in using the term 'monolatry' to describe Israel's worship. This captures the idea of holistic devotion to and worship of YHWH, expressed individually and corporately. We shall now explore how Deuteronomy's emphasis on monolatry sits in its wider ANE context.

Deuteronomy in its ANE context

Israel's distinctiveness was to demonstrate wisdom to the surrounding nations (Deut. 4:5–8). In particular love for God and love for neighbour were the twin foci of Israel's Torah obedience. Here we shall examine how Israel's love for God is distinctive in relation to the law codes of the nations around them.[190] The argument depends on the fact that Israel's code *is* distinctive and not, in large part, dependent upon, or derivative from, the law codes around them. David Wright has argued at length that Israel's law drew heavily from the laws

---

186. Heiser, 'Monotheism', pp. 2–13.

187. Ibid., pp. 18–27.

188. Larry W. Hurtado, *One God, One Lord: Early Christian Devotion and Ancient Jewish Monotheism* (London: SCM, 1988), p. 39.

189. W. Randall Garr, *In His Own Image: Humanity, Divinity, and Monotheism*, Culture and History of the Ancient Near East 15 (Leiden: Brill, 2003), p. 83.

190. The law codes considered can be found in *ANET*. They are Lipit-Ishtar, Eshnunna, Hammurabi, Middle Assyrian, Hittite and Neo-Babylonian.

of Hammurabi.[191] Deuteronomy's literary and historical formation is apparently complex and it seems likely that there were common oral traditions and wisdom regarding law, governance, crime and punishment.[192] Overlap in themes and structures should be expected, but noteworthy is the dissimilarity in form and content between Deuteronomy and the other ANE law codes.[193] Admittedly the evidence for the other codes is incomplete but Deuteronomy would appear longer than other codes. Deuteronomy's narrative introduction is considerably longer than, for example, Hammurabi's.[194] The Middle Assyrian Laws and the Hittite Laws contain no prologue or epilogue.[195] Deuteronomy's themes and emphases are also different. For example, it is YHWH, rather than the king, who

---

191. David P. Wright, *Inventing God's Law: How the Covenant Code of the Bible Used and Revised the Laws of Hammurabi* (Oxford: Oxford University Press, 2009).

192. Jackson argues for the evolutionary development of law codes but this fails to account for some significant differences and developments. For example, the Middle Assyrian Laws appear less humanitarian than earlier counterparts. See Bernard S. Jackson, *Essays in Jewish and Comparative Legal History*, SJLA 10 (Leiden: Brill, 1975), pp. 11–23; Malul argues for the literary dependence of Israel's law on Mesopotamian counterparts, but this view does not address how Israel might have accessed such laws. See Meir Malul, *The Comparative Method in Ancient Near Eastern and Biblical Studies*, AOAT 227 (Neukirchen-Vluyn: Neukirchener Verlag, 1990), pp. 13–159. Indeed, as Cook notes, if Hammurabi's code was well known in Israel, account must be given for the comparatively small use which has been made of it. See Stanley A. Cook, *The Laws of Moses and the Code of Hammurabi* (London: Adam and Charles, 1903), p. 273. Westbrook argues against both the evolutionary and the literary dependence model and suggests that the similarities that do exist are based on some shared oral tradition. See Raymond Westbrook, 'Biblical and Cuneiform Law Codes', *RB* 92.2 (1985), pp. 247–264; Raymond Westbrook, 'The Laws of Biblical Israel', in *Law from the Tigris to the Tiber: The Writings of Raymond Westbrook*, 2 vols. (Winona Lake: Eisenbrauns, 2009), vol. 2, pp. 317–340.

193. Westbrook notes the common tripartite structure of prologue, rules and epilogue, and the significant amount of overlap and recurrence in themes. Raymond Westbrook, 'The Character of Ancient Near Eastern Law', in *A History of Ancient Near Eastern Law*, 2 vols., Handbook of Oriental Studies 72 (Leiden: Brill, 2003), vol. 1, pp. 1–24.

194. Hammurabi's prologue, the longest in *ANET*, runs to twenty lines. Deuteronomy's prologue runs to 161 verses in the first four chapters of the book.

195. *ANET*, pp. 180–197. The Hittite treaties do contain a prologue and epilogue but are more formal in character and much briefer than Deuteronomy.

is credited with national blessing. The blessing and curse section at the end of Deuteronomy is also longer than any of its counterparts. Most significant for this section, religious instruction is unique to Deuteronomy among ANE legal codes and treaties. None of the other law codes or treaties contains such instruction. The closest analogue is Hammurabi's prologue. There we are told that King Hammurabi purified the cult of Eabzu, designed the temple of Ebabbar, made secure the great shrines of Inanna, provided bountiful sacrifices for Eninnu and banquets for Ninazu, installed Ishtar in Eulmash, and prayed fervently to the gods.[196] In the epilogue Hammurabi also commands people to pray.[197] However, this is considerably less detail than that given in Deuteronomy, and it could be argued that Hammurabi is concerned with promoting his own name rather than those of the deities, as the rest of the prologue and epilogue would suggest. The treaties, likewise, contain some similarity in ordering but are not as long as Deuteronomy and do not contain the same themes.[198] The comparison may be unfair as other nations do have separate religious texts, but it is noteworthy that Deuteronomy is to some degree *sui generis* in its interweaving of narrative, treaty-like material, legal code and cultic instruction. It is this last element that is of present interest. Even a comparison with other ANE cultic texts demonstrates that Deuteronomy is unusual. Egyptian, Akkadian and Hittite ritual texts are more concerned with the priests than the people, and address the individual more than the corporate body.[199] Other ANE ritual texts are interested in how the individual can find relief rather than how the community should worship.[200] As Walton notes, 'The people sought the gods for protection and assistance, not for relationship.'[201] Van der Toorn's study observes the variegated nature of worship in the ANE. Sometimes worship is linked to the gods of the ancestors and honouring their memory; sometimes worship is linked to local gods, who were considered somehow more proximate.[202] Bottéro states:

196. *ANET*, pp. 164–165.

197. *ANET*, p. 178.

198. See the Egyptian and Hittite treaties in *ANET*, pp. 199–206.

199. *ANET*, pp. 207, 325–361.

200. Examples include charms against snakes, the magical protection of children, and rituals against pestilence, impotence and domestic quarrel. See *ANET*, pp. 326–350.

201. John H. Walton, *Ancient Near Eastern Thought and the Old Testament* (Nottingham: Apollos, 2007), p. 161.

202. Karel van der Toorn, *Family Religion in Babylonia, Syria and Israel: Continuity and Change in the Forms of Religious Life*, Studies in the History and Culture of the Ancient Near East 7 (Leiden: Brill, 1996), pp. 66–93.

> One of Moses' great revolutions in Israel: to replace the purely material maintenance
> of the gods with the single and sole 'liturgical' obligation in life to obey a moral law,
> thereby truly rendering to God the only homage worthy of him.[203]

It must be reiterated that the evidence for comparison is limited and fragmentary, but examining the available evidence suggests a distinctive emphasis and shape to Israel's cultic life.

The shape of Israel's monolatry

A significant feature of the legal instruction given in Deuteronomy is the amount of space given to prescriptions concerning right worship. Deuteronomy 12 is devoted to the centralization of the cult. Deuteronomy 16 describes the various festivals along with instructions on how to celebrate them. Deuteronomy 17 – 18 provides instruction for dealing with idolatry, and serves to establish appropriate authority for kings and prophets. Deuteronomy 26 – 27 contains instructions for special acts of worship upon entering the land. Even the song of Deuteronomy 32 appears to function as a type of national anthem to be remembered and rehearsed. The instructions cover the individual and the corporate, and the regular and special acts of worship. The importance of Israel's liturgical life should not be underplayed, and we shall examine its impact in due course.

I have already argued in examining Deuteronomy 1 – 11 that a suitable summary of Israel's missional ethic is love for God and love for neighbour. We also observed that Deuteronomy 6 – 11 is an exposition of the first and second commandments. It is the way in which Israel were to uphold the commands that is of interest here. Deuteronomy 12, 16, 17 – 18 and 26 provide more specific instruction regarding Israel's monolatry through liturgical praxis.

Deuteronomy 12

Just as 'the decrees and laws' (*haḥuqqîm wĕhammišpāṭîm*) have run through chapters 4–11, so now they frame chapters 12–26, holding together the paraenetic and legal sections.[204] Following the lengthy exposition of the first and second commandments (Deut. 6 – 11), the statutes of chapters 12–26 begin with instructions regarding the proper worship of YHWH. Block notes that instructions

---

203. Jean Bottéro, *Religion in Ancient Mesopotamia*, tr. Teresa Lavender Fagan (Chicago: University of Chicago Press, 2001), p. 169.

204. See Deut. 4:1, 5, 8; 5:1, 31; 6:1, 20; 7:11; 11:32; 12:1; 26:16–17. J. Gary Millar, *Now Choose Life: Theology and Ethics in Deuteronomy*, NSBT 6 (Leicester: Apollos, 1998), p. 82.

regarding proper worship bookend the entire section running from chapter 12 to 26.[205] Right worship frames right living. Placing these instructions at the start of the code identifies Israel as a sacral community first and foremost.[206]

Deuteronomy 12:1–3 begins with five imperatives regarding Canaanite worship: *destroy* the high places; *break* the altars; *smash* the sacred stones; *burn* the Asherah poles; *cut down* the idols. Israel are not to worship YHWH as the Canaanites worship their gods (v. 4). These five negative imperatives are mirrored with five positive imperatives in verses 4–7: *seek* YHWH's place; *go* to that place; *bring* the burnt offerings; *eat*; and *rejoice* in the presence of YHWH.[207] The people are no longer to do as each sees fit (v. 8) but are to bring the offerings to the place YHWH chooses. This place of worship is to be for the whole community, including the servants, and is to have a strong element of rejoicing (vv. 11–14). The inclusion of servants and Levites in the worship places social and ethical demands on the people to provide for and include those who cannot provide for themselves.[208] The wholehearted rejoicing is festal in character and looks backward and forward. As well as remembering all that YHWH has done for the people, there is an eschatological foreshadowing of destination and vocation.[209] Regulations and concessions are outlined and then repeated with the emphasis on bringing the tithes and offerings to the central place. The importance of obedience is stressed and the command not to worship as the nations is reiterated. The repetition and reiteration underscores the importance of right worship for the community.[210] They are to come together, as the whole community, to worship YHWH.

Centralization is intended to unite the people and eradicate the memory of Canaanite worship. As Nelson notes, centralization is not about political control but about the prevention of apostasy.[211] 'The place' (*hammāqôm*, 12:5) is the context for devoted obedience and is a picture of the whole land in microcosm.[212]

---

205. Block, *Deuteronomy*, p. 301.

206. Gerhard von Rad, *Old Testament Theology*, 2 vols. (London: SCM, 1975), vol. 1, p. 228.

207. I am indebted for the insight regarding the five negative and five positive imperatives to James Robson's unpublished lecture notes on Deuteronomy.

208. McConville, *Deuteronomy*, p. 231.

209. McConville says, 'This rejoicing of the people of God is no accidental extra, but is essential to the picture, and even has an eschatological quality.' Ibid., p. 231.

210. Wright, *Deuteronomy*, p. 162.

211. Nelson, *Deuteronomy*, p. 149. Millar notes that the chapter is not about centralization per se, but about obedience to YHWH. *Now Choose Life*, p. 114.

212. Millar, *Now Choose Life*, p. 102.

There is a repeated emphasis on 'rejoicing' (śāmaḥ), which is designed to unite the people around thanksgiving for the blessings divinely bestowed.[213] As Block describes:

> The redeemed anticipate worship with both delight and sobriety. On the one hand those who worship God in spirit and in truth realize the incredible grace that God has lavished on them first in His redemption and second in His invitation to feast in His presence (cf. Ps. 95:1–5). On the other hand those who worship God in spirit and in truth are to acknowledge their unworthiness to come before Him and to recognize that in worship what He says is always more important than what believers have to say to Him (cf. vv. 6–11).[214]

The continued practice of gathering at the place the Lord will choose 'brings for ever into Israel's life the principle that the covenant must always be renewed in a life of decision'[215] – the place the Lord will choose is a perpetual place of decision. Israel's worship is to be unified and exclusive, wholehearted and joyful, and corporate and inclusive.[216]

Deuteronomy 16
Having addressed issues surrounding false prophets (ch. 13), food laws (ch. 14) and laws of release (ch. 15), chapter 16 provides instructions regarding the three great annual pilgrimage festivals: the Passover (vv. 1–8), the Feast of Weeks (vv. 9–12) and the Feast of Tabernacles (vv. 13–17).[217] Wright notes the 'sabbatical themes of rest, remembrance, and concern for the poor are all woven into Deuteronomy's summary of the three festivals'.[218]

The original Passover was celebrated by family or clan groups (Exod. 12) but here, on the border of Canaan, the instruction is that it be celebrated centrally

---

213. Christensen, *Deuteronomy 1:1–21:9*, pp. 244–245.
214. Daniel I. Block, 'The Joy of Worship: The Mosaic Invitation to the Presence of God (Deut. 12:1–14)', *BSac* 162.646 (2005), pp. 148–149.
215. McConville, *Deuteronomy*, p. 232.
216. Wright, *Deuteronomy*, pp. 167–168.
217. Surrounding nations also had festivals. The Babylonians had a festival to purify their temple, *ANET*, pp. 331–334, and a pageant for the statue of Anu. *ANET*, p. 342. The Hittites performed a festival of the Warrior God. *ANET*, pp. 358–359. These festivals involved the priests and sometimes the king, but the obligation and participation of the laity are nowhere mentioned.
218. Wright, *Deuteronomy*, p. 198.

and corporately.[219] It appears that the two feasts of Passover and Unleavened Bread are brought together into one central festival. Millar suggests that the combining of the festivals brings together 'the significance of the exodus for Israel's life in the land, and the enjoyment of that life with Yahweh . . . This is the essence of Deuteronomic theology: the exodus and enjoyment of the land must go hand in hand.'[220]

This is the only feast of the three that does not mention the presence of outsiders. This may be due to the fact that while all in the land are beneficiaries of the blessings of harvest, only Israel's ancestors experienced the blessing of deliverance at the first Passover. Another notable feature of this festival is its length. In duration it lasts an entire week. It begins with the Passover meal, which is then followed by six days of eating unleavened bread, and finishes with an assembly before YHWH. It would have been an immersive experience for the community, performed every year. As such its performative value for shaping the community should not be underestimated. The purpose of the festival is made explicit in Deuteronomy 16:3: 'that all the days of your life you may *remember* the time of your departure from Egypt'. Remembrance has been a key theme of Deuteronomy (e.g. Deut. 6:10–12; 8:11–14), and the festivals function to prevent theological amnesia. Christensen suggests that 'what happened once on a historical or national level also happens on an individual psychic level for each participant, and it happens every year'.[221]

The Feast of Weeks (vv. 9–12) begins midway through the harvest. As with the Passover and the Feast of Tabernacles the number seven regulates the calendar; hence a number of commentators link the festivals with the fourth commandment regarding the Sabbath. As with the Passover the feast is centralized and remembrance of slavery in Egypt is to the fore (v. 12). Here the children, servants, Levites, aliens, orphans and widows are present to participate. As with the other festivals the worship prescribed required commitment. There would have been a considerable cost involved in providing for one's own family, and for those who were unable to provide for themselves.

The Feast of Tabernacles (vv. 13–17) occurs after harvest has finished, as a grateful celebration of YHWH's material provision. Nelson notes the use of the description of Tabernacles as *your* feast, as opposed to simply *the* feast.[222] '*Your* feast' is an appropriation of YHWH's blessing, not simply an impersonal or

---

219. J. A. Thompson, *Deuteronomy*, TOTC 5 (Leicester: Inter-Varsity Press, 1974), p. 193.

220. Millar, *Now Choose Life*, p. 123.

221. Christensen, *Deuteronomy 1:1–21:9*, p. 336.

222. Nelson, *Deuteronomy*, p. 210.

abstract duty to be observed. As with the Passover it is a seven-day feast at the place the Lord will choose; and as with the Feast of Weeks the whole community is involved in the festival. Deuteronomy 16:14 connects the presence of the whole community with the joyful celebration of the community. The implication is that Israel's joy was incomplete in the absence of the vulnerable and the outsider.[223]

At the three major festivals in Israel's calendar there is an emphasis on remembrance of former times, joy in the present and care for the vulnerable.[224] Joy and gratitude are to be at the heart of the festivals. In all these things they remember God's kindness to Israel when Israel was marginalized, and they imitate YHWH in their generous response towards others. Their actions are in this way formative for their identity as God's distinctive people. Israel's 'deepest convictions are to be found, not in systematic doctrinal or ethical formulations, but in doxology, the language of worship'.[225] The cult is practically pedagogical. Even the deliberate rhythms of time through the Sabbath, seasons, tithes and festivals all serve to teach the goodness of YHWH in delivering and blessing Israel. Such worship serves to shape the identity and vocation of Israel, and to convict the 'alien' of the goodness of YHWH.

Deuteronomy 17 – 18

Deuteronomy 17 continues the theme of Deuteronomy 16 in prescribing punishment for idolatry. The people are not to set up Asherah poles or sacred stones (Deut. 16:21–22), they are not to sacrifice defective animals and they are not to worship other gods (Deut. 17:1–4). Those caught doing so must be taken to the gates of the city and put to death that the evil may be purged from their midst (17:5–7).

Instruction surprising in an ANE context concerns the king and the prophet in Deuteronomy 17 – 18. The king, unlike some kings from surrounding nations, is not divinized, but is subject to YHWH (Deut. 17:15).[226] He is forbidden great wealth and many wives (17:16–17). He is to read the Torah daily so that 'he may

---

223. For this insight I am indebted to Dr Tim Davy and his lecture 'Looking for Orphans: Approaches for Understanding the Place of Vulnerable Children in the Old Testament', delivered at the Tyndale Fellowship Quadrennial Conference, July 2016.

224. Wright, *Deuteronomy*, p. 201.

225. Wright, *Old Testament Ethics*, p. 45.

226. See the discussion in David Janzen, *The Necessary King: A Postcolonial Reading of the Deuteronomistic Portrait of the Monarchy*, HBM 57 (Sheffield: Sheffield Phoenix, 2013), pp. 57–85.

learn to revere the LORD his God and follow carefully all the words of this law and these decrees, and not consider himself better than his fellow Israelites and turn from the law to the right or to the left' (17:19–20). The chief responsibility of the king is the same as that of his fellow Israelites – to obey the law.[227] He is to 'exemplify and demonstrate true obedience to the Lord for the sake of the well-being of both the dynasty and the kingdom'.[228] He is to be, primarily, a model Israelite.[229] The king does not create the law, but is rather subject to it, in the same way he is subject to YHWH.[230] In an ANE context the Israelite king's power is surprisingly limited.[231]

By contrast the prophet is esteemed as possessing the words of YHWH. The Lord will raise up a prophet and the people must listen to him (Deut. 18:15). YHWH's words will be in the prophet's mouth, and if he is genuine his words will come to pass (18:18–22). YHWH's prophet possesses YHWH's words and so even the king is subject to him. In the ANE the king ruled over all and was frequently divinized.[232] In Israel YHWH is the only God and ruler and he rules through his word, which all people, including the king, are to obey. To any outside observer Israel's relationship to authority figures, and their devotion to YHWH alone as king, would have been strikingly distinctive.

Deuteronomy 26

Millar describes Deuteronomy 26 as a 'carefully crafted conclusion' to the whole law code running from chapter 12.[233] As noted in examining Deuteronomy 12,

---

227. Millar, *Now Choose Life*, p. 127.

228. Miller, *Deuteronomy*, p. 149.

229. Norbert Lohfink, 'Distribution of the Functions of Power: The Laws Concerning Public Offices in Deuteronomy 16:18–18:22', in *A Song of Power and the Power of Song: Essays on the Book of Deuteronomy* (Winona Lake: Eisenbrauns, 1993), p. 349; Wright, *Old Testament Ethics*, p. 232.

230. Norbert Lohfink, 'Tora und Gewaltenteilung in den Ämtergesetzen', in *Studien zum Deuteronomium und zur deuteronomistischen Literatur I*, SBAB 8 (Stuttgart: Katholisches Bibelwerk, 1990), p. 318.

231. One Egyptian inscription not only has the king, Amen-hotep III, as working alongside the god, Amon-Re, but even concludes with the god singing a hymn of praise to the king. See *ANET*, pp. 375–376.

232. For example, Hammurabi in his prologue counts himself among the Igigi – the lesser gods. See *ANET*, p. 164. Evidence for the divinization of Pharaohs can also be seen in *ANET*, pp. 378–379.

233. Millar, *Now Choose Life*, p. 143.

both the opening and the closing to the law code of Deuteronomy 12 – 26 focus on right worship. Right worship is the framework within which neighbour love takes place. Interspersed throughout chapters 12–26 are further instructions to right worship, further reinforcing this Deuteronomic emphasis on right worship as central to life as God's people. In Deuteronomy 26 material from chapters 14:22–28 and 16:9–12 appears to be restated, explicitly connecting the first-fruits with covenant renewal.[234] Greater detail as to the administration of such gifts is found elsewhere (Deut. 14:22–29; 15:19–23; 18:1–8), but here, at the end of the code, the emphasis is on the cultic aspect of the gift. Later Jewish tradition connected the date of First-fruits with the giving of the law at Sinai. Instructions in Deuteronomy 26 link the action with remembrance of deliverance and inheritance of the land, so, as a complex of ideas, it would be natural to link the festal offering with a ceremony of covenant renewal.[235] Biddle notes that the passage is concerned principally with three confessions of faith.[236]

In verses 1–5a the Israelites are instructed to take some of the first-fruits of the produce of the land to the place the Lord will choose as a dwelling for his name, and to present them to the priest. Here the worshipper is to make the first of the three confessions before the Lord (v. 3), affirming both the faithfulness of YHWH and the gift of the land.

After the priest has taken the basket and set it down before the Lord the worshipper recites the second of the three confessions (vv. 5b–10). This second confession is a recital of Israel's sacred history.[237] It moves from the wanderings of Jacob, to settlement and subsequent oppression in Egypt, to deliverance by YHWH's mighty hand, and finally to settlement in the land flowing with milk and honey. Von Rad argues that the prescribed litany here functioned as Israel's credo – a credo found in similar form in Deuteronomy 6:20–24 and Joshua 24:2–13.[238] It was a statement expressing the essence of Israel's identity and

---

234. Merrill, *Deuteronomy*, p. 331.

235. Ibid., p. 331.

236. Mark E. Biddle, *Deuteronomy*, SHBC (Macon: Smyth & Helwys, 2003), p. 380.

237. The historical credo is unusual among the ANE literature. A Sumero-Akkadian prayer supports Walton's earlier cited view that ANE religion was concerned with individual and immediate relief: 'May the god who is not known be quieted toward me; may the goddess whom I know or do not know be quieted toward me.' *ANET*, p. 391. Israel's corporate and historic prayer is without parallel in the ANE religious texts.

238. Gerhard von Rad, *The Problem of the Hexateuch and Other Essays*, tr. E. W. Trueman Dicken (Edinburgh: Oliver & Boyd, 1966), pp. 3–8. Von Rad describes the creedal recital of vv. 5–10 as the 'hexateuch in miniature'.

purpose.[239] This recitation was not a one-off act for the first generation in the land: it was to be repeated annually as part of Israel's cultic life. The 'wandering Aramean' most likely refers to Jacob (cf. Gen. 24:10; 25:20, 26; 31:41–42), with the participle 'wandering' carrying overtones of lack or danger. Of particular interest is the use of the first person plural pronoun throughout verses 6–9: 'the Egyptians ill treated *us*'; '*we* cried out'; 'the LORD heard *our* voice'; 'the LORD bought *us* out'.[240] Only Joshua and Caleb, of the entire exodus generation, saw the land of Canaan. The rest died in the wilderness. The intent of the creed is generational unity. Israelites throughout the generations identify as those redeemed from slavery by YHWH and given the land as a gift. The themes of sojourn and slavery are important reminders to remember those who have no portion of their own – the Levites, aliens, widows and orphans. They too are to join the communal festival rejoicing in all the good things the Lord has given (v. 11).

In verses 12–15 there is further instruction regarding the third-year tithe which was to be given to 'the Levite, the foreigner, the fatherless and the widow, so that they may eat in your towns and be satisfied' (v. 12). In Israel's cultic life they are reminded of the daily obligation to imitate YHWH in their care, concern and provision for the disadvantaged and dependent. Their worship of YHWH has a vertical and a horizontal dimension. They offer vertically as they rejoice in gratitude before YHWH, and they distribute God's blessings horizontally to those in material need. As Block states, 'care for the marginalized is not merely a noble humanitarian issue; it is expressive of one's covenant relationship with Yahweh'.[241]

The third confession of the ceremony requires the worshippers to affirm adherence to the commandments in their distribution of the tithe to the community's dependants. This is then followed by a final prayer asking YHWH to look down and bless the people of Israel. Biddle notes the three dimensions of fellowship the community is drawn into in its worship. They stand in fellowship with YHWH supremely; they stand in fellowship with previous generations; and they stand in fellowship with the various community members within their generation.[242]

---

239. Merrill, *Deuteronomy*, p. 333.

240. A number of scholars question the absence of Sinai from the creed and propose various source- or form-critical solutions. These are unnecessary, as the creed is only reciting elements of Israel's history that are pertinent to the themes of first-fruits and land. See Jerry Hwang, *The Rhetoric of Remembrance: An Investigation of the 'Fathers' in Deuteronomy*, Siphrut 8 (Winona Lake: Eisenbrauns, 2012), p. 68.

241. Block, *Deuteronomy*, p. 605.

242. Biddle, *Deuteronomy*, p. 385.

In return YHWH's declaration in verses 18–19 is that Israel is his treasured possession (*lĕ'am sĕgullâ*) and a 'holy people' (*'am-qādōš*), phrases reminiscent of Exodus 19:5–6. As a result, Israel will be set above the nations in praise, fame and honour. YHWH's fame is mediated through the Torah-shaped lives of the community, as anticipated in Deuteronomy 4:5–8.[243]

Summary

Deuteronomy 12 commands centralization for the unity and purity of Israel's worship. Deuteronomy 16 outlines the costly communion of three annual pilgrimage festivals. Deuteronomy 17 – 18 regulates the authority of the king and the prophet under the supreme authority of YHWH. Deuteronomy 26 links the creedal remembrance to present worship. Key to Israel's worship was remembrance reinforcing identity. The marginalized were welcomed and provided for, and the feasts were characterized by joy. The shape of Israel's monolatry was to be unified and exclusive, wholehearted and joyful, corporate and inclusive.[244] The personal aspect of Israelite religion was evidenced through obedience, reverence and trust. The communal aspect of Israelite religion was seen in their liturgical life of feasts and festivals involving offering, sharing, sojourning and rejoicing.[245] It is this communal aspect, expressed in the annual pilgrimage festivals in particular, that is distinctive in its ANE context. Worship in other ANE contexts was primarily concerned with personal benefit or appeasement of deities.[246] State religion in the cities was differentiated from localized family religion in which each worshipped his or her own ancestral gods.[247] In Israel the worship of YHWH was a corporate celebration and expression of love for God and love for neighbour. To the surrounding nations it is the corporate and the celebratory that would have been strikingly distinctive.

The impact of Israel's monolatry

The argument thus far leads to the question of impact. If missional ethics has the two-pronged emphasis of loving God and loving neighbour it raises the question of how love for God encourages love for neighbour. How does the intracommunal act of worship impact the outsider?

---

243. Miller, *Deuteronomy*, p. 188.

244. Wright, *Deuteronomy*, pp. 167–168.

245. John Goldingay, *Old Testament Theology*, 3 vols. (Downers Grove: IVP Academic, 2003), vol. 3, pp. 53–190.

246. Walton, *Ancient Near Eastern Thought*, p. 161.

247. Ibid., p. 143.

In answer there are two major ways in which Israel's monolatry should have affected those outside the covenant community – directly and indirectly. Directly it appears that some outsiders were present and were encouraged to participate in some aspects of Israel's cultic life. Aliens working as slaves for a family might have been circumcised and therefore regarded as covenant members. In reality the boundaries might have been blurred, particularly with regard to female slaves, their children and those from certain surrounding nations (cf. Deut. 23:3–8). Many of these people would have witnessed family life and community worship, and might have been directly affected. Praise of YHWH functions horizontally as well as vertically.[248] Miller, commenting on Israel's cultic life, says the following:

> That is the purpose of praise – to respond to the experience of God's grace and power, to exalt the one who is seen and known to be gracious and powerful, and to bear witness to all who hear that god is God. In that sense the praise of God in the Old Testament is always devotion that tells about God, that is, theology, and proclamation that seeks to draw others into the circle of those who worship this God, that is, testimony for conversion . . . one might even speak of a missionary aim if that did not risk distorting the material by suggesting a program of proselytizing to bring individuals in to the visible community of Israel.[249]

Second, the effect on those outside the covenant community is indirect. The affective element of Israel's cultic life was primarily to be on Israel themselves. The liturgical and festal practices were designed to shape Israelite identity, and then, as a consequence, affect the watching nations around. A number of related disciplines shed light on this exploration: liturgics, linguistics, ethics and world-view studies. These areas address the way in which worship, language, behaviour and narrative all serve to shape individual and corporate identity.

Liturgics
Smith, Klingbeil and MacDonald have all produced work exploring the effect of liturgy on the faith community.

---

248. Christopher J. H. Wright, *The Mission of God: Unlocking the Bible's Grand Narrative* (Downers Grove: InterVarsity Press, 2006), pp. 126–133.
249. Patrick D. Miller, '"Enthroned on the Praises of Israel": The Praise of God in the Old Testament Theology', *Int* 39.1 (1985), p. 9.

Smith's *Desiring the Kingdom* describes liturgies as pedagogies of desire.[250] He argues for an Augustinian anthropology where the 'person-as-lover' leads not with the head but with the heart.[251] He states, 'liturgies – whether "sacred" or "secular" – shape and constitute our identities by forming our most fundamental desires and our most basic atunement to the world'.[252] Ritual and liturgy create the 'social imaginary'.[253] The 'imaginary' is constructed from the sorts of things that fuel the imagination: stories, images, legends, myths, rites and rituals, and so on. All of the things that constitute Israel's festivals – remembrance, enacted experience, communal praise and joy – serve to shape identity and desire. Israel's cultic practice forms them as the people of God.

Klingbeil, employing concepts from social science, identifies three functions of ritual: social function (or social glue), repression of deviance, and a lens on the significant (phenomenological).[254] These functions form community identity and vocation. He argues that structure, order, time and space are all important elements of ritual contributing to ritual being a 'meaning-laden communicator'.[255] He concludes, 'Rituals are the "Sistine chapels" of communication. They form intricately-tuned, meaning-loaded masterpieces of inter-communication on both an interpersonal and a societal level.'[256] Rituals are more than obedient acts: they are teachers of ultimate realities. As such they serve to reinforce identity and purpose. Applied to Deuteronomy these insights support the claim that Israel's liturgical praxis shapes them to be the people YHWH would have them be, namely a distinctively holy missional community.

MacDonald similarly sees Israel's rituals, as described in Deuteronomy, as 'inscribed and incorporated memories' that lead to 'embodied experience'.[257] The great danger for Israel, as repeated throughout the book of Deuteronomy,

---

250. James K. A. Smith, *Desiring the Kingdom: Worship, Worldview, and Cultural Formation* (Grand Rapids: Baker Academic, 2009), p. 87.

251. Ibid., p. 47.

252. Ibid., p. 25.

253. Ibid., p. 216.

254. Gerald A. Klingbeil, *Bridging the Gap: Ritual and Ritual Texts in the Bible*, BBRSup 1 (Winona Lake: Eisenbrauns, 2007), pp. 29–37.

255. Ibid., p. 55.

256. Ibid., p. 241.

257. Nathan MacDonald, *Not Bread Alone: The Uses of Food in the Old Testament* (Oxford: Oxford University Press, 2008), p. 96.

is that they 'forget'. Cultic meals are at minimum concerned with memory.[258] MacDonald states:

> Israelite festivals are a particularly important expression of Israel's historical memory as understood by Deuteronomy. Through the course of the year the journey from Egypt to the Land is memorialized and celebrated . . . for Deuteronomy life in the land can only truly be appreciated through a memory of the past.[259]

The combination of performance, experience and memory has the potential to shape beliefs, values and behaviour, as they are formative for the communal and individual sense of identity and vocation. The pedagogy of Israel's liturgy directs the community towards being the Torah-morphic people, attracting the interest of the surrounding nations.

Linguistics
We noted the performative nature of speech acts in the methodology. Vanhoozer states, 'The fact of the matter is that speakers, and authors as well, are both perlocutionary and illocutionary agents. Interpreting texts is thus a matter of understanding purposive action – communicative and strategic.'[260] As Briggs notes, 'many of the most significant aspects of human life are governed in profound ways by language and its uses and effect . . . human interactions are irreducibly linguistic'.[261] Performative utterances have power to energize, change, alienate or sap.[262] These rhetorical elements can also be fruitfully applied to ritual and liturgy. Just as with speech or writing, so with ritual there is the action performed, the meaning of the action and the effect of the action on the performer and observer. Vanhoozer notes, 'Drama . . . provides a salient reminder that we should not draw too fine a distinction between "word" and "act." '[263] Ritual becomes a 'Theo-drama' in which people move from observers to participants through performance.[264] Celebrating the Passover, as an example,

---

258. Ibid., p. 85.

259. Ibid., p. 99.

260. Kevin J. Vanhoozer, *Is There a Meaning in This Text?* (Leicester: Apollos, 1998), p. 224.

261. Richard S. Briggs, 'Speech-Act Theory', in *Words and the Word: Explorations in Biblical Interpretation and Literary Theory* (Nottingham: Apollos, 2008), p. 85.

262. Ibid.

263. Kevin J. Vanhoozer, *The Drama of Doctrine: A Canonical Linguistic Approach to Christian Theology* (Louisville: Westminster John Knox, 2005), p. 48.

264. Ibid., p. 409.

should be more than empty ritual. The embodied and enacted experience communicated and reminded the participant of the goodness of God and all that YHWH had done for them. As a consequence the ritual should affect the participant to resolve to live a life of love for YHWH and others in his service. Acts, like texts, inform, affect and effect response from the performers. As Brueggemann has noted, 'praise is the performance of faith', and, as with any performative speech, there is a perlocutionary effect on those who participate or perform.[265] It is interesting to note that some of Israel's ritual practice involved care for outsiders as part of the festival. For example, in Deuteronomy 26 the third-year tithe was to be given to the Levite, widow, orphan and alien. The very performance of faith reinforces identity and vocation in practical ways.

Ethics

The performance of faith is character-forming in something preceding but akin to Aristotle's virtue ethics. Aristotle posited that a virtuous life was lived in pursuit of well-being (*eudaimonia*). The path to *eudaimonia* was through identification and practice of the virtues. Aristotle gives the following analogy:

> For the things we have to learn before we can do them, we learn by doing them, for example, men become builders by building and lyre players by playing the lyre: so do we become just by doing just acts, temperate by doing temperate acts, brave by doing brave acts.[266]

The problem for Aristotle was that defining virtues required the definition of human purpose, a topic that elicited vigorous debate. For Israel the purpose was already determined. They were to be a kingdom of priests and a holy nation (Exod. 19:6), and were to obey the statutes that the nations might observe their wisdom (Deut. 4:5–8). This is significant, as many modern ethicists view Old Testament religion as deontological (divine command theory), and miss the existential/virtue aspect, and the consequentialist aspect of Israel's ethics. The deontological aspect is provided for in the laws, decrees and statutes. The consequentialist aspect was the witness to the nations. It is the function of existential/virtue ethics that is of particular interest here. Hauerwas has criticized what he sees as the historical tendency within Protestantism to discuss

---

265. Walter Brueggemann, *Old Testament Theology: An Introduction*, LBT (Nashville: Abingdon, 2008), p. 240.

266. Aristotle, *The Nichomachean Ethics*, ed. D. Ross, repr. (Oxford: Oxford University Press, 1998), p. 1103b.

ethics in individualistic and occasionalistic application of the command metaphor.[267] He argues for character as the overarching theme for understanding Christian ethics. He raises the interesting question of whether character determines action or vice versa.[268] His proposal is that 'Christian ethics cannot be construed as an ethical program or goal or even subscription to "Christian principles" such as love or benevolence.'[269] Rather it is 'a mode of being to be lived out'.[270] Hauerwas argues that a life of growth in character is a community project: 'character is formed by his association with the community that embodies the language, rituals, and moral practices from which this particular form of life grows'.[271] The virtue aspect is developed *through* ritual and liturgical practice *inter alia*. For Hauerwas, ethical discussion primarily concerned with the discrete acts of the individual has lost its biblical roots. The Bible is much more concerned with the embodiment of truth within and by the community of God's people.[272]

Birch develops the idea of virtue ethics and character formation in ritual practice under the rubric of emulation and imitation. He argues character formation requires emulation, which is exactly what is happening in Deuteronomy 26:12–15 (cf. Deut. 10:18).[273] For Birch the various laws 'establish and preserve an identity with Israel's memory of themselves as delivered slaves, and an identification with (imitation of) God in certain specified ways (identifying with the oppressed, resting on the Sabbath, embodying holiness)'.[274] Willis argues that the bridge between celebrative response and everyday obedience is in part fuelled by inclusion of dependent groups in liturgical gatherings.[275] Community praxis, and particularly liturgical praxis, can define individual and corporate identity and behaviour.

---

267. Stanley Hauerwas, *Character and the Christian Life: A Study in Theological Ethics* (San Antonio: Trinity University Press, 1975), pp. 3–4.

268. Ibid., p. 9.

269. Ibid., p. 180.

270. Ibid., p. 182.

271. Ibid., p. 210.

272. Ibid., p. 232.

273. Bruce C. Birch, 'Moral Agency, Community, and the Character of God in the Hebrew Bible', *Semeia* 66 (1995), pp. 23–41.

274. Ibid., p. 36.

275. Timothy M. Willis, '"Eat and Rejoice Before the Lord": The Optimism of Worship in the Deuteronomic Code', in *Worship and the Hebrew Bible: Essays in Honor of John T. Willis*, JSOTSup 284 (Sheffield: Sheffield Academic Press, 1999), pp. 276–294.

World view

World view is concerned with 'the comprehensive belief-framework that colors all of a person's activities. It is a communal direction of the heart, a framework of belief commitments commonly held by a community of like mind.'[276] Naugle traces the development of the idea from Kant's *Weltanschauung* (world view) in relation to the *mundus sensibilis* (intelligible world) through the eighteenth, nineteenth and twentieth centuries.[277] Naugle notes that the *Weltanschauung* had its 'roots sunk deeply in German soil, [but] its rapid transcontinental transplantation manifests the amazing fertility of the concept'.[278] From Hegel to Foucault the source and function of *Weltanschauung* have stimulated much debate. Strange notes the communal and religious elements of world view: 'activities of culture and world view are shaped by our "vertical" relationship: that which we as human beings believe to be most basic, most ultimate, *a se*'.[279] Culture is the exteriorization of the cult.[280]

N. T. Wright's work on world-view construction is helpful, as it contains, like Deuteronomy, the elements of story, symbol, question and praxis. Identity formation is intimately connected to world view, and world view is intimately connected to one's narrative, symbol and praxis. All three of these elements (narrative, symbol and praxis) are taken up in Israel's various corporate liturgies.[281] Stories are the vehicle by which human beings view reality.[282] Stories

---

276. Harvie M. Conn, *Eternal Word and Changing Worlds: Theology, Anthropology, and Mission in Trialogue* (Phillipsburg: P&R, 1984), p. 319. Sire defines world view as 'a set of presuppositions which we hold about the basic make-up of the world'. James Sire, *The Universe Next Door* (Leicester: Inter-Varsity Press, 1988), p. 17. Similar definitions can be found in Brian J. Walsh and J. Richard Middleton, *The Transforming Vision: Shaping a Christian World View* (Downers Grove: InterVarsity Press, 1984); Paul A. Marshall, Sander Griffioen and Richard J. Mouw (eds.), *Stained Glass: Worldviews and Social Science* (Lanham: University of America Press, 1989).

277. David K. Naugle, *Worldview: The History of a Concept* (Grand Rapids: Eerdmans, 2002), pp. 58–186.

278. Ibid., p. 67.

279. Daniel Strange, *'For Their Rock Is Not as Our Rock': An Evangelical Theology of Religions* (Nottingham: Apollos, 2014), p. 69.

280. Ibid.; John M. Frame, *The Doctrine of the Christian Life* (Phillipsburg: P&R, 2008), p. 857.

281. Wright, *People of God*, pp. 122–126.

282. Ibid., p. 123.

enable people to answer questions of ultimate concern regarding origin, purpose and destiny.[283] Stories and the answers to questions of ultimate concern are expressed in cultural symbols, in particular festivals and gatherings.[284] Rituals are both shaped by, and in turn shape, world views.

Summary

In Deuteronomy love for God was supposed to be one arm of a compelling missional ethic to the nations. In this section I have argued that Israel's worship was a significant part of their life. Israel's monolatry was not so much concerned with philosophical discussions of ontological uniqueness as with a statement of relational exclusivity in devotion to YHWH. It is this aspect of the Deuteronomic code that is distinctive in its ANE context. Not only were the surrounding nations polytheistic, but their law codes and treaties contained almost nothing regarding worship of their gods. The little information available from the explicitly religious texts addresses religious worship in terms of personal benefit rather than corporate celebration.[285] The shape of Israel's monolatry was primarily structured around the three annual centralized pilgrimages. The effect of their liturgical practice was intended to form a community whose identity and vocation were rooted in YHWH and service of him.

Braulik affirms, 'Reform of worship and reform of the community are very closely related in Deuteronomy.'[286] Worship shapes the community into that which YHWH has called them to be. Love for God provides the necessary foundation for a compelling love for neighbour. Worship is a central component of missional ethics.

Deuteronomy and love for neighbour

In the first section of this chapter the examination of Deuteronomy 1 – 11 led to the thesis that an exegetical description of missional ethics can be

---

283. Ibid.

284. Ibid.

285. Assmann describes the distinctive of Israelite religion in contrast to that of the surrounding nations as 'deep religion' – not just serving a god for what he might give you, but worshipping God because he is worthy of worship in himself. *Of God and Gods*, pp. 140–141.

286. Braulik, *Theology of Deuteronomy*, p. 81.

summarized as love for God and love for neighbour. In the previous section the shape and impact of love for God was developed and outlined. Israel's love for God had a direct impact on outsiders observing the community's worship, and an indirect impact as Israel's worship served to shape them as a community for the outsider.

This section will seek to outline the shape of Israel's love for neighbour in its ANE context. Most space will be given to a direct comparison of ANE law with Deuteronomy with special regard to laws that address concern for neighbour. Areas of similarity and dissimilarity will be considered as well as the general purpose of the laws and the motivation to obey. This section will argue that Deuteronomy's distinctive lies in the purpose and motivation of the laws, as well as a more humanitarian tone when compared with other ANE codes.

The social vision of Deuteronomy 12 – 26 in ANE context

Much has been written on the relationship between Israel's legal code and the legal codes of surrounding nations. There is clearly overlap of themes and concerns. Large sections of these legal codes address issues of interest for this section, namely laws concerning neighbourly interaction, including laws addressing vulnerable members of society. Here Deuteronomy 12 – 26 will be examined with particular consideration of areas of similarity or dissimilarity with other ANE legal codes.

Deuteronomy 15: release of debts and slaves

In the first half of Deuteronomy 15 the issue of debt-release is addressed. There is some evidence of debt-cancellation in the ANE, but these examples seem to accompany accession to the throne by a new king. It could be argued that such edicts serve the interests of monarchical propaganda more than they serve the poor or the economy more generally.[287] Hamilton notes the occurrence of *mišarum* edicts. These were royal decrees issued early in a king's reign.[288] One example is the edict of Ammiṣaduqa in which he remits arrears in the interest of equity.[289] The evidence from ANE cultures suggests that the remission of

---

287. One example of debt-cancelling can be found in the later Egyptian wisdom literature. The instruction of Amen-Em-Opet recommends writing off two-thirds of a large debt. *ANET*, p. 423.

288. Jeffries M. Hamilton, *Social Justice and Deuteronomy: The Case of Deuteronomy 15*, SBLDS 136 (Atlanta: Scholars Press, 1992), pp. 48–53.

289. *CoS*, p. 362.

debt was unusual and arbitrary, whereas excessive charging of interest was common and widespread.[290]

By contrast Deuteronomy requires that every seven years debts were to be cancelled. The sabbatical cycle functions as a 'holy rhythm' combining worship of YHWH with love for neighbour.[291] Those who see Deuteronomy 12 – 26 as being structured as an extended exposition of the Decalogue link the laws of Deuteronomy 15 to the fourth commandment regarding the observance of the Sabbath. The law stipulates that loans given to fellow Israelites be cancelled every seventh year. Wright argues that the law of release probably refers to pledges made in lieu of a debt (e.g. portions of land), and the law may refer to suspension rather than cancellation.[292] Whichever is in view the law provides alleviation from the greatest cause of poverty which is debt.[293] Payment may still be required from a foreigner but the fellow Israelite's debt must be cancelled. Lundbom suggests the reason for this as being that foreigners may still enter the land for trade purposes and therefore this law would not apply to the non-resident.[294] Additionally, Tigay suggests that the law did not apply to unpaid wages, bills owed to shopkeepers for merchandise or business loans.[295] The ideal outcome of such an approach would be that there were no poor among

---

290. Similar instruction is found in Deut. 23:19–20, which includes the prohibition on charging interest on a loan to a 'brother' Israelite. This is unique in the ANE context. CH §§88–100 addresses the issue of lending and interest. CH fixes the rate of interest at one-sixth of the amount loaned. *ANET*, p. 169. Exactly the same rule can be found in CE. *ANET*, p. 162. Evidence for loaning at interest can also be seen in Sumerian and Neo-Assyrian legal documents. *ANET*, pp. 217, 221. The latter example cites a loan of three minas increasing to six shekels a month, which equates approximately to an 18% annual interest rate. Loewenberg suggests that throughout ancient Mesopotamia, Assyria and Egypt loans exceeding 20% were not uncommon. See Frank M. Loewenberg, *From Charity to Social Justice: The Emergence of Communal Institutions for the Support of the Poor in Ancient Judaism* (New Brunswick: Transaction, 2001), p. 111.

291. Brad A. Pruitt, 'The Sabbatical Year of Release: The Social Location and Practice of Shemittah in Deuteronomy 15:1–18', *RQ* 52.2 (2010), p. 82.

292. Wright, *Deuteronomy*, p. 188.

293. Ibid.

294. Jack R. Lundbom, *Deuteronomy: A Commentary* (Grand Rapids: Eerdmans, 2013), p. 489.

295. Tigay, *Deuteronomy*, p. 145. Tigay notes the parallel to the *mišarum* edict of King Ammiṣaduqa, which also did not include the cancellation of business loans.

them (v. 4). The ideal is counter-balanced with the real in verse 11: 'There will always be poor people in the land'. This law acts to protect the poor by limiting the power of the strong.[296]

The outcome of obeying the law is that the people will be economically prosperous and blessed by YHWH, and will in turn become a blessing to the nations (v. 6). The imperative is spelled out in verses 7–8: be open-handed and not hard-hearted or tight-fisted. The command is grounded in an appeal to divine authority and to Israel as a community of 'brothers'.[297] This generous sharing within the covenant community is rooted in the generosity of YHWH in what Brueggemann terms 'covenant economics'.[298] The purpose of the law is to shape a society in which citizens truly love their neighbour by ensuring that there is no permanent underclass of those perpetually in debt.[299] Westbrook sees the cyclical nature of the law as ineffective – nobody would have wanted to loan money in the sixth year, and he therefore views the law as utopian.[300] Pruitt suggests that there is good evidence for some kind of practice of Shemittah law, though it was perhaps not widespread.[301] Deuteronomy 15:10 promises that the open-handed will be blessed with prosperity. Loaning in the sixth year was as much an act of faith as generosity.

The second half of Deuteronomy 15 addresses the issue of manumission. Comparing Deuteronomy with its ANE counterparts some similarities can be observed. As with CH §117 slaves are to be released after a certain period of time – three years with Hammurabi, six years in Deuteronomy 15:12. The length of time served probably reflects the sabbatical cycle as evidenced in Deuteronomy 15:1–11. It could be argued that in terms of time served Hammurabi appears more humane.[302] However, the remainder of the instruction in

---

296. Gershon Brin, *Studies in Biblical Law: From the Hebrew Bible to the Dead Sea Scrolls*, JSOTSup 176 (Sheffield: Sheffield Academic Press, 1994), p. 86.

297. Martin J. Oosthuizen, 'Deuteronomy 15:1–18 in Socio-rhetorical Perspective', *ZAR* 3 (1997), p. 68. The term 'brother' occurs six times in vv. 1–11.

298. Brueggemann, *Deuteronomy*, p. 168.

299. Ibid.

300. Raymond Westbrook, 'Social Justice in the Ancient Near East', in *Social Justice in the Ancient World* (Westport, Conn.: Greenwood, 1995), p. 160.

301. Pruitt, 'Sabbatical Year', pp. 87–92.

302. CH §117 commands the release of such 'pledges' after three years of service. *ANET*, pp. 170–171. Hamilton observes the occurrence of *andurārum* edicts, which decree manumission by royal fiat. *Social Justice and Deuteronomy*, pp. 53–56. CH §§117 and 280 are good examples of laws that decree the release of slaves.

Deuteronomy 15:12–18, along with the motive clauses, reveals some unique features of the Deuteronomic code when compared to its ANE counterparts.[303]

The use of the term 'brother', as with the laws regarding lending in Deuteronomy 15:1–11, reinforces the notion of equality before YHWH, and neighbourliness in treatment of one another.[304] Upon release the slaves gain not only their freedom but a liberal supply from the flock, threshing-floor and winepress of their master. This instruction would have provided economic viability for the emancipated and prevented a newly released slave from having to borrow, incurring debt, to begin a new life.[305] Generosity is required in line with the generosity experienced at the hand of YHWH.[306] Carmichael suggests that the gifts given tie into the reminder of verse 15: 'Remember that you were slaves in Egypt and the LORD your God redeemed you.'[307] The people are to remember the slave drivers of Egypt and Pharaoh's unwillingness to grant release, and they are to remember the plunder received upon liberation.[308] Manumission is a forceful visual aid reinforcing the liberation of Israel in the exodus, and therefore the restriction on any sort of slavery for the subsequent

---

303. Gregory C. Chirichigno, *Debt-Slavery in Israel and the Ancient Near East*, JSOTSup 141 (Sheffield: Sheffield Academic Press, 1993), pp. 256–301.

304. McConville, *Deuteronomy*, p. 262. In some cases in ANE legislation slaves appear to have been treated as property. In Lipit-Ishtar the laws relating to slaves come immediately after the laws relating to boats and land, and like those laws deal with proper reimbursement for loss. *ANET*, p. 160. Moreover, CE and CH distinguished between the freeman and the slave. In CH §116 the punishment for causing the death of a 'pledge' is given. If the pledge is the son of the freeman, the one who causes the death will have his own son put to death. If the pledge is the slave of the freeman, the perpetrator pays one third of a mina of silver. *ANET*, p. 170.

305. Tigay, *Deuteronomy*, p. 149.

306. Wright, *Old Testament Ethics*, p. 168.

307. Calum Carmichael, 'The Three Laws on the Release of Slaves', *ZAW* 112 (2000), pp. 520–523.

308. Ibid. Chirichigno suggests the phrase 'empty handed' carries allusions to both Gen. 31:42 and Exod. 3:21–22. In the first account Jacob claims Laban would have sent him away 'empty handed' after his six years' service. In the latter account YHWH promises that Israel will not leave Egypt 'empty handed'. The miserliness of Pharaoh and Laban serve as negative examples. Instead Israel, on account of YHWH's generosity, should exercise open-handed generosity. Chirichigno, *Debt-Slavery*, pp. 287–294.

generations. Further the promise is one of blessing at YHWH's hand for those who exercise generosity (v. 18).

There is the possibility of the slave willingly remaining with the family, which itself would have served to encourage slave masters towards humane treatment of their slaves.[309] However, if the slave wished to leave, the master should consider the worth of the servant's labour. Another distinctive feature of Deuteronomic legislation concerning slaves can be seen in the Sabbath law. Tigay states, 'The *torah*, unique among ancient law codes, insists that servants be given rest on the Sabbath, be included in the festivals, and be protected from physical abuse and harm by their masters.'[310]

A further difference can be observed in the laws concerning runaway slaves. In ANE culture runaways could be punished, and compensation was required from the person who sheltered such a slave. In contrast Deuteronomy simply states in 23:15–16 that a runaway slave is not to be returned to a master. Not only that, but the slave is free to choose where he will dwell. Lundbom describes this law as 'remarkable, having no equivalent in slave legislation of the ANE'.[311] It is difficult to understand the context for this law, since it appears to allow slaves to run away with impunity. McConville and Lundbom suggest the law refers to foreign slaves fleeing to Israel for refuge.[312] In such a case they are to be offered asylum.

Deuteronomy 19: lex talionis *and false witness*
The principle of *lex talionis* is found in Deuteronomy 19:11–21. In verses 13 and 21 the phrase 'show no pity' occurs.[313] Verses 13 and 19 give the reason as the

---

309. McConville, *Deuteronomy*, p. 264.

310. Tigay, *Deuteronomy*, p. 148.

311. Lundbom, *Deuteronomy*, p. 655. In the Hittite Laws (HL) slaves must not be stolen. Runaway slaves must be returned to their masters, or compensation be made for slaves that are stolen. *ANET*, p. 190. One example of Nuzi-Akkadian treatment of slaves is a document in which a Hebrew woman, Sin-balti, enters the house of Tehip-tilla as a slave. The contract states 'if Sin-balti defaults and goes into the house of another, Tehip-tilla shall pluck out the eyes of Sin-balti and sell her'. *ANET*, p. 220.

312. See Lundbom, *Deuteronomy*, pp. 654–655; McConville, *Deuteronomy*, pp. 350–351.

313. In CE §§42–47 various compensations are ordered in accordance with the severity of the injury inflicted. For example, a broken hand or foot commands half a mina, a damaged eye a whole mina and a slap in the face costs ten shekels. *ANET*, p. 163. Similar instructions can be found in CU §§18–22. *CoS*, p. 410.

necessary 'purge' of guilt or evil from the midst of the community. Tigay notes the seriousness with which the taking of human life is viewed: 'since life is infinitely precious, no economic value can be assigned to it'.[314] The law has a communal function. It is not exclusively for the justice of wronged individuals. The law is also designed to protect and promote a whole community of justice.

The need for two or three witnesses (vv. 15–20) protects the accused from malicious false accusation. The requirement of standing before the Lord in the presence of the priests and the judges suggests the seriousness of the crimes under consideration.[315] Standing before the Lord emphasizes the vertical as well as the horizontal dimension to justice. The purpose clause is that the evil be purged, and that the community should hear and be afraid. As with the previous laws addressing personal injury it is the communal and individual, horizontal and vertical aspects of justice that are emphasized. The problem is not simply that the false witness has lied, but that he or she has lied in the presence of God and wilfully sought to damage a neighbour.[316] False witnesses fail in their duty to love God and neighbour. McConville's conclusion notes the distinctive of Israelite law: 'The prince or tycoon must take the consequences of his destruction of the pauper. This is the absolute difference between biblical and other ancient laws.'[317]

While often viewed as vengeful and barbaric, the law of *talion*, as McConville notes, has the advantage of treating all people equally and limiting retribution.[318] Punishment is not determined by class or wealth, and the victim is not permitted to take excessive retribution.[319] As Wright notes, the common misunderstanding

---

314. Tigay, *Deuteronomy*, p. 183.

315. Lundbom, *Deuteronomy*, p. 573.

316. Brueggemann, *Deuteronomy*, p. 205.

317. McConville, *Deuteronomy*, p. 314.

318. Ibid., p. 313. In Middle Assyrian Laws (MAL), in cases where a man publicly and falsely accuses another man of adultery the punishment is flogging, castration and a month's service to the king. *ANET*, p. 181.

319. CH §§195–217 provides an extensive list of personal injury offences and appropriate penalties. There is a class distinction between personal injury inflicted on the aristocracy, the commoner and the slave. In the case of someone of equal class the principle of *lex talionis* applies. In the case of injury of a slave or commoner monetary restitution is adequate. *ANET*, p. 175. Tablet 1, §§1–18, of the HL contains extensive legal material relating to cases of personal injury. Unlike other law codes the principle of *lex talionis* is not present and monetary compensation is instead prescribed. There is, like other codes, a difference in the amount of compensation depending on whether the injured party is a freeman or a slave.

of this law is that it was vengeful, whereas it was intended to restrain the powerful. The law is 'designed to ensure that penalties in law are strictly proportionate to offenses committed'.[320] Jesus' refutation of *lex talionis* is concerned with the violent application of the principle in his own context.[321] The law of Deuteronomy exists to 'curb the excessive barbarism among those bent on vengeance'.[322] One may ask how Deuteronomy's law is distinctive with its legislation regarding personal injury. It appears to be more barbaric than surrounding legal codes. There is a distinctive here that will be returned to later – the distinctive relates to the differing views on the value of life and property. Deuteronomy is less severe in the case of property, but more severe with regard to human life.[323] There is a distinctive value of people more prevalent in Deuteronomy than in other ANE legal codes.

Deuteronomy 22:1–4: laws concerning property
Of interest in the context of this work is Deuteronomy 22:1–4. Here the law stipulates personal responsibility for a neighbour's property not only when borrowed but also when found.[324] The law states that if a citizen finds a neighbour's ox or sheep going astray that person should return it to his neighbour. Moreover if the neighbour is unknown or far off the person who found the animal is to take it in and look after it until the neighbour comes to collect. The law covers any lost property and the one who finds it is not permitted to ignore it. The word translated 'ignore' (*wĕhitʿallamtā*) can carry the sense of hiding or disregarding. Either way, it is the personal responsibility to love one's neighbour that comes to the fore. Brueggemann observes the importance of such laws in small agrarian communities, where mutual protection and care are paramount.[325] The language of 'brotherhood' (*'āḥîkā*) is present, and, as with other laws, is motivational since such a law would be difficult to

---

320. Wright, *Deuteronomy*, pp. 226.

321. D. A. Carson, 'Matthew', in EBC, vol. 8 (Grand Rapids: Zondervan, 1984), pp. 155–156.

322. Brueggemann, *Deuteronomy*, p. 206.

323. Leon Epsztein, *Social Justice in the Ancient Near East and the People of the Bible*, tr. John Bowden (London: SCM, 1986), p. 136.

324. Laws regarding property are common among ANE codes and occupy significant space within their legal codes. Compensation for damage or destruction can be as high as thirtyfold. If the thief is unable to make amends the death penalty is, in some places, prescribed. *ANET*, p. 166.

325. Brueggemann, *Deuteronomy*, p. 219.

enforce.[326] The section from Deuteronomy 22:1–4 closes with the command to look out for the well-being of a neighbour's animals; if any fall down by the way the Israelite is to help his brother in lifting the animal up. The spirit of the law goes above and beyond the standard of surrounding law codes. Love for neighbour motivates the Israelite to go the extra mile. A similar spirit, it would appear, is present in Deuteronomy 22:8, where the Israelite is commanded to build a parapet for his roof. Lundbom, paraphrasing Calvin, says, 'it is not enough simply to abstain from evil . . . one must also strive to do good'.[327]

Deuteronomy 21 – 25: laws concerning the treatment of women

Treatment of women in Deuteronomy has elicited much debate. Carolyn Pressler has said of Deuteronomy, 'these texts do what rape does. They eliminate women's will from consideration and erase women's right to sexual integrity.'[328] Similarly Washington sees the texts as viewing women as property, and a discourse in male power.[329] Carol Meyers on the other hand views Deuteronomy as giving women dignity and honour within their own cultural milieu.[330]

---

326. McConville, *Deuteronomy*, p. 337.

327. Lundbom, *Deuteronomy*, p. 614.

328. Carolyn Pressler, 'Sexual Violence and Deuteronomic Law', in *A Feminist Companion to Exodus to Deuteronomy* (Sheffield: Sheffield Academic Press, 1994), p. 103.

329. Harold Washington, 'Lest He Die in Battle and Another Man Take Her: Violence and the Construction of Gender in the Laws of Deuteronomy 20–22', in *Gender and Law in the Hebrew Bible and the Ancient Near East*, JSOTSup 262 (Sheffield: Sheffield Academic Press, 1998), pp. 185–213.

330. Carol Meyers, *Discovering Eve: Ancient Israelite Women in Context* (Oxford: Oxford University Press, 1988), pp. 173–181. Some examples of ANE material on the treatment of women are as follows: CE depicts not just slaves, but women as property. In CE §18 the law states, 'If he takes her (the girl) and she enters his house, but *afterward* the young woman should decease, he (the husband) shall get refunded.' *ANET*, p. 162. Emphasis original. CL promotes the support of second wives, slave wives or 'harlot wives'. In some cases children born from such unions also have a claim on support. *ANET*, p. 160. Ur-Nammu differentiates between the 'first-ranking' wife and the widow. If a man divorces the former he must pay her sixty shekels; if he divorces the latter he must pay her thirty shekels. CH §§129–132 covers accusations of infidelity directed primarily at women. In order for the wife to prove her innocence, and 'for the sake of her husband', she must submit to the river ordeal. *ANET*, p. 171. The MAL contain some of the harshest punishments for all people, and women in particular. The first eight laws concern infringements

Four passages are worthy of brief consideration. First, Deuteronomy 21:10–14 addresses a soldier who wishes to take a female captive as his wife. The law addresses the male and regulates his behaviour. He is not permitted to have intercourse with her until she has left her family, completed her mourning rituals, stayed in her new home for a full month and he has supplied her with new clothes. Only then is he permitted to take her as his wife. The thirty-day period and the associated rituals suggest an assimilation of the foreign woman into her new culture, and ensure the appropriate intention of the man.[331] Tigay argues that the overriding concern of the law is the respect of the personhood and dignity of the woman.[332] Abuse is prohibited; respect and fidelity are endorsed. If the man changes his mind he is not to sell her, as he has caused her dishonour.

A second group of laws occurs in Deuteronomy 22:13–30. Various offences are covered and may be further subdivided into issues of virginity (vv. 13–21), adultery (vv. 22–24) and rape (vv. 25–29). The first issue concerns a man who slanders his new bride, casting doubt over her virginity. On first reading it seems that the law is harsh towards women. If the elders determine the man is lying he is fined; if the accusation is upheld the woman is stoned to death. Scholars note the discrepancy with Deuteronomy 19:16–19, which stipulates the false accusation results in the punishment sought being meted out on the one who brought the false accusation – in this case, death. However, a number of scholars note that this situation is more likely an attempt to defraud the father-in-law, with financial incentive in mind.[333] It is the parents, in verse 15, who bring the case to the elders. Therefore the talionic principle is upheld – if the accusation proves false then the accuser will pay the money sought to the family. As such the law

---

(note 330 *cont.*) a woman might have committed, including blasphemy, theft and assault on a man. Punishments include death, tearing out eyes and cutting off ears and nose. *ANET*, pp. 180–181. Perhaps the most disturbing law from MAL concerning women is §55, which also employs *lex talionis*, but in this case for rape. If a virgin is raped, the offended party's father is permitted to give the perpetrator's wife over to be raped in retribution. *ANET*, p. 185. Additionally MAL states that 'apart from the penalties . . . which [are prescribed] on the tablet . . . a seignior may pull out (the hair of) his wife, mutilate (or) twist her ears, with no liability attaching to him'. *ANET*, p. 185.

331. Tigay, *Deuteronomy*, p. 195.

332. Ibid., p. 194.

333. Hilary B. Lipka, *Sexual Transgression in the Hebrew Bible*, HBM 7 (Sheffield: Phoenix, 2006), p. 93; Bruce G. Wells, 'Sex, Lies, and Virginal Rape: The Slandered Bride and False Accusation in Deuteronomy', *JBL* 124 (2005), pp. 41–72.

serves to protect young brides from economic exploitation, along with the social consequences entailed.[334] However, if the accusation proves true the severity of the punishment matches the severity with which covenant breach is viewed.

In the case of rape (vv. 25–29) the marital status of the woman determines the punishment. If she is married or betrothed the man must die. If she is neither married nor betrothed the crime is not considered adultery, and therefore the man is required to pay a fine to the girl's father and marry her. Washington expresses a common view – that it is barbaric to force the victim to marry her assailant.[335] However, Tigay argues that the text allows for the possibility that the father may refuse such a marriage.[336] Additionally the fate of women (and children born from such unions) in such circumstances was parlous. They would have been in danger of becoming 'untouchables' and could have ended up in poverty and prostitution.[337] As difficult as it is for modern readers to understand, the law offers protection to abused women and forces men to take responsibility for their actions.

The third law of interest here is in Deuteronomy 24:1–4 and concerns divorce. The reason for divorce is unclear. The 'displeasing thing' ('erwat dābar) is not grave enough to warrant death, nor so serious as to prohibit remarriage.[338] Should the same thing happen again, the first man is not permitted to remarry her. If that were to happen it would be an 'abomination' (tôʿēbâ), the only sexual transgression described as such in Deuteronomy. There are a number of things this law could be seeking to address. Clements argues the law prevents 'fickle marital exchange'; McConville suggests that the law prevents economic exploitation; and Wright suggests this law 'prevents a woman from becoming the victim of sexual football between feckless men'.[339]

---

334. Eckhart Otto, 'False Weights in the Scales of Biblical Justice? Different Views of Women from Patriarchal Hierarchy to Religious Equality in the Book of Deuteronomy', in *Gender and Law in the Hebrew Bible and the Ancient Near East*, JSOTSup 262 (Sheffield: Sheffield Academic Press, 1998), p. 135.

335. Washington, 'Lest He Die in Battle', p. 212.

336. Tigay, *Deuteronomy*, p. 208.

337. Daniel I. Block, 'Marriage and Family in Ancient Israel', in *Marriage and Family in the Biblical World* (Downers Grove: InterVarsity Press, 2003), p. 72; Wright, *Old Testament Ethics*, p. 332.

338. McConville, *Deuteronomy*, p. 342.

339. R. E. Clements, *The Book of Deuteronomy: Introduction, Commentary, and Reflections*, NIB 2 (Nashville: Abingdon, 1998), p. 468; McConville, *Deuteronomy*, p. 359; Wright, *Old Testament Ethics*, p. 332.

The fourth and final law in Deuteronomy to be considered here is found in Deuteronomy 25:5–10, the law of levirate marriage. Its intent seems threefold: to preserve the name of the deceased, to retain the land and property within the family and to provide for the widow and orphan.[340] The expectation of the male *levir* is that he will fulfil his family obligation in regard to the law. While he is within his legal right to refuse, the morality of such a decision is clearly questioned.

In summary, Deuteronomic legislation regarding women is undeniably patriarchal, patrilineal and patrilocal.[341] However, in the context of the ANE, Israelite law seems to provide women with greater rights and protection than the law codes of surrounding nations.

Laws regarding other vulnerable people
There are a number of general laws in the cuneiform codes encouraging the protection of the orphan and the widow, reflecting a widespread awareness of, and concern for, the vulnerable in society.[342]

Deuteronomy picks up this pairing and adds, uniquely, a third party – the alien. Deuteronomy 10 provides the basic principle of care towards the vulnerable in society, and one particular law, which could also be considered under laws addressing lending, comes in Deuteronomy 24:10–15. These verses give three commandments, the first two negative, and the third positive. The first prohibition concerns entering the house of another to claim a pledge. This likely

---

340. Block, *Deuteronomy*, pp. 580–581. Ellens thinks the woman's welfare is incidental to the law, an ancillary accomplishment, rather than a primary concern. Deborah L. Ellens, *Women in the Sex Texts of Leviticus and Deuteronomy* (London: T&T Clark, 2007), pp. 249, 266–267. Pressler, on the other hand sees the woman's welfare as part of the design of the law. Carolyn Pressler, *The View of Women Found in the Deuteronomic Family Laws*, BZAW 216 (Berlin: de Gruyter, 1993), p. 67, n. 17.

341. These are the terms used by Block to sum up what he calls 'patricentrism'. Block, 'Marriage and Family', pp. 40–41.

342. The earliest available account of what may be termed social justice comes in the reforms of Uru-inimgina or Uru-Kagina (c. 2351–2342 BC). He states that 'he made a compact with the divine Nin-Girsu that the powerful man would not oppress the orphan (or) widow' (*CoS*, p. 408). His successor Ur-Nammu (CU) also claims, in his prologue, to have protected the orphan, the widow and the poor (*CoS*, p. 409). CH prevents the children of slaves or adopted orphans being reclaimed (*ANET*, pp. 174–175).

refers to defaulting on a loan.[343] The creditor is to wait outside and the pledge is to be brought out. Lundbom suggests this prevents further humiliation of the debtor and prevents the creditor from excessive reclamation.[344] As McConville says, 'humane regard for a neighbour prevails over economic imperatives . . . economic calculation is to be subordinate to compassion'.[345] The second prohibition concerns the return of a garment pledged. This must be done before sundown so that the person may sleep in it. A creditor may not take a debtor's handmill (24:6), so options on what to seize would be limited. While the taking of a garment may encourage repayment it may not be kept to the detriment or harm of the debtor. Tigay notes the spirit of such laws: 'These restrictions considerably reduce the creditor's leverage in securing a repayment, but they are consistent with the Bible's position that loans to the poor are acts of charity that may well turn into outright gifts.'[346] The law here treats the poor with dignity and restrains the hand of the strong. The law does not simply create a just order in society, but is pleasing to YHWH and is thus bound up with service and worship. McConville states, 'oppression of the poor is the parade example in the OT of social sin, the antithesis of the spirit of the covenant'.[347]

Summary

From this brief survey and comparison of Deuteronomic law with its ANE equivalents it can be seen that there are elements of both similarity and dissimilarity. All codes share a certain cultural heritage and work with that shared capital to produce legal texts that have varying degrees of overlap. Other ANE law codes, like Deuteronomy, have a concern to protect the orphan and widow, to protect the vulnerable from the powerful, to freeze interest, to release slaves, and to pursue justice. These major themes are common across ANE legal material.[348] Baker notes the similarities between the ANE codes and Old

---

343. Jacob Milgrom, *Cult and Conscience: The Asham and the Priestly Doctrine of Repentance*, SJLA (Leiden: Brill, 1976), pp. 95–98.

344. Lundbom, *Deuteronomy*, p. 686.

345. McConville, *Deuteronomy*, p. 362.

346. Jeffrey H. Tigay, 'A Talmudic Parallel to the Petition from Yavneh-Ham', in *Minhah le-Nahum*, JSOTSup 154 (Sheffield: Sheffield Academic Press, 1993), pp. 330–331.

347. McConville, *Deuteronomy*, p. 362.

348. Enrique Nardoni, *Rise up, O Judge: A Study of Justice in the Biblical World*, tr. Sean Charles Martin (Peabody: Hendrickson, 2004), pp. 5–37.

Testament law as being protection from theft or damage to property, legislation regarding chattel slavery, justice, honesty and fairness.[349]

However, this is not to conclude that the claims of Deuteronomy 4:6–8 are empty idealism. There are some distinctive features to Israelite law. Baker notes seven distinctives in Israelite law:

1. Penalties for infringing property rights are more humane.
2. Land belongs to the people not the king.
3. Greater protection for slaves (since they are people, not property).
4. Greater concern for the vulnerable.
5. Interest on loans is forbidden.
6. Remission of debt and slavery is regular.
7. The Sabbath commandment.[350]

Epsztein notes that while Israel's law is more humane concerning property it is more severe in punishing crimes against humanity (made in the image of God).[351] Greenberg explains this difference in terms of the 'basic difference in the evaluation of life and property'.[352] Corcoran suggests that as a nation of 'resident aliens' their property rights are already limited. Israel are tenants of God's land and, as such, are a microcosm of all people.[353] The purpose of the law and the motivation to obey will be considered shortly, but first a discussion of Deuteronomic legislation in its ANE context requires some consideration of those features of Deuteronomic legislation that are unique.

Features of Deuteronomic law without ANE parallel

So far we have examined features of Deuteronomic law that have some parallel with ANE counterparts. There are, however, laws in Deuteronomy that have

---

349. David L. Baker, *Tight Fists or Open Hands? Wealth and Poverty in Old Testament Law* (Grand Rapids: Eerdmans, 2009), p. 306.

350. Ibid., pp. 307–310.

351. Epsztein, *Social Justice*, p. 136.

352. Moshe Greenberg, 'Some Postulates of Biblical Criminal Law', in *A Song of Power and the Power of Song: Essays on the Book of Deuteronomy*, Sources for Biblical and Theological Study 3 (Winona Lake: Eisenbrauns, 1993), p. 294.

353. Jenny Corcoran, 'The Alien in Deuteronomy 29 and Today', in *Interpreting Deuteronomy: Issues and Approaches* (Nottingham: Apollos, 2012), p. 237.

no ANE counterpart.[354] Five types of laws are worthy of note as they provide a framework for considering the purpose of Deuteronomic law.

First, as previously observed, a considerable amount of space in the legal code is given to instruction regarding worship. Such instruction comes in chapters 12–13, 16–18 and 26. Instructions regarding worship frame legal texts concerning neighbour. This reminds the reader that Torah is not simply legal material, but instruction for life in the community of YHWH's people. Observing the law in the societal sphere is part of what it means to love YHWH and serve him. David Pleins notes, 'biblical law, unlike other Near Eastern codes, regularly blends ritual and social obligations'.[355] He continues:

> the social visions spawned by Israel's variegated legal traditions are inextricably intertwined with the liturgical programs of the tradents . . . social well being is not simply a product of royal or judicial fiat but finds its deepest roots in the community's worship response to Israel's divine sovereign.[356]

Second, there are the enigmatic laws of Deuteronomy 22:9–12 regarding mixed fabrics, planting a field with two kinds of seed, and yoking an ox and donkey together, concluding with a single instruction to make tassels for garments. Wright suggests these rules are symbolic 'badges' of distinctive identity.[357] The clue to understanding lies in the concept of defilement in verse 9. To maximize profit by sowing seed between the rows of vines expresses ingratitude and a lack of faith in YHWH to provide. Such action renders first-fruits unacceptable to YHWH at the sanctuary. Similarly oxen and donkeys must not be yoked together since one is clean and the other unclean (cf. Lev. 11:1–8).[358] The wearing of mixed fabric, argues Block, is something reserved for priests; hence the reason why the laity may not wear such garments.[359] Finally, the instruction to fasten tassels to the four corners of a garment would have functioned as a

---

354. These include laws regarding worship (Deut. 12 – 13; 16 – 18; 26); laws regarding charity (14:22–29; 24:19–22); laws regarding firstborn animals (15:19–23); laws regarding the appointment of kings (17:14–20); laws regarding idolatry (18:9–22); laws regarding warfare (20); and laws regarding mixed fabric/seed, etc. (22:9–12).

355. J. David Pleins, *The Social Visions of the Hebrew Bible: A Theological Introduction* (Louisville: Westminster John Knox, 2001), p. 44.

356. Ibid.

357. Wright, *Deuteronomy*, p. 242.

358. Ibid.

359. Block, *Deuteronomy*, p. 515.

reminder to Israel of their missional vocation, set at the centre of the four corners of the earth.[360] The laws of Deuteronomy are about more than minimal justice – they are about holiness, a distinctive quality of life before the nations.

Third, unique to Deuteronomy are laws commending charity. The basis for this is Deuteronomy 10:18–19 – YHWH's love for the widow and alien, and Israel's remembrance of their former status as resident aliens in a foreign land.[361] The remembrance of former identity shapes the social concern of Deuteronomy.[362] Charity begins with the memory of slavery. Deuteronomy 15:11 instructs Israel to be 'open-handed' towards the poor. In 15:14 slave owners are commanded to be liberal in generosity when releasing slaves. In Deuteronomy 24:19–22 the Israelites are instructed to leave the edges of fields for the alien, the orphan and the widow. The enforcement of specifics with such law would have been difficult to enact. It is an appeal to charity and generosity. Distinctive lives of love unveil the distinctive purpose of Israel's law.

Fourth, the people of Israel, including resident aliens, are commanded to observe Sabbath. There is no parallel commandment among neighbouring peoples.[363] The Sabbath displays a humanitarian concern for welfare and well-being: no longer are people to be expendable commodities. Additionally, each and every Sabbath is a reminder of redemption. Sabbath contains horizontal and vertical aspects. Braulik says Sabbath is about physical rest, social restructuring and theological reflection.[364]

Finally, the addition of 'alien' to the 'orphan and widow' is unique to Deuteronomy. Surrounding law codes frequently mention 'orphans and widows' but the addition of 'alien' is a 'literary innovation' unique to Deuteronomy.[365] Its conspicuous presence indicates an intentional addition to the surrounding traditions. Israel's history as foreign slaves should motivate a special concern for resident aliens.[366] Israel is to be a deliberate and intentional 'paradigm of hospitality' where strangers are concerned.[367]

---

360. Ibid., p. 516.

361. F. Charles Fensham, 'Widow, Orphan, and the Poor in Ancient Near Eastern Legal and Wisdom Literature', *JNES* 21.1 (1962), p. 135.

362. Corcoran, 'Alien in Deuteronomy 29', p. 236.

363. Nardoni, *Rise up, O Judge*, p. 71.

364. Braulik, *Theology of Deuteronomy*, p. 138.

365. Mark A. Awabdy, *Immigrants and Innovative Law: Deuteronomy's Theological and Social Vision for the גר*, FZAT 267 (Tübingen: Mohr Siebeck, 2014), p. 249.

366. Nardoni, *Rise up, O Judge*, p. 42.

367. Corcoran, 'Alien in Deuteronomy 29', p. 237.

The purpose of the law

Walton argues for a dual function in ANE law. On the one hand there is a desire for the king to legitimate his rule.[368] As such the law codes, particularly the ones with extended epilogues, serve as royal propaganda. Second, they exist to maintain some sort of community stability.[369] Walton suggests that one of the fundamental differences between ANE law and biblical law lies in the purpose of the law. In the ANE law is frequently concerned with royal legitimation, self-glorification and control through fear. In Israel the law is given in the context of a covenantal relationship.[370] Only in Israel does the deity initiate a covenantal relationship with a people group. The people do not exist to relieve the gods of burdensome chores; the people exist to bring glory to YHWH.

In Mesopotamia the king's role was to maintain justice and order, through divine authentication.[371] Homeric heroes and Mesopotamian kings are divinized.[372] There is an 'intentional quest' for fame.[373] Not only does this 'divinization' give credence to their law; it also glorifies the king. The king wants justice in so far as it magnifies his name. Israel's quest is also for intentional fame, but in this case the fame of YHWH among the nations. Block notes the framework for the whole of the law – a framework with Exodus 19:5–6 and Deuteronomy 26:16–19 as bookends.[374] Exodus 19:5–6 describes Israel as a treasured possession (səgullâ) and holy nation (gôy qādôš). As we have already noted, Deuteronomy 26:18–19 similarly describes Israel as a treasured possession (lĕʿam səgullâ) and a holy people (ʿam qādôš). Israel will be a treasured possession and a holy people, and their holiness will be the praise of the surrounding nations.[375] YHWH's renown is mediated through the Torah-shaped

---

368. Walton, *Ancient Near Eastern Thought*, p. 295.

369. Ibid.

370. Ibid., p. 299.

371. Dale F. Launderville, *Piety and Politics: The Dynamics of Royal Authority in Homeric Greece, Biblical Israel, and Old Babylonian Mesopotamia* (Grand Rapids: Eerdmans, 2003), p. 336.

372. Ibid., pp. 142–143.

373. Ibid., p. 168.

374. Daniel I. Block, 'The Privilege of Calling: The Mosaic Paradigm for Missions (Deut. 26:16–19)', in *How I Love Your Torah, O Lord* (Eugene: Wipf & Stock, 2011), pp. 144–145.

375. Ibid., pp. 154–156. Block argues that the praise belongs to God, not Israel.

lives of the community. The purpose of the law is sanctification;[376] the purpose of sanctification is mission. This explains the frequent purpose clause in Deuteronomy – to purge the evil from their midst. Israel were to be a 'sacred community, different from all the nations, yet with a mission to them as they exercise a priestly function among the nations by being the very model of a just society'.[377]

The motivation to observe the law

Bottéro argues that 'the observance of moral laws [in Mesopotamia] did not stem from piety but from prudence'.[378] There was a fear that disobedience would lead to wrath. It was therefore prudent to observe the law, which the king claimed had come from the gods.[379] Once each person (including the king) had performed the necessary duty in appeasing the gods he or she was 'free to go'.[380] As quoted earlier, Bottéro states:

> [O]ne of Moses' great revolutions in Israel: to replace the purely material maintenance of the gods with the single and sole 'liturgical' obligation in life to obey a moral law, thereby truly rendering to God the only homage worthy of him.[381]

Again Bottéro highlights the link between worship and ethics. To obey the law is in some sense a 'liturgical' act since it is in the service of YHWH. In Israel YHWH was honoured; in Mesopotamia the gods were provided for.[382] Saggs argues that for Israel man's role was to have dominion in the *imitatio Dei*, whereas in Mesopotamia man was created to relieve the gods of their chores.[383] Sonsino agrees with this view that the primary function of the law was to curry favour with the gods. He summarizes as follows:

---

376. Shalom Paul, *Studies in the Book of the Covenant in the Light of Cuneiform and Biblical Law*, VTSup 18 (Leiden: Brill, 1970), pp. 36–41.

377. Nardoni, *Rise up, O Judge*, p. 85.

378. Bottéro, *Religion in Ancient Mesopotamia*, p. 169.

379. Launderville, *Piety and Politics*, pp. 142–143.

380. Bottéro, *Religion in Ancient Mesopotamia*, p. 170.

381. Ibid., p. 169.

382. Launderville, *Piety and Politics*, p. 145.

383. H. W. F. Saggs, *The Encounter with the Divine in Mesopotamia and Israel* (London: Athlone, 1978), p. 164.

It is noteworthy that, unlike biblical laws, no cuneiform law is ever motivated by reference to an historic event, a promise of well-being or, for that matter, a divine will. In fact, in these laws the deity is completely silent, yielding its place to a human lawgiver whose main concern is economic rather than religious. Biblical law, on the other hand, ascribed in its totality to God both in terms of source and authorship, displays a concern that goes beyond the economic, enveloping all aspects of community life, whether past, present or future, and incorporating both the strictly cultic/sacral and that which remains outside of it.[384]

Deuteronomy's law is for the good of the people (Deut. 4:1–2) and for the honour of God's name among the nations (Deut. 4:6–8). Justice in ancient Israel has 'a basically religious stamp'.[385] Not only is Deuteronomy's law, in many respects, more humane than ANE equivalents, but its purpose and motivation are radically different in creating a worshipful community that loves God and loves neighbour for the well-being of Israel and the nations.

Conclusion

Deuteronomy is a constitutive document for Israel as the people belonging to YHWH. It sets out a vision for a Torah-shaped community who, through their distinctive ethic, would bear witness to the greatness of YHWH among the nations. That witness was to be twofold in form: love for God and love for neighbour.

In the first section of this chapter we considered the vocation of Israel as laid out in Deuteronomy 1 – 11. We noted the repeated emphasis on YHWH's mighty acts of deliverance remembered and anticipated, and the call to live a life of covenantal loyalty to YHWH. Covenantal loyalty and obedience result in an attentiveness to one's neighbour. Concern for those on the other side of the covenantal boundary is repeatedly stressed in the opening chapters of Deuteronomy. Israel's experience as strangers and aliens is the motivation to care for aliens in their midst. Love for YHWH, displayed through obedience to Torah, causes the surrounding nations to take notice.

In the second section of this chapter the shape and impact of Israel's monolatry was explored. Israel's monolatry is concerned with relational

---

384. Rifat Sonsino, *Motive Clauses in Hebrew Law: Biblical Forms and Near Eastern Parallels*, SBLDS 45 (Chico, Calif.: Scholars Press, 1980), p. 175.

385. Epsztein, *Social Justice*, pp. 104–105.

exclusivity in devotion to YHWH. This aspect of the Deuteronomic code is distinctive in its ANE context. Not only were surrounding nations polytheistic, but their law codes and treaties contained almost nothing regarding worship. The information available from explicitly religious texts describes worship in terms of personal benefit rather than corporate celebration.[386] The effect of their liturgical practice was intended to form a community whose identity and vocation were rooted in service of YHWH. To the surrounding nations it is the corporate and the celebratory that would have been strikingly distinctive.

In the third section of this chapter the social vision of Deuteronomy 12 – 26 was considered within its ANE context. Elements of similarity and dissimilarity were explored. Shared cultural inheritance has produced texts with a varying degree of overlap. Like Deuteronomy, other ANE law codes have a concern to protect the orphan, widow and the vulnerable from the powerful, to freeze interest, to release slaves and to pursue justice.[387] However, we also noted Baker's seven distinctives of Israelite law, including Sabbath observance and love for the alien.[388] Israel's law is more humane concerning property, and it is more severe in punishing crimes against humanity.[389] This is due to a 'basic difference in the evaluation of life and property'.[390]

Israel's law was a combination of moral, religious and legal principles to govern all of life as the covenant community.[391] Deuteronomic law exists not simply to maintain order, nor as royal propaganda, but rather to create a holy people whose social ethic is inextricably connected to their worship of YHWH. This holy nation existed for the sake of the nations. The motivation to obedience was not appeasement of capricious deities, but rather to honour YHWH in the sight of the nations. Israel's Torah was to have a distinctive inclusivity to the marginalized and a distinctive exclusivity to YHWH.

Israel, as a Torah-morphic community, was commissioned to bear witness to the greatness of YHWH among the nations in liturgical observance (love for God) and social care (love for neighbour). The outsider should have seen a distinctively joyous and inclusive worship of YHWH, and a distinctive social ethic

---

386. Assmann, *Of God and Gods*, pp. 140–141.

387. Nardoni, *Rise up, O Judge*, pp. 5–37.

388. Baker, *Tight Fists*, pp. 307–310.

389. Epsztein, *Social Justice*, p. 136.

390. Greenberg, 'Some Postulates', p. 294.

391. James Phillip Ashmore, *The Social Setting of the Law in Deuteronomy* (Detroit: UMI, 1997), pp. 152–157.

towards the vulnerable. The unfolding narrative of the Old Testament demonstrates Israel's failure in this regard, and the need for a new heart and new spirit for the ideal to be realized. We now turn to the prophetic critique of, and hope for, Israel's missio-ethical vocation.

3. MISSIONAL ETHICS IN THE MAJOR PROPHETS

Introduction

In the previous chapter we examined the Deuteronomic vision for missional ethics, with love for God and love for neighbour providing a summary of the exegesis. Now we turn to consider the extent to which Israel fulfilled their missio-ethical vocation. The prophets provide a window on Israelite religion, presenting, in Deuteronomic terms, both a critique of, and a vision for, Israel's missional ethic.

Some view the prophets as ecstatic eccentrics presenting radically new ideas and ideals.[1] Others, however, suggest that they are conservatives appealing to the Sinaitic covenant.[2] The prophetic office is regulated by the Torah

---

1. For example, Klaus Koch, *The Prophets: The Assyrian Period*, 2 vols. (London: SCM, 1982), vol. 1, pp. 1–32; J. Lindblom, *Prophecy in Ancient Israel* (Oxford: Blackwell, 1963), pp. 6–12.

2. Clements states, 'For the prophets and the psalmists the covenant tradition formed the heart of their religion.' R. E. Clements, *Prophecy and Covenant* (London: SCM, 1965), p. 18. Lundbom observes that 'Behind all the indictments and judgments of the prophets lay a broken Sinai covenant.' Lundbom connects the message of the prophets with the message of Deuteronomy. The prophets,

(Deut. 18:15–22) and is therefore 'covenant-centered'.[3] Prophets were covenant mediators concerned with covenant breach and its ramifications.[4] As such their reflection on the covenantal traditions is of interest in the consideration of Israel's plight and call. We have noted Deuteronomy's vision of a Torah-shaped community capturing the admiring interest of the surrounding nations. Any investigation of the theme of missional ethics must consider the extent to which it transcends one tradition and finds its way into others. It is this relationship between Deuteronomy and the Major Prophets that occupies this chapter, and in particular the way in which the notion of missional ethics is employed and developed.

It is beyond the scope of this work to consider the entire prophetic corpus; and so the Major Prophets will be the focus, since they contain and 'embody some of the boldest and most eloquent theological probing in the Old Testament'.[5] Further, these three, more than any others, proclaim hope – something new, which YHWH will do in and among his people for his glory among the nations.[6]

Therefore this chapter will seek to elucidate missio-ethical themes that have arisen out of the covenantal tradition, and will focus on the sections within Isaiah, Jeremiah and Ezekiel that are of most relevance to the wider discussion of this book. As the exploration proceeds it will become evident that Israel has been an anti-witness due to their failure to fulfil the basic Deuteronomic requirement to love God and love neighbour. However, there is hope for a future restoration that will enable Israel to fulfil their missio-ethical vocation.

---

according to Lundbom, are 'basically conservatives', and he notes 'Jeremiah's big word is not "change," but "return".' Jack R. Lundbom, *The Hebrew Prophets: An Introduction* (Minneapolis: Fortress, 2010), pp. 33–34. VanGemeren too argues that the prophets 'formed a tradition that was founded on covenantal structure'. Willem A. VanGemeren, *Interpreting the Prophetic Word: An Introduction to the Prophetic Literature of the Old Testament* (Grand Rapids: Zondervan, 1990), p. 68.

3. William J. Dumbrell, *The Faith of Israel: A Theological Survey of the Old Testament*, 2nd edn (Grand Rapids: Baker Academic, 2002), p. 107.

4. Ibid.

5. Walter Brueggemann, *Hopeful Imagination: Prophetic Voices in Exile* (Philadelphia: Fortress, 1986), p. 1.

6. Gerhard von Rad, *Old Testament Theology* (London: SCM, 1975), vol. 2, pp. 112–119.

Isaiah

Isaiah's great concern is with regard to the sin and judgment of rebellious Israel (chs. 1–39), and their subsequent redemption and restoration (chs. 40–66). Of particular interest is Isaiah's depiction of Israel's covenant breaking (and its missio-ethical impact), and his description of restored Israel's vocation among the nations. Sections of Isaiah's prophecy that are especially relevant to the aims of the thesis are chapters 1–2; 9–12; 24–27; 40–55; 56–66.

Isaiah 1 – 2

The opening to Isaiah's prophecy contains, according to Brueggemann, an 'overture of the main themes'.[7] Schultz similarly notes the way in which Isaiah 1 – 2 and 65 – 66 frame the book, presenting the major emphases.[8] The prophecy opens with a summons for the heavens and the earth to witness the charges laid against Israel. Oswalt notes the echo of Deuteronomy 32:1 and 30:19, where Moses summons the heavens and earth to witness the summons to covenant obedience.[9] The merismus of 'heavens and earth' expresses totality and satisfies the requirement for two or more witnesses as outlined in Deuteronomy 19:15. Israel is charged with forsaking YHWH, and persisting in rebellion (vv. 3–5). As the opening chapter unfolds Israel's rebellion is twofold: false worship and injustice.

In 1:13 their worship is described as being 'meaningless' (*šāw'*). This same term appears in Deuteronomy 5:11 (taking YHWH's name in vain) and 5:20 (concerning false witness). It is not the cult itself that is problematic, but rather the false heart of the worshippers.[10] The verdict on their worship is 'abomination' (*tô'ēbâ*), a word that also appears with reference to false worship in Deuteronomy (Deut. 7:25–26; 12:31; 17:1–4; 27:15; 32:16).[11] Their false worship is exacerbated

---

7. Walter Brueggemann, *Isaiah 1–39*, WBC (Louisville: Westminster John Knox, 1998), p. 10.

8. Richard L. Schultz, 'Nationalism and Universalism in Isaiah', in *Interpreting Isaiah: Issues and Approaches* (Nottingham: Apollos, 2009), pp. 122–144.

9. John N. Oswalt, *The Book of Isaiah: Isaiah 1–39*, NICOT (Grand Rapids: Eerdmans, 1986), p. 85.

10. Ibid., p. 97.

11. Hans Wildberger, *Isaiah 1–12: A Commentary*, tr. Thomas H. Trapp (Minneapolis: Fortress, 1991), p. 43. The word *tô'ēbâ* appears seventeen times in the covenant code of Deuteronomy. Preuss notes that Deuteronomy contains the first 'clear concentration of the noun' and suggests this usage is formative for the Dtr/Dtn and prophetic literature. H. D. Preuss, 'תּוֹעֵבָה', in *TDOT*, vol. 15, pp. 595–604.

by the blood on their hands (v. 15) – a reference to social injustice (vv. 16–17).[12] The people have failed to defend the orphan and the widow (*yātôm* and *'almānâ*, vv. 17, 23), and have ignored the plight of the oppressed.[13] Isaiah confirms the connection established by the Deuteronomist between social ethics and worship. YHWH makes it clear that failure to love one's neighbour renders cultic activity meaningless. Isaiah's opening functions as a summary of the prophetic witness – Israel have failed with regard to the fundamentals of the Torah, love for God and love for neighbour expressed in the cult and in social ethics.

Though justice must be delivered for Israel's rebellion, there is a glimmer of hope in the opening chapter for forgiveness and restoration (vv. 18–20, 25–28). The people may be cleansed and washed (vv. 16–18), and a City of Faithfulness and Righteousness may be established. Such restoration will, of necessity, involve purification, renewed cultic activity and a reformed social ethic.[14]

Isaiah 2:1 resumes and expands upon the theme introduced in 1:26 – the vision of a righteous place. The vision portrays the establishment of YHWH's temple mountain to which the nations will stream. Zion traditions characterize the mountain as a place of justice, righteousness, peace and of YHWH's beneficent rule through his appointed king.[15] Such a picture is the reverse of the situation depicted in Isaiah 1, where false worship and injustice run rampant. Significantly, true worship and justice in Zion will serve to attract the nations. Many will desire to go to the mountain of YHWH that they might learn his ways and walk in his paths. The mountain and its inhabitants have centripetal and centrifugal qualities; centripetal in the attraction of the nations towards Zion, and centrifugal in that the law (*tôrâ*) will go out from Zion, the word of YHWH from Jerusalem (v. 3), and YHWH himself will bring peace, causing swords to be beaten into ploughshares (v. 4). Watts describes Isaiah 2:1–4 as expressing the 'condensed and controlling theme of the entire Vision'.[16] Tull notes that this passage 'cuts right through oppositions between nationalism and universalism,

---

12. The hendiadys of 'justice and righteousness' appears a number of times in Isaiah (1:27; 5:7, 16; 28:17; 32:1; 33:5; 59:9, 14) and Jeremiah (9:24; 22:3, 15; 23:5; 33:15), and contains 'political, social, theological, moral, and legal dimensions'. Patricia K. Tull, *Isaiah 1–39*, SHBC (Macon: Smyth & Helwys, 2010), p. 68.

13. Deuteronomic laws concerning the orphan and widow can be seen in Deut. 14:28–29 and 24:19–21. As we have seen, these laws are rooted in YHWH's concern for such groups as expressed in Deut. 10:18.

14. Brueggemann, *Isaiah 1–39*, p. 19.

15. Jon D. Levenson, 'Zion Traditions', *ABD*, vol. 6, pp. 1098–1102.

16. John D. W. Watts, *Isaiah 1–33*, WBC 24 (Waco: Word, 1985), p. 29.

emphasizing that Jerusalem's unique calling comes from God not for her sake alone, but so that in her all the nations of the earth will be blessed'.[17] With YHWH's Torah at its centre, the City of Righteousness and Faithfulness (cf. 1:26) will be 'like a magnet, drawing all the nations of the world toward its peculiar authority'.[18] Mission and ethics are held together in Deuteronomic terms. The eschatological vision ushers in the ethical imperative of verse 5: 'Come, descendants of Jacob, let us walk in the light of the LORD.' In discussing the relationship between the national and universal aspects of Isaiah's prophecy, Schultz concludes, 'Israel's punishment and exile as well as its restoration and salvation as God's elect people both involve and ultimately transform the nations.'[19]

Isaiah 9 – 12

Isaiah 9 opens with words of consolation for those experiencing 'darkness and fearful gloom' as a consequence of idolatry (cf. Isa. 8:19–22). The promise is that there will be no more gloom for those in distress (v. 1). While Zebulun and Naphtali have experienced a degree of humbling at YHWH's hand, in the future he will honour Galilee of the nations, beyond the Jordan (9:1).[20] The darkness of 8:22 will give way to a great light (9:2), which will be accompanied by the enlarging of the nation and great rejoicing.[21] The years of oppression, slavery and war will be no more. These things will come to pass when a child is born to rule – a child who will bear the titles 'Wonderful Counsellor', 'Mighty God', 'Everlasting Father', 'Prince of Peace' (v. 6).[22] The Davidic king who will bring perpetual peace is a repeating theme indicative of Israel's restoration to their calling. He will establish and uphold the throne through a rule of 'justice and righteousness' (bĕmišpāṭ ûbiṣdāqa, v. 7). The 'throne names' of this king correlate to his functions.[23] It is only a rule of justice and righteousness that can bring lasting shalom.[24] Like other prophets Isaiah sees the solution to Israel's plight

---

17. Tull, *Isaiah 1–39*, p. 85.

18. Brueggemann, *Isaiah 1–39*, p. 24.

19. Schultz, 'Nationalism and Universalism', p. 143.

20. Tull notes that Galilee is both geographically marginal and, it seems, at least partially Gentile. *Isaiah 1–39*, p. 208.

21. Themes of light and darkness run throughout Isaiah. See 2:5; 5:20; 10:17; 42:6–7; 45:7; 58:10; 59:9; 60:1–3.

22. Wildberger notes the parallels in Egyptian literature in terms of the 'throne names' bestowed on royalty. *Isaiah 1–12*, pp. 403–405.

23. Willem A. M. Beuken, *Jesaja 1–12*, HTKAT (Freiburg: Herder, 2003).

24. Wildberger, *Isaiah 1–12*, p. 406.

resting with the restoration of the Davidic monarchy – in particular a great Davidic king, who will bring true justice and righteousness.[25] This in turn leads to the prosperity of Israel and the blessing of the nations (v. 1). Where Israelite and Assyrian rule had failed, YHWH himself would establish the sort of rule he desired through his appointed and anointed ruler.

Isaiah 11 further develops the theme of a Davidic king with the promise of a shoot arising from Jesse's stump. In Isaiah 10:15 Assyria is likened to an axe in YHWH's hands. Since the axe has attempted to raise itself above the one who swings it, YHWH will cut down not only Israel but Assyria also (10:32–34). While only a remnant of Israel's great forest remains (10:20–21) there is a glimmer of hope that comes from the stump of a felled tree. From the stump a shoot will grow and bear fruit.[26] The notion of fruitfulness is itself suggestive of earlier covenants with YHWH's people.[27] Fruitfulness sits hand in hand with blessing and speaks of right relationship with God, fellow creatures and the creation.[28] This descendant of Jesse will possess the Spirit of YHWH, with three pairs of gifts attendant – wisdom and understanding, counsel and might, knowledge and fear (11:2). The first word pair, 'wisdom and understanding' (ḥokmâ ûbînâ), first occurs in Deuteronomy 4:6 as a description of what the Torah-shaped life of the community would look like to those outside the covenant community. As Israel obeyed the Torah it would demonstrate their wisdom and understanding in the sight of the nations. This 'wisdom and understanding' is a missional ethic, a *fruitful* ethic.[29] As the pericope demonstrates, this wisdom and understanding is not simply related to intellectual ability but issues in a social ethic of establishing 'righteousness' (ṣedeq) and 'justice' (mîšôr) for the poor (11:4). Verses 6–9 paint a picture of eschatological harmony, with nature's enmities past. Watts deems it a poetic 'picture of a return to Eden's tranquillity

---

25. For other prophecies of a Davidic king in the Major Prophets see Isa. 11; Jer. 23; Ezek. 37.

26. Watts suggests that the stump imagery primarily refers to a 'broken, cut-off dynasty'. *Isaiah 1–33*, p. 171.

27. See Gen. 1:22, 28; 9:1, 7; 17:6; 35:11; 48:4; 49:22; Exod. 1:7; Lev. 26:9. Similar promises occur in Jer. 23:3 and Ezek. 36:11.

28. Christopher J. H. Wright, *The Mission of God: Unlocking the Bible's Grand Narrative* (Downers Grove: InterVarsity Press, 2006), pp. 208–209.

29. As we later consider Luke–Acts and the outpouring of the eschatological Spirit we will return to consider the ways in which the believing community receives this same Spirit and enacts the charismatic gifting in ethical and fruitful ways.

and innocence'.[30] If an Edenic allusion is intended there may be a further parallel between the stump of verse 1 and the tree of life in the Garden of Eden. The man with YHWH's 'Spirit' (*rûaḥ*) may be intended as a second Adam charged with fruitful stewardship.[31] Davidic and Adamic ideals are interwoven to speak of a restored creation.

In 11:9–10 the mountain of Isaiah 2:1–4 returns into view as the place of peace and knowledge that fills the earth. In that day the Root of Jesse will be a banner for the people and nations will seek him. The repetition in verse 10 of 'root' from verse 1 is demonstrative of the function and significance of the root as universal, and not simply local.[32] The remnant will return from their exile (v. 11) and the promise is reiterated: he will raise a banner for the nations and gather the exilic remnant (v. 12). Isaiah 11:16 characterizes the return from exile as being like a new exodus: 'there will be a highway for the remnant of his people that is left from Assyria, as there was for Israel when they came up from Egypt'.[33] Isaiah 11 recapitulates and develops the themes of Isaiah 9. After Israel's judgment for their idolatry and injustice YHWH will gather the exilic remnant through his Davidic king, a king who will rule in justice and righteousness, bringing peace. This new exodus will include not just the remnant of Israel but the nations of the earth, all making pilgrimage to Mount Zion (Isa. 2:1–4; 11:9). The imagery of Eden, the exodus and the Davidic king are brought together to provide a rhetorically powerful vision of Israel's restoration.

Isaiah 12 presents a final hymn of praise that closes the section running from chapter 1 to 12.[34] The introductory phrase 'in that day' (*bayyôm hahû'*) commences a vision of a day when people will praise YHWH for his salvation and make known among the nations YHWH's name and deeds (v. 4). The praise of YHWH is to be universally heard (*běkol-hā'āreṣ*, v. 5). As noted in the previous chapter, one aspect of missional ethics is the love for God displayed through worship in the cultic sphere. The cult epitomizes Israel's relationship to YHWH, which in turn should serve to shape Israel's relationship with their neighbours.[35] In the wider context of Isaiah 1 – 12 it should also be noted that a significant aspect

---

30. Watts, *Isaiah 1–33*, p. 174.

31. Brueggemann, *Isaiah 1–39*, p. 102.

32. Kirsten Nielsen, *There Is Hope for a Tree: The Tree as Metaphor in Isaiah*, JSOTSup 65 (Sheffield: JSOT Press, 1989), p. 141.

33. Wildberger, *Isaiah 1–12*, p. 497.

34. Beuken terms Isaiah 12 'Das Finale'. *Jesaja 1–12*, p. 327.

35. Hemchand Gossai, *Justice, Righteousness and the Social Critique of the Eighth-Century Prophets*, AUS 7.141 (New York: Peter Lang, 1993), pp. 310–311.

of the restoration includes peace, justice and righteousness.[36] It is not simply the restored community's praise that reaches the ears of the nations; it is their restored and righteous community, in right relationship with both God and neighbour, that serves to impact the nations.

Isaiah 24 – 27

Chapters 13–23 contain a number of prophecies against various surrounding nations, culminating in chapters 24–27 with Isaiah's 'little apocalypse' – a vision of YHWH's ultimate deliverance of his people that employs a number of evocative images and metaphors. Before examining the 'little apocalypse', it is worth commenting on Isaiah 14:1–2 and 19:16–25, which both present an international vision for the covenant people. Deuteronomic associations are present in both of these short pericopes. In Isaiah 14:1–2 YHWH promises once again to have compassion (*rāḥam*; cf. the promise of Deut. 30:3) on Jacob, and to settle them in their land. Mention of Jacob recalls the song of Moses in Deuteronomy 32 – 33.[37] Israel as 'chosen' (*bāḥar*) echoes Deuteronomy 4:37; 7:6–7; 10:15; and 14:2. The gift of 'rest' reminds the hearer of Deuteronomy 3:20; 12:10; and 25:19; and the promise of land also alludes to Deuteronomy.[38] At that time 'the foreigner' (*haggēr*) will unite with them, as suggested by Deuteronomy 4:4–6. Additionally these nations will take Israel to their own lands with the implication that Israel will govern in those places (v. 2). The notion of possession may also refer back to YHWH's promises in Deuteronomy 12:10; 19:3, 14; 31:7. The rule envisaged in 14:2 is not revenge but peace, settlement and relief, as outlined in 14:3.[39]

In Isaiah 19:16–25 there is a prophecy against Egypt followed by the promise of rescue (vv. 17–20). In that day Egypt will swear allegiance to YHWH (v. 18), an altar to YHWH will be erected (v. 19) and he will send a saviour to rescue them when they cry out to him (v. 20). The altar and stone of witness

---

36. Isa. 1:17, 21, 26–27; 5:7, 16, 23; 9:6–7; 10:2; 11:4–5. Thomas L. Leclerc, *Yahweh Is Exalted in Justice: Solidarity and Conflict in Isaiah* (Minneapolis: Fortress, 2001), pp. 47–70.

37. Mention of Jacob alone (without mention of Abraham and Isaac) appears twice in Isa. 14:1 and, likewise, occurs four times in Deut. 32 – 33 (32:9; 33:4, 10, 28). The use of 'Jacob' alone in Isa. 14:1 would allude to Israel's special identity as YHWH's people as described in the song and benediction of Moses in Deut. 32 – 33.

38. Deut. 4:40; 5:16; 6:15; 7:13; 11:9, 17, 21; 12:1, 19; 25:15; 26:2, 15; 28:11, 21, 63; 30:18, 20; 31:13, 20; 32:47.

39. Gary V. Smith, *Isaiah 1–39*, NAC 15A (Nashville: B&H, 2007), p. 307.

are reminiscent of instructions given to Israel in Deuteronomy 27, and the crying out linked to a saviour alludes to the first exodus. As Brueggemann observes, 'upon crying out and being heard and saved, Egypt will come to *know* Yahweh, *worship* Yahweh, and *make vows* to Yahweh; that is, fully join the community of Yahweh'.[40] After YHWH has judged them he will heal them and they will turn to him (v. 22). The vision extends beyond the borders of Egypt as Isaiah prophesies a highway between Assyria and Egypt, with both groups worshipping YHWH together (v. 23). Of particular note is the promise that Israel, along with Assyria and Egypt, will be a blessing on the earth (v. 24). The chapter closes with YHWH's surprising use of covenantal language to include Assyria and Egypt: 'Blessed be Egypt my people, Assyria my handiwork, and Israel my inheritance' (v. 25).[41] Blenkinsopp suggests echoes of Genesis 10 in the tripartite division of the future world, and Genesis 12 in the blessing formula of verse 25.[42] Isaiah 14:1–2 and 19:16–25 depict the restoration of Israel to true worship and the consequent international reach of YHWH's salvation.

Isaiah's 'little apocalypse' (chs. 24–27) begins with a harrowing vision of YHWH's devastation of the earth. The opening verse depicts the judgment as cosmic and catastrophic, with allusions to the Noachic flood and Tower of Babel.[43] The 'earth' (*'eres*) is mentioned fourteen times in the chapter and it is the disobedience of its inhabitants that brings judgment.[44] In particular they have defiled the earth, disobeyed the laws, violated the statutes and broken the everlasting covenant (24:5). The de-creation serves to pave the way for a new creation anticipated in the song of the jubilant (vv. 14–16) and the reign of YHWH in Zion (v. 23).

Chapter 25 begins by picking up the song of praise begun in 24:14. YHWH is to be praised for his faithfulness in executing judgment, particularly with reference to his care for the poor and needy. The prophecy then looks forward to a feast on a mountain (vv. 6–8), recalling the words of Isaiah 2:1–4 and

---

40. Brueggemann, *Isaiah 1–39*, p. 163. Emphases original.

41. Oswalt notes the radical nature of this vision and the fact that the Targums severely altered these statements. Oswalt, *Isaiah 1–39*, p. 381, n. 28.

42. Joseph Blenkinsopp, *Isaiah 1–39*, AB 19 (New York: Doubleday, 2000), pp. 319–320.

43. Carol J. Dempsey, 'Words of Woe, Visions of Grandeur: A Literary and Hermeneutical Study of Isaiah 24–27', in *Formation and Intertextuality in Isaiah 24–27* (Atlanta: SBL, 2013), p. 210.

44. Ibid., p. 211.

picking up on the promise of 24:23.[45] It is a place of paradise that requires moral integrity to ascend (cf. Ps. 24:3–4).[46] Further it is the centre of the world from which blessing flows outwards.[47] Millar notes the richness of feast imagery, drawing in the themes of covenant, cult, garden and exodus, all pointing towards a revitalization of a barren creation.[48] All nations and peoples are the invited beneficiaries of this feast (v. 7), and the feast will consume not only choice meats and aged wine, but death itself will be swallowed up. Cho and Fu note that grammatically the subject should be death; therefore threatening to devour the guests at the feast.[49] However, they argue that since God is the subject through the rest of the pericope, he is the implied subject here, with the verb in the future tense.[50] Cho and Fu argue for a deliberate ambiguity that creates dramatic tension for the listener.[51] Death arrives uninvited and threatens to devour, but death itself is devoured as soon as it appears. Death appears hard on the heels of the covenant feast, but is swiftly swallowed up. As Cho and Fu conclude, 'this triumph over death by consumption both symbolically and in fact enacts the inauguration of YHWH's kingdom'.[52]

Chapter 26 moves from the mountain to the city YHWH is building (cf. 1:26). This city stands in contrast to the lofty city of verses 5–6, which will be brought low because of its oppression of the poor. The righteous nation is invited to inhabit and enjoy the peace, justice and righteousness of the city. The identity of the 'righteous nation' (*gôy ṣaddîq*) in verse 2 is not given, but instead characterized as those who are righteous and 'remain faithful' (*šōmēr 'ĕmunîm*). The inhabitants of the city wait as they walk in the way of YHWH's judgments (v. 8). Indeed when YHWH's judgments are in the earth the inhabitants learn righteousness (v. 9).

---

45. It is also worth noting that Ezek. 28:13–14 links YHWH's mountain with the Garden of Eden. Beth Steiner, 'Food of the Gods: Canaanite Myths of Divine Banquets and Gardens in Connection with Isaiah 25:6', in *Formation and Intertextuality in Isaiah 24–27* (Atlanta: SBL, 2013), pp. 99–115.

46. Ibid.

47. Ibid.

48. William R. Millar, *Isaiah 24–27 and the Origin of Apocalyptic*, HSMS 11 (Missoula: Scholars Press, 1976), pp. 112–114.

49. Paul Kang-Kul Cho and Janling Fu, 'Death and Feasting in the Isaiah Apocalypse (Isaiah 25:6–8)', in *Formation and Intertextuality in Isaiah 24–27* (Atlanta: SBL, 2013), pp. 117–142.

50. Ibid., pp. 118–120.

51. Ibid., p. 120.

52. Ibid., p. 142.

While other 'lords' have ruled over them it is only YHWH the people revere (v. 13). The lords (*běʻālûnû ʼădōnîm*) may be a reference to human rulers or perhaps the gods of Babylon. Given Israel's trust in human rulers, coupled with the ANE view of royalty as in some sense divine, there may be deliberate *double entendre* here. The people now recognize their previous 'lords' to be dead and express complete devotion to YHWH alone. In verses 15–18 the song praises YHWH for enlarging the borders, and at the same time the people confess their failure to bring salvation to the earth (v. 18).[53]

Isaiah 27 transitions from the city to the vineyard – a vineyard that will be fruitful because YHWH himself will tend it. The chapter opens with a promise regarding the fate of the Leviathan – the 'primordial mythological chaos dragon'.[54] The slaying of the serpent enables order to be brought once again to the garden. The vineyard imagery appears also in Isaiah 5:1–7, where the vineyard's failure to bring forth fruit was to result in its destruction. Here we have the reversal.[55] This vineyard is fruitful due to YHWH's care for it. This vineyard will bud and blossom and fill the entire world with fruit (v. 6). Jacob's guilt is atoned for when he rejects the idol altars and Asherah poles and worships YHWH alone (v. 9). The chapter closes by recalling the promise that all those from Egypt to Assyria will come and worship on YHWH's holy mountain.

> Thus, through the poetics of Hebrew Poetry, Isa 24–27 conveys a story about destruction and salvation that is cosmic in scope, a story that includes all the nations with special attention drawn to Israel and Judah . . . The defeat of the city of chaos (Isa 24:10) and the turning of a city into a heap (Isa 25:2) paves the way for the restoration of Jerusalem – a new city in Isa 27:1, the place of God's holy mountain – a home for all nations.[56]

Isaiah's 'little apocalypse' is the story of Moses' song (Deut. 32) in mythological terms.[57] A number of themes need drawing together from Isaiah's 'little

---

53. Oswalt suggests an intertextual echo here of Israel's larger mission to be a blessing to the nations as promised to Abraham in Gen. 12:3. John N. Oswalt, *Isaiah*, NIVAC (Grand Rapids: Zondervan, 2003), p. 300.

54. Dempsey, 'Words of Woe', p. 220.

55. John T. Willis, 'Yahweh Regenerates His Vineyard: Isaiah 27', in *Formation and Intertextuality in Isaiah 24–27* (Atlanta: SBL, 2013), pp. 201–207.

56. Dempsey, 'Words of Woe', p. 223.

57. See some of the intertextualities observed by Donald C. Polaski, *Authorizing an End: The Isaiah Apocalypse and Intertextuality* (Leiden: Brill, 2001), pp. 268–270; Steiner, 'Food of the Gods', pp. 112–114.

apocalypse'. First, restoration is promised through a number of pictures, including a mountain feast, a new city and a fruitful vineyard. Second, the purpose of this activity is the fruitfulness of Israel and the ingathering of the nations. Third, this restoration is YHWH's sovereign activity. Fourth, it comes to pass when righteousness fills the earth, when justice is done and when YHWH is worshipped and idols rejected. Fifth, its fulfilment is future from Isaiah's perspective. Themes of restoration, mission and ethics are again entwined. A restored community will live out justice, resulting in the nations learning righteousness and coming to the feast.[58] YHWH's restorative economy trades in the currency of the redeemed community's missional ethic.

Isaiah 40 – 55

Isaiah 40 marks a turning point in the tone of Isaiah.[59] The section begins with a double imperative – 'Comfort, comfort my people' (naḥămû naḥămû 'ammî) – for Jerusalem's sin has been pardoned. The prophecy now looks forward to a future beyond judgment and exile in which Jerusalem's glory is restored. 'All flesh' (kol-bāśār, Isa. 40:5) will see the 'glory of the LORD' (kĕbôd yhwh, Isa. 40:5). The emphases of the section are on the supremacy of YHWH as the unique creator, the folly of the nations in their worship of idols, and the promise of restoration for YHWH's covenant people.

At the centre of Deutero-Isaiah is the servant of YHWH.[60] The language of 'servant' ('ebed) appears repeatedly, referring to different individuals or groups, and has stimulated much debate regarding the identity or identities of the 'servant'.[61]

---

58. Dempsey, 'Words of Woe', p. 221.

59. Smith outlines the various compositional issues that surround Isa. 40 – 55 and 56 – 66, as well as the various approaches employed. He suggests an approach that is aware of the critical issues, yet that focuses on the final canonical form. Gary V. Smith, *Isaiah 40–66*, NAC 15b (Nashville: B&H, 2009), pp. 27–41.

60. Kaiser identifies the four Servant Songs as Isa. 42:1–4[9]; 49:1–6[13]; 50:4–9[11]; 52:13 – 53:12. Walter C. Kaiser Jr, 'The Identity and Mission of the "Servant of the Lord"', in *The Gospel According to Isaiah 53: Encountering the Suffering Servant in Jewish and Christian Theology* (Grand Rapids: Kregel, 2012).

61. Scholars propose a number of alternatives. Blenkinsopp suggests Isa. 42:1–4 refers either to Jacob as ancestor and representative or to another prophetic figure. Joseph Blenkinsopp, *Isaiah 40–55: A New Translation with Introduction and Commentary*, AB 19 (New York: Doubleday, 2002), p. 24. Orlinsky argues that all of the twenty-one instances of 'ebed refer to the people of Israel or to Deutero-Isaiah himself. Harry

In the opening song (Isa. 42:1–4) YHWH's Spirit-anointed servant is introduced. According to Poulsen, the 'central task of the servant in verses 1–4 concerns the promotion of justice to the nations'.[62] It may be that this is a justice to be meted out upon rebellious nations; but given 42:4, 'in his teaching the islands will put their hope', it would seem that this 'justice' (*mišpāṭ*, vv. 1, 3, 4) will be enjoyed by the nations. In context this appears to be ethical guidance for the good of the nations.[63] Brueggemann roots the prophetic notion of justice in the Mosaic law, pertaining particularly to the most vulnerable.[64] Further, the establishment of justice has implications beyond the borders of Israel. The task of promoting justice leads to the servant being

> a light for the Gentiles,
> to open eyes that are blind,
>   to free captives from prison
>   and to release from the dungeon those who sit in darkness.
> (42:6–7)

(note 61 *cont.*) M. Orlinsky, *Studies on the Second Part of the Book of Isaiah: The So-Called 'Servant of the Lord' and 'Suffering Servant', in Second Isaiah*, VTSup 14 (Leiden: Brill, 1977), p. 96. Lindblom views the Servant Songs as allegorical, applying to the nation. J. Lindblom, *The Servant Songs in Deutero-Isaiah* (Lund: Gleerup, 1951), pp. 102–103. Clines considers the servant prophecies to be ambiguous and open-ended, permitting multiple referents and fulfilments. David J. A. Clines, *I, He, We and They: A Literary Approach to Isaiah 53*, JSOTSup 1 (Sheffield: JSOT Press, 1976), pp. 59–65. Similarly North argues for a certain 'fluidity' in the concept embracing Israel, the prophet and messianic expectation. Christopher R. North, *The Suffering Servant in Deutero-Isaiah: An Historical and Critical Study* (London: Oxford University Press, 1948), p. 215. The approaches of North and Clines perhaps best preserve the ambiguity present. There is the legitimate possibility of triperspectivalism regarding the servant. The ambiguity permits, even suggests, that Deutero-Isaiah himself is the servant – an anointed prophet who brings a message of light into a dark situation and suffers rejection. The prophet-servant also represents and stands for the nation (or at least a righteous remnant), who are to be a light to the nations – all of which foreshadows a particular individual, a Messiah, who fulfils these roles and as a consequence draws in and empowers the covenant people to fulfil their universal mandate.

62. Frederik Poulsen, *God, His Servant, and the Nations in Isaiah 42:1–9*, FZAT 2.73 (Tübingen: Mohr Siebeck, 2014), p. 196.

63. Ibid.

64. Walter Brueggemann, *Isaiah 40–66*, WBC (Louisville: Westminster John Knox, 1998), p. 42.

The promise is repeated in 49:6: the servant will be 'a light for the Gentiles, that my salvation may reach to the ends of the earth'. The same theme appears for a third time in 51:4–6. YHWH promises that his 'justice will become a light to the nations' and 'the islands will look to me [YHWH] and wait in hope for my arm'. The establishment of justice is a means of light to the Gentile nations. Lind compares the trial speeches (41:21–29; 43:8–13; 45:18–25), the Cyrus poems (41:1–4, 21–29; 42:5–9; 44:24–28; 45:9–13; 46:9–11; 48:12–15) and the Servant Songs, and concludes, regarding the 'justice' (*mišpāṭ*) of 42:1–4:

> [It] can be understood only in terms of the tradition of biblical Torah in which Deutero-Isaiah speaks, a tradition which places law within the structures of covenant and worship . . . [and] in the servant's mission the moral quality of Yahweh's Torah-justice guarantees both the continuity of the community and the acclaim of the nations.[65]

The call to the idol-worshipping nations is:

> Turn to me and be saved,
>   all you ends of the earth;
>   for I am God, and there is no other.
> (45:22)

In Isaiah 52:7–10 YHWH promises that 'all of the nations' (*kol-haggôyîm*) and the 'ends of the earth' (*kol-'apsê-'āreṣ*) will see shalom, good things, and the salvation of YHWH. In the best-known Servant Song, Isaiah 53, the servant acts to represent the people by somehow bearing sin, punishment and suffering in the place of the people.[66] His actions procure forgiveness, healing and peace. Exactly how

---

65. Millard C. Lind, 'Monotheism, Power, and Justice: A Study in Isaiah 40–55', *CBQ* 46 (1984), pp. 445–446.

66. Hägglund considers the servant of Isa. 53 to be the people in exile, as this best explains the motifs of death and resurrection. Fredrik Hägglund, *Isaiah 53 in the Light of Homecoming After Exile*, FZAT 2.31 (Tübingen: Mohr Siebeck, 2008). Whybray suggests that Isa. 53 refers to Second Isaiah's own experience of prison escape. R. N. Whybray, *Thanksgiving for a Liberated Prophet: An Interpretation of Isaiah Chapter 53*, JSOTSup 4 (Sheffield: JSOT Press, 1978), pp. 136–137. Laato suggests that the 'death' of the servant may be compared to Ezek. 37, and the death in view, on behalf of the people, could refer to an exiled minority, a pious remnant, in some sense bearing the sin of the majority. Antti Laato, *The Servant*

the first recipients understood the prophecy is an interesting question. At the very least it seems as though the punishment of exile is not fully over, and deliverance is not fully complete until the servant has suffered and made intercession for the people (53:12). Only then can justice and salvation become increasingly manifest to the nations.

The final chapter of Deutero-Isaiah begins with an invitation. The double imperative 'comfort' of 40:1 has become the threefold imperative 'come' (*lĕkû*) of 55:1. YHWH has established an everlasting and unbreakable covenant (54:9–10), and his covenant people will be a witness to the peoples. YHWH's covenant people will summon the nations, and the nations will come because YHWH has endowed his people with splendour. The link between an everlasting covenant and the nations is reminiscent of the Abrahamic covenant (Gen. 17:7–13).[67] Just as Deuteronomy 4:6–8 promised that the nations would be impressed by Israel's Torah, so now the nations will be impressed by the people's God-given splendour.

Throughout Deutero-Isaiah creation and redemption are held together. Redemption is seen as an act of recreation or new creation.[68] This recalls the creation mandate to bless, and the Abrahamic promise that his offspring would be a blessing. Stuhlmueller, noting the creation theme that runs through Isaiah 40 – 55, suggests:

(note 66 *cont.*) *of YHWH and Cyrus: A Reinterpretation of the Exilic Messianic Programme in Isaiah 40–55*, CBOTS 35 (Stockholm: Almqvist & Wiksell, 1992), p. 19. However, Kaiser gives five reasons why the 'servant' in Isa. 53 is better understood as the Messiah. First, in Isa. 49:5–6 the servant is distinct from Jacob in his role of restoring Jacob. Second, in Isa. 42:6 the servant is a 'covenant for the people', where the people are juxtaposed to the Gentiles; therefore the servant in this case cannot be equated with the people (Israel). Third, in Isa. 53:8 the servant is cut off for the people, again implying a distinction between them. Fourth, the description of the servant in Isa. 52:13 – 53:12 includes the ascription 'done no violence, nor was any deceit in his mouth' (53:9), which could not be said of the nation. Fifth, the servant is to be a guilt offering (53:10), suggesting representative substitution of an innocent, which would not apply to the nation. For these reasons Kaiser suggests that the Messiah is the most likely candidate for the ascription 'servant' in Isa. 52:13 – 53:12. Kaiser, 'Identity and Mission', pp. 89–92.

67. Smith, *Isaiah 40–66*, p. 498.

68. Carroll Stuhlmueller, *Creative Redemption in Deutero-Isaiah*, AnBib 43 (Rome: Biblical Institute, 1970), pp. 67–70.

> The purpose of creation is to provide a promised land of happy life with God, first of all for Israel, and through Israel for all mankind . . . he has given life – a full life of *šālôm* – so that all hearts 'sing for joy, . . . shout from the mountain tops, give glory to the Lord,' . . . 'your Maker . . . your husband' (42, 10–12; 54, 5).[69]

Deuteronomy puts form to the blessing with the embodiment of the divine will in the Torah. Creation and redemption are for the purpose of love for God and love for neighbour. Themes of salvation and justice are also brought together by means of YHWH's anointed servant. They are not two distinct aspects of YHWH's work but are rather related parts of the whole. Deliverance and justice belong together and the ultimate *telos* is that the 'ends of the earth' will put their hope in the justice that comes with the deliverance.

Noteworthy also is the ambiguity of the servant as both singular and collective. The light to the nations is mediated by a representative or representatives of YHWH. As Lee observes, 'the coming of YHWH as the creator and redeemer of Israel also marks a new sense of mission for Israel as YHWH's servant and witness'.[70] Israel's failure to be a light to the nations necessitates the sending of the servant, but by the end of Deutero-Isaiah the focus has shifted back to servants, plural (54:17).[71] The servants, following *the* Servant, undertake the same task empowered by the same Spirit – to be a light to the Gentiles by promoting justice.[72]

Finally, in considering Deutero-Isaiah, it is also worth observing that this new work is rooted firmly in Israel's redemptive history. Abraham is mentioned, as is Jacob; so too the exodus.[73] Deuteronomic ideas and vocabulary are also evident. YHWH's future work of deliverance is rooted in his earlier deliverance and commissioning of his covenant people. This new work of salvation will enable the covenant people, empowered by YHWH's Spirit, to fulfil the original divine mandate. Anderson summarizes: 'Israel's "obligation" is to be a witness

---

69. Carroll Stuhlmueller, 'The Theology of Creation in Second Isaias', *CBQ* 21 (1959), pp. 466–467.

70. Stephen Lee, *Creation and Redemption in Isaiah 40–55*, JDDS 2 (Hong Kong: Alliance Bible Seminary, 1995), p. 189.

71. Smith, *Isaiah 40–66*, p. 492.

72. Poulsen, *God, His Servant*, pp. 211–226.

73. Stuhlmueller identifies direct or implicit allusions to the exodus in Isa. 40:3–11; 41:17–20; 42:14–17; 43:1–7, 16–21; 44:1–5, 27; 48:20–21; 49:8–12; 50:2; 51:9–10; 52:11–12; 55:12–13. *Creative Redemption*, p. 66.

to grace which is freely given, "without price," and thereby to attract nations to Zion, the world centre from which the word or *tôrâ* of Yahweh goes forth.'[74]

Isaiah 56 – 66

Isaiah 56 – 66 contains some of the most exalted eschatological imagery in the Old Testament. However, among the lofty visions of the New Jerusalem there are direct instructions regarding the practical ethic of her inhabitants.[75] Isaiah 56 – 66 is 'primarily concerned with the future Jerusalem . . . [and whether it] will or will not be a practice of neighbour ethic, will or will not manifest a passion for justice'.[76] Brueggemann, commenting on the section as a whole, notes that it contains 'remarkable ethical claims, an insistence that Judaism must practice a *tôrâ* obedience that transcends self-protective punctiliousness'.[77]

Third Isaiah opens with a call to 'Maintain justice and do what is right' (*šimrû mišpāṭ waʿăśû ṣĕdāqâ*, Isa. 56:1).[78] The opening to the Servant Songs (42:1–4) similarly emphasized the theme of justice. Polan considers this a 'summons to embrace the ways of right relationship with God and with neighbor'.[79] The people are called to live in the light of YHWH's coming salvation. The next verse (56:2) incorporates the cultic within the ethical, calling the people to 'observe Sabbath' (*šōmēr šabbāt*).[80] The combination of justice, righteousness and Sabbath observance echoes Israel's legal traditions as given in the Torah.[81] The prophecy issues a call to return and reform in the light of those traditions. Isaiah 56:3

---

74. Bernard W. Anderson, 'Exodus and Covenant in Second Isaiah and Prophetic Tradition', in *Magnalia Dei: The Mighty Acts of God* (New York: Doubleday, 1976), p. 356.

75. Childs outlines the various issues surrounding authorship, dating and redaction of Isa. 56 – 66. Brevard S. Childs, *Isaiah*, OTL (Louisville: Westminster John Knox, 2001), pp. 439–449.

76. Brueggemann, *Isaiah 40–66*, p. 167.

77. Ibid., p. 165.

78. Watts describes this as a summary of the whole law, as in Mic. 6:8. John D. W. Watts, *Isaiah 34–66*, WBC 25 (Waco: Thomas Nelson, 2005), p. 820.

79. Gregory J. Polan, *In The Ways of Justice Toward Salvation*, AUS 13 (New York: Peter Lang, 1986), p. 330.

80. Hrobon argues that the Sabbath contains both cultic and ethical dimensions appealing to Deut. 5:15; 10:19; 24:18–22. Bohdan Hrobon, *Ethical Dimension of Cult in the Book of Isaiah*, BZAW 418 (Berlin: de Gruyter, 2010), pp. 163–165.

81. Wells outlines many of the correspondences between Deuteronomy and Isa. 56:1–8. Roy D. Wells, 'Isaiah as an Exponent of Torah: Isaiah 56:1–8', in *New Visions of Isaiah*, JSOTSup 214 (Sheffield: Sheffield Academic Press, 1996), pp. 140–155.

extends the invitation to the 'foreigner' (*ben-hannēkār*), promising that if they too observe the Sabbath, choose what pleases YHWH and hold fast to his covenant they will be welcomed and not excluded. In Knight's words the Sabbath becomes an 'instrument of mission'.[82] The place of welcome is YHWH's 'holy mountain' (*har qodšî*), thus tying Isaiah 2 and 25 with Isaiah 56. The mountain-sanctuary (v. 7), as in Isaiah 2 and 25, has an international draw and will be a 'house of prayer for all nations'. In 56:3–8 there is an 'insistence of a large *inclusiveness* in the community, presumably an attempt to counter and resist any narrow exclusivism . . . The advocacy of both *inclusiveness* and *neighbourly needs* is an important ethical passion' for the future of YHWH's people.[83] The desire for justice, mandated in Isaiah 56:1–2, is echoed in 57:8, 11, 14, 15. The faithful community must be a just community.

Isaiah 56:9 – 58:5 laments Israel's failure to live out the cultic and ethical requirements of Isaiah 56:1–8. The injustice, immorality and idolatry account for their present experience of judgment. The people complain, in 58:3, that YHWH has not responded to their fasting, yet they have failed to consider the exploitation and violence that accompanies their fasts (58:3–4). Brueggemann argues that the fast is linked to provision for those without.[84] Fasting therefore has both horizontal and vertical dimensions. In 58:6–7 YHWH declares the sort of fasting he has chosen: to loose the chains of injustice, to free the oppressed, and to provide for the poor, hungry and naked. If YHWH's covenant people enact such justice then their light will dawn and righteousness go before them (vv. 8, 10). It is noteworthy in Isaiah 58:8 that light, healing and righteousness emanate from Israel. Given the association with light and blessing the nations elsewhere in Isaiah (42:6; 49:6; 51:4), it is possible this verse refers to restored Israel's impact on the nations. Similarly verse 10 contains the possibility of light as something that radiates out from the renewed covenant people. As with Isaiah 56, cult and ethics are woven together such that Hrobon concludes, 'metaphorically speaking, ethics, and cult in Isa 58 are two sides of the same coin'.[85]

Isaiah 59 continues the alternation of imploration and rebuke, piling up the charges of injustice. The solution to Israel's persistent rebellion is twofold: YHWH himself will put on the armour to fight for salvation, and, as in Ezekiel 36 and Jeremiah 31, will give his Spirit to his people to enable true confession of YHWH (Isa. 59:16–21), in fulfilment of Deuteronomy 30:1–10.

---

82. George A. F. Knight, *Isaiah 56–66*, ITC (Grand Rapids: Eerdmans, 1985), p. 4.

83. Brueggemann, *Isaiah 40–66*, p. 165. Emphases original.

84. Ibid., p. 189.

85. Hrobon, *Ethical Dimension*, p. 216.

Isaiah 60 – 62 functions as the 'nucleus' of Trito-Isaiah and is concerned with the restoration and glorification of Zion/Jerusalem.[86] The theme of light reappears as that which has dawned on Israel, and will attract the nations (60:3). The nations will be so impressed that they will come to serve the light of the nations (vv. 4–14), and then the righteousness of the people will display the splendour of YHWH (v. 21). The display of YHWH's splendour is repeated in 61:3 as a consequence of YHWH's favour. In Isaiah 61:8–11 the renewed covenant people will be known among the nations as YHWH causes righteousness and praise to spring up before all nations. Isaiah 62:1–2 continues the theme, with Israel's righteousness a 'brightness' and their salvation like a blazing torch. As righteousness shines forth, the nations pay attention.[87] YHWH's proclamation over his people is that they are holy and redeemed – a banner for the nations (vv. 10–12).

The concluding chapters continue to alternate between rebuke, encouragement and comfort, but close with the promise that some of the redeemed Gentiles will proclaim YHWH's glory among the nations and bring the nations to his holy mountain (66:18–21).[88] The vision of Isaiah 2 is finally brought to fruition through the redeemed, restored and renewed covenant people.[89] Brueggemann, commenting on 66:18–21, draws the threads of the larger narrative together:

> As the ultimate imagery of inclusiveness, in verse 21 it is asserted that from among these *goyim*, these Gentile nations, some will be designated and ordained as priests and Levites . . . This paragraph is a most astonishing refusal to settle for sniggling, punctilious sectarianism. The vision is as large and comprehensive as the invitation to Pentecost . . . If we push the birth metaphor of verses 7–9 back into the book of Genesis, it will not surprise us to remember that the promise to father Abraham and mother Sarah was 'in you all the families of the earth shall be blessed' (Gen. 12:3).[90]

86. Brooks Schramm, *The Opponents of Third Isaiah: Reconstructing the Cultic History of the Restoration*, JSOTSup 193 (Sheffield: Sheffield Academic Press, 1995), p. 143.

87. Knight, *Isaiah 56–66*, p. 62.

88. Dim suggests that the unusual list of nations to which these emissaries are sent is symbolic, designed to create a sense of mission to the farthest reaches of the earth. Emmanuel Uchenna Dim, *The Eschatological Implications of Isa 65 and 66 as the Conclusion of the Book of Isaiah* (Bern: Peter Lang, 2004), p. 185.

89. Tomasino notes the links in theme and vocabulary between Isaiah 1 – 2 and 63 – 66. Anthony J. Tomasino, 'Isaiah 1.1–2.4 and 63–66, and the Composition of the Isaianic Corpus', *JSOT* 57 (1993), pp. 81–98.

90. Brueggemann, *Isaiah 40–66*, p. 259.

In concluding his study of justice in Isaiah 56 – 66 Leclerc argues that doing righteousness and justice is a précis of covenant responsibilities.[91] This restored covenant community is characterized by people who fulfil covenant responsibilities, particularly in the cultic and social settings – 'cultic practice and moral conduct must be practiced in tandem'.[92] Williamson sees a connection between Israel's ethical and cultic practice, and the universal blessing that issues forth from YHWH's covenant people.[93] Trito-Isaiah adds a third element, however. The messianic Servant of Deutero-Isaiah is the Warrior of Trito-Isaiah. The people's rebellion necessitates divine intervention as YHWH's 'own arm achieved salvation' for his people (59:16; 63:5), and his gift of the Spirit (as in Ezek. 36 and Jer. 31) enables the people to be that light to the nations. The reformation of the people will lead to the blessing of the nations, but only after YHWH has decisively intervened.

Summary

Isaiah 1 – 2 and 65 – 66 frame the book, providing two ends of a narrative arc that moves from the faithless city to the Faithful City (1:21, 26). The covenantal and legal context of Deuteronomy has been noted throughout, as well as the promise of restoration (Deut. 30:1–10). In order for the vision to become a reality Israel must first be judged, then redeemed and restored. YHWH himself will achieve a new-exodus salvation for his people (Isa. 11; 19; 59:16–19), but will do so by raising a Royal Branch (Isa. 9; 11) and a Servant (Isa. 42 – 53). YHWH's Spirit will empower the restored and redeemed community to maintain justice and righteousness (Isa. 56:1–4; 59:21). As a consequence the nations will be attracted to Israel's 'light' (Isa. 51:4; 58:8–10; 60:1–3) and will stream to Mount Zion to enjoy peace, a feast and worship (Isa. 2; 25; 56). Israel's missional ethic is a significant and pervasive theme throughout Isaiah's prophecy.

Jeremiah

Jeremiah, like Isaiah, is chiefly concerned with the judgment and restoration of Israel. Wright notes Jeremiah's concern with Israel's restoration is connected to

---

91. Leclerc, *Yahweh Is Exalted in Justice*, p. 158.

92. Ibid., p. 159.

93. H. G. M. Williamson, 'Promises, Promises! Some Exegetical Reflections on Isaiah 58', *WW* 19.2 (1999), p. 155.

their wider purpose in election, and the blessing for the nations.[94] Jeremiah
brings together the missional and the ethical, with Deuteronomy the foundation
for lament, rebuke, instruction and hope. Sections to be considered are as
follows: Jeremiah 1; 3 – 5; 7 – 11; 13 – 18; 23 – 24; 30 – 31; 32 – 33. These sections
are pertinent to the wider discussion of this book as they bring together missio-
ethical elements in a Deuteronomic framework. Wright notes, 'There is nothing
in Jeremiah that remotely compares with the symphony of universality and hope
for the nations that we find in Isaiah. But still, there are some significant notes
from the same score.'[95] It is these 'similar notes' to which we turn.

Jeremiah 1

Jeremiah's call (1:4–19) is significant, as twice in the opening chapter the reader
is informed that his ministry is to extend beyond the borders of Judah or Israel.
In 1:5 Jeremiah is told of his appointment to be 'a prophet to the nations' (*nābî'
laggôyîm*). The preposition could carry the sense of 'to' the nations, but, given
Jeremiah's location, it is preferable to understand Jeremiah's call as 'for' the
nations. The ambiguity allows for Jeremiah's ministry concerning the nations
to be potentially both positive and negative.[96] The call is reiterated in Jeremiah
1:10 along with a fuller description of Jeremiah's prophetic call: 'to uproot
and tear down, to destroy and overthrow, to build and to plant'. Negative and
positive images are both present. Jeremiah does not literally tear down
and overthrow kingdoms: his uprooting and planting are declarative and
prophetic. Jeremiah was to be a 'proclaimer of Yahweh's comprehensive work
that was to involve not only destruction but also reconstruction'.[97]

Jeremiah 3 – 5

The opening chapters of Jeremiah's prophecy chart the idolatrous rebellion
of Israel against YHWH in terms of forgetfulness and adultery. Jeremiah 3 – 5
outlines Israel's failure as YHWH's covenant people, but also hints at their historic
purpose to bless the nations.

---

94. Christopher J. H. Wright, *The Message of Jeremiah*, BST (Nottingham: Inter-Varsity
    Press, 2014), p. 36.

95. Christopher J. H. Wright, '"Prophet to the Nations": Missional Reflections on the
    Book of Jeremiah', in *A God of Faithfulness: Essays in Honour of J. Gordon McConville
    on His 60th Birthday*, LHB/OTS 538 (London: T&T Clark, 2011), p. 117.

96. Terence E. Fretheim, *Jeremiah*, SHBC (Macon: Smyth & Helwys, 2002), p. 50.

97. Leslie C. Allen, *Jeremiah: A Commentary*, OTL (Louisville: Westminster John Knox,
    2008), p. 28.

The opening verses of the section describe the sin of both Israel and Judah. Israel has committed spiritual adultery at the high places and under the spreading trees (3:1–10), which appears to be a reference to rural shrines (cf. 2:20; 3:2).[98] A hoped-for return to YHWH never materialized and so YHWH issued the certificate of divorce to Israel, as prescribed in Deuteronomy 24:1.[99] In imagery similar to Ezekiel 16 and 23 Judah, the younger sister, rather than heeding the warning from Israel's wayward behaviour, followed suit and likewise went to commit adultery with stone and wood (v. 9). YHWH's charge against Judah is that their recent return, in accordance with Josiah's reforms, is in pretence only and not with their heart. The rhetorically shocking conclusion in 3:11 is that Israel is *more* faithful than Judah, presumably because Israel's behaviour is at least consistent.[100]

Continuing the marital imagery, YHWH calls Israel to return to their true 'husband' (*ba'al*) with the promise that he will provide 'shepherds after my own heart, who will lead you with knowledge and understanding' (3:15).[101] The language of 3:16 suggests the invitation to return will become a reality, not just a possibility, with the Deuteronomic introduction 'In those days'. The absence of the ark may anticipate the law written on hearts (Jer. 31:31–34) or may suggest God's presence to all the people, not just the priesthood (cf. Ezek. 48).[102] In language similar to Isaiah 2 and Micah 4, Jeremiah 3:17–18 gives a vision of the nations streaming to Jerusalem once the nation is restored and the people no longer 'follow the stubbornness of their evil hearts'.[103] A reunified kingdom

---

98. Ibid., p. 56.

99. Shields argues that Deut. 24:1–4 stands in the background to the whole of Jer. 3. Mary E. Shields, *Circumscribing the Prostitute: The Rhetorics of Intertextuality, Metaphor and Gender in Jeremiah 3.1–4.4*, JSOTSup 387 (London: T&T Clark, 2004).

100. William L. Holladay, *Jeremiah 1*, Hermeneia (Philadelphia: Fortress, 1986), p. 118.

101. The word 'turn' or 'return' (*šûb*) is a key word in Jer. 3:1 – 4:4, occurring eight times. J. A. Thompson, *The Book of Jeremiah*, NICOT (Grand Rapids: Eerdmans, 1980), p. 200.

102. Fretheim, *Jeremiah*, pp. 83–84.

103. The word translated as 'stubbornness' (*šĕrîrût*) is unusual in the OT. It appears at the covenant-renewal ceremony of Deut. 29 as a warning to those who would consider the covenant a guarantee in spite of persistent rebellion. It also appears in Ps. 81:13, and then in Jeremiah eight times (3:17; 7:24; 9:13; 11:8; 13:10; 16:12; 18:12; 23:17). In each occurrence in Jeremiah it is connected closely with idolatry and infidelity. See H. J. Fabry and N. van Meeteren, 'שְׁררוּת', in *TDOT*, vol. 4, p. 487.

and a faithful people will accompany the flow of the nations to Jerusalem.[104] Once again the covenantal fidelity of the people is linked to the mission of God to the nations.

Jeremiah 4:1 picks up the *Leitmotif* 'turn' (*šûb*) from chapter 3, calling the people to put aside their idols. Part of Judah's turning involves cultic reform, turning away from high places, fertility rites and Canaanite rituals.[105] If the people confess YHWH in a truthful, just and righteous way, then 'the nations will invoke blessings by him and in him they will boast' (4:2). The threefold description of Israel's return as 'in truth, in justice and in righteousness' (*be'emet bĕmišpāṭ ûbiṣdāqâ*) implies a genuine profession that is ethically enacted.[106] Wright observes, 'it was not just a matter of purging the religious landscape of false gods. It was also a matter of purging the social, economic and political landscape of lies, injustice and oppression. The two things are integrally intertwined.'[107]

Jeremiah 4:2b connects the transformation of the people with the blessing that comes to the nations (*wĕhitbārkû bô gôyîm*). While the connection between verses 2a and 2b is not explicit, there is the implication that the blessing to the nations comes *through* a restored and transformed Israel. The religious and ethical transformation of Israel has consequences not only for them but for all nations.[108]

The true, just and righteous confession of verse 2 will require the people to break the unploughed ground and circumcise their hearts to the Lord. The first metaphor implies the need for inner transformation. Sowing seed on top of thorns is superficial and ineffective. What is required is the uprooting of the thorns. The metaphor of circumcision of the heart is an idea that is distinctive to, and provides connections between, Deuteronomy and Jeremiah. In Deuteronomy 10:16 the people are called to circumcise their hearts. In Deuteronomy 30:6 YHWH promises that *he* will be the one to perform the necessary surgery after the people have borne the curse of exile. Jeremiah later depicts the people as being uncircumcised of heart (Jer. 9:26). The connection here between circumcised hearts and unploughed ground suggests (as in Deuteronomy) an

---

104. Cf. Isa. 2:2–4; Mic. 4:1–2.

105. Robert P. Carroll, *Jeremiah*, OTL (London: SCM, 1986), p. 156.

106. The only other place in the OT where these three terms appear together is Isa. 59:14. Two out of the three can be found in Isa. 48:1; 56:1; Jer. 33:15; Amos 6:12. In each case the ethical dimension of the terms is to the fore.

107. Wright, *Jeremiah*, p. 88.

108. Jack R. Lundbom, *Jeremiah 1–20*, AB 21A (New York: Doubleday, 1999), p. 326; Holladay, *Jeremiah 1*, pp. 128–129.

ethical dimension to the true, just and righteous confession. Intertextual echoes with the Abrahamic promises and the Deuteronomic material sound throughout Jeremiah 3:14–18 and 4:1–4 as the people are called to cultic and ethical renewal for the sake of the nations.

In addition to the people's idolatry the final section of Jeremiah 5 highlights the injustice present in Judah. The missional ethic of Deuteronomy required love for God and love for neighbour, and, as with the other prophets, Jeremiah describes the people's failure in both spheres. Jeremiah 5:26 characterizes the wicked as those who snare birds. Their houses are full of deceit in the same way the fowler's cage is full of birds. Such people are described as wealthy and powerful, and fat and sleek. Their evil knows no limit. Deuteronomic themes are present in the charges of verse 28: they have failed the orphan and the poor, the priests rule by their own authority and the prophets prophesy lies.[109] As Lundbom puts it, 'the clergy . . . are scarcely better than the criminals'.[110] The opening chapters of Jeremiah describe Judah's rebellion in terms of idolatry and injustice, the key twin-foci of Deuteronomy. As a consequence of a stubborn heart, Israel's witness before the nations is mute (Jer. 3:17; 4:2).

Jeremiah 7 – 11

Jeremiah's 'Temple Sermon' in 7:1–8 presents the reader with 'the clearest and most formidable statement we have of the basic themes of the Jeremiah tradition'.[111] With Deuteronomy in the background, the covenantal formula serves to summon the people to face their transgression.[112] In Jeremiah 7:1–8 the prophet is instructed to stand at the gates of the temple and proclaim a message to the worshippers there. The message itself picks up on a number of Deuteronomic themes, including worship and ethics.[113] The speech begins with a call to the people to make good their ways and deeds, with the promise that if they do, YHWH will let the people live in this place. The deceptive words of the leaders have led the people into false assurance based on the presence of the

---

109. The theme of justice for the orphan and the poor can be seen in Deut. 10:18; 24:17; 27:19. Relevant material on priests and prophets can be found in Deut. 17:8–12; 18:1–22.

110. Lundbom, *Jeremiah 1–20*, p. 411.

111. Walter Brueggemann, *A Commentary on Jeremiah: Exile & Homecoming* (Grand Rapids: Eerdmans, 1998), p. 77.

112. Deuteronomic themes include the summons to 'hear', to do justice and not to oppress the alien, orphan or widow.

113. Holladay notes the 'Deuteronomistic' style. *Jeremiah 1*, p. 241.

Lord in Jerusalem (v. 4). Jeremiah challenges such false assurance (v. 8) and calls
the people to reject idolatry and injustice (vv. 5–6). The call to amend their ways
takes two forms. First, the people are called to 'oppress the alien, fatherless or
widow no longer' (gēryātôm wĕ'almānâ lō' ta'ăšôqû) – a clear echo of Deuteronomy.[114]
Second, the people are called to follow other gods no longer, which also echoes
the fundamental principle of the Shema (Deut. 6:4). The basic call to love God
and love neighbour has been abandoned by Jeremiah's generation.

As the oracles of judgment continue into Jeremiah 9 there is further evidence
of Israel's failure to exercise covenant fidelity according to the terms of Deuteronomy. In Jeremiah 9:13 it is reiterated that judgment has fallen because the
people have forsaken YHWH's law, which he set before them, and have followed
after the stubbornness of their hearts in worshipping the Baals. The verb
'forsake/abandon' ('āzab) is often used of relationship breakdown, particularly
in the context of the covenant.[115] The people's disobedience is not portrayed in terms of a minor misdemeanour, but rather in terms of wilful infidelity
towards their covenant partner.

In Jeremiah 9:23–24 the people are summoned to boast not in wisdom,
strength or riches, but rather in the knowledge of YHWH, who 'exercises
kindness, justice and righteousness' ('ōśeh ḥesed mišpāṭ ûṣĕdāqâ). To know YHWH
means to understand something of his character. This is, presumably, not just
intellectual cognizance but an experience and lived reality of the imitatio Dei. As
Lundbom states, 'the implication is that Yahweh, who himself practices steadfast
love, justice, and righteousness in the world, expects the same from his covenant
people'.[116]

Israel's problem is graphically highlighted by means of another Deuteronomic
metaphor – that of the circumcised heart. Circumcision in flesh alone will bring
punishment (v. 25). Naturally the hearers' minds applaud the idea of punishment
upon Egypt, Edom, Moab and Ammon (v. 26). The surprise comes when Judah
is included in the judgment, and when the whole house of Israel is graphically
described as having foreskin on their hearts. The heart is a key theme in Jeremiah.
Stubborn, uncircumcised hearts are at the root of Israel's failure to love God
and love neighbour. Their only hope, it appears, is that YHWH will give them a
new heart.

In between the two covenantal sermons of the section (chs. 7, 11) Jeremiah
gives a poetic satire instructing the people not to learn the idolatrous ways of

---

114. Cf. Deut. 10:18; 14:29; 16:11, 14; 24:17, 19, 20–21; 26:12–13; 27:19.

115. Robert L. Alden, 'עזב', in NIDOTTE, vol. 3, pp. 364–365.

116. Lundbom, Jeremiah 1–20, p. 572.

the nations (Jer. 10:2; cf. Deut. 7:1–6).[117] Rather than learn the ways of the nations, the people are instructed to speak to the nations: 'These gods, who did not make the heavens and the earth, will perish from the earth and from under the heavens' (Jer. 10:11). Israel, as far as religion is concerned, ought to be the teachers of the nations, not their pupils. Yet, as Jeremiah 7:6 and 11:10 make clear, *reverse mission* has been the reality. The people have learned the nations' ways and followed their gods in antithesis of Deuteronomy 4:4–6.

Finally, under this section, we see further reiteration of the reasons for Israel's judgment at the hands of YHWH in chapter 11. Brueggemann terms this section of prose a 'highly stylized statement of covenant theology'.[118] Affinities between Jeremiah 11 and 7 are noted by Lundbom as is the theme of 'covenant preaching'.[119] The original terms of the covenant are appealed to (v. 2) and the curses are the consequence of disobedience (v. 3).[120] The use of 'curse' (*'ārûr*) recalls its use in Deuteronomy 27:15–26, where it occurs twelve times.[121] In case the people are in any doubt Jeremiah is explicit – these are the terms commanded when YHWH brought the people out of Egypt and called them to '"Obey me and do everything I command you, and you will be my people, and I will be your God. Then I will fulfil the oath I swore to your ancestors, to give them a land flowing with milk and honey" – the land you possess today' (vv. 4–5). Jeremiah repeats the 'terms of this covenant' and their redemptive history in verses 6–7. Mercy has been shown via repeated warnings but the people have refused to listen and (as in 9:14) have followed the stubbornness of their hearts (v. 8). As a consequence YHWH is bringing upon them all the covenantal curses. The particular manifestation of covenant breaking highlighted in 11:9–13 is idolatry, where the people are said to have 'as many gods as you have towns' and 'the altars you have set up to burn incense to that shameful god Baal are as many as the streets of Jerusalem' (v. 13).

Throughout Jeremiah 7 – 11 Israel's rebellion is described in terms of covenant breach. The manifestation of their covenant breaking is seen primarily in idolatry and injustice. The root of their covenant breaking is their stubborn and uncircumcised hearts. As a consequence, rather than teaching the nations,

---

117. Hetty Lalleman, *Jeremiah and Lamentations*, TOTC 21 (Nottingham: Inter-Varsity Press; Downers Grove: IVP Academic, 2013), p. 126.

118. Brueggemann, *Commentary on Jeremiah*, p. 109.

119. Lundbom, *Jeremiah 1–20*, p. 615.

120. As with Jer. 7:1–8, Holladay notes that 'the present passage [Jer. 11:1–17] imitates the diction of Deuteronomy 27:15–26'. *Jeremiah 1*, p. 353.

121. Allen, *Jeremiah*, p. 138.

they have been taught by the nations (Jer. 10:2, 11). Within the broader contours of Israel's story, covenant faithfulness is antecedent to their role in blessing the nations. As Wright says, 'recalling Israel to their covenant monotheism was thus profoundly missional in its *shaping* function'.[122]

Jeremiah 13 – 18

Jeremiah 13 – 18 is bookended by two parables – that of the linen belt and the potter. In Jeremiah 13 the prophet is told to buy a linen belt to wear for a period before hiding it in the rocks (vv. 1–5). Sometime later the prophet is instructed to retrieve the belt and observe its ruin. In 13:11 the explanation is given. The belt represents Israel, worn around YHWH's waist to be a people for his 'renown, praise and honour' (*ûlĕšēm wĕlithillâ ûlĕtip'āret*). These three terms – 'name', 'praise', 'honour' – occur together in Deuteronomy 26:19 and Jeremiah 33:8–9.[123] The people existed to display the splendour of YHWH, but instead are like a ruined belt to be discarded: 'Israel, far from displaying the splendour of YHWH, were rotting in their own disgrace. They were failing to be and do what they had been bought for. They were denying their mission, their reason for existence.'[124]

In Jeremiah 16 there is a reiteration of YHWH's determination to judge Judah for idolatry (Jer. 16:1–8). When the people enquire as to the cause of their misfortune Jeremiah cites their idolatry (vv. 11–13). There is, however, in spite of Israel's rebellion, a promise that YHWH will restore his people in a new exodus (vv. 14–15).[125] After Israel's restoration the nations will come from the ends of the earth to confess the folly of their own idolatry and learn from YHWH (vv. 19–21). There is a heavy irony in the confession of the nations, a confession Judah has rejected.[126] Wright observes the logic of Jeremiah 16:14–21: 'Israel must be judged, but beyond judgment there lies the restoration of Israel, and beyond that the ingathering of the nations.'[127] Jeremiah 16:14–21 'concerns the new historical beginning made possible by Yahweh's sovereign resolve'.[128]

The promise of Jeremiah 16:14–21 leads into the depiction of the present situation in chapter 17 and the inability of Judah to be a fruitful witness to

---

122. Wright, 'Prophet to the Nations', p. 122. Emphasis original.

123. Ibid., pp. 116–117.

124. Wright, *Jeremiah*, p. 159.

125. Brueggemann, *Commentary on Jeremiah*, p. 154.

126. Wright, *Jeremiah*, p. 194.

127. Ibid.

128. Brueggemann, *Commentary on Jeremiah*, p. 157.

YHWH.[129] Picking up the theme of Jeremiah 9:26, the opening of chapter 17 likens Israel's hearts to tablets, upon which is engraved their sin. There is an obvious allusion to the stone tablets upon which the Decalogue was engraved.[130] A further echo comes from the words that followed the Shema (Deut. 6:5–9), instructing the people to have Torah upon their hearts.[131] These fleshy tablets, instead of bearing YHWH's Torah, bear only the engraving of the people's sin. Here is one of Jeremiah's key themes – that of the human heart. The root problem with the people is their hearts. Jeremiah describes their hearts as unwashed (4:14), stubborn (11:8), deceitful (17:9), uncircumcised (9:26) and engraved with sin (17:1).[132] The solution to their plight is picked up later in Jeremiah (24:7; 31:31–34; 32:39), which will be examined in due course.[133]

The nature of that heart sin is expounded further in 17:2 with mention of the altars and Asherah poles.[134] The high places and the spreading trees have already been mentioned and identify Judah's chief sin as idolatry (Jer. 3:1–13). Their failure to honour YHWH rightly will result in their judgment (vv. 3–4).[135]

A contrast is developed in 17:5–8 between the one who trusts in man for his salvation (a reference to military alliance with Egypt) and the person who trusts in YHWH. The latter will be like a tree planted beside a stream. As with the heart, illustrations involving water are also a favourite of Jeremiah. In chapter 2:13 he denounces the people for forsaking YHWH, the spring of living water, and digging their own cisterns that can hold no water. The same charge is levelled here, and in verse 13, where water is used as an image of life and flourishing. The tree that sends out roots by the stream never fails to bear fruit (v. 8). In the wider canon trees and streams are often used to speak of life and health, and

---

129. Kidner, in his commentary on Jeremiah, has Jer. 17:1–4 as the anticlimax of the section running from 14:1 onwards. Derek Kidner, *Jeremiah* (Downers Grove: IVP Academic, 1987), p. 71.

130. Note the parallel terminology in Exod. 32:16. Holladay, *Jeremiah 1*, p. 486.

131. Lundbom, *Jeremiah 1–20*, p. 777.

132. Holladay suggests that the 'heart' refers to the centre of the nation, in particular the priesthood. *Jeremiah 1*, p. 486. While this is possible, the references to the heart seem, at least by implication, to include the sin of the people more broadly (9:26; 11:8; 17:9).

133. Cf. also Ezek. 36:26.

134. Lundbom, *Jeremiah 1–20*, p. 777.

135. Meadors notes the heart problem represents covenant apostasy, and the remedy is the new covenant of Jer. 31 and Ezek. 36. Edward P. Meadors, *Idolatry and the Hardening of the Heart: A Study in Biblical Theology* (New York: T&T Clark, 2006), pp. 56–76.

often in the context of blessing the nations. Holladay suggests that Jeremiah may be alluding to Psalm 1 here, though the contrast between the blessed and the cursed is reversed.[136] Creach notes the association of water, trees, leaves and fruit in a number of poetic texts and their signification of life, healing and restoration for God's people and beyond.[137]

In verse 12 Jeremiah reaffirms the sanctuary as the place of hope. Here again we see the contrast between idolatry and worship of YHWH put into cultic terms. Worship must be practised as the outward manifestation of the heart's intent.

The call to true worship is continued in the second half of Jeremiah 17, with a particular focus on the Sabbath. As with Jeremiah's preaching in 7:3–7 and 11:3–5 the themes of covenant and temple are prominent in 17:19–26.[138] Jeremiah is to announce at the city gates YHWH's command that the Sabbath is to be appropriately observed. It is to be kept 'holy' as was commanded to their forefathers (v. 22). The mention of carrying loads into the city refers to commercial activity and may therefore have a humanitarian thrust.[139] Economic greed both results from and leads to a failure to love God and love neighbour. The promise (vv. 24–25) is that if the people keep the Sabbath holy, then the Davidic kings will enter the gates of the city and dwell on the throne.[140] Alternatively disobedience will result in YHWH's judgment upon Jerusalem and her fortress (v. 27). As noted in examining Deuteronomy, the law regarding Sabbath was unique within its ANE context. It served as a reminder of both creation and redemption and was to be enjoyed by all within the community. Sabbath functioned on both the horizontal and vertical dimensions. It offered humanitarian concern and an opportunity for worship of YHWH. The Sabbath enables the people to remember their *raison d'être*.[141]

---

136. Holladay, *Jeremiah 1*, pp. 489–490.

137. See Gen. 1 – 2; Pss 46:2–4; 52:8; 65:6–10; 92:13–15; Isa. 30:25; 32:2; 44:4; Ezek. 47:12. Jerome F. D. Creach, 'Like a Tree Planted by the Temple Stream: The Portrait of the Righteous in Psalm 1:3', *CBQ* 61 (1999), pp. 34–46.

138. Lundbom, *Jeremiah 1–20*, p. 809.

139. Jerry A. Gladson, 'Jeremiah 17:19–27: A Rewriting of the Sinaitic Code?', *CBQ* 62 (2000), p. 37.

140. Similar promises regarding Sabbath observance were noted in Isa. 56.

141. Louis Stulman, *Jeremiah*, Abingdon Old Testament Commentaries (Nashville: Abingdon, 2005), p. 180. Tsevat argues that Sabbath, at its most basic, is the 'acceptance of the sovereignty of God'. Matitiahu Tsevat, 'The Basic Meaning of the Biblical Sabbath', in *The Meaning of the Book of Job and Other Biblical Studies: Essays on the Literature and Religion of the Hebrew Bible* (New York: Ktav, 1980), p. 49.

Lundbom observes the connection between reform of worship and social concern. Commenting on the importance of Sabbath observance for covenant fidelity he writes:

> Violation of this commandment goes much deeper than absenteeism in public worship. It is an evil rooted in greed, which, according to Amos 8:4–6, is the handmaiden of social injustice and what leads to the breakdown of community well-being.[142]

Brueggemann also discerns the pivotal nature of the Sabbath for the existence of the covenant community:

> It is the dramatic act whereby this people asserts to itself and announces to the watching world that this is Israel, a different people with a different way in the world, who will not behave according to the expectations of the imperial world. In the purview of covenant, the stability of political life (v. 25) and the effectiveness of worship (v. 26) depend on sabbath, an act that hands life back to God in trusting obedience.[143]

The future dynasty and well-being of the people depend upon faithful Sabbath observance. As in Deuteronomy, right worship (love for God) and love for neighbour secures a perpetual inheritance. Failure in these areas brings YHWH's judgment. Restoration and renewal are the necessary preconditions for the ingathering of the nations envisaged in Jeremiah 16:19–21.

In Jeremiah 18:1–17 we read the parable of the potter and its explanation. The parable speaks of the potter's right to do as he pleases with the clay. When the clay becomes 'marred in his hands' (v. 4) he reshapes it as seems best. The explanation links the clay to the response of any nation, but Israel in particular. Israel's rebellion has resulted in their present crisis. Jeremiah 18:13–17 draws out the missional implications, namely that the nations are horrified by Israel's actions and current condition. Israel's behaviour has served as an anti-missional ethic before the surrounding nations. As Wright concludes, 'God's mission to the nations is being hindered because of Israel's continual spiritual and ethical failure.'[144]

---

142. Lundbom, *Jeremiah 1–20*, p. 810.

143. Brueggemann, *Commentary on Jeremiah*, p. 166.

144. Wright, 'Prophet to the Nations', p. 124.

Jeremiah 23 – 24

Jeremiah 23:1–8 concludes the kingship cycle (Jer. 21:1 – 23:8), which laments the failure of Judah's kings.[145] It begins with another 'woe' directed against the faithless kings of Israel and Judah.[146] Their failure is outlined in 22:13–30 in terms of injustice and unrighteousness. As a consequence the people suffer under the mistreatment of their leaders, and under the punishing hand of YHWH (vv. 28–30). Their failure is put in ethical terms and will result in their punishment, while YHWH himself will gather the flock and be the Shepherd of his people.[147] At the same time, in 23:4 YHWH declares that he will appoint shepherds over the people who will tend them rightly. The result, in 23:3, is that the regathered people will be 'fruitful and increase in number' (*ûpārû wĕrābû*), an allusion to the repeated phrase within Genesis.

All of this will come to pass when YHWH establishes the 'righteous branch' (*ṣemaḥ ṣaddîq*) from David's line, who will 'reign wisely and act justly in the earth' (*wĕʿāśâ mišpāṭ ûṣĕdāqâ bāʾāreṣ*).[148] Baldwin, picking up on the term *ṣemaḥ* (branch), also used in Isaiah 4:2, Jeremiah 33:15 and Zechariah 3:8 and 6:12, argues that the term brings together both kingly and priestly functions.[149] The term *ṣemaḥ* therefore refers to a special sort of priest-king. In his era Judah will be 'saved', and his name will be 'YHWH, our righteousness' (*yhwh ṣidqēnû*) (v. 6).[150] As Wright observes, '*this* son of David will be the one who will combine a reign of righteousness and justice with the blessing of salvation'.[151]

The deliverance of the people will be a new exodus, not from Egypt, but from 'the land of the north'. The implication of verses 7–8 is that the return from exile, the new exodus, will be so great that it will eclipse the first exodus, such that people will no longer say, 'As surely as the LORD lives, who brought

---

145. W. J. Wessels,'The Fallibility and Future of Leadership According to Jeremiah 23:1–4', *OTE* 6 (1993), p. 330.

146. Jack R. Lundbom, *Jeremiah 21–36*, AB 21B (New York: Doubleday, 2004), p. 164.

147. Holladay, *Jeremiah 1*, pp. 614–615. Holladay suggests that Ps. 23 lies in the background to this passage, and further notes the links with Ezek. 34:1–16; Mic. 2:12; Isa. 40:11; John 10:1–18.

148. This is reminiscent of Isaiah's similar theme in Isa. 11:1–5.

149. Joyce G. Baldwin, '*Ṣemaḥ* as a Technical Term in the Prophets', *VT* 14 (1964), pp. 93–97.

150. Lundbom argues that the name of this new king is a deliberate reversal of Zedekiah's name and is, therefore, an indirect censure on Zedekiah's rule. *Jeremiah 21–36*, p. 176.

151. Wright, *Jeremiah*, p. 244. Emphasis original.

the Israelites up out of Egypt.'[152] The people's confession of faith will no longer be centred on the first exodus, but on this new exodus.[153] As Holladay notes, 'If Israel is to swear by a God of the new exodus, then that new exodus will have to overshadow the old, just as the new covenant (31:31–34) will overshadow the old.'[154] Wright notes the importance of holding the twofold promise of verses 5–8 together. Only when the righteous Branch reigns is the exile over and the new exodus accomplished. These two events together will form the definitive moment of redemption and the inauguration of a new creation, with the Davidic King and his subjects fulfilling the creation mandate to bring blessing to the whole earth.[155]

Moving into Jeremiah 24, Lundbom states, 'Chapter 24 anticipates some of the most important themes preached by Jeremiah before and after the fall of Jerusalem: a return from Babylon and rebuilding the land; a new covenant; and judgment on those seeking refuge in Egypt.'[156] After Jehoiachin along with the artisans and craftsmen is exiled to Babylon, Jeremiah sees a vision of two baskets of figs, placed in front of the temple. One basket has good figs, while the other contains figs that are inedible. The good figs represent the exiles living in Babylon. YHWH promises to watch over them and bring them back to the land. Niditch explores the symbolic use of agricultural elements, likening Jeremiah's vision to Pharaoh's dreams in Genesis 41.[157] In both cases the agricultural element represents either flourishing or languishing. Figs in the Old Testament often symbolize blessing; therefore the symbolic usage here suggests a future for the rescued exiles that will include blessing and flourishing.[158] As with Jeremiah 23 the key note to observe is that blessing and flourishing are creational motifs. There may be here a further hint towards a blessing or flourishing beyond the borders of Israel and Judah. He will plant them and not uproot them.[159] He will give them a heart to know YHWH, and, in an echo of earlier covenant formulas, YHWH declares, 'They will be my people, and I will

---

152. Holladay notes the new-exodus theme and the similarities with Isa. 45:15–21; 51:9–11. *Jeremiah 1*, p. 623.

153. Fretheim, *Jeremiah*, p. 327.

154. Holladay, *Jeremiah 1*, p. 623.

155. Wright, *Jeremiah*, p. 245.

156. Lundbom, *Jeremiah 21–36*, p. 223.

157. Susan Niditch, *The Symbolic Vision in Biblical Tradition*, HSMS (Chico, Calif.: Scholars Press, 1983), pp. 67–70.

158. See Num. 13:23; Deut. 8:8; 1 Kgs 4:25; Joel 2:22; Mic. 4:4; Zech. 3:10.

159. Cf. Jer. 1:10; 18:9; 24:6; 29:5, 28; 31:4–5, 28; 35:7; 42:10; 45:4.

be their God, for they will return to me with all their heart' (24:7).[160] As Holladay observes, 'those who return will not simply replicate the past – they will be given a new heart, so that in a basic sense it will be a new start, and in that new start the covenant will be secure'.[161] By contrast the poor figs represent Zedekiah and his officials, who will suffer the punishment of the various covenant curses for their rebellion and unfaithfulness.[162]

Suffice to note, as we move into the 'Little Book of Consolation', that the remedy for the people is a new covenant and a new heart. Only YHWH can provide such a transformation, and only then will they truly be YHWH's people, able to fulfil their covenant calling to bring blessing to the nations.

Jeremiah 30 – 31

Bozak suggests that the 'Little Book of Consolation' is a unit structured around an introduction (30:1–4), followed by six short poems (30:5 – 31:22), finished with a two-part conclusion (31:23–40).[163] The plight outlined in the judgment oracles is reversed, with much of the earlier language and imagery present.[164] Additionally the promises contained in Jeremiah 30 – 31 (and 32 – 33) have much in common with Ezekiel 33 – 37, and Isaiah 40 – 55.[165]

The 'Little Book of Consolation' (Jer. 30 – 33) begins with the promise of restoration (30:3). The phrase 'restore the fortunes/captives' (wĕšabtî 'et-šĕbût) occurs seven times in Jeremiah 30 – 33.[166] Significantly Wright notes that an almost identical phrase occurs in Deuteronomy 30:3 (wĕšāb yhwh 'ĕlōhêkā 'et-šĕbûtkā), and he suggests that Jeremiah 30 – 33 is a prophetic and poetic

---

160. Similar formulas occur in Exod. 6:7; Lev. 26:12; Deut. 29:12–13. As with previously examined sections of Jeremiah, the 'heart' is a key theme, and Jer. 24:7 is an anticipation of Jer. 31:31–34.

161. Holladay, *Jeremiah 1*, p. 660.

162. This message would have constituted a reversal in expectation: those exiled were favoured, while those left behind would come under judgement. As Lalleman states, 'Unexpectedly that hope lies with the exiles!' Lalleman, *Jeremiah and Lamentations*, p. 200.

163. Barbara A. Bozak, *Life 'Anew': A Literary-Theological Study of Jer 30–31*, AnBib 122 (Rome: Editrice Pontificio Istituto Biblico, 1991), pp. 19–20.

164. Joshua N. Moon, *Jeremiah's New Covenant: An Augustinian Reading*, JTISup 3 (Winona Lake: Eisenbrauns, 2011), pp. 202–203.

165. Walter Brueggemann, *The Theology of the Book of Jeremiah*, OTT (Cambridge: Cambridge University Press, 2007), p. 121.

166. See Jer. 30:3, 18; 31:23; 32:44; 33:7, 11, 26.

expansion of that passage.[167] Israel may be in process of enduring the covenant curses of Deuteronomy 28, but they can hope in the promised restoration of Deuteronomy 30. Elements of Israel's restoration, according to Jeremiah 30, will include a return to the land (v. 3), freedom from captivity (v. 8) and a renewed relationship with YHWH under his Davidic king (v. 9). Wright, noting the language of verses 8–9, says, 'For them the message of the exodus liberation rings forth . . . God alone will act, as he did in the exodus.'[168] A feature of the book of consolation is the fusing of Abrahamic, Mosaic and Davidic motifs. This future Davidic king, Lundbom observes, will not simply be a king *like* David, but will be 'a David *redivivus*'.[169] Here is a promise of a messiah in David's line, who will lead a new exodus. The enemies of YHWH's people will be destroyed, and, in words reminiscent of the Abrahamic covenant, the people will increase. Further, historical links to Abraham, Jacob, Moses and David cover the entirety of the covenant people, not just Israel, and point forward to a reunified kingdom.[170] In verses 19–20 the establishment of the community before YHWH may refer to a restored worshipping community within a restored cultic setting.[171] What is in view is not simply material prosperity but the restoration of a community that loves YHWH with heart, soul, mind and strength, and lives out the liturgical requirement of Deuteronomy 12, 16 and 26. The promise of a faithful ruler is reiterated in verse 21 with the addition that he will be one who draws near to YHWH. This suggests a future ruler who will combine royal and priestly roles.[172] The section concludes with the covenant formula 'you will be my people, and I will be your God' (v. 22). The formula, repeated throughout Jeremiah 30 – 33, is the basis upon which YHWH's deliverance and transformation can occur.

The opening of chapter 31, 'at that time', commences what Bozak considers to be the fourth poem of the cycle and reiterates the theme of the reunification of Israel under YHWH (v. 1).[173] The initial result of YHWH's restorative work will be the joyful celebration of the people (v. 7). This in turn will spread the news of YHWH's salvation beyond the borders of Israel. The people's praise of YHWH will be heard by the surrounding nations (v. 7). The syntax of 31:10 suggests

---

167. Wright, *Jeremiah*, p. 301.

168. Ibid., p. 305.

169. Lundbom, *Jeremiah 21–36*, p. 390.

170. Ibid., pp. 404–405.

171. Ibid.

172. Ibid., p. 408.

173. Bozak, *Life 'Anew'*, p. 72.

that the nations who hear of YHWH's salvation are themselves to announce it to those even further afield (*šim'û děbar-yhwh gôyîm wěhaggîdû bā'iyyîm*). Just as the nations were called to witness Israel's judgment (6:18), so now they will witness Israel's liberation.[174]

YHWH's people will be gathered from the ends of the earth (v. 8). This may refer to the exiles scattered in various parts of the ANE, or it could allude to a much greater ingathering at a future unspecified time.[175] Among those who return will be the blind and the lame (v. 8), the young and the old (v. 13). The imagery of the restoration includes streams, level paths, bounty, new wine, a well-watered garden, with mourning turned to gladness (vv. 10–14). YHWH will shepherd his people himself, since the appointed shepherds have been found wanting (cf. Jer. 23:1–4). Moon describes the restoration as 'idyllic' – things are not just put back to how they were pre-exile, but are restored to what they always ought to have been.[176] The hyperbolic description suggests something radically new in Israel's future.

The next oracle continues the theme of repentance and restoration, employing the evocative image of Rachel's weeping over her children (v. 15). The final clause of Jeremiah 31:22 is enigmatic, but key is the preceding phrase: 'The LORD will create a new thing on the earth' (*kî bārā' yhwh ['ādōnāy] ḥădāšâ bā'āreṣ*).[177] This restoration is described as containing elements of a new creation. The verb 'create' (*bārā'*) occurs only here in Jeremiah and naturally alludes to Genesis 1. The agrarian imagery continues as YHWH promises to watch over his people as they rebuild and plant, and no longer to tear down and uproot (cf. Jer. 1:10).

The themes of Jeremiah 30:1 – 31:29 provide an important context for the well-known new-covenant promise of Jeremiah 31:31–34. These promises, following those depicting the totality of restoration, speak specifically of a new covenant and new heart for YHWH's redeemed people. The oracle builds from a statement of how a new/renewed covenant will be dissimilar to that which

---

174. Wright, *Jeremiah*, p. 318.

175. Bozak, *Life 'Anew'*, p. 83.

176. Moon, *Jeremiah's New Covenant*, p. 223.

177. For discussion of the interpretative possibilities see Bernard W. Anderson, '"The Lord Has Created Something New": A Stylistic Study of Jer 31:15–22', in *Prophet to the Nations: Essays in Jeremiah Studies* (Winona Lake: Eisenbrauns, 1984), pp. 367–380; Alice Ogden Bellis, 'Jeremiah 31:22B: An Intentionally Ambiguous, Multivalent Riddle-Text', in *Uprooting and Planting: Essays on Jeremiah for Leslie Allen*, LHB/OTS 459 (New York: T&T Clark International, 2007), pp. 5–13.

preceded, followed by a positive description of the new covenant's characteristics, climaxing with the reason for the possibility of the new covenant. Some
debate whether *ḥādāšâ* should be translated 'new' or 'renewed'.[178] Either translation is possible; it is the content of the covenant that is of interest.

First, in verses 31–32 it is described as being unlike the covenant made with
the forefathers. Moon notes that in Jeremiah the 'new covenant' is never
contrasted with the 'old' or 'first' covenant.[179] The contrast presented is between
'broken' and, implicitly, unbreakable. Moon states, 'the way in which that
contrary covenant is presented is as a broken covenant . . . the contrast to the
new covenant is infidelity'.[180] The 'Book of Consolation' promises to overturn
the state of affairs created by the people's infidelity. As Moon states, 'universal
infidelity is overturned into universal fidelity'.[181]

This leads to the positive description of this new covenant (vv. 33–34). The
emphasis is on what YHWH will do to transform his people from covenant
breakers to faithful covenant people. He will put his Torah (*'et-tôrātî*) in their
inner parts (*bĕqirbām*) and write it upon their hearts (*wĕ'al-libbām 'ektăbennâ*). The
former, *bĕqirbām*, could mean 'in the midst', but given the parallel in the second
half of the promise, 'inner parts' seems the more likely sense.[182] Given the
imagery of a written Torah perhaps the Decalogue is in view, though this is
unspecified.[183] This action overwrites the sin engraved on the people's hearts

---

178. Verhoef asserts that the new covenant would not be 'a mere renewal of the
     covenant, which occurred several times in Israel's history . . . Only a radically new,
     God-given change of mentality would suffice, and to this end God lit. "cut" a new
     covenant with both houses of Israel.' Pieter A. Verhoef, 'חדש', in *NIDOTTE*,
     vol. 2, p. 35. Lundbom agrees with Verhoef in stressing the discontinuity of this
     'new' covenant. *Jeremiah 21–36*, p. 466. Fretheim, on the other hand, argues for a
     fundamental continuity between the 'old' and the 'new', the difference being one
     of efficacy, not content. *Jeremiah*, pp. 441–443. Both Fretheim and Lundbom agree
     that Jer. 31 is neither supercessionist nor mere renewal. This covenant is new but
     not novel. Moon is correct to suggest 'too much has been made of the rendering
     of this term . . . The English term "new" is sufficiently vague for our purposes
     and functions well in the semantic role taken up by חֲדָשָׁה'. *Jeremiah's New Covenant*,
     p. 229.
179. Moon, *Jeremiah's New Covenant*, p. 185.
180. Ibid., pp. 185–186.
181. Ibid., p. 226.
182. Lundbom, *Jeremiah 21–36*, p. 469. LXX translates *bĕqirbām* with *eis tēn dianoian autōn*.
183. Ibid., p. 468.

referred to in Jeremiah 17:1. The internalization of Torah is the fulfilment of Deuteronomy 6:6: 'these commandments that I give you today are to be on your hearts'. YHWH will be their God and they will be his people. No longer will a man teach his neighbour saying 'know YHWH' for they will all know YHWH, from the smallest to the greatest. Lundbom suggests that the phrase 'know YHWH' is an echo of Jeremiah's own mission to the people outlined in Jeremiah 5:4. This would further suggest that to 'know YHWH' was akin to the calls in Deuteronomy to listen, remember and obey.[184] Jeremiah envisions a day when his role, calling people back to covenant fidelity, will no longer be necessary. Wright observes that in Jeremiah, to 'know the LORD' has socio-ethical implications, as seen in Jeremiah 9:23–24 and 22:16: 'It means to value what God delights in: "kindness, justice and righteousness." It means to do what is right and just and to defend the poor and needy: "is that not what it means to know me?"'[185]

The phrase 'least to the greatest' (*lĕmiqṭannām wĕ'ad-gĕdôlām*) appears in 6:13 and 8:10, where the whole community is characterized as greedy for gain. This is contrasted with the new covenant, 'where the *whole community* will be characterised by the knowledge of God'.[186] The 'for' (*kî*) at the end of verse 34 is causal, giving the actuating principle for this new-covenant arrangement: complete and ongoing forgiveness of sins.[187] Forgiveness is the prerequisite for the new relationship.[188] As Brueggemann puts it, 'this line states the basis for all the foregoing'.[189] In other words, YHWH's decisive act of forgiveness makes the new covenant possible, and the associated blessings follow. Clements summarizes the thrust of Jeremiah 31:31–34:

> The unspoken question that underlies what it [the new covenant] has to declare is this: If Israel's sins in the past brought such fearful judgment upon the nation so that it came close to total annihilation, what assurance can there be that after a future restoration has taken place the same fate will not befall Israel again? The theologically conceived response to this is that God will, by the very creative power of his love, write the law of the covenant upon the hearts of the men and women who make up Israel.[190]

---

184. Ibid., p. 469.

185. Wright, *Jeremiah*, p. 330.

186. Ibid.

187. Bozak, *Life 'Anew'*, p. 122.

188. Moon, *Jeremiah's New Covenant*, p. 242.

189. Brueggemann, *Commentary on Jeremiah*, p. 294.

190. R. E. Clements, *Jeremiah*, Int (Atlanta: John Knox, 1988), p. 190.

The promise is confirmed in verses 35–40 by the divine oath in which YHWH assures the people of his decree by the movement of the sun, moon and stars. Only if the laws of nature cease need Israel be concerned that YHWH may renege on his promise. As with Ezekiel's temple vision (chs. 40–48), the whole city, and not just the temple area, will be holy to the Lord (v. 40). Even the place of death (v. 40) will become holy.

Jeremiah 32 – 33

Themes from chapters 30 to 31 are here repeated and expanded upon. Jeremiah's purchase of the field and the storage of the accompanying legal document is on the basis that YHWH will restore the people to the land, and property will again be bought and sold (Jer. 32:13–15). It is thus an enactment of hope. Although Nebuchadnezzar and the Babylonians are on the brink of capturing the city, YHWH promises return and restoration (Jer. 32:26–29). Jeremiah 32:38–41 contains similar themes to Jeremiah 31:31–34. YHWH will give the people singleness of heart and action, and his covenant with them will be everlasting. In Jeremiah 33:8 there is the promise of cleansing from sin and forgiveness for rebellion. The result, again, is that the renown, praise and honour of YHWH will come before all nations on earth – that which Brueggemann terms the 'doxological agenda' (Jer. 33:9).[191] As already noted, the triplet – name, praise, honour – has appeared before in Jeremiah 13:11 and Deuteronomy 26:19.[192] They will hear of all the good things YHWH does for his people and will be in awe (Jer. 33:9). Brueggemann concludes, 'Thus healed Jerusalem becomes a theological datum which requires the nations to reposition themselves vis-à-vis Yahweh.'[193]

The sounds of joy and gladness will fill the restored city (33:10–11) and, as previously, a Davidic king will bring security to all the people (vv. 15–16). David will never fail to have a man sit on the throne, and the priests and Levites will never fail to have a man to stand continually to offer sacrifices (vv. 17–18). In verse 22 the promise concerning David and the Levites is given Abrahamic overtones: 'I will make the descendants . . . as countless as the stars in the sky and as measureless as the sand on the seashore.'[194]

Throughout Jeremiah 30 – 33 the covenants with Abraham, Moses and David are all appealed to and, to some degree, fused together. The promise of this

---

191. Brueggemann, *Book of Jeremiah*, p. 131.

192. Wright, 'Prophet to the Nations', pp. 116–117.

193. Brueggemann, *Commentary on Jeremiah*, p. 315.

194. See Gen. 15:5; 22:17; 26:4; 32:12.

section is the reversal of the covenant curses, and the fulfilment of the covenantal blessings and promises stretching back through David and Moses to Abraham.

Although the immediate perspective of the prophet is with the restoration of Israel, the wider perspective regarding the nations lies in the background. The promises regarding the nations are not as explicit in Jeremiah as they are in either Isaiah or Ezekiel, but they are nonetheless present.

Summary

Jeremiah's rebuke of Israel centres on their failure to 'obey the terms of this covenant' (11:3), and in particular the oppression of widows, orphans and aliens (7:6), and worship of Baal and other gods (7:9; 11:12). Their rebellion is cast in familiar Deuteronomic terms, as is their root problem – uncircumcised hearts (9:26). Their hearts are instead engraved with their sin (17:1). The solution to Israel's plight resides in a new Davidic king (30:9; 33:15–16) and a new covenant with the law engraved on hearts (31:31–34). The tearing down and uprooting (1:10) will turn into building and planting (31:28). The redeemed will serve YHWH with 'singleness of heart and action' (32:39) and the nations will hear of his kindness and come with shouts of joy (31:12; 33:9). Jeremiah shares with Isaiah a concern for justice and true worship. They both look forward to a restoration involving a Davidic king, a new exodus, the work of the Spirit and the blessing of the nations. Wright's conclusion summarizes the missio-ethical thrust of Jeremiah:

> The missional purpose of the text of Jeremiah, then, was to bring Israel back to their covenant shape. But the longer-distant purpose of *that* was to enable them to fulfil their mission of bringing blessing to the nations . . . there is a fundamental, inextricable connection between the ethical quality of life of the people of God and their mission to the nations.[195]

Ezekiel

Ezekiel has been described as 'a strange visionary'.[196] The book bearing his name has been termed cold, lacking in *pathos* and as being parochial.[197] Such

---

195. Wright, 'Prophet to the Nations', p. 124.
196. Koch, *Prophets*, p. 84.
197. See Brueggemann, *Hopeful Imagination*, pp. 69–87; Daniel I. Block, *The Book of Ezekiel: Chapters 1–24*, NICOT (Grand Rapids: Eerdmans, 1998), p. 47.

assessments, however, fail to notice the way in which a pervasive theme throughout the prophecy, YHWH's name among the nations, relates to Israel among the nations. Repeatedly Ezekiel alerts the reader to the reason for Israel's exile. It is because YHWH's name has been blasphemed among the nations and he must act for the sake of his name.[198] Israel was set in the centre of the nations to witness positively to YHWH, but instead their behaviour in the sight of the nations served as an anti-witness. These themes will be explored and developed as we examine the text. Key sections for the purpose of this section are as follows: Ezekiel 5; 16 – 20; 36 – 37.

Ezekiel 5

The opening four chapters of Ezekiel's prophecy set the scene and include his vision of YHWH's throne chariot (ch. 1), his call to prophesy the contents of the scroll (chs. 2–3) and a prophetic drama symbolizing the judgment to come on Jerusalem (ch. 4). Chapter 5 brings the drama of chapter 4 to completion as Ezekiel shaves his head and beard, and weighs and divides the hair.[199] Such an act is a picture of defilement, forbidden by the law (Deut. 14:1), and a sign of disgrace (2 Sam. 10:4).[200] Israel, a once holy chosen nation, is now an object of humiliation. Odell suggests that Ezekiel here relinquishes any priestly role and subjects himself to contact with mourning and death. The 'waves of death' must wash over the people.[201] Only then can the breath of resurrection life come. Ezekiel is to take a third of the hair and burn it, symbolizing those who will die as a result of the siege. A third is to be struck with the sword, again picturing the events of the siege. And a final third is to be scattered to the winds, symbolizing those driven into exile. A number of these people will be judged by fire and a few strands will be kept as a remnant, symbolized by being tucked into Ezekiel's garment.

The remainder of the chapter explains the reasons for YHWH's fierce judgment against Jerusalem beginning, significantly, with the affirmation of Jerusalem's centrality among the nations. Ezekiel 5:5b reads, 'This is Jerusalem, which I have set in the centre of the nations.' Wright states:

> Israel's centrality is not merely geographical but theological and, in a sense,
> missiological . . . It was a shorthand way of expressing all the universality of

---

198. In particular Ezek. 36:20–23; 39:7.

199. Block suggests there may be an allusion to Isa. 7:20 in the act of shaving. *Ezekiel 1–24* , p. 192.

200. Ralph H. Alexander, 'Ezekiel', in EBC, vol. 7 (Grand Rapids: Zondervan, 2010), p. 678.

201. Margaret S. Odell, *Ezekiel*, SHBC (Macon: Smyth & Helwys, 2005), p. 67–68.

God's purposes among the nations that was bound up in the particularity
of Israel's election.[202]

In Hummel's words, Israel are the 'locus of his [God's] salvation'.[203] The
problem is that the people have been an anti-witness through their idolatry. In
Ezekiel 5:6 God's charge against the people is revealed: 'she has rebelled against
my laws and decrees more than the nations and countries around her. She has
rejected my laws and has not followed my decrees.' The combination, twice
iterated, of 'laws and decrees' is reminiscent of the language of Deuteronomy.[204]
Worse, Jerusalem has not even lived up to the standards of the nations around
it (v. 7; cf. Jer. 10:2). As Block describes, 'Instead of being a light to the world,
by failing to live in the light of God's revelation, his chosen city had become
the world's darkest blot.'[205]

Therefore YHWH's punishment will be in the sight of the nations (v. 8) and
will come because of their 'abominations' (v. 9). The word 'abomination' (tô'ēbâ)
in verse 9, already noted elsewhere, is 'a word of central theological importance in Ezekiel (found on thirty-five occasions), an aspect of his indebtedness
to Deuteronomistic influence'.[206] Jerusalem's vile images and detestable practices
will bring the judgments promised in Deuteronomy and now prophetically
enacted by Ezekiel (vv. 10–12). Jerusalem will become a warning, reproach,
taunt and object of horror among the surrounding nations (v. 15). The themes
of judgment that run through the chapter echo the covenant curses of Deuteronomy 28, making clear that covenant violation is the reason for judgment.
Greenberg makes a strong case for seeing the concluding judgments spoken of
in verse 17 as alluding to Deuteronomy 32:23–24.[207] In a tragic way Jerusalem
will witness to the holiness and greatness of YHWH; not through their obedience

---

202. Christopher J. H. Wright, *The Message of Ezekiel*, BST (Leicester: Inter-Varsity Press,
     2001), pp. 87–88.

203. Horace D. Hummel, *Ezekiel 1–20*, Concordia (St. Louis: Concordia, 2005), p. 180.

204. The word 'laws' (*mišpāṭim*) appears 5 times in Ezek. 5:6–8, 5 times in Deut. 4 and 37
     times in Deuteronomy as a whole. The word 'statutes' (*ḥuqqim*) appears 3 times in
     Ezek. 5:6–7 and 6 times in Deuteronomy. Israel's role at the 'centre' of the nations
     is related to Torah observance, or in this case a failure so to do. See Moshe
     Greenberg, *Ezekiel 1–20*, AB 22 (New York: Doubleday, 1983), p. 111.

205. Block, *Ezekiel 1–24*, p. 199.

206. Paul M. Joyce, *Ezekiel: A Commentary*, LHB/OTS 482 (New York: T&T Clark,
     2007), p. 89.

207. Greenberg, *Ezekiel 1–20*, pp. 116–117.

to YHWH's wisdom and goodness, but rather by their wickedness incurring his punishment before the eyes of the nations. The nations should observe, understand, and learn from YHWH's judgment on Jerusalem. YHWH's judgment does not simply teach Israel a lesson, but 'constitutes a major historical object lesson for the nations'.[208]

As Deuteronomy 6 – 11 emphasized the necessity of obeying the first commandment, so Ezekiel cites (and will cite repeatedly) the breaking of the first commandment as the nature of Israel's anti-witness, and the reason for God's judgment.

Ezekiel 16

In the chapters following Ezekiel 5 the oracles of judgment have continued, the glory of YHWH has left the temple (ch. 10) and the false prophets have been condemned (ch. 13). Ezekiel 16 – 20 charts the narrative of redemption, rebellion and renewal. These central chapters contain *in nuce* the message of the book.

In chapter 16 Ezekiel employs an allegory of betrothal to symbolize the relationship between YHWH and Israel. Its parallel is in Ezekiel 23, which picks up and develops similar themes. Chapter 16 is the longest prophecy in the book and has four major divisions: first, there is the extended metaphor of Jerusalem as a 'nymphomaniacal adultress'[209] (vv. 3–34); second, there is the pronouncement of judgment on Jerusalem for her harlotry (vv. 35–43); third, there is the surprising comparison of Jerusalem with her sisters Sodom and Samaria (vv. 44–58); fourth, there is the promise of an everlasting covenant for a restored Jerusalem, which will include her sisters Sodom and Samaria (vv. 59–63).

Gile argues that the building blocks of Ezekiel 16 are found in the Song of Moses in Deuteronomy 32.[210] He outlines the similarities in terms of plot structure, thematic links, synonyms and shared motifs. In both Deuteronomy 32 and Ezekiel 16 YHWH discovers Israel and delivers them; they prosper, but then forsake YHWH in pursuit of other gods; YHWH is provoked to anger, and Israel is judged before ultimately being restored. Ezekiel uses the plot structure of the Song of Moses (Deut. 32) and actualizes it using the motif of harlotry to shocking rhetorical effect.[211] The allusions to Deuteronomy are also present

---

208. Wright, *Ezekiel*, p. 93.
209. Greenberg, *Ezekiel 1–20*, p. 292.
210. Jason Gile, 'Ezekiel 16 and the Song of Moses: A Prophetic Transformation?', *JBL* 130.1 (2011), pp. 87–108.
211. Ibid., p. 108.

in the judgment curses for covenant breaking spelled out in verses 35–43. As a whole the chapter depicts the graciousness of God, the sinfulness of Jerusalem, God's righteous anger and his determination to provide restoration through atonement.

The opening of the chapter sets the tone as Ezekiel is summoned to make known to Jerusalem her abominations. A number of scholars suggest that the form of the chapter is 'dispute' (*rîb*), with YHWH as plaintiff and prosecutor, and Israel as defenceless defendant.[212] Israel's infancy is recalled to throw their rebellion into stark relief. The Hebrew word *zōnâ* (prostitution) functions as a *Leitwort* for the chapter, occurring twenty-one times and depicting Israel's harlotry.[213] Jerusalem's origins, in Ezekiel's oracle, are not with Abraham and Sarah, but with the nations they were supposed to drive out during the conquest. Their covenantal compromise in the days of Joshua means that they owe more to the Canaanites, Amorites and Hittites for their current condition than they do the patriarchs. These nations, which symbolize rebellion against YHWH, are Israel's spiritual parents, who left them to die.[214] YHWH's intervention is thus life saving.[215] As Zimmerli puts it, 'Into this hopeless beginning Yahweh's pitying love has intervened.'[216]

In verses 8–14 protection becomes betrothal. A covenant is entered into and the bride is given the best provisions.[217] Galambush has noted that the terms used for the clothes and garments appear elsewhere only in the descriptions of the furnishings of the tabernacle and temple.[218] That suggests that the harlotry depicted is not purely political, but also religious. The adulterous relationships lead to idolatry and defile the people, temple and covenant. The bride became a queen and YHWH declares, 'your fame spread among the nations on account of your beauty, because the splendour I had given you made your beauty perfect'. Wright notes that Israel's international fame and beauty was for the purpose of enhancing YHWH's reputation among the nations. Further the

---

212. Walther Zimmerli, *Ezekiel 1*, Hermeneia (Philadelphia: Fortress, 1979), p. 336.

213. Block, *Ezekiel 1–24*, pp. 465–466.

214. Ibid., p. 475.

215. Meir Malul, 'Adoption of Foundlings in the Bible and Mesopotamian Documents: A Study of Some Legal Metaphors in Ezekiel 16:1–7', *JSOT* 46.1 (1990), pp. 97–126.

216. Zimmerli, *Ezekiel 1*, p. 339.

217. Greenberg notes that the covering of a woman with a garment expresses the acquiring of her. *Ezekiel 1–20*, p. 277.

218. Julie Galambush, *Jerusalem in the Book of Ezekiel: The City as Yahweh's Wife*, SBLDS 130 (Atlanta: Scholars Press, 1992), p. 95.

tabernacle/temple imagery is suggestive of Israel's priestly role to make YHWH known among the nations.[219]

The power of attraction is abused as Israel used her allure to sell herself to the surrounding nations (vv. 15–29). There is an escalation through the verses as Israel's abominations progress through adultery to child sacrifice to public promiscuity. Their place at the 'centre' of the nations (5:5) is being used to erect brothels in the public square.[220] Their hope was in the other nations rather than YHWH and the emphatic double 'woe' (v. 23) intensifies the horror at Jerusalem's harlotry. Israel is accused of being worse than a prostitute since she pays others to engage her (vv. 32–34).

Verses 35–43 proclaim the judgment: because of Israel's promiscuity, child sacrifice and idolatry, Israel will suffer the punishment of the adulteress – death by stoning (cf. Deut. 22). YHWH himself will enact the punishment and then the 'lovers' will come and strip Jerusalem and hack her to pieces (vv. 39–40). Election required covenant loyalty. Idolatry brought disgrace. Those at the centre are now scattered to the periphery.[221]

In verses 44–58 Jerusalem is compared to her sisters Sodom and Samaria. The connection with Samaria would not have surprised Ezekiel's audience, but the sisterhood of Sodom would have shocked the recipients. Sodom's sins are listed in verses 49–50 as arrogance, gluttony, complacency and social irresponsibility. It is possible that this list of sins mirrors in part Jerusalem's sins. Her ethical failure relates to her pride, complacency and neglect of social justice. Strikingly YHWH promises to restore Sodom and Samaria, and this theme is picked up in the final section of the oracle. Wright notes that similar Old Testament prophecies of restoration for named nations are not to be understood in a literal sense, but rather 'points to the extension of Israel to include the nations – a fulfilment that the New Testament describes through the Gentile mission of the church'.[222]

In the final section (vv. 59–63) YHWH promises to remember the covenant he made with Jerusalem in her youth, and to establish an eternal covenant with her. In all this 'it becomes quite clear that this promise for Jerusalem's future does not mean a superficial and hasty glossing over of the past under the impact of a miracle of social and architectural reconstruction in Jerusalem'.[223] It will take something far greater to restore Jerusalem and her sisters.

---

219. Wright, *Ezekiel*, pp. 134–136.

220. Block, *Ezekiel 1–24*, p. 494.

221. Zimmerli, *Ezekiel 1*, pp. 348–349.

222. Wright, *Ezekiel*, p. 152, n. 77.

223. Zimmerli, *Ezekiel 1*, p. 353.

Ezekiel 17

The imagery of the vine has already been used in Ezekiel 15 as an omen of judgment on Jerusalem. Here in chapter 17 that judgment is made more explicit, but only after Ezekiel has challenged his audience to interpret a riddle. Ezekiel's riddle speaks of two eagles and a vine and 'presupposes the conspiracy of Judah with Egypt and Zedekiah's defection from Babylonian overlordship'.[224] The eagle, a symbol of royalty, represents Babylon's earliest attacks on Jerusalem (vv. 12–13), when Nebuchadnezzar took Jehoiachin, along with some of the nobility, as captives back to Babylon (2 Kgs 24:10–17). Ezekiel 17:5 alludes to Zedekiah's installation as a puppet king in Jerusalem, prospering to some degree so long as he remains in subjection to the great eagle king of Babylon.[225] In verse 7 a second eagle is introduced into Ezekiel's riddle. The second eagle (v. 7) most likely refers to the Egyptian ruler Psammetichus II.[226] The second eagle is not described with the same grandiose terminology of the first, but surprisingly the vine (Zedekiah) now begins to stretch its roots towards this other 'eagle' for some kind of help or nourishment. In the light of these events Ezekiel invites his hearers in verse 9 to 'decide whether the conduct of the vine can be expected to prosper'.[227] As Block observes, 'by the time Ezekiel had finished telling the story, the sympathies of his hearers would undoubtedly have been on the side of the first eagle'.[228]

In verses 11–21 Ezekiel provides the interpretation of the fable. The king of Judah's political folly will have consequences for himself and the nation. The problem, as Ezekiel presents the allegory and interpretation, is covenant breaking. The king of Judah made a covenant treaty with the king of Babylon, which he subsequently broke. As a consequence of his infidelity he would incur Babylon's wrath.

In the penultimate section of Ezekiel's oracle (vv. 19–21) the message of the riddle is further revealed and applied. The introductory 'therefore' in verse 19 links Jerusalem's covenant infidelity towards Babylon to the covenant relationship between Judah and YHWH. Just as judgment follows the breaking of international covenants, so judgment is the inevitable consequence of breaking covenant with YHWH. The king of Babylon is not only acting in response to the

---

224. Ibid., p. 361.
225. Block, *Ezekiel 1–24*, p. 524.
226. Zimmerli argues that the setting and description best fits Psammetichus II. *Ezekiel 1*, p. 362.
227. Ibid., p. 363.
228. Block, *Ezekiel 1–24*, p. 532.

covenant Judah broke with him, but is also YHWH's agent of judgment for Judah's unfaithfulness to YHWH. Only at the end of the explanation can the audience appreciate the *double entendre*. For those among Ezekiel's audience familiar with the imagery of the eagle and the vine there is an allusion to YHWH's deliverance, covenant and blessing upon Israel, which outstripped anything Babylon or Egypt could offer (cf. Exod. 19:4; Deut. 32:11; Isa. 5:1–7). For those with ears to hear, the implications of Ezekiel's message begin to dawn. YHWH is the one who bought out the vine, cleared the ground and planted. The vine then took root and filled the land, sending out its boughs to the sea. The principal crime presented is not human folly in the international political arena, but rather infidelity to the covenant with *the* great Eagle. The riddle's ambiguity invites the hearer to reflect on its message on both the human and divine plane.[229] Their plight is not just before Nebuchadnezzar, but before YHWH.

The final section of Ezekiel's prophecy in chapter 17 offers hope of restoration. Ezekiel presents YHWH's promise that he will again take and plant his people on the mountain heights. This tree will bear fruit and the birds will find shelter in its branches. The other peoples and empires will know that this is a work of YHWH. Imagery of growing vines or trees is also applied to other nations besides Judah (cf. Ezek. 31:3–9), and it is clear in each case that YHWH causes the growth, and YHWH cuts them down for their wickedness. The unique promise to Jerusalem is restoration after judgment to new and greater heights. Bauckham notes that Ezekiel's vision of this giant tree has universal overtones; this is a 'mythological world-tree' whose roots run deep under the earth, whose branches reach to the heavens, and whose fruits are visible to the whole earth.[230] Additionally, planting the tree on a mountain speaks of security, visibility and fertility.[231] The lofty mountain is the locus of God's blessing to renew the whole world.[232] Eichrodt comments on these verses:

> The eyes of the nations are opened to the wonderful world-power of Yahweh which, by annihilation and revivification, by abasing and exalting, by the downfall of mighty empires and the establishment of an apparently quite devastated kingdom

229. Greenberg, *Ezekiel 1–20*, pp. 320–323.

230. Richard Bauckham, 'The Parable of the Vine: Rediscovering a Lost Parable of Jesus', *NTS* 33 (1987), pp. 87–90.

231. Robert L. Cohn, *The Shape of Sacred Space: Four Biblical Studies*, AARSR 23 (Chico, Calif.: Scholars Press, 1981), pp. 25–41.

232. 'Mountains', in Leland Ryken, James C. Wilhoit and Tremper Longman III, *Dictionary of Biblical Imagery* (Downers Grove: IVP Academic, 1998), p. 574.

to a position of world-wide significance, shows that the world-plan announced in his word is being carried out.[233]

This chapter, as with previous chapters examined, hints once more at the universal hope through this particular people. YHWH's ultimate purpose is to bless the nations through his chosen 'shoot'.[234]

Ezekiel 18

Joyce observes that Ezekiel 18 contains 'the most elaborate statement of the responsibility of Israel to be found in the book'.[235] If there remains any doubt, Ezekiel's disputation with his opponents makes clear that their plight is directly linked to their disobedience.[236] Block observes structurally that there are 'three strategically placed quotations of the popular opinion (vv. 2, 19, 25), each of which serves as a preface to a lengthy prophetic speech'.[237] The three inter-locutions provide the occasion for Ezekiel's disputation with his opponents.

Ezekiel begins his oracle by quoting a popular proverb. Lust argues that the proverb is most likely uttered by those who remain in the land and contest possession.[238] The inhabitants think it right that the children of those in exile should suffer, and therefore make claim to the land. They are, in Lust's words, 'convinced that the exilic people, including their children, forfeited their rights to the land. In their view, the children rightly suffer for the sins of their parents.'[239] In this context Ezekiel is refuting such a view of moral determinism by bringing a message of divine sovereignty over personal and corporate morality. Such a

---

233. Walther Eichrodt, *Ezekiel: A Commentary*, tr. Cosslett Quin, OTL (London: SCM, 1970), p. 229.

234. Similar themes of shoots, branches and trees (and their associated blessing for the nations) have been observed in Isa. 11 and Jer. 23 – 24.

235. Paul M. Joyce, *Divine Initiative and Human Response in Ezekiel*, JSOTSup 51 (Sheffield: Sheffield Academic Press, 1989), p. 61.

236. Matthies examines the genre of the passage and concludes it is best categorized as a disputation, though unique among disputations as offering repentance at the conclusion. Gordon H. Matthies, *Ezekiel 18 and the Rhetoric of Moral Discourse*, SBLDS 126 (Atlanta: Scholars Press, 1990), pp. 46–60.

237. Block, *Ezekiel 1–24*, p. 554.

238. Johan Lust, 'The Sour Grapes: Ezekiel 18', in *Scripture in Transition: Essays on Septuagint, Hebrew Bible, and Dead Sea Scrolls in Honour of Raija Sollamo*, JSJSup 126 (Leiden: Brill, 2008), pp. 233–234.

239. Ibid., pp. 236–237.

message challenges the opponents not only with regard to the exiles, but also in regard to their own perceived self-righteousness.

The notion of intergenerational responsibility originates in the Decalogue (cf. Exod. 20:5–6; Deut. 5:9–10) and was originally addressed to parents that they should guard their conduct. If this proverb is spoken by those remaining in the land as a claim to it, Ezekiel's words echo Deuteronomy 24:16: 'Parents are not to be put to death for their children, nor children put to death for their parents; each will die for their own sin.' This verse complements rather than contradicts the statement made in the Decalogue, for in the Decalogue the administrator of such justice is YHWH, whereas Deuteronomy 24:16 refers to human administration of the law. In other words, the proverb stemming from Deuteronomy 5 is being misapplied by the people in Ezekiel 18. Ezekiel does not reject the proverb, but rather the application of it by his interlocutors.

Ezekiel presents three almost identical catalogues of vice and virtue to illustrate three test cases relating to a man, his son and then his grandson. His cumulative argument builds to force agreement with his conclusion. Ezekiel's interest here in the socio-moral laws, suggests Greenberg, 'stems from the distinctively prophetic appreciation of them as the essence of God's requirement of Israel'.[240] If Deuteronomy spells out the ethical content of a life that wins the interest of the nations Ezekiel 18 provides the antithesis. Common to all three lists are eating at mountain shrines, defiling another's wife, exploitation of the needy, theft, idolatry and usury. These practices violate the basic ethic of love for God and love for neighbour.

The first list concerns the case of the righteous man who lives a virtuous life in regard to the Torah. The conclusion in verse 9 is that he shall live. The second case concerns the wicked son who is portrayed in antithetical terms to his father. His case is concluded with a rhetorical question, 'will such a man live?', in verse 13b. Ezekiel answers, 'He is to be put to death; his blood will be upon his own head.' In the third case Ezekiel introduces the grandson who reflects on the life of his father and lives instead like his grandfather. The conclusion is that he will surely live, and not die for his father's sin.

Verse 19 provides the second quotation of Ezekiel's interlocutors: 'Why does the son not share the guilt of his father?' If it is correct to view Ezekiel's opponents as those possessing the land, then Ezekiel is addressing their desire that those in exile should be viewed as receiving just punishment at YHWH's hand, and therefore the claim to the land is now theirs alone. Ezekiel, in response, demonstrates that in their zeal to apply Deuteronomy 5:9–10 they

---

240. Greenberg, *Ezekiel 1–20*, p. 347.

have overlooked Deuteronomy 24:16. YHWH takes no delight in the death of the wicked. Ezekiel rejects their 'deterministic notion of intergenerational accountability'.[241]

The third interjection appears in verse 25, where the people claim that YHWH's way is unjust, a charge that Ezekiel returns against them. It is not YHWH who is acting capriciously but the people in the land who seek and rejoice in the judgment on the exiles. It is the house of Israel whose way is out of order.

The final section of the oracle (vv. 30–32) calls the people to repent, rid themselves of their offences and get a new heart and a new spirit. Block observes that YHWH desires the people's obedience, and the use of 'heart' (*lēb*) and 'Spirit' (*rûaḥ*) demonstrates the fundamental nature of Israel's problem, a problem that will be addressed again in Ezekiel 36:26–27.[242]

Sakenfeld concludes, 'Here there is no "cheap grace"; repentance is seen in action, as the sample catalogues of behaviour in the earlier parts of the chapter make very plain.'[243] As Block says:

> Instead of theologizing about Yahweh's (mis)administration of justice, they need to repent of their rebellious ways and to reorder their lives according to *tôrâ*. The same *tôrâ* that determines the principles of divine judgment offers the only hope of escape and points the way to the future.[244]

The individualistic thread of the chapter points towards an important theme: a Torah-shaped community requires every individual to be shaped by Torah.[245] The restoration of Israel to their original calling will require personal transformation, as will be seen in Ezekiel 36 – 37. Matthies helpfully concludes his study of Ezekiel 18 as follows:

> Ezekiel 18 stands as a testimony to the liminal moment between Ezekiel's harsh announcements of judgment and bold eschatological vision . . . Its goal is the reconstitution of the peoplehood among whom the divine presence is known and made known through the integrity of character in the practice of justice and righteousness.[246]

---

241. Block, *Ezekiel 1–24*, p. 580.
242. Ibid., pp. 588–589.
243. Katharine Doob Sakenfeld, 'Ezekiel 18:25–32', *Int* 32.3 (1978), p. 299.
244. Block, *Ezekiel 1–24*, p. 557.
245. Matthies, *Ezekiel 18*, p. 158.
246. Ibid., p. 224.

The call to take responsibility, to repent and seek a new heart is a call back to the Torah-shaped way of life laid down in Deuteronomy.

Ezekiel 19

Ezekiel 19 employs two metaphors – a lioness and her cubs, and a vine and its branches/fruit – to portray the fate of a mother and her offspring. This overarching picture is itself a metaphor depicting Israel through recent generations. The use of the 'lament' (qînâ) in Ezekiel is noteworthy. This is the first occurrence in Ezekiel and it most often refers to the downfall of other nations and cities. Further, Ezekiel's lament here does not contain the usual elements of death or eulogy. This raises questions over the function of the lament in Ezekiel, which we shall return to after examining the chapter.

The structure of the lament falls into two sections relating to the two major metaphors and uses the 'once . . . now' formula to highlight past honour and present shame.[247] The opening verse of the lament summons the people to take up a lament concerning the princes of Israel and launches into the dominant theme – the former glory of their mother. The exact identity of 'your mother' (and her cubs) is debated. Ezekiel uses 'your mother' to refer both to the monarchy (Ezek. 23:2) and to the city of Jerusalem (Ezek. 16:44–45).[248] Identifying a particular individual from history is not necessary to understand Ezekiel's message.[249] The figure in view is likely a symbolic representation of both Jerusalem and her leaders.[250]

The first image of the lion is suggestive of royalty and power.[251] In verse 3 the cub grows, becomes strong and devours men. Whether this is expressive of mistreatment of others or simply a depiction of power is debatable.[252] When

---

247. Panc C. Beentjes, 'What a Lioness Was Your Mother: Reflections on Ezekiel 19', in *On Reading Prophetic Texts: Gender-Specific and Related Studies in Memory of Fokkelien van Dijk-Hemmes*, BIS 18 (Leiden: Brill, 1996), p. 23.

248. Ibid., p. 25.

249. Most commentators are confident to assert that the first cub refers to Jehoahaz (his mother being Hamutal) but are less confident regarding the second young lion, who could be Jehoiachin or Zedekiah. See Greenberg, *Ezekiel 1–20*, pp. 355–356.

250. See the evidence laid out in Beentjes, 'What a Lioness', pp. 26–29.

251. G. T. M. Prinsloo, 'Lions and Vines: The Imagery of Ezekiel 19 in the Light of Ancient Near-Eastern Descriptions and Depictions', *OTE* 12.2 (1999), pp. 339–346.

252. Zimmerli considers these descriptions as pictorial of 'awesome royal majesty'. *Ezekiel 1*, p. 395. However, Block considers the language to refer to the barbaric rules of Judah's kings (cf. 2 Kgs 24:4). *Ezekiel 1–24*, p. 605.

the nations hear about this lion (v. 4) they capture and transport him to Egypt. Then, in verse 5, the lioness, observing her frustrated hopes, produces another powerful lion that, like his predecessor, grows strong, tears prey and devours men. Verse 7 suggests that this lion was even more powerful than the first. Odell suggests that 'Ezekiel may be the first to accuse Jerusalem of being a terror not only to herself but to the other nations . . . the surrounding nations react to her with alarm.'[253] Yet again the lion is captured and taken away. Strikingly it is the nations who are the liberators in preventing the lion's predatory behaviour on the mountains of Israel.[254] With the two young lion-kings taken, the implications for the 'mother' are disquieting.[255]

The second image of the vine is likely drawn from the ANE picture of the *Weltenbaum* (world tree) or *Lebensbaum* (life tree) and communicates themes of order, life and prosperity.[256] The vine is described in similar terms to Ezekiel 17:5, 8 as being well watered and fruitful. Its branches are strong and its height great. However, in verses 12–14 the tree is uprooted by an unidentified assailant, and burned in a violent and catastrophic end. Carvalho argues that it is the 'mother' and her death which bind the two halves of the lament together.[257] While the lament may be making reference to particular individuals, it works on multiple levels such that the imagery can refer to Judah more generally. The overall point is clear – what once was is no more.

The purpose of the lament is less clear and requires reflection on the rhetoric of the riddle. The occasion of the riddle-lament appears to relate to the behaviour of Judah, and particularly their rulers. The sin for which the people suffer is not made explicit in the lament. It may relate to harsh treatment of others (vv. 3, 6–7) and it could refer to haughtiness (v. 11).[258] These are themes explicit elsewhere in Ezekiel but merely alluded to here. This behaviour provokes the fury of an unidentified power that utterly destroys them. This may refer to the nations or even Judah's own self-destruction, but the wider context of Ezekiel's prophecy makes YHWH the most likely executor of justice. Botha

---

253. Odell, *Ezekiel*, p. 239.

254. Block, *Ezekiel 1–24*, p. 603.

255. Zimmerli, *Ezekiel 1*, p. 396.

256. Prinsloo, 'Lions and Vines', pp. 346–351.

257. Corrine Carvalho, 'Putting the Mother Back in the Center: Metaphor and Multivalence in Ezekiel 19', in *Thus Says the Lord: Essays on the Former and Latter Prophets in Honor of Robert R. Wilson*, LHB/OTS 502 (New York: T&T Clark, 2009), pp. 212–213.

258. Greenberg, *Ezekiel 1–20*, p. 358.

suggests that the themes of honour and shame that run throughout Ezekiel 19 explain YHWH's fury: 'The only possible reason was that Israel's prominence among the nations made her self-assured and belligerent, thereby infringing on the honour of Yahweh.'[259] Already, in Ezekiel 5, Jerusalem's role at the centre of the nations has been emphasized, and repeatedly throughout the prophecy it is Judah's behaviour that dishonours YHWH's name among the nations. It is for the sake of his name that he comes to judge. Twice the 'nations' (*gôyîm*) are mentioned in Ezekiel 19 (vv. 4, 8) and implied therein is Judah's responsibility towards them.

The purpose of this unusual lament is to cause Judah to reflect and repent. Beentjes states that Ezekiel 19, unlike chapters 18 and 20, offers no hope of restoration. It simply ends with destruction.[260] Yet this fails to allow for the rhetorical effect envisaged in the communal liturgical recital of the *qînâ* (v. 14). The lament is to be taken up by those who are, in some sense, already dead. As Duguid notes, 'to conduct a "funeral service" for a still-living patient may not always be considered in the best of taste, but it is an effective way of communicating the certainty with which a death is anticipated'.[261] The use of lament to address those who are, in fact, still living means that rhetorically 'lament is transformed into accusation'.[262] This powerful and evocative dirge should cause the people to acknowledge their failure and to seek restoration. Carvalho's conclusion is helpful:

> Ezekiel 19 functions on three rhetorical levels. As a city lament sung while the city still stands, it functions as an oracle of condemnation . . . As a *qînâ* to be used in the future, as suggested by the end of the chapter, the text also functions as an oracle of restoration: that is, the form implies a function for the exilic audience of the book. As a text halfway between the scroll of lamentation and the final vision of the book, it reminds Israel of the choice laid before them.[263]

Their anti-witness through idolatry and social injustice will mean death, but death may not be the final word. YHWH's purpose to bless the nations through his chosen people is smouldering but not extinguished.

---

259. P. J. Botha, 'The Socio-Cultural Background of Ezekiel 19', *OTE* 12.2 (1999), p. 259.
260. Beentjes, 'What a Lioness', p. 21.
261. Iain M. Duguid, *Ezekiel*, NIVAC (Grand Rapids: Zondervan, 1999), p. 247.
262. Beentjes, 'What a Lioness', p. 22.
263. Carvalho, 'Putting the Mother Back', p. 221.

Ezekiel 20

Ezekiel 20 begins with the elders approaching Ezekiel, presumably for a hopeful word regarding a return to Jerusalem after seven years in exile. Ezekiel's reply is that YHWH will not allow them to enquire of him, and Ezekiel recounts Israel's history to show why. Block categorizes the genre of Ezekiel 20 as a parody:

> With painstaking precision, incontrovertible logic, and deliberate skewing and
> distorting of the sacred traditions, Ezekiel turns his people's history on its head.
> Employing ancient theological and historical motifs but infusing them with new
> content he calls his audience to critical self-evaluation.[264]

A number of structural outlines have been proposed for Ezekiel 20.[265] Patton suggests that the first half of the chapter (vv. 1–29) follows the exodus-narrative pattern of sojourn (vv. 5–8), deliverance (vv. 9–10), wilderness (vv. 10–25) and entry into the land (vv. 26–29).[266] The second half of the chapter (vv. 30–44) looks forward to a day that will provide restoration through judgment.

The first half of the chapter recounts three cycles of deliverance and rebellion with the 'exile' being the climactic word in verses 23–26. Ezekiel is clearly familiar with the Deuteronomic thinking and uses the exodus narrative to conduct a review focusing not primarily on YHWH's mighty acts of deliverance but rather on the pervasiveness of Israel's sin.[267] Noting the use of Deuteronomistic vocabulary throughout the chapter Block states:

> Ezekiel's use of this vocabulary is intentionally polemical, replacing the
> Deuteronomist's vision of hope . . . with a picture of persistent idolatry from
> the nation's earliest beginnings. If the desert had represented a place of divine
> judgment in the past, the same is true of the diaspora in the present . . . hope
> is to be found only in a new creative act of God.[268]

Patton notes that, as a historical review, it matches the historical review material found in Deuteronomy 1 – 11, though uses such a review for different purposes.

---

264. Block, *Ezekiel 1–24*, pp. 613–614.
265. See Leslie C. Allen, 'The Structuring of Ezekiel's Revisionist History Lesson', *CBQ* 54 (1992), pp. 448–462.
266. Corrine Patton, '"I Myself Gave Them Laws That Were Not Good": Ezekiel 20 and the Exodus Traditions', *JSOT* 69 (1996), pp. 73–74.
267. Ibid., p. 75.
268. Block, *Ezekiel 1–24*, p. 615.

Rather than looking forward to future obedience, it looks back over generations of rebellion.[269]

The first cycle (vv. 4–9) records the exodus from Egypt, and the call to rid themselves of Egypt's idols (vv. 4–7). But in verse 8 we hear that the people rebelled and would not rid themselves of those idols. As a result God determines to judge the people but relents for the sake of his name in the sight of the surrounding nations.

The second cycle (vv. 10–17) brings the people to the foot of Mount Sinai, where YHWH again presents the people with his righteous requirements. Ezekiel repeatedly emphasizes the Sabbaths as divine gifts designed to be a reminder of YHWH's deliverance and covenant.[270] Again the people rebel and reject the law, incurring YHWH's wrath, which he again restrains for the sake of his name in the eyes of the nations. Yet because of the people's idolatry they are prevented from entering the land until the rebellious generation has died out. A consistent theme through the chapter is rebellion in the form of idolatry and Sabbath desecration. The rejection of idolatry was the first and most basic commandment, spelled out in Deuteronomy 6 – 11, and here is a hint that their idolatry took a liturgical form, both influenced, and perhaps witnessed, by the nations.

The third cycle (vv. 18–26) addresses the children of the wilderness generation, calling them to forsake idols and follow YHWH's decrees and statutes. The children, like their parents, rebelled. YHWH again determined to judge them yet withheld his hand of judgment for the sake of his name among the nations. Instead there would come a day when they would be dispersed among the nations as judgment upon their rebellion. There is debate around the meaning of verses 25–26, which refer to YHWH's giving the people statutes that were 'not good'. Hahn and Bergsma think this refers to aspects of the Deuteronomic code that were being misused; though it seems more likely, in context, to see these laws as being those the other nations follow.[271] In verse 23 YHWH swears to disperse the people among the nations; in verses 25–26 he gives them over to laws that are defiling and involve sacrifice of the firstborn; and the result in verse 26 will be that the people will be horrified and recognize YHWH as Lord. Ezekiel's rhetorical point is that YHWH is sovereign even over

---

269. Patton, 'I Myself Gave Them Laws', p. 75.

270. Block, *Ezekiel 1–24*, p. 632.

271. Scott W. Hahn and John Sietze Bergsma, 'What Laws Were "Not Good"? A Canonical Approach to the Theological Problem of Ezekiel 20:25–26', *JBL* 123.2 (2004), pp. 201–218.

Israel's desire to follow pagan laws. YHWH wants to show his people the contrast between the destructive laws of the nations (v. 26) and his own life-giving laws (vv. 11, 13).[272]

The conclusion of verses 27–29 answers the request of verse 1: YHWH will not respond to those who continue in the present that which has been repeatedly condemned in the past.[273] In verse 30 the prophecy begins to turn towards themes of restoration already seen in Ezekiel's previous oracles. The cyclical nature of Israel's rebellion is not fated to continue *ad infinitum*: YHWH will make a way out.[274] The desire to be 'as the nations' in their polytheism will not be allowed to continue. The motif of the new exodus comes in verse 33 with the promise that YHWH will rule over his people 'with a mighty hand and an out-stretched arm'.[275] Judgment followed by a new-exodus restoration must occur for the sake of YHWH's name among the nations. Ezekiel prophesies a day when the people of YHWH will no longer profane his holy name – YHWH will show himself holy among the people, in the sight of the nations (vv. 39–41). As Blenkinsopp notes, 'To speak of the name in this context is to say that Israel exists not for itself but to fulfil the divine purpose in history. That is why Israel must on all occasions sanctify the name.'[276] Verses 39–40 tell the reader what that will look like among the restored people. They will no longer offer false worship to idols, and will instead bring acceptable offerings, gifts and sacrifices.

Ezekiel 20 presents one of the clearest diagnoses of the reason for Judah's exile. Idolatry is the fundamental problem, and it expresses itself in wrong forms of worship, which in turn are an 'anti-witness' to YHWH in the sight of the nations. Equally clear in the chapter is YHWH's desire for his own reputation among the surrounding nations. It is 'for the sake of my name in the sight of the nations' (vv. 9, 14, 22) that he holds back judgment before eventually acting in both judgment and restoration. YHWH's people are revelatory agents and their idolatry has served as an anti-witness to YHWH in the eyes of the nations. YHWH will act to ensure that his chosen people manifest his holiness to outsiders. Particular election is for a universal purpose, and that purpose is that YHWH's

---

272. Ellen F. Davis, *Swallowing the Scroll: Textuality and the Dynamics of Discourse in Ezekiel's Prophecy*, BLS 21 (Sheffield: Sheffield Academic Press, 1989), p. 114.

273. Greenberg, *Ezekiel 1–20*, p. 376.

274. Contra Eslinger who sees no end to the cyclical theme within Ezek. 20. Lyle Eslinger, 'Ezekiel 20 and the Metaphor of Historical Teleology: Concepts of Biblical History', *JSOT* 81 (1998), pp. 116–118.

275. Ibid., p. 101.

276. Joseph Blenkinsopp, *Ezekiel*, Int (Louisville: John Knox, 1990), p. 88.

name may be made known through the religious – missional – ethics of the believing community.

Ezekiel 36

Following the prophecy of punishment on Mount Seir (ch. 35), chapters 36–37 offer (along with 40–48) the greatest visions of restoration for Israel. Chapter 36 begins with a prophecy of restoration for the mountains of Israel (v. 1).[277] The promise begins with the fate of the surrounding nations that sought to plunder the land of Israel. Since the land has suffered scorn, YHWH will act in retribution (vv. 4–7). Once the enemies of the land have been dealt with the land will again bear fruit, be sown and ploughed, and be inhabited (vv. 8–12). The reference to increase and fruitfulness (wĕrābû ûpārû, v. 11) echoes Genesis 1:22, 28, but this time the land will not reject or deprive its inhabitants.[278] It is the first time that Ezekiel's oracles have addressed the land in a personal fashion.[279] Addressing the land recalls the promises made to Abraham and his descendants: the people of Israel were to be YHWH's own people, blessed by him and possessing a land given by him. The rebellion of Israel against YHWH has meant forfeiture of all three elements – relationship, blessing and land. YHWH has left the temple, the people experience judgment instead of blessing and have been taken from the land. The renewal envisaged by Ezekiel necessitates the reformation of all three elements.

In verses 16–23 Ezekiel declares the twofold reason for YHWH's judgment on his people. First there is the now familiar double sin of injustice and idolatry (v. 18), and second they had profaned the name of YHWH among the nations (v. 20). It is primarily for the sake of YHWH's own name that he acts to restore his people.

A consequence of their restoration is that 'the nations will know that I am the LORD, declares the Sovereign LORD, when I am proved holy through you before their eyes' (v. 23b). Verses 24–38 provide the explanation of what is meant by verse 23. YHWH will gather his people, sprinkle and cleanse them from false worship. Israel has been likened to a woman considered unclean (v. 17), but now, having been made pure again, she may return to the presence of her husband (v. 25).[280] Profanation gives way to sanctification so that the light for the

---

277. Moshe Greenberg, *Ezekiel 21–37*, AB 23 (New Haven: Yale University Press, 2007), p. 717.

278. Daniel I. Block, *The Book of Ezekiel: Chapters 25–48*, NICOT (Grand Rapids: Eerdmans, 1998), p. 334.

279. Block, *Chapters 25–48*, p. 327.

280. Greenberg, *Ezekiel 21–37*, p. 728.

nations comes *through* Israel.[281] The people will receive a new heart and a new spirit. Joyce suggests that the 'heart' (*lēb*) in Ezekiel refers to the 'locus of the moral will' and a 'symbol of inner reality as distinct from more outward appearance'.[282] Robson, examining the term 'Spirit' (*rûaḥ*), suggests that it refers to the animating 'driving force' of applied understanding.[283] This suggests more than merely the capacity to respond; it suggests that YHWH himself will move the people to follow his decrees and be careful to keep his laws.[284] The phraseology is reminiscent of Deuteronomy. Moral renewal will serve to protect and proclaim the name of YHWH to the surrounding nations.[285] Although the word 'covenant' is not explicitly used here the phrase 'you will be my people, and I will be your God' is a covenantal formula. Robson states, 'What Jeremiah sees as achieved by Yahweh writing the Torah on the heart (Jer. 31:33), what Deuteronomy ascribes to Yahweh circumcising the heart (Deut. 30:6–8), Ezekiel ascribes to the giving of the divine רוּחַ.'[286] Greenberg observes the major themes of the restoration oracles as being gathering, cleansing, implanting (a new heart), settling and multiplying, with a return to Eden as the *telos* (v. 35).[287] As a result Israel and the nations will know that YHWH is the true Lord.[288] Wright suggests that the 'they' of verse 38 should probably be taken to include all observers – Israel *and* the nations.[289] A combination of cultic renewal, moral renewal and the consequent prosperity of the place serve to demonstrate the holiness of YHWH. This is a vision for missional ethics. Launderville's conclusion is as follows:

> In Ezekiel's view, the primary way to understand the character of sovereign power in the cosmos was to observe living symbols of the personal reality that ruled the cosmos … Yhwh's Spirit in the Israelites would enable them to be obedient and thus to send a true picture of what Yhwh is like through their collective existence.[290]

---

281. Eichrodt, *Ezekiel*, p. 495.

282. Joyce, *Divine Initiative*, pp. 108–109.

283. James Robson, *Word and Spirit in Ezekiel*, LHB/OTS 447 (London: T&T Clark, 2006), p. 252.

284. Ibid.

285. Joyce, *Ezekiel*, p. 205.

286. Robson, *Word and Spirit*, p. 262.

287. Greenberg, *Ezekiel 21–37*, p. 734.

288. Walther Zimmerli, *Ezekiel 2*, Hermeneia (Philadelphia: Fortress, 1979), p. 251.

289. Wright, *Ezekiel*, p. 303.

290. Dale F. Launderville, *Spirit and Reason: The Embodied Character of Ezekiel's Symbolic Thinking* (Waco: Baylor University Press, 2007), p. 381.

Ezekiel 37

Ezekiel 37:1–14 reaches 'a new and dramatic height'.[291] As with chapter 36 'Spirit' (*rûaḥ*) is a *Leitwort* of the chapter, occurring ten times, and it is the 'Spirit of YHWH' who leads Ezekiel to his vision of the valley of dry bones.[292] The vision of an ancient battlefield expresses the horror at the fate of the deceased.[293] The bones are many and described as 'very dry'. These are not the remains of the recently deceased. Life is long gone, making YHWH's question to Ezekiel in verse 3 appear ridiculous. Ezekiel's response suggests that he is aware that with God nothing is as straightforward as it appears. In verse 4 Ezekiel is commanded to prophesy to the bones. The word of YHWH is that he will put *rûaḥ* into the bones and make them live. Bones and tendons and flesh will reverse the process of decay in a process of recreation or new creation animated by YHWH's *rûaḥ*. As Ezekiel begins to prophesy (v. 7) the bones come together, tendons and flesh clothe the skeletons, but there is, as yet, no breath in them. The two-stage process heightens the drama and brings the focus onto the *rûaḥ*.[294] In verse 9 Ezekiel is commanded twice to prophesy to the *rûaḥ* to come and animate the bones, further expressing urgency and tension.[295] The scene is an echo of Genesis 2:7.[296] Here we have a new Israel, animated by the *rûaḥ* of YHWH. The valley of death may become a garden of life again.[297] A vast army rises, and the explanation is given in verses 11–14.

Block suggests that the valley of dry bones represents those from the house of Israel slain by Nebuchadnezzar's army. The reason for their lack of burial is bound up with the covenant curses of Deuteronomy 28:25–26.[298] In verses 11–14 YHWH explains what the vision refers to: it is a metaphor for the experience of Israel in exile – those who lament, 'Our bones are dried up and our

---

291. Block, *Chapters 25–48*, p. 372.

292. Ibid., p. 373.

293. Greenberg, *Ezekiel 21–37*, p. 748.

294. Block, *Chapters 25–48*, p. 377.

295. Greenberg, *Ezekiel 21–37*, p. 744.

296. For links between Ezek. 37 and Gen. 2 see John F. Kutsko, *Between Heaven and Earth: Divine Presence and Absence in the Book of Ezekiel*, Biblical and Judaic Studies 7 (Winona Lake: Eisenbrauns, 2000), pp. 129–134.

297. Christopher R. Seitz, 'Ezekiel 37:1–14', *Int* 46 (1992), p. 53.

298. Block, *Chapters 25–48*, pp. 377–378. So too F. Charles Fensham, 'The Curse of the Dry Bones in Ezekiel 37:1–14 Changed to a Blessing of Resurrection', *JNSL* 13 (1987), pp. 59–60.

hope is gone; we are cut off' (v. 11). The vision refers not to the physically slain in Judah, but the whole house of Israel living in exile.[299] The promise of verse 14 then refers not to a final physical resurrection for those slaughtered by Nebuchadnezzar's forces; rather it refers to the restoration of YHWH's people who are, in a metaphorical sense, dead, and require YHWH's *rûaḥ* to make them alive. In Ezekiel 36 – 37 we have observed repeatedly the crucial role of the Spirit in the renewal of Israel.[300] Ezekiel's vision of the dry bones is a picture of what Lapsley calls 'inherent human incapacity'.[301] There is a need for 'total transformation by God, who graciously provides a new moral nature capable of obeying the divine commandments'.[302]

In verses 15–28 a new sign act that develops the theme of restoration takes place. Ezekiel is commanded to take two sticks and inscribe them with the names pertaining to the southern and northern kingdoms. He is then to join them together in an act that will cause his fellow countrymen to ask the meaning of the action. The pieces of wood may refer to vines, shepherds' staffs, sceptres or writing tablets.[303] The referent is ambiguous, but the interpretation from YHWH in verses 21–23 is clear: YHWH himself will gather his people and unite them again as one nation with one king. Perhaps unexpectedly the reunification of the nation will not only include unity in terms of ethnicity, territory and government, but will also involve religious unity, purity and cleansing. The restored people will no longer worship idols; they will be cleansed, and, in a repeat of the covenant formula of 11:20 and 14:11, YHWH declares that 'They will be my people, and I will be their God' (v. 23). The resanctification of land and people is a prerequisite to YHWH's returning to his sanctuary.[304]

---

299. Sabine van den Eynde, 'Interpreting "Can These Bones Come Back to Life?" in Ezekiel 37:3: The Technique of Hiding Knowledge', *OTE* 14.1 (2001), p. 162.

300. Greenberg, *Ezekiel 21–37*, p. 749.

301. Jacqueline E. Lapsley, *Can These Bones Live? The Problem of the Moral Self in the Book of Ezekiel*, BZAW 301 (Berlin: de Gruyter, 2000), p. 106.

302. Ibid.

303. See the discussion in Block, *Chapters 25–48*, pp. 397–406. Connections between Ezekiel's 'sticks' and the vines of Ezek. 15, 17, 19 are under-developed. It is possible that Ezekiel is taking shoots and grafting them into one – an image that would resonate with vine imagery used elsewhere in Scripture.

304. Marvin A. Sweeney, 'The Royal Oracle in Ezekiel 37:15–28: Ezekiel's Reflection on Josiah's Reform', in *Israel's Prophets and Israel's Past: Essays on the Relationship of Prophetic Texts and Israelite History in Honor of John H. Hayes*, LHB/OTS 446 (New York: T&T Clark, 2006), p. 240.

The final section (vv. 24–28) presents an even more glorious picture of Israel's future, using images from their past. A Davidic king will rule over an undivided kingdom; the people will keep YHWH's laws and decrees; they will inhabit the land promised to the patriarchs in perpetuity; an eternal covenant will be established; and YHWH will be in the midst of his people again. Duguid notes that the Davidic king in Ezekiel 37 is the same as the shepherd of Ezekiel 34. Here is a ruler who will deal with the failure of godly leadership by bringing a 'continuing state of righteous rule'.[305] And then in verse 28 is the conclusion of this work of YHWH: 'Then the nations will know that I the LORD make Israel holy, when my sanctuary is among them for ever.' As elsewhere in Ezekiel YHWH's reputation among the nations is of prime importance. He will establish that reputation through a restored Israel's inhabiting God's place, under the leadership of the Davidic king, living lives of obedience and true worship. The failure of Ezekiel 5:5 will be remedied only when YHWH cleanses and empowers his people with his *rûaḥ*.[306]

Summary

Ezekiel reaffirms the Deuteronomic vision that Israel were commissioned to witness to the nations concerning YHWH through a Torah-shaped life. Ezekiel reminded the people that they had been set in the centre of the nations (ch. 5) to be a living exhibit of the glory of YHWH. His chosen people were to be the vine (chs. 15, 17, 19) – the *Lebensbaum* or *Weltenbaum* – to spread, influence and provide blessing for the surrounding nations. Yet Israel failed to live out a missional ethic. Their idolatry and injustice is graphically portrayed (chs. 16–20) and is the reason for the departure of YHWH's glory from the temple. Israel's behaviour blasphemed YHWH's name among the nations (20:9, 14, 22; 36:20–23). However, YHWH will not abandon his plan to make his name known among the nations through his chosen people. He will restore Israel, granting new hearts, a new spirit and new life, with the Davidic king ruling and shepherding his people (chs. 36–37). YHWH's people will be enabled and equipped to follow his decrees and statutes, and, as they do so, will bear positive witness to the name of YHWH (36:24–38; 37:24–28).

---

305. Iain M. Duguid, *Ezekiel and the Leaders of Israel*, VTSup 56 (Leiden: Brill, 1994), p. 49.
306. Eichrodt, *Ezekiel*, p. 515.

Conclusion

The Major Prophets provide an insight into Israel's vocation, failure and hope. All three frame their critique in Deuteronomic terms; all three identify Israel's problem in terms of idolatry and injustice; all three note Israel's vocation to mediate YHWH's blessing to the nations; all three look forward to the redemption and restoration of Israel; and all three share a vision for a Davidic king who will restore and transform the people, with universal implications.

The *telos* of YHWH's restorative action is the creation of a community that effectively bears authentic witness to YHWH. That witness is described in the Major Prophets in terms of true worship and the promotion of justice; in terms of cultic reform and care for the widow, orphan and alien; and, in short, in the terms of the Deuteronomic summary of love for God and love for neighbour. What the Major Prophets lament in the absence of that witness, and promise in the eschaton, is the communal living out of a missional ethic. We turn now to the New Testament to chart the beginning of the end of that story.

4. MISSIONAL ETHICS IN LUKE–ACTS

Introduction

As we consider the canonical trajectory of the theme of missional ethics, Luke–Acts lends itself as a text for consideration. Recall Hays's description of Luke's narrative world as 'thick with scriptural memory'.[1] He states:

> [Luke's] vision allows for a comprehensive appropriation of the things about Jesus 'in all the scriptures' . . . He shows Jesus to be precisely the Lord of Israel who passionately seeks the redemption of the poor and downtrodden. And he also shows how the mission to the Gentiles is the outworking of God's longstanding plan for Israel as a light to the nations.[2]

In chapter 1 we noted Hays's outline of Luke's three distinctive emphases. These were his concern with the fulfilment of the plan of God, God's plan of salvation beyond the borders of Israel and Luke's concern for the poor and marginalized.

---

1. Richard B. Hays, *Reading Backwards: Figural Christology and the Fourfold Gospel Witness* (London: SPCK, 2015), p. 59.
2. Ibid., p. 100.

These three Lukan distinctives together provide a case for the consideration of Luke–Acts in the canonical narrative trajectory of the theme of missional ethics. This chapter will include examination of Luke 1 – 4, 6, themes within the travel narrative (chs. 11–19), and Luke 19 – 24. In Acts most space will be given to Acts 1 – 6, as these chapters set the pattern for the believing community's life beyond Jerusalem.

Luke's Gospel

Luke 1 – 2

Bock suggests that Luke's opening chapters serve as an overture giving a theological overview of the whole of Luke–Acts, and contain all the main themes and emphases.[3] Luke's opening words demonstrate his central concern: 'the things that have been fulfilled [*peplērophorēmenōn*] among us'.[4] The events do not stand alone but must rather be understood in terms of an 'antecedent web of activity'.[5] Luke is concerned to demonstrate 'that this "new" story, the story of Jesus, joins the "old" scriptural story as its ongoing manifestation and, indeed, as the realization of God's ancient plan'.[6] Luke aims to persuade the reader that in Jesus the promises made to Abraham, David and the nation as a whole regarding their post-exilic redemption and restoration have come to fulfilment.

Following Luke's prologue (1:1–4) his account begins with Zechariah and Elizabeth who, Luke notes, are 'righteous in the sight of God, observing all the Lord's commands and decrees blamelessly' (Luke 1:6). At the outset of Luke's narrative he presents two model Israelites through whom God will prepare a people (1:17). Yet Elizabeth is barren, paving the way for a reprise of Old Testament stories of miraculous conception linked to God's salvation.[7] The

---

3. Darrell L. Bock, *Luke 1:1–9:50*, BECNT (Grand Rapids: Baker, 1994), p. 69.

4. Fitzmyer notes Luke's repeated use of 'fulfilment' language related to OT prophecy. For *plēroō* see Luke 1:20; 24:44. For *pimplēmi* see Luke 21:22. Joseph A. Fitzmyer, *The Gospel According to Luke I–IX*, AB 28 (New York: Doubleday, 1981), p. 293.

5. Joel B. Green, *The Theology of the Gospel of Luke*, New Testament Theology (Cambridge: Cambridge University Press, 1995), p. 30.

6. Ibid.

7. For example, Abraham and Sarah (Gen. 17:16), Jacob and Rachel (Gen. 30:22–24), Manoah and his wife (Judg. 13:3–25), Elkanah and Hannah (1 Sam. 1:1–20). David E. Garland, *Luke*, ECNT 3 (Grand Rapids: Zondervan, 2011), p. 65.

announcement is given to Zechariah that his wife will bear a son who will be a prophet like Elijah. The wording of Luke 1:17 echoes Malachi 4:5–6, which refers to an Elijah figure who will prepare the way for Israel's restoration.[8]

A second angelic announcement is given to Mary that she will bear a child who, in echoes of Isaiah 7:14 and 9:6–7, will be called the Son of the Most High, and will sit on David's throne to rule over a perpetual kingdom (1:32–33). Rowe notes that the word *kyrios* (lord) occurs twenty-five times in the infancy narratives.[9] The majority of these instances refer to God, but, significantly, two refer directly to Jesus. The first occurs in Luke 1:43 where, on Mary's arrival at Elizabeth's house, Elizabeth exclaims, 'why am I so favoured, that the mother of my Lord should come to me?'

Mary's Magnificat 'declares with exultant joy that God the Saviour has acted decisively for Israel. This decisive help is best explained as the coming of Jesus Christ.'[10] The hymn closes with allusion to the Abrahamic promises, implying that some kind of fulfilment is at hand (1:55).[11] Strauss notes that Mary, having been promised that she will give birth to the son of David (1:32–33), praises God for fulfilling his promise to Abraham.[12] The promised blessing, as the fulfilment of the Abrahamic promise, will extend not just to Israel but to all the peoples of the earth.[13] Abraham and David are brought together to emphasize that Jesus is the fulfilment of the entire Old Testament story.[14] Strauss concludes, 'Luke places the fulfilment of the promise to David at the heart of his promise–fulfilment scheme – not in isolation, but as the epitome and summation of the promises, oaths and covenants which God made to his people.'[15]

Zechariah's Benedictus also picks up on the theme of prophecy and fulfilment. He interprets the miraculous events as meaning that God has come to redeem; he has raised up a horn of salvation for us in the house of his servant

---

8. Bock, *Luke 1:1–9:50*, p. 99.

9. C. Kavin Rowe, *Early Narrative Christology: The Lord in the Gospel of Luke*, BZNW 139 (Berlin: de Gruyter, 2006), p. 31.

10. Stephen Farris, *The Hymns of Luke's Infancy Narratives: Their Origin, Meaning and Significance*, JSNTSup 9 (Sheffield: JSOT Press, 1985), p. 126.

11. Ibid., p. 126.

12. Mark L. Strauss, *The Davidic Messiah in Luke–Acts: The Promise and Its Fulfillment in Lukan Christology*, JSNTSup 110 (Sheffield: Sheffield Academic Press, 1995), p. 97.

13. Garland, *Luke*, p. 96.

14. Nils A. Dahl, 'The Story of Abraham in Luke–Acts', in *Studies in Luke–Acts* (Nashville: Abingdon, 1966), pp. 139–158; Strauss, *Davidic Messiah*.

15. Strauss, *Davidic Messiah*, p. 97.

David, as promised by the prophets; and has remembered his covenant with Abraham (1:68–75). The covenants with Abraham and David feature heavily in the promises of the Major Prophets with the new exodus also to the fore. For Luke, Jesus is the fulfilment of all of these promises. Additionally, in the final verse of Zechariah's Benedictus (v. 79), the theme of light shining in darkness echoes Isaiah 58:8 and 60:1,[16] and the way of peace alludes to Isaiah 59:8.[17]

Luke's interest in the fulfilment of Old Testament prophecy continues into chapter 2, where he notes that Jesus was born in Bethlehem, the town of David (2:4–7). An angel appears to the shepherds to announce the birth of a Saviour who is the Messiah, the Lord (Luke 2:11). The annunciation, the Benedictus and the birth narrative all explicitly connect the Davidic Messiah to the infant Jesus, leading Strauss to suggest that 'Davidic messiahship represents the controlling Christology of Luke's introductory scene.'[18] Also here is the second occurrence of the word *kyrios* referring directly to Jesus. Luke's use of *kyrios* to refer to both God and Jesus binds them together in a shared identity.[19]

When Jesus is presented at the temple Luke introduces two more characters – Simeon and Anna. Simeon, like Zechariah and Elizabeth, is 'righteous and devout' and is awaiting the consolation of Israel, having been promised that he would see the Messiah before he died (2:25–27).[20] Simeon is the sixth person in the opening two chapters who is described as filled or empowered by the Holy Spirit (2:25–27).[21] This 'enabling presence' of the Spirit echoes the prophetic promises concerning Israel's restoration in Isaiah 59:21, Jeremiah 31:31–34 and Ezekiel 36:26–27.[22] When Simeon sees Jesus he praises God in words reminiscent of Isaiah 49:6:

> my eyes have seen your salvation,
>   which you have prepared in the sight of all nations:
> a light for revelation to the Gentiles,
>   and the glory of your people Israel.
>
> (2:30–32)

---

16. Garland, *Luke*, p. 108.
17. Fitzmyer, *Luke I–IX*, p. 388.
18. Strauss, *Davidic Messiah*, p. 123.
19. Rowe, *Early Narrative Christology*, p. 27.
20. Fitzmyer notes the connection between Simeon's awaited 'consolation' (*paraklēsin tou Israēl*) and the LXX of Isa. 40:1 (*parakaleite parakaleite ton laon*). *Luke I–IX*, p. 427.
21. Cf. Jesus, 1:15; Mary, 1:35; Elizabeth, 1:41–42; Zechariah, 1:67; John, 1:80.
22. Green, *Gospel of Luke*, pp. 41–47.

Like Mary's Magnificat and Zechariah's Bendictus, Simeon's Nunc Dimittis asserts that God has acted decisively for Israel's salvation in fulfilment of his promise. The Nunc Dimittis adds a new theme introducing Gentiles as recipients of blessing.[23] Luke's major concern in his opening two chapters is with the redemption of Israel, and both John and Jesus will play a crucial role.[24] Anna too gave thanks to God and 'spoke about the child to all who were looking forward to the redemption of Jerusalem' (2:38). Bovon suggests that the word *lytrōsis* (redemption) possesses salvation-historical, legal and cultic dimensions.[25] It is a holistic vision of redemption.

In case the readers were slow to comprehend Luke's intention, his opening chapters close with an account of Jesus as an adolescent at the temple who, when found by his parents, explains 'I had to be in my Father's house' (2:49). The climax of Luke's introduction sets the scene for that which is to follow, with Jesus' self-identification as God's son.[26]

It is evident that Luke understands the events around the birth of Jesus as the fulfilment of Old Testament messianic prophecies concerning the restoration of Israel. As Schweizer states, 'the eschatological coming of God is thus identified with the coming of Jesus'.[27] At the centre of the action is worship, ethics and the Spirit. The action occurs in and around the temple. Minear notes the prevalence of liturgical practice and the emphasis on worship, fasting, prayer, joy and peace.[28] The liturgical life of the people is important for Luke. The characters involved are depicted as righteous, blameless or devout. And the Spirit is at work in and among the central characters. Further, at the outset Luke has made it clear that this redemption will include the Gentiles. Mission, ethics (including worship), the Spirit and a Messiah-Saviour all pick up on the themes explored in the previous chapters on missional ethics in the Old Testament. This is the inauguration of the new exodus in fulfilment of the

---

23. Farris, *Hymns*, p. 150.

24. David Ravens, *Luke and the Restoration of Israel*, JSNTSup 119 (Sheffield: Sheffield Academic Press, 1995), p. 50.

25. See Isa. 43:3–4; 45:14; 49:26; 54:1–8. François Bovon, *Das Evangelium nach Lukas*, 4 vols., EKK 3 (Zürich: Benziger Verlag, 1989), vol. 1, p. 149.

26. Mark Coleridge, *The Birth of the Lukan Narrative: Narrative as Christology in Luke 1–2*, JSNTSup 88 (Sheffield: JSOT Press, 1993), p. 213.

27. Eduard Schweizer, *The Good News According to Luke* (Atlanta: John Knox, 1984), p. 65.

28. Paul S. Minear, 'Luke's Use of the Birth Stories', in *Studies in Luke–Acts* (Nashville: Abingdon, 1966), p. 116.

ancient prophecies. Luke is going to chart *inter alia* the inaugurated fulfilment of the covenant community's missio-ethical vocation.

Luke 3 – 4

Luke 1 – 2 narrated the prophecies and births of John the Baptist and Jesus. Luke 3 – 4 narrates the birth of their respective ministries beginning, as in Luke 1 – 2, with John. He appears in the wilderness preaching a baptism of repentance for the forgiveness of sins (Luke 3:3). John's ministry commences with his quotation of Isaiah 40:3–5, a poignant and significant quotation concerned with consolation and restoration. Understood in its broader context it speaks of the new exodus (cf. Isa. 42:13; 43:16–19; 48:21; 52:12).[29] John is claiming that the fulfilment of that which Isaiah foresaw is now at hand. Noteworthy is John's application of his message of repentance (vv. 3, 10–14). When the crowd enquire as to how they should respond John replies in terms of the sharing of goods, and financial integrity and contentment. John's 'repentance' bears practical ethical implications.[30] The children of Abraham were supposed to bring forth fruit (v. 8).[31] As Bock states, 'true repentance responds to God and treats fellow humans justly . . . a concern for him [God] is expressed through concern for others'.[32] Indeed it is the force of John's ethical message that results in his imprisonment (3:19–20). The crowds understand the significance of John's message and wonder if he is the Messiah, a claim he is quick to correct, alluding instead to one who is to follow (3:15–18).

This leads to the baptism and genealogy of Jesus (3:21–38). Luke notes the presence of the Holy Spirit and the heavenly voice identifying Jesus as God's son.[33] The genealogy traces Jesus' lineage through David and Abraham all the way back to Adam. David and Abraham are key figures in Luke's infancy narrative, and the tracing of the genealogy all the way back to Adam demonstrates Jesus' connection to the monarchy, to Israel and to all humanity.[34] He fulfils the creation mandate and covenantal commissions to bring blessing to the world.

---

29. Bock notes the 'highway' imagery as it appears also in Isa. 57:14–17 and 62:10 in connection with a people who are humble and lowly: 'the imagery has ethical dimensions'. *Luke 1:1–9:50*, pp. 292–293.

30. John Nolland, *Luke 1–9:20*, WBC 35a (Dallas: Word, 1989), p. 154.

31. Garland, *Luke*, p. 156.

32. Bock, *Luke 1:1–9:50*, p. 315.

33. Fitzmyer, *Luke I–IX*, p. 481.

34. Bock, *Luke 1:1–9:50*, p. 350.

As Luke 4 commences Jesus is led immediately from the Jordan into the wilderness where he is tested for forty days by the devil. Just as Israel was tested for forty years in the wilderness so Jesus, as the messianic representative, is also tested. As Nolland notes, 'Echoes of the testing of God's son Adam (3:38) in the garden and of God's son Israel in the wilderness permeate the account.'[35] The difference is that Jesus passes the test. His citation of Deuteronomy 6:13, 16; 8:3 demonstrates him to be a model Israelite.[36] As Talbert notes, Jesus' experience is antitypical of Israel and Adam and Eve, making Jesus the 'true culmination of Israel's heritage . . . reversing Adam's fall and Israel's sin'.[37] He is the obedient Son of God who, by succeeding where Adam and Israel failed, is able to represent both the nation and all humanity.[38]

His Galilean ministry commences with his synagogue sermon at Nazareth in which he quotes a combination of Isaiah 58:6 and 61:1–2.[39] Talbert notes that Luke brings these events forward in his account – he fronts them since this event has 'programmatic significance for the whole'.[40] Kimball describes this passage as 'the most important for Luke–Acts; it is almost universally held to be programmatic for the two-part work'.[41] Furnish describes this passage as a 'charter and program for everything that follows'.[42]

Isaiah 58:6 is part of a larger passage addressing the subject of true fasting. Israel claim to have fasted, yet YHWH exposes their hypocrisy in their having exploited workers and fought with one another during their fasts (Isa. 58:3–5). YHWH admonishes:

---

35. Nolland, *Luke 1–9:20*, p. 182.

36. Fitzmyer, *Luke I–IX*, pp. 510–512.

37. Charles H. Talbert, *Reading Luke: A Literary and Theological Commentary on the Third Gospel* (Macon: Smyth & Helwys, 2002), p. 50.

38. Bock, *Luke 1:1–9:50*, p. 368.

39. Patrick D. Miller, 'Luke 4:16–21', *Int* 29 (1975), p. 418. For a discussion of sources, text critical issues and differences between Luke's citation and the LXX of Isa. 58:6 and 61:1–2 see the discussion in Thomas S. Moore, 'Luke's Use of Isaiah for the Gentile Mission and Jewish Rejection Theme in the Third Gospel', PhD diss., Dallas Theological Seminary, 1995, pp. 81–86.

40. Jesus' rejection in his hometown of Nazareth appears later in the accounts of Matthew (13:53–58) and Mark (6:1–6).Talbert, *Reading Luke*, p. 57.

41. Charles Kimball, 'Jesus' Exposition of Scripture in Luke 4:16–30: An Inquiry in Light of Jewish Hermeneutics', *PRSt* 21 (1994), p. 180.

42. Victor Paul Furnish, *The Love Command in the New Testament*, NTL (London: SCM, 1973), p. 44.

Is not this the kind of fasting I have chosen:
to loose the chains of injustice
    and untie the cords of the yoke,
to set the oppressed free
    and break every yoke?
Is it not to share your food with the hungry
    and to provide the poor wanderer with shelter –
when you see the naked, to clothe them.
(Isa. 58:6–7)

Isaiah 61:1–2 prophesies a Spirit-anointed servant who will proclaim good news to the poor, freedom for captives, sight for the blind and the year of the Lord's favour. The 'poor' (*ptōchois*) likely refers to those who were disadvantaged and marginalized in economic and sacred realms. Green describes them as dishonourable and excluded.[43] Pilgrim suggests, 'the poor were not receiving the attention, compassion and help, as God had plainly intended. They were despised by the religious teachers and excluded from the most sacred precincts.'[44]

Chad Hartstock, having conducted an analysis of the 'physiognomic consciousness' that pervaded the ancient world, concludes that 'blindness' was used as a characterization of spiritual status and widely understood as such.[45] Jesus' ministry is not less than concern for the physically blind but is certainly more – a concern and plan to open spiritual eyes to God's salvation. Roth argues that the poor, captive, blind and oppressed should be taken as a whole rather than as disconnected groups.[46] If both Roth and Hartstock are correct in their respective observations then there is an overlap between the physical and spiritual. Jesus' ministry is concerned to remedy both physical and spiritual impairment. Jesus is not concerned merely with souls and uninterested in physical suffering; neither is Jesus simply interested in physical liberation without a concern for the spiritual. The physical and the spiritual belong together as two aspects of an interconnected whole. Green suggests that the language of 'release' or 'freedom' (*aphesis*; twice in verse 18 referring to the captive and

---

43. Green, *Gospel of Luke*, p. 82.

44. Walter E. Pilgrim, *Good News to the Poor: Wealth and Poverty in Luke–Acts* (Minneapolis: Augsburg, 1981), p. 46.

45. Chad Hartstock, *Sight and Blindness in Luke–Acts: The Use of Physical Features in Characterization*, BIS 94 (Leiden: Brill, 2008), p. 207.

46. S. John Roth, *The Blind, the Lame, and the Poor: Character Types in Luke–Acts*, JSNTSup 144 (Sheffield: Sheffield Academic Press, 1997), p. 26.

oppressed) 'signifies wholeness, freedom from diabolic and social chains, acceptance'.[47] As Patrick Miller has said:

> The Old Testament passages enable us – indeed force us – to understand that which God began in Jesus not simply as release from sin but as all those concrete kinds of physical, social and economic liberation of which the Old Testament speaks. At the same time Luke will not allow us to assume that those things which oppress the souls and minds and lives of people are tied wholly to their physical situation. The gospel reminds us that the freedom God intends through Christ is at root release from the entanglement and dominance of sin in our lives.[48]

The final clause of the prophecy (v. 19) proclaims the 'year of the LORD's favour'. Green states, 'The emphasis on "release," together with the final appeal to "the year of the Lord's favour," inscribes the present text not only in Isa. 58:6; 61:1–2, but, more deeply, in legislation related to the Jubilee in Leviticus 25.'[49] Green notes that the *Melchizedek Scroll* (11QMelch) attests an 'eschatological re-interpretation of Leviticus 25, likening the epoch of salvation to the eschatological Jubilee'.[50] Jesus is announcing his ministry as the new Jubilee. In verse 21 he claims that today the fulfilment of Isaiah's eschatological prophecy has arrived.[51] His subsequent rejection (Luke 4:24–30) and the citation of Elisha's healing of Naaman (2 Kgs 5) foreshadow the movement towards the Gentiles.[52]

In Luke's account he seeks to persuade the reader that Jesus of Nazareth is the son of David, son of Abraham and son of God – the long-awaited Jewish Messiah who will, in fulfilment of Isaiah's prophecy, bring freedom and favour to the poor and oppressed, and restore Israel's missio-ethical vocation.

Luke 6

Luke's account of the Sermon on the Plain is equivalent to Matthew's Sermon on the Mount. Similar material is covered, though Lukan distinctives are of

---

47. Green, *Gospel of Luke*, p. 79. So too Hays, who considers the good news to the poor to include material and spiritual nuances. Christopher M. Hays, *Luke's Wealth Ethics*, WUNT 275 (Tübingen: Mohr Siebeck, 2010), pp. 110–111.

48. Patrick D. Miller, 'Luke 4:16–21', *Int* 29 (1975), p. 420.

49. Green, *Gospel of Luke*, p. 78.

50. Ibid. So too Nolland, *Luke 1–9:20*, p. 197.

51. Moore, 'Luke's Use of Isaiah', p. 94.

52. Garland, *Luke*, p. 210.

particular interest. Beck notes that this is the first section of sustained teaching for the disciples and therefore has the 'quality of a manifesto'.[53] Its placement, immediately after the selection of the twelve, suggests a restatement of the Torah as issued to the twelve tribes of Israel. The sermon commences with the Lukan Beatitudes. Pilgrim notes that, while not explicit, many connect the Beatitudes with the theological and eschatological vision of Isaiah 61 and the associated vision of Jubilee.[54] If correct that implies that Jesus' own mission, as outlined in Luke 4:18–19, is something to be shared with his followers. Although Luke's Beatitudes are briefer than Matthew's (four macarisms to Matthew's nine) they are more focused on the poor, the hungry, the grieving and the persecuted.[55] The downtrodden and outcast are the focus of the Lukan macarism, and the promise is one of the kingdom, satisfaction and joy.[56] The final clause of the section connects the sufferings of the 'blessed' (makarioi) with the Son of Man. It is those who suffer because they follow Jesus who will be rewarded for their faithfulness. This is amplified in verse 23, where the suffering faithful are compared to the Old Testament prophets. Unlike Matthew's account, Luke follows the four blessings with a series of four woes that parallel the blessings. Woe is pronounced on the rich, the well fed, those who laugh now and those of whom others speak well. In verse 26 we see the parallel amplification (cf. v. 23) that their ancestors so treated the false prophets. Luke is connecting ethics and religion. Those faithful to God suffer at the hands of the unfaithful. Jesus' disciples should expect opposition but their charge is to be faithful to the master, rather than compromise for the sake of worldly comfort.

---

53. Brian E. Beck, *Christian Character in the Gospel of Luke* (London: Epworth, 1989), p. 181.

54. Pilgrim, *Good News*, p. 74.

55. Beavis states, 'the idea of sympathy for the poor and outcast was alien to Greco-Roman ways of thinking'. Mary Ann Beavis, 'Expecting Nothing in Return', *Int* 48 (1994), p. 363.

56. As in the Nazareth synagogue sermon (Luke 4:18–19) the poor are best identified in Isaianic terms of socio-economic oppression and the poor in spirit awaiting eschatological deliverance. For differing viewpoints see the discussion in David P. Seccombe, *Possessions and the Poor in Luke–Acts*, SNTU 6 (Linz: Fuchs, 1982), pp. 24–43; L. John Topel, *Children of a Compassionate God: A Theological Exegesis of Luke 6:20–49* (Collegeville: Liturgical Press, 2001), pp. 67–85. Both unnecessarily opt for either materially or spiritually poor, failing to see the way in which Luke (and Isaiah) employs the terms holistically.

In verse 27 Jesus transfers his attention from his disciples (cf. v. 20) to the crowd and begins with the instruction to 'love your enemies, do good to those who hate you, bless those who curse you, pray for those who ill-treat you'. Bock describes the command as unparalleled in terms of its emphatic tone.[57] The golden rule in verse 31 is 'Do to others as you would have them do to you.'[58] Garland notes that in a culture of patronage and honour this command would seem 'bizarre . . . [it] effectively erases the social distinctions between the giver and the receiver'.[59] The implication of what follows is that the community of Jesus' disciples should be distinctive within their own culture.[60] Jesus notes that 'the sinners' (*hoi hamartōloi*) practise love and good deeds to those who do so reciprocally (vv. 32–34).[61] Jesus promises that for those who love their enemies expecting nothing in return their reward will be great and they will be called 'children of the Most High' (v. 35). They are to be 'merciful, just as your Father is merciful' (v. 36) in words reminiscent of Leviticus 11:44–45, 19:2 and 20:26

---

57. Bock, *Luke 1:1–9:50*, p. 588.

58. Topel cites Lysias' conclusion in *For the Soldier* 20: 'I consider it established that one should do harm to one's enemies and be of service to one's friends.' Cited in Topel, *Children*, p. 137.

59. Garland, *Luke*, p. 280. Topel agrees: 'No one but the Cynics considered poverty or hunger a blessing . . . Hence Jesus' beatitudes and woes would have evoked in Luke's Gentile reader as much incredulity as they did in his Jewish reader.' *Children*, p. 232.

60. 2 Clement 13.4, commenting on the command to love enemies, says, 'when they hear this they wonder at this extraordinary goodness; but when they see that we not only do not love those who hate us, but do not even love those who love us, they laugh us to scorn, and the name is blasphemed.' Cited in 'An Ancient Christian Sermon', in J. B. Lightfoot and J. R. Harmer (tr.), *The Apostolic Fathers*, 2nd edn, repr. (Grand Rapids: Baker, 1989), pp. 74–75.

61. Talbert notes that during the Hellenistic era the benefactor–beneficiary relationship consisted of reciprocal obligations such that lending to the poor was uncommon, as it elicited no reward. *Reading Luke*, pp. 76–77. There are numerous examples where a law of reciprocity was enacted in Jewish and Graeco-Roman culture. See *m. Bab. Qam.* 8.6; 1QS 2.4–9; 9.21–23; 11Q19 61.12–14; Lysias, *For the Soldier* 20. For something akin to Jesus' instruction see *b. Šabb.* 31a; 1QS 10.17–18; Thucydides, *History of the Peloponnesian War* 4.19.1–4; Herodotus, *The Histories* 3.142; Seneca, *On Benefits* 2.1.1. Even where a more loving ethic is practised it is done for self-centred reasons contra Jesus' instruction to love without expecting anything in return. See Topel, *Children*, pp. 137, 158.

('be holy, because I am holy').[62] The root of Judaeo-Christian ethics is the *imitatio Dei* and the *imitatio Dei* is a means towards the *missio Dei*.

In verse 37 the subject moves from love to judgment with the instruction 'Do not judge, and you will not be judged. Do not condemn, and you will not be condemned. Forgive, and you will be forgiven.' In verse 41 Jesus uses the illustration of the plank and speck to demonstrate the hypocrisy of a judgmental spirit. In between the command and the illustration is the insertion of an intriguing mini-parable that does not, at first glance, seem to fit the flow of the argument. In verses 39–40 Luke tells the reader, 'He also told them this parable: "Can the blind lead the blind? Will they not both fall into a pit? The student is not above the teacher, but everyone who is fully trained will be like their teacher."' The implication in Jesus' teaching is that his disciples are being trained so as to be guides for those who are in some sense blind. Given my discussion of blindness and physiognomy in Luke 4:18, and Luke's explicit description of Jesus' teaching as a parable, it appears Jesus' ethical teaching is missio-telic. The purpose of his extended ethical instruction is that his followers will be able to be guides for the 'blind'. Green notes that when the twelve are appointed (6:12–16) there is no explicit missionary assignment until 9:1–2.[63] At this stage the instruction is preparatory.

In verse 43 Jesus gives a positive example of righteousness in contrast to the example of hypocrisy just cited. Good trees bear good fruit and each tree is therefore recognized by the quality of its fruit.[64] As with the parable of verses 39–40 the implication is that Jesus expects his followers to be fruitful in some sense, and that fruitfulness is inextricably intertwined with their character.

Jesus' closing illustration is of the wise and foolish builders who lay foundations on top of two different materials, one solid and reliable, the other shaky and unstable. The difference between the two is not the hearing (*akouō*, vv. 47, 49) of the words but the practising (*poieō*, vv. 46, 47, 49) of them. The man on shaky ground is the one who hears the words of Jesus and does not put them into practice. The man on solid ground is the one who hears what Jesus says and puts it into practice. Here we see the twin themes of love for God and love for neighbour brought together as a summary of Jesus' sermon.

The twelve have been assembled and charged in the hearing of the crowd. That charge consists of reassurance and exhortation. The exhortation is to live

---

62. Fitzmyer, *Luke I–IX*, p. 641.

63. Green, *Gospel of Luke*, p. 109.

64. Fruit used figuratively to refer to deeds can be seen in Isa. 3:10; Jer. 17:10; 21:14. Fitzmyer, *Luke I–IX*, p. 643.

distinctively counter-cultural lives of love for God and love for neighbour. As they do the implication is that they will become guides for the blind. Jesus' manifesto is in part a charter for missional ethics. As Beck concludes in his study of character in Luke's Gospel, 'the character of the disciple is testimony to the good news of God'.[65] More properly, given the context of Jesus' teaching, the character of the *community* is testimony to the good news of God.

Luke 10

Luke 10 groups together three narratives that express Jesus' priorities for mission and discipleship. Taken together they reveal missio-ethical discipleship. Nolland notes that Luke 9:51 marks a turning point in the narrative as Jesus sets his face towards Jerusalem. This subsequent section is concerned with initiating the disciples into the ways of Jesus.[66]

Chapter 10 opens with the sending out of the seventy.[67] The sending out of the twelve has already occurred in 9:1–6.[68] Fitzmyer suggests that Luke's 'second sending' emphasizes that mission will be undertaken by a broader community than just the twelve – here is a missionary charge for the Christian community of Luke's day.[69] Though the seventy are sent within Israel's borders, the number 70 along with the surrounding context of Samaritan opposition (9:51–56) and the parable of the good Samaritan (10:25–37) suggest the beginnings of a mission beyond the borders of Israel. The disciples are sent, like John the Baptist, ahead of Jesus (v. 1) to announce, 'The kingdom of God has come near to you' (v. 9). The long-awaited and anticipated eschatological reality, spoken of by the prophets, has broken into the present.[70] The imagery of a plentiful harvest has Old Testament connotations.[71] In verse 3 the disciples

---

65. Beck, *Christian Character*, p. 186.

66. John Nolland, *Luke 9:21–18:34*, WBC 35B (Dallas: Word, 1993), p. 533.

67. The number 70 or 72 is symbolic of the nations in antiquity. See J. Massyngbaerde Ford, *My Enemy Is My Guest: Jesus and Violence in Luke* (Maryknoll: Orbis, 1984), p. 92.

68. Morton S. Enslin, 'The Samaritan Ministry and Mission', *HUCA* 51 (1980), p. 32. Enslin notes that the twelve are sent to the twelve tribes of Israel (9:1–6) and now the seventy are sent to the seventy nations of the world (10:1–24).

69. Joseph A. Fitzmyer, *The Gospel According to Luke X–XXIV*, AB 28A (New York: Doubleday, 1985), pp. 844–845.

70. Nolland, *Luke 9:21–18:34*, p. 554.

71. Nolland suggests that the image combines the eschatological motifs of judgment and gathering as seen in Mic. 4:1–11; Isa. 27:12–13; 63:1–6; Jer. 25:30–31; and Joel 3:13. Ibid., pp. 550–551.

are described as sheep among wolves, another evocative Old Testament image, speaking of hostility from surrounding nations (cf. Isa. 40:11; Ezek. 34:11–31) and the hope of reconciliation and harmony (cf. Isa. 11:6; 65:25).[72] In verse 24 Jesus confirms to the disciples that they have seen that which the prophets longed to see. As Bock says, 'the promises of old are now being fulfilled'.[73]

Immediately following the sending of the seventy is the parable of the good Samaritan, another hint of Jesus' wider mission beyond the borders of Israel.[74] Placing the parable of the good Samaritan immediately after the sending of the seventy displays a different facet of the mission, or, as Nolland puts it, 'the ways of Jesus'.[75] Jesus' parable of the good Samaritan is instructive as it provides both a summary of the law and an exposition of its meaning. It begins with a question regarding the entry requirements for eternal life (v. 25). Jesus refers the enquirer to the law and his understanding of it (v. 26). The lawyer responds by quoting a combination of the Shema (Deut. 6:5–6) and Leviticus 19:18.[76] Jesus commends the lawyer's answer and instructs him, 'do this and you will live' (v. 28). Desiring self-justification the lawyer asks, 'And who is my neighbour' (v. 29). In reply Jesus tells the parable of the good Samaritan. Jewish antipathy towards Samaritans is well attested.[77] The twist in the tale is that where the Jewish elite failed, the Samaritan succeeded. The law is practised by someone widely considered to be outside the covenant community, who becomes a symbol of Jesus' boundary-breaking mission.[78] As Fitzmyer notes, 'even the Samaritan has found his way to eternal life'.[79] The lawyer in verse 37 cannot even say the name, preferring to identify the Samaritan as 'The one who had mercy on him' (v. 37). Jesus' final instruction is, 'Go and do likewise' (v. 37).[80]

---

72. Darrell L. Bock, *Luke 9:51–24:53*, BECNT (Grand Rapids: Baker, 1996), p. 996.

73. Bock, *Luke 9:51–24:53*, p. 993.

74. Massyngbaerde Ford, *My Enemy Is My Guest*, p. 92.

75. Nolland, *Luke 9:21–18:34*, p. 533.

76. Jesus himself gives this summary of the law in Mark 12:29–31. There are similarities in *T. Iss.* 5.1–2; *T. Dan* 5.3; *T. Ben.* 3.3; *Jub.* 36.4–8; Philo, *On the Special Laws* 2.15 §63.

77. See John 4:9; *m. Šeb.* 8.10; *b. Sanh.* 57a. Bock describes the contemporary Jewish view of Samaritans as those who were unclean and to be avoided. Bock, *Luke 9:51–24:53*, p. 1031.

78. Nolland, *Luke 9:21–18:34*, p. 598.

79. Fitzmyer, *Luke X–XXIV*, p. 884.

80. The witness regarding Graeco-Roman attitudes to 'neighbours' is varied, according to Downey. A positive view can be seen in Thucydides, *History of the Peloponnesian War* 2.40, 51; Plato, *Republic* 1.335; *Laws* 729e. Examples of a more negative view

Salo summarizes: 'Salvation includes ethical demands of correct conduct toward neighbours.'[81] Given the preceding literary context we could rephrase Salo's conclusion as *mission* includes the ethical demands of correct conduct towards neighbours.

Immediately following this pericope is Jesus' arrival at the home of Mary and Martha. Mary sat at Jesus' feet listening to what he said (v. 39), while Martha was distracted by the necessary preparations (v. 40). As Martha rebukes Jesus for not telling Mary to assist, Jesus affirms Mary's action as 'necessary' and 'better' (*henos de estin chreia*, v. 42). If the good Samaritan fulfils the law's requirement to love one's neighbour, Mary fulfils the law's requirement to love God. Wall argues for a Deuteronomic background to the wider section (10:25–42) and suggests that 'Martha, like Israel, is in danger of "living by bread alone," while Mary "lives by every word that proceeds from God's mouth"' (cf. Deut. 8:3).[82] Love for God (10:38–42) and love for neighbour (10:25–37) are to be the ethical shape of the community's mission of witness (10:1–24).

These three stories bring together three themes. First, we observe Jesus' priority for mission. In sending out the seventy he anticipates their subsequent commission to go not just to Israel but to the nations (Acts 1:8).[83] Second, we see Jesus' emphasis on practical social ethics expressed in love for neighbour (cf. Deut. 7:12; 10:18–20). Third, we see the necessity of devoted listening to Jesus (cf. Deut. 8:3). At the heart of Luke 10 we read the summary of the law – love for God and love for neighbour (cf. Deut. 6:5–6). Evans has argued that Luke's central section (10:1 – 18:14) has parallels with the legal material of Deuteronomy 1 – 26.[84] For Evans the purpose of such a parallel is to

---

of outsiders can be seen in Plutarch, *Solon* 24; Seutonius, *Claudius* 25; Theognis 209. Downey suggests that while kindness to strangers was on occasion idealized, in reality status and class consciousness were pervasive such that the story of the good Samaritan would have proved to be a 'novelty' in its historical contexts. Glanville Downey, 'Who Is My Neighbour? The Greek and Roman Answer', *ATR* 47 (1965), pp. 3–15.

81. Kalervo Salo, *Luke's Treatment of the Law: A Redaction-Critical Investigation*, AASFDHL 57 (Helsinki: Suomalainen Tiedeakatemia, 1991), p. 111.

82. Robert W. Wall, 'Martha and Mary (Luke 10:38–42) in the Context of a Christian Deuteronomy', *JSNT* 35 (1989), p. 24.

83. Nolland, *Luke 9:21–18:34*, p. 549; Enslin, 'Samaritan Ministry', p. 37.

84. C. F. Evans, 'The Central Section of St. Luke's Gospel', in *Studies in the Gospels: Essays in Memory of R. H. Lightfoot* (Oxford: Blackwell, 1955), pp. 42–50. Evans parallels all of Deut. 1 – 26 with Luke 10:1 – 18:14.

demonstrate that Jesus is a prophet like Moses.[85] That this is Luke's intent is likely, but should be supplemented to include Jesus' disciples as being the fulfilment of all that Israel were supposed to be as described in Deuteronomy. In particular Evans argues for the parallel progression in Luke 10 from the great commandment (10:27; cf. Deut. 5 – 6) to love for neighbour (10:30–37; cf. Deut. 7) to love for God (Deut. 8). Thus for Evans Luke 10 recapitulates Deuteronomy 5 – 8.[86] Evans's thesis is persuasive but may be supplemented by seeing the first half of Luke 10 in parallel to Deuteronomy 4, as it is also concerned with mission that begins to look beyond the borders of Israel. To modify Evans's argument, Luke 10 parallels Deuteronomy 4 – 8, providing the commission and the character required for fulfilment of their missional calling. Luke 10 provides a snapshot of the shape of discipleship with all the ingredients of a missional ethic (cf. Deut. 4:6–8). As Jesus sets his face towards his own death he provides instruction for his followers regarding the shape of their task before the nations.

Luke 11 – 19

Having examined Luke 10, the wider travel narrative (9:51 – 19:44) is worth considering as a whole since it contains a variety of Jesus' teachings, parables and exchanges, much of which pertains to the relationship between mission and ethics. Talbert suggests the section as a whole is concerned with the way of discipleship, with some of the material prefiguring the wider mission to be narrated in Acts.[87] Evans suggests the entire section is analogous to Moses' final instructions to Israel before his own death.[88] There are a number of key recurring themes throughout the section as follows.

Pharisees and false righteousness

Luke 11:37–54 contains an extended rebuke by Jesus of his dinner hosts, the Pharisees. In particular Jesus draws attention to their outward expressions of devotion, which mask a neglect of justice and love for God (11:42). Worse, they actually hinder others from entering the kingdom of God (11:52). In Luke 15 Jesus tells the parables of the lost coin, sheep and son in response to their accusation 'This man welcomes sinners, and eats with them' (15:2). In 16:14–15 Jesus again rebukes the Pharisees for their self-justification, since God knows their hearts. In Luke 18:9–14 Jesus recounts a parable of a Pharisee and a tax collector

---

85. Ibid., p. 50.

86. Ibid., p. 43.

87. Talbert, *Reading Luke*, p. 119.

88. Craig A. Evans, *Luke*, NIBC 3 (Peabody: Hendrickson, 1990), pp. 160–161.

to demonstrate that those who humble themselves will be exalted, while those who exalt themselves will be humbled. The Pharisees' self-righteousness, and mistreatment of those they considered outsiders, is an anti-missional ethic, akin to that of their forefathers.[89]

Wealth

Jesus repeatedly addresses the issue of wealth in Luke's travel narrative with the parable of the rich fool (12:16–21), the story of the rich man and Lazarus (16:19–31), the rich young ruler (18:18–30), closely followed by the story of Zacchaeus (19:1–10). He instructs his disciples to give to the poor (12:33), to give up everything (14:33), and in the parable of the shrewd manager concludes by saying, 'You cannot serve both God and Money' (16:13). Wealth may signify both economic and spiritual realities.[90] The man who stores up treasures for himself is not rich towards God (12:21). The instruction to his disciples a few verses later regarding almsgiving is a constructive contrast, which both protects against spiritual poverty and gains treasure in heaven (12:33).[91] God's abundant generosity, as outlined in 12:22–32, is the motivation for the *imitatio Dei*.[92] Zacchaeus embodies this in his encounter with Jesus. His practical response, and Jesus' declaration 'Today salvation has come to this house' (19:9), are inextricably intertwined. To many people Zacchaeus was a 'sinner'. Jesus declares him to be a true son of Abraham. Jesus' concluding statement functions as a challenge to Luke's community to 'become a beachhead of the kingdom, where lost human beings can find welcome and new life in the grasp of a hospitable God'.[93] Zacchaeus, in contrast to the rich man (18:18–30), acts as an exemplar of repentance and discipleship.[94]

Further, Green notes a social dimension to wealth to add alongside the economic and spiritual. He observes that Luke 14:12 links together rich neighbours with friends and family, the 'inner circle' – those with whom 'one enjoys relationships of equality and mutuality'.[95] The terms 'rich' and 'poor'

---

89. Cf. Isa. 1:13–17; Jer. 7; 11; Ezek. 20.

90. Matthew S. Rindge, *Jesus' Parable of the Rich Fool: Luke 12:13–34 Among Ancient Conversations on Death and Possessions*, ECL 6 (Atlanta: SBL, 2011), p. 198.

91. Rindge, *Rich Fool*, p. 204.

92. Ibid., p. 205.

93. Brendan Byrne, *The Hospitality of God: A Reading of Luke's Gospel* (Collegeville: Liturgical Press, 2000), p. 152.

94. Hays, *Luke's Wealth Ethics*, p. 178.

95. Green, *Gospel of Luke*, p. 82.

do not simply relate to economic status, but speak of social status also. Jesus' instruction then encompasses the spiritual, the economic and the social aspects of wealth and poverty.

Hospitality
In Luke's Gospel Jesus is often criticized by the Pharisees for eating with the wrong people (see Luke 15:1–2; 19:7). In Luke 14:1–14 Jesus attends a banquet and, observing the desire for the places of honour among the guests, teaches them not only to take the lowest place at the table, but also to invite the poor, crippled, lame and blind to their meals since 'you will be blessed'.[96] Although 'they cannot repay you, you will be repaid at the resurrection of the righteous' (14:14). As Green notes:

> In the ancient Mediterranean world, mealtimes were a social event . . . To welcome people at the table had become tantamount to extending to them intimacy, solidarity, acceptance; table companions were treated as though they were of one's extended family.[97]

Esler demonstrates the ancient Jewish antipathy to dining with those considered outsiders.[98] Esler argues that Luke's emphasis on table fellowship in Luke–Acts legitimates Jew–Gentile fellowship and goes some way to explaining the break between the *ekklēsia* and the synagogue.[99] Esler describes table fellowship as a 'vital arch' in Luke's 'symbolic universe'.[100] If table fellowship is an arch, that which it supports is mission. Jesus' table practices are about more than the need to satisfy hunger or enjoy social gathering. They are an example of his mission to cross boundaries in welcoming outsiders.

In Luke 16:19–31 the unnamed rich man is chastised for failing to listen to Moses and the Prophets. As Bauckham observes, 'To perceive the situation of the rich and the poor as radically unjust the rich need only listen to Moses and the prophets.'[101] Hays has suggested that, in addition to the Deuteronomic

---

96. Fitzmyer suggests Deut. 14:28–29, 16:11–14 and 26:11–13 provide the OT background to Jesus' instruction. *Luke X–XXIV*, p. 1048.

97. Green, *Gospel of Luke*, p. 87.

98. Philip Francis Esler, *Community and Gospel in Luke–Acts: The Social and Political Motivations of Lucan Theology* (Cambridge: Cambridge University Press, 1987), pp. 73–86.

99. Ibid., pp. 108–109.

100. Ibid., p. 109.

101. Richard Bauckham, 'The Rich Man and Lazarus: The Parable and the Parallels', *NTS* 37 (1991), p. 246.

requirements regarding justice for outsiders, Isaiah 58:6–7 looms large in the background of the wider section.[102] Rooted in the Old Testament, Jesus' teaching on hospitality is about more than food; it is about an ethic of inclusivity.

The mission

At the centre of the travel narrative are three stories which depict Jesus' ministry to seek and save the lost – the lost sheep, the lost coin and the lost son (Luke 15). Jesus' mission to seek and save the lost is reiterated in Luke 19:10: 'For the Son of Man came to seek and to save the lost' (cf. Luke 5:27–32). Additionally Jesus' parable of the great banquet (14:15–23) ends with the charge 'Go out to the roads and country lanes and compel them to come in, so that my house will be full' (14:23).[103] Who are those people? Undoubtedly Jesus' primary concern is with the Jews. Nevertheless there is an anticipation of Gentile mission seen in 13:29, where Jesus tells the crowd that many will come from north, south, east and west.[104]

Service

In Luke 12:35–48 Jesus encourages his followers to be 'dressed ready for service' like servants waiting for their master to return from a wedding banquet (12:35–36). Peter is confused as to who exactly is being addressed, so Jesus follows with another parable about the wise manager who serves the master faithfully (12:41–48). In Luke 14:25–35 Jesus teaches the crowds about the cost of discipleship and the requirement to give up everything (14:33). Jesus concludes his teaching with the words 'Salt is good, but if it loses its saltiness, how can it be made salty again?' (14:34). At the end of the travel section Luke concludes with Jesus' parable of the ten minas (Luke 19:11–27), which acts as both a warning to the Pharisees and an encouragement to Jesus' followers to be at the master's work.

Beck notes Luke's editorial hand in this central section in which a number of important themes have been interwoven: 'wealth, arrogance, the interpretation of the law against the advantage of those in need, hostility to sinners contrasted with their welcome in the kingdom of God as expressed by Jesus'.[105] A number of scholars have noted the way in which Deuteronomy has influenced

---

102. Hays, *Luke's Wealth Ethics*, p. 157.

103. Bock suggests this refers to the future Gentile mission, possibly alluding to Isa. 49:6. *Luke 9:51–24:53*, p. 1276.

104. Fitzmyer, *Luke X–XXIV*, p. 1023.

105. Beck, *Christian Character*, pp. 155–156.

Luke's shaping of his travel narrative.[106] His purpose in so doing is to present Jesus as the prophet like Moses (Deut. 18:15–19), and to subvert contemporary Jewish ideas surrounding election. As Evans notes, 'those who are assumed to be the non-elect (such as Gentiles, Samaritans, the poor) may in fact be included in the kingdom and may even serve as examples for others to follow'.[107] Luke's presentation of his central section holds together the Deuteronomic vision for mission and ethics. The mission of Jesus to reach outsiders and the ethics that accompany discipleship belong together and cannot be neatly separated. Humility, care for the poor and hospitality are part of what it looks like to seek and welcome the lost into the kingdom, and disciples are to imitate the master in exercising a missional ethic.

Luke 19 – 24

A number of fulfilment themes as Luke's narrative draws towards its climax are worth observing. At the conclusion of the triumphal entry Jesus enters the temple courts, driving out the merchants (Luke 19:45). He then quotes from two significant Old Testament passages that we considered in the previous chapter. He first quotes Isaiah 56:7: 'my house will be called a house of prayer'. This passage, in context, combines the themes of justice (Isa. 56:1–2) and the welcome of all nations (Isa. 56:3–8).[108] The second quotation in Luke 19:46 is from Jeremiah 7:11, Jeremiah's first temple sermon, which itself draws on Deuteronomic ideas and language; in particular the oppression of the alien, orphan and widow (Jer. 7:6). While both of these prophetic texts speak of justice and outsiders, one promises judgment (Jer. 7:1–11) while the other looks

---

106. Evans, 'Central Section', pp. 42–50; James A. Sanders, 'The Ethic of Election in Luke's Great Banquet Parable', in *Essays in Old Testament Ethics* (New York: Ktav, 1974), pp. 245–271; J. Duncan M. Derrett, *Law in the New Testament* (London: Darton, Longman & Todd, 1970), pp. 126–155.

107. Craig A. Evans, 'Luke's Use of the Elijah/Elisha Narratives and the Ethic of Election', *JBL* 106.1 (1987), p. 82.

108. However, it is noteworthy that, in contrast to Mark's account (11:15–17), Luke omits the final phrase 'for all nations'. The omission could be because at the time of writing the temple no longer existed and the Gentiles were finding their way into the church. Fitzmyer, *Luke X–XXIV*, p. 1261; Geir Otto Hólmas, '"My House Shall Be a House of Prayer": Regarding the Temple as a Place of Prayer in Acts Within the Context of Luke's Apologetical Objective', *JSNT* 27.4 (2005), p. 407. Alternatively it could be to make the contrast between 'house of prayer' and 'robbers' sharper. Garland, *Luke*, p. 775.

forward to salvation (Isa. 56:1–8).[109] Luke brings them together on the lips of Jesus, providing, in the context of the triumphal entry, a tantalizing ambiguity. Jesus' words are more than mere rebuke: they also contain something of announcement and promise. And if the crowd's estimation of Jesus is correct how might he bring both judgment and salvation?

Luke provides further messianic credentials in chapter 20 as Jesus cites Psalms 118:22 and 110:1; and again in Luke 22, where Jesus claims that Isaiah 53:12 must be fulfilled in him (22:37). Luke is explicit in his conviction that Jesus is the Messiah – Isaiah's suffering servant come to bring restoration to Israel. Further messianic allusions appear throughout Luke's account of Jesus' trial, crucifixion and resurrection appearances. In Luke 24:26–27 Jesus claims that he is the *telos* to which Moses and all the Prophets testify.[110] Luke's claim is that Jesus is the fulfilment of the narrative trajectory that I have traced from Deuteronomy and the Major Prophets (and the rest of the Old Testament). This is repeated a few verses later (24:44), followed by his commission to his disciples to be witnesses to these things.[111] As we observed in considering missional hermeneutics in the methodology, Luke 24:44 requires us to under-stand the Bible's narrative messianically *and* missionally.[112] The prophetic hints towards Gentile mission now receive explicit provision.[113] In the wider context of Luke's Gospel their witness will consist of more than a verbal testimony.[114] Their way of life, as spoken of in Jesus' teaching in the travel section, will be an integral part of their discipleship and witness. Meanwhile there is one more prophetic promise to be fulfilled before they take up their task. They need to

---

109. Hiers notes, with reference to Ezek. 40 – 48: 'Temple reform and renewal were associated with the inauguration of a new era, and at least in some of the literature, as preparatory to the beginning of the Messianic Age.' Richard H. Hiers, 'Purification of the Temple: Preparation for the Kingdom of God', *JBL* 90 (1971), p. 86.

110. Garland notes the way in which Jesus also began his public ministry with a claim to be fulfilling Scripture (4:16–17). *Luke*, p. 954.

111. They are to begin in Jerusalem, and then go to all nations, which is reminiscent of two important OT texts: Ezek. 5:5 and Isa. 2:3. Garland, *Luke*, p. 968.

112. Christopher J. H. Wright, *The Mission of God: Unlocking the Bible's Grand Narrative* (Downers Grove: InterVarsity Press, 2006), p. 30.

113. Richard J. Dillon, *From Eye-Witnesses to Ministers of the Word*, AnBib 82 (Rome: Biblical Institute, 1978), p. 168.

114. Bock states, 'Their [the disciples'] faith is not just an ethic or a morality. It is the testimony of God's activity in history.' *Luke 9:51–24:53*, p. 1942.

wait for the divine empowerment (24:49).[115] As Luke opened his account in the temple courts (1:8), so too he closes his account with a depiction of the disciples worshipping in the temple courts in the final verse (24:53).[116]

Acts

Acts 1

The opening of Acts continues the narrative of the disciples' preparation to witness outlined in Luke 24. Acts 1 provides a number of allusions to the Old Testament, supporting the view that Luke–Acts is portraying the new-exodus restoration spoken of in the Major Prophets. As Turner notes, 'Acts 1:3–8 is ... one of the most subtle and concentrated pieces of theological writing in Luke's whole enterprise.'[117] We will note here a number of scriptural allusions that reveal something of the identity and mission of Jesus' disciples. First, there is the waiting period of forty days (1:3), a number symbolic of waiting or preparation.[118] Second, they are told to wait in Jerusalem (1:4) – a city rich in historical and theological significance.[119] Jerusalem was the place where God ruled over and blessed his people through his king, and the place to which nations would stream to hear the word of the Lord.[120] In Acts, Jerusalem is the launch city of mission (1:8), and each new wave of expansion circles back to Jerusalem.[121] Jerusalem is a symbol of restoration, and a centre from which

---

115. Fitzmyer notes the emphatic placing of δύναμιν at the end of the verse. *Luke X–XXIV*, p. 1580.

116. Bock, *Luke 9:51–24:53*, p. 1946.

117. M. M. B. Turner, *Power from on High: The Spirit in Israel's Restoration and Witness in Luke–Acts*, JPTSup 9 (Sheffield: Sheffield Academic Press, 1996), pp. 294–295.

118. F. Scott Spencer, *Journeying Through Acts* (Peabody: Hendrickson, 1994), p. 35. Moses spent forty years in preparation for his mission. For forty days Moses was on the mountain receiving commandments (Exod. 24:18). For forty years Israel wandered in the wilderness before taking the land (Exod. 16:35). Forty days is also the number of days Jesus was tested before his own public Spirit-anointed ministry began (Luke 4:2, 18–19). Horst Balz, 'τεσσεράκοντα', in *TDNT*, vol. 8, p. 136.

119. Joseph A. Fitzmyer, *The Acts of the Apostles*, AB 31 (New York: Doubleday, 1998), p. 204.

120. Isa. 2:2–4; 40:1–2; 65:18–25; Zech. 8:20–23; Mic. 4:1–8. David G. Peterson, *The Acts of the Apostles*, PNTC (Nottingham: Apollos, 2009), p. 107.

121. Acts 12:5; 15:2; 18:22; 19:21; 21:17. Luke Timothy Johnson, *The Acts of the Apostles*, SP 5 (Collegeville: Liturgical Press, 1992), p. 15. In Acts there is a distinction to be

salvation flows.[122] Third, we hear mention again of John the Baptist (1:5), the figure who fills with expectation (Luke 1:17; 3:15), and announces the coming day of the Lord (Luke 3:16–17; Mal. 4:5–6). Fourth, there is a more explicit reference in the question of verse 6, 'Lord, are you at this time going to restore the kingdom to Israel?' It is a natural question given the Lukan connection between the pouring out of the Spirit and the coming of the kingdom (Acts 1:3–5), and also in view of the allusion to John the Baptist's prophecy in Luke 3:16–17 with its eschatological overtones.[123] Menzies suggests the question is included as a literary device, anticipating misconception and inviting further clarification.[124] The interpreter must decide whether the 'but' (*alla*) at the start of verse 8 is contrastive or continuative. The latter is preferable given the Isaiah allusions in verse 8, and the positive allusion to restoration made by Peter in Acts 3:20–21.[125] Jesus' answer suggests that kingdom restoration *is* on the agenda but in a broader and more all-encompassing way than was expected.[126] Fifth, Acts 1:8, taken together with Luke 24:49, contains an allusion to Isaiah

made between the symbolic and topographic cartography of Jerusalem. Luke portrays Jerusalem both positively and negatively. Positively, Jerusalem is a centre of restoration and messianic hope (2:38). Luke's Gospel begins and ends in Jerusalem (2:22; 24:52), with Jerusalem the destination city (9:51). Negatively, Jerusalem is the city that kills prophets, and the city in which the Messiah is killed (Luke 13:33–34) and will be judged accordingly (Luke 21:24). Weatherly points out that it is more specifically the leaders in Jerusalem who are responsible for the death of Jesus. Jon A. Weatherly, *Jewish Responsibility for the Death of Jesus in Luke–Acts*, JSNTSup 106 (Sheffield: Sheffield Academic Press, 1994), pp. 54–90.

122. Mikael C. Parsons, 'The Place of Jerusalem on the Lukan Landscape: An Exercise in Symbolic Cartography', in *Literary Studies in Luke–Acts* (Macon: Mercer University Press, 1998), pp. 155–171.

123. Peterson, *Acts*, p. 108; Fitzmyer, *Acts*, p. 205; contra Pervo, who describes the question as 'excruciatingly inept'. Richard I. Pervo, *Acts*, Hermeneia (Minneapolis: Fortress, 2009), p. 41.

124. Robert P. Menzies, *The Development of Early Christian Pneumatology*, JSNTSup 54 (Sheffield: Sheffield Academic Press, 1991), p. 200.

125. Robert C. Tannehill, *The Narrative Unity of Luke–Acts: A Literary Interpretation*, 2 vols. (Minneapolis: Fortress, 1994), vol. 2, pp. 15–16; David Gooding, *True to the Faith: A Fresh Approach to the Acts of the Apostles* (London: Hodder & Stoughton, 1990), p. 41.

126. Johnson, *Acts*, p. 29; Robert W. Wall, *Acts*, NIB 10 (Nashville: Abingdon, 2002), p. 42. Recall also the emphasis in Luke 2:25, 38, 22:29–30 on the restoration of Israel.

32:15 (the Spirit poured out from on high), a verse that speaks of the restoration of Israel.[127] Similarly the mention of witnesses picks up Isaiah 43:10–12, and witnessing 'to the ends of the earth' alludes to Isaiah 42:6 and 49:6 (again cited by Paul in 13:47), which are also sections about the restoration of Israel.[128] Pao outlines three stages in the new-exodus restoration: '(1) the dawn of salvation upon Jerusalem; (2) the reconstitution and reunification of Israel [Judea and Samaria] . . . (3) the inclusion of Gentiles within the people of God'.[129] Thus the commission of Acts 1:8 is not only locational but also theopolitical in the restoration of Israel.[130] Sixth, another Old Testament allusion is seen in the ascension of Christ (1:9). Fitzmyer observes that the cloud in the Old Testament was 'used in the sense of an apocalyptic stage prop'.[131] A number of scholars notice the parallels to the rapture stories of Enoch,[132] Moses[133] and Elijah.[134] Also noted are possible allusions to the cloud of God's presence during the exodus (Exod. 16:10; 19:9; 24:15–18).[135] When we recall the association of Moses and Elijah in the transfiguration (Luke 9:30) it seems likely that Luke is presenting Jesus as the prophet like Moses who ascends to God in order to receive and then give a new community-forming 'covenant law'.[136]

---

127. Fitzmyer, *Acts*, p. 206.

128. Turner, *Power*, p. 300; Menzies, *Development*, p. 199.

129. David W. Pao, *Acts and the Isaianic New Exodus* (Grand Rapids: Baker Academic, 2000), p. 95.

130. Ibid.

131. Fitzmyer, *Acts*, p. 210.

132. Gen. 5:21–24; *1 En.* 39.3; *2 En.* 3.1. Johnson, *Acts*, p. 27.

133. Josephus, *Jewish Antiquities* 4.8.48; Philo, *On the Life of Moses* 291; Anthony B. Robinson and Robert W. Wall, *Called to Be Church: The Book of Acts for a New Day* (Grand Rapids: Eerdmans, 2006), p. 35; John F. Maile, 'The Ascension in Luke–Acts', *TynB* 37 (1986), p. 40.

134. 2 Kgs 2:1–18. Thomas L. Brodie, 'Luke–Acts as an Imitation and Emulation of the Elijah–Elisha Narrative', in *New Views on Luke–Acts* (Collegeville: Liturgical Press, 1990), pp. 78–85. For an outline of all three rapture traditions (Enoch, Moses and Elijah) see Arie Zwiep, *The Ascension of the Messiah in Lukan Christology*, NovTSup 87 (Leiden: Brill, 1997), pp. 41–76.

135. Robinson and Wall, *Called to Be Church*, p. 36; Beverly Roberts Gaventa, *Acts*, ANTC (Nashville: Abingdon, 2003), p. 66.

136. Cf. also Acts 3:22 and 7:37. By 'law' here, I am drawing a connection between the law given at Sinai and the law written on hearts in Jer. 31:31–34. In Acts 1 – 2 we see Luke fusing Mosaic, Davidic and Elijah Christologies, as Christ is the perfect

Finally, the selection of Matthias to replace Judas reconstitutes the twelve (1:21–26) – a further Lukan allusion to the renewal, reconstitution and restoration of Israel.[137] With the leader ascended to the Father, and 'Israel' waiting below, the administration of the fiery covenant-gift may commence.

Acts 2

Although the events of Ascension and Pentecost are separated by several days, thematically and structurally these events are tied together by celestial events (1:9; 2:2) and the pattern of prophecy and fulfilment (1:4–8; 2:17–18).[138]

The parallels between the starts of Luke's Gospel and Acts are noteworthy. In both there is a promise of baptism in the Spirit (Luke 3:16; Acts 1:5), followed by the descent of the Spirit (Luke 3:21–22; Acts 2:1–4), then a programmatic sermon (Luke 4:16–30; Acts 2:14–40), followed finally by witness (in words and wonders) to the Jews (Luke 4:31–44; Acts 3 – 4). These parallels support the special place of the Twelve as Jesus' witnesses, already seen in Acts 1:2–3, 21–26.[139]

There are further new-exodus or new-restoration motifs present in Acts 2, beginning with the Sinai *déjà vu* in Acts 2:1–4.[140] Bock thinks that a 'Mosaic background is not significant at all for the Pentecost event'.[141] However, there are a number of strands of evidence that suggest a Sinai backdrop to the Pentecost event. First, the Jewish festival of Pentecost is considered by some to have become a remembrance and celebration of the giving of the law at Sinai.[142]

---

fulfilment of them all and the end to which they all point (Luke 24:27). Matthias Wenk, *Community Forming Power: The Socio-Ethical Role of the Spirit in Luke–Acts*, JPTSup 19 (Sheffield: Sheffield Academic Press, 2000), p. 247.

137. Arie Zwiep, *Judas and the Choice of Matthias* (Tübingen: Mohr Siebeck, 2004), pp. 159–179.

138. Spencer, *Acts*, p. 33.

139. Ben Witherington III, *The Acts of the Apostles* (Grand Rapids: Eerdmans, 1998), p. 128.

140. Spencer, *Acts*, p. 42.

141. Darrell L. Bock, *Proclamation from Prophecy and Pattern: Lucan Old Testament Christology*, JSNTSup 12 (Sheffield: Sheffield Academic, 1987), pp. 182–183; Bock is more sympathetic to a Mosaic background in his later commentary. Darrell L. Bock, *Acts*, BECNT (Grand Rapids: Baker Academic, 2007), pp. 95–96.

142. Mikael C. Parsons, *Acts*, Paideia Commentaries on the New Testament (Grand Rapids: Baker Academic, 2008), p. 36; O. Betz, 'φωνή', in *TDNT*, vol. 9, p. 296.

There is some evidence of this in the intertestamental literature.[143] Second, there are obvious Sinai parallels in the description of the events of 2:1–13. The sound and fire provide conceptual parallels to the giving of Torah at Sinai (Exod. 19:18–20).[144] As Johnson points out, 'nowhere is the same cluster of symbols found all together except in the LXX description of Sinai'.[145]

Having been filled with the Spirit (1:5; 2:4), the disciples begin to speak (1:8; 2:4). Many scholars see an allusion to Genesis 11.[146] If there is a sense in which Babel is reversed this would further support the restoration motif already argued for as nations stream to Jerusalem (Mic. 4:1–2). A reversal, recapitulation or even parody of Babel fits with the view that the list of nations in 2:9–11 has some relationship to the table of nations in Genesis 10.[147]

There are various interpretations regarding the list of nations in 2:9–11. Interpreters consider the list of nations to be a random list,[148] representative of universality,[149] representative of the table of nations in Genesis 10[150] or a

---

143. *Jub.* 1.1, 6.17–19 and 14.20 associate covenant renewal with Pentecost (Feast of Weeks). See Geza Vermes, *The Dead Sea Scrolls: Qumran in Perspective* (London: Collins, 1977), pp. 177–178.

144. Peterson, *Acts*, p. 131.

145. Johnson, *Acts*, p. 46.

146. See particularly Gary Gilbert, 'From Eschatology to Imperialism: Mapping the Territory of Acts 2', in *The Gospels According to Michael Goulder* (Harrisburg: Trinity, 2002), pp. 84–110; James M. Scott, 'Luke's Geographical Horizon', in *The Book of Acts in Its First Century Setting*, 5 vols. (Grand Rapids: Eerdmans, 1994), vol. 2, pp. 483–544.

147. Green argues that Pentecost is a parody of Babel, as diverse languages are brought together not for preservation from scattering (Gen. 11:4) but for the purpose of scattering. Joel B. Green, '"In Our Own Languages": Pentecost, Babel, and the Shaping of Christian Community in Acts 2:1–13', in *The Word Leaps the Gap: Essays on Scripture and Theology in Honor of Richard B. Hays* (Grand Rapids: Eerdmans, 2008), pp. 198–213.

148. Fitzmyer, *Acts*, p. 240.

149. Spencer, *Acts*, p. 44. He considers the list to be descriptive of the four corners of the earth. Metzger argues that the list represents universality under the twelve signs of the zodiac, but the connections are unconvincing. Bruce M. Metzger, 'Ancient Astrological Geography and Acts 2:9–11', in *Apostolic History and the Gospel: Biblical and Historical Essays Presented to F. F. Bruce* (Exeter: Paternoster, 1970), pp. 123–133.

150. Parsons, *Acts*, pp. 39–40. Scott, 'Luke's Geographical Horizon', p. 530. This understanding might fit particularly well if Pentecost were to be understood as a reversal of Babel.

political statement.[151] The last three options together provide the most plausible answer. We are told in 2:5 that men had gathered from 'every nation under heaven'. Heaven, in Acts, is the place from which the risen and ascended Christ exercises his universal rule. In terms of Genesis 10, the linguistic connections between Acts 2 and Genesis 11 extend back to Genesis 10 (LXX *glōssa*, Gen. 10:5, 20, 31). Genesis 10 also gives us a list of all the nations under the heavenly rule of YHWH. And politically, just as the writer of Genesis lists the nations of the earth under YHWH, so too Rome lists the nations of the earth under Caesar.[152] Luke is making a theopolitical statement by reconstituting the nations 'under heaven', that is, under *Christ's* rule,[153] as well as perhaps drawing on Old Testament prophecies about the ingathering of the exiles (Isa. 11:11–12; Acts 2:5–11).[154]

In response to the events Peter delivers a message that many see as, in some sense, programmatic for the rest of the narrative.[155] Peter's speech begins with the citation of Joel 3:1–5 (LXX). Significantly Peter modifies the LXX, replacing the more general *meta tauta* (after these things) with the more redemptively significant 'in the last days' (*en tais eschatais hēmerais*).[156] These words place the Pentecost event within God's final stage of redemption.[157] Peter is injecting a sense of eschatological urgency into the events.[158]

The speech explains the events just witnessed by the crowd in terms of the resurrection, ascension and exaltation of the Messiah, Jesus. The purpose of citing Joel 3:1–5 (LXX) is clear – it explains the prophetic events just witnessed by the crowd. However, it goes beyond a justification for the events and sets up a proclamation of the heavenly author of the events. 'Wonders and signs' are

---

151. Gilbert, 'Eschatology to Imperialism', pp. 84–110.

152. This is similar to the argument Gilbert makes, linking Gen. 10 – 11, Acts 2 and the political propaganda of Luke's day. Luke's point is theopolitical. Ibid., pp. 94–95.

153. There may also be a movement through time as well as space, as the empires listed span those from the Parthians to the Romans. This may further highlight Christ's superiority over Caesar. Laura Nasrallah, 'The Acts of the Apostles, Greek Cities, and Hadrian's Panhellenion', *JBL* 127.3 (2008), pp. 533–566.

154. Pao, *Acts*, pp. 130–131. We also must remember the strong influence the Gen. 10 table of nations exerts on the OT and other Jewish literature. See Scott, 'Luke's Geographical Horizon', p. 520.

155. Tannehill, *Narrative Unity*, p. 29.

156. Witherington, *Acts*, p. 142.

157. C. K. Barrett, *Acts 1–14*, ICC (London: T&T Clark, 1994), p. 136.

158. Spencer, *Acts*, p. 45; Johnson, *Acts*, p. 49.

accredited to Jesus in 2:22, further demonstrating the Christological application of the quote. The miraculous as authenticating is constitutive of Lukan Christology.[159]

Peter moves from Jesus' life to his foreordained death to his resurrection. The quotation from Psalm 16 (LXX 15):8–11, cited in verses 25–28, demonstrates that the resurrection of Jesus, witnessed by his disciples, is the vindication of him as the 'Holy One' of God. Jesus is shown to be the Messiah and David's eschatological heir.[160] Notes of restoration again resound as a Davidic King is returned to the throne (v. 30). This is a key aspect of Luke's soteriological enterprise (cf. Acts 15:16).[161]

Here we begin to see how 'exodus' and 'restoration' themes converge. When we recall that there had not been a king on David's throne since the exile we can see why the Jews still considered themselves in exile.[162] A new exodus provides both liberation and restoration. With the throne occupied and the covenant ratified, liberation and restoration can begin, and have in fact already begun (vv. 30–33). Turner suggests that in Jesus' exaltation (vv. 33–36) we have a fusion of 'Davidic and Mosaic Christologies together in a New Exodus soteriology'.[163] The argument is built partly on seeing an allusion in verse 33 to the Jewish Targum on Psalm 68:19 (MT), which interprets the verse as referring to the giving of the law at Sinai.[164] The Targum on Psalm 68:19 (MT) reads, 'You have ascended to the firmament, O prophet Moses, you took captives, you taught the words of the Law, you gave them as gifts to the sons of man.'[165]

---

159. See also Luke 4:36; 19:37. Fitzmyer, *Acts*, p. 20.

160. Turner, *Power*, p. 275.

161. Mark Lee, 'An Evangelical Dialogue on Luke, Salvation, and Spirit Baptism', *The Journal of the Society for Pentecostal Studies* 26.1 (2004), p. 87.

162. Judah had of course had self-acclaimed priest-kings in the Hasmonean dynasty and puppet kings in the Herodian, but Davidic kings these were not. For evidence of early Jews viewing themselves as still in exile see Sir. 36; Bar. 2.7–10; Tob. 13.5; 2 Macc. 2.18; *1 En.* 89; *T. Mos.* 4.8–9; see also N. T. Wright, *The New Testament and the People of God*, COQG 1 (London: SPCK, 1992), pp. 157–161, 268–269.

163. Turner, *Power*, p. 279. I have already argued above that the fusion also includes an Elijah Christology seen in the ascension.

164. J. Dupont, 'Ascension du Christ et don de l'Esprit d'après Actes 2:33', in *Christ and Spirit in the New Testament: Studies in Honour of Charles Francis Digby Moule* (Cambridge: Cambridge University Press, 1973), pp. 219–228.

165. David M. Stec, *The Targum of Psalms*, 16 vols., ArBib (London: T&T Clark, 2004), vol. 16, p. 131.

While rabbinic exegesis of the psalm celebrates the gift of the law through the ascended Moses, now it is replaced by the gift of the Spirit through the ascended Christ.[166] It is the figures of David and Moses *together* who play the part.[167]

The use of 'right hand' in verse 33 leads into the quotation from Psalm 110:1 (LXX Ps. 109:1).[168] The risen and exalted Messiah has taken his place on the throne at the right hand of God as both Lord and Christ. The final appeal to the audience takes us back to Joel 3:1–5 (LXX) with mention of the 'name' (now clearly identified as Jesus Christ) and the promise of the Spirit. The promise in Acts 2:39 is said to be 'for you and your children and for all who are far off' echoing another promise of covenant renewal and restoration in Isaiah 59:19–21.[169] The final call to save themselves from this crooked generation once again alludes to the wilderness generation, which Moses addressed in Deuteronomy 32:5.

Following Peter's Pentecost sermon is the first description of the corporate life of this new community (Acts 2:42–47).[170] Keener states, 'The goal of the Pentecost experience, with its empowerment for mission, includes a community modelling the ideal, proleptically eschatological lifestyle of the kingdom.'[171] Just as the Spirit empowered missionally effective preaching, so the Spirit empowers missionally effective living.[172] Luke reports their devotion to the apostolic 'teaching' (*didachē*), the 'fellowship' (*koinōnia*),[173] the 'breaking

---

166. Dupont, 'Ascension', p. 229.

167. Turner, *Power*, p. 289.

168. Johnson, *Acts*, p. 52.

169. Jon Ruthven, 'This Is My Covenant with Them: Isaiah 59:19–21 as the Programmatic Prophecy of the New Covenant in the Acts of the Apostles (Part II)', *JPT* 17.2 (2008), pp. 219–237.

170. These summary passages in Acts serve as an apologia of the community for Theophilus, and also as an example to imitate. Schnabel suggests, 'These summaries are located in the early part of Acts, probably because there was a need at the beginning to describe the identity and ministry of the church. The summaries function to generalize and thus make the experience of individuals normative.' Eckhard J. Schnabel, *Acts*, ECNT 5 (Grand Rapids: Zondervan, 2012), p. 175.

171. Craig S. Keener, *Acts: An Exegetical Commentary*, 4 vols. (Grand Rapids: Baker, 2012), vol. 1, p. 991.

172. Craig S. Keener, *Acts 1:1–2:47* (Grand Rapids: Baker, 2012), p. 1038.

173. Dupont suggests that the idea of the 'fellowship' incorporates both the practical sharing of goods and the enjoyment of close relationship. Dupont argues that

of bread' (*klasei tou artou*),[174] and 'prayers' (*proseuchais*).[175] The periphrastic construction, and the present active participle 'continually' (*proskarterountes*, 2:42), suggest an ongoing perseverance in a way of life.[176] Additionally, apostolic signs and wonders are performed and the whole community share possessions, meeting daily in the temple courts, eating together and praising God.[177] Several studies note the various parallels of such a community ideal in Hellenistic and Qumran literature, but Keener suggests that the primary influence on Luke's community is Jesus and the literature of the Old Testament.[178] Johnson notes the positive effect that this Hellenistic style of narrative would have for Gentile readers, but also notes that for Luke it is more important to present the new community as the fulfilment of the promise to restore Israel.[179]

(note 173 *cont.*) Luke's description is based on both Graeco-Roman and Jewish ideals. Jacques Dupont, 'Community of Goods in the Early Church', in *The Salvation of the Gentiles: Studies in the Acts of the Apostles* (New York: Paulist Press, 1979), pp. 85–102.

174. Whether the breaking of bread refers to simple shared meals or a more formal 'Lord's Supper' is debated. Keener suggests that these common meals were based on Jesus' teaching on hospitality (Luke 14:1–14) and the Last Supper (Luke 22:7–23). The primitive Lord's Supper would have been part of a meal in which people shared food and gave thanks to God for, among other things, the cross-work of Jesus. Keener, *Acts 1:1–2:47*, pp. 1004–1005. So too Philippe H. Menoud, 'The Acts of the Apostles and the Eucharist', in *Jesus Christ and the Faith: A Collection of Studies by Philippe H. Menoud*, tr. Eunice M. Paul (Pittsburgh: Pickwick, 1978), pp. 84–106.

175. The 'prayers' likely refer to the set times of prayer at the temple (cf. Acts 3:1). See Daniel K. Falk, 'Jewish Prayer Literature and the Jerusalem Church in Acts', in *The Book of Acts in Its First Century Setting*, 5 vols. (Grand Rapids: Eerdmans, 1995), vol. 4, pp. 267–301.

176. BDAG, p. 881; Bock, *Acts*, p. 149.

177. Bock suggests that care for the needy here may be rooted in Jesus' teaching in Luke 6:30–36 or taken from Deut. 15:4–5. *Acts*, p. 153.

178. Keener, *Acts 1:1–2:47*, p. 1021. See also David L. Mealand, 'Community of Goods and Utopian Allusions in Acts II–IV', *JTS* 28 (1977), pp. 96–99; Pieter W. van der Horst, 'Hellenistic Parallels to the Acts of the Apostles', *JSNT* 25 (1985), pp. 49–60. Hellenistic parallels can be seen in Plato, *Republic* 449c; *Critias* 110c–d; Aristotle, *Nicomachean Ethics* 1168b; Ovid, *Metamorphoses* 1.88–111. Qumran parallels can be seen in 1QS 5.1–3; CD 9.1–15.

179. Johnson, *Acts*, pp. 62–63. VanderKam, noting the Sinai links with the day of Pentecost, extends the links to the summary at the end of Acts 2 by suggesting,

Significantly, the result of this community life is they were 'enjoying the favour of all the people. And the Lord added to their number daily those who were being saved.'[180] There is a translation question with the phrase 'enjoying the favour of all the people' (*echontes charin pros holon ton laon*, 2:47).[181] It is possible that the 'grace/favour' (*charin*) is received or given. Both senses carry missional overtones, but, as Andersen observes, the literary context supports the majority translation – the 'favour' is received *from* all the people.[182] As a consequence many people are added to the number of the believing community. The community ethic is explicitly missional. Keener suggests a possible chiastic arrangement, which brings out the missional emphasis:

A   Effective evangelism (through preaching, 2:41)
   B   Shared worship and meals (2:42)
      C   Shared possessions (2:44–45)
   B' Shared worship and meals (2:46)
A' Effective evangelism (through lifestyle, 2:47)[183]

Keener's suggestion fails to account for the miracles of 2:43, but does draw out Luke's emphasis on both the lifestyle of the community and its missional consequences. As Bock observes, 'A vibrant community extends itself in two

---

'the nature of the community formed by the first Christians may also be paralleled by Jewish understandings of events at Sinai . . . the Bible itself gave rise to the idea of imagining the situation as ideal when Israel encamped at Mt. Sinai and received the Torah'. James VanderKam, 'Covenant and Pentecost', *CTJ* 37 (2002), p. 252.

180. The church, like Jesus, in its infancy wins the favour of the people (cf. Luke 2:52). Pervo notes this favour does not last, and opposition grows through Acts 3 – 7, culminating in the death of Stephen, the *ekklēsia*'s first martyr. *Acts*, pp. 94–95. Nevertheless the nature of the passage as a summary transposes it from description to paradigm.

181. Andersen notes it is the only occurrence of the phrase in the NT, with the preposition *pros* plus the accusative (*holon ton laon*) ordinarily designating the recipients of the 'grace/favour' (*charis*). T. David Andersen, 'The Meaning of ECHONTES CHARIN PROS in Acts 2.47', *NTS* 34 (1988), pp. 604–610.

182. Ibid., p. 607. See Acts 4:21; 5:13. Further, BDAG (874b) indicates that *pros* plus the accusative can mean 'with' or 'before' (i.e. favour with/before all the people).

183. Keener, *Acts 1:1–2:47*, p. 992.

directions: toward God and toward neighbour ... Their life as a community
was a visible part of their testimony.'[184]

Acts 3 – 4

Immediately following Luke's portrayal of the life of the community the reader
is introduced to a specific situation that depicts a new wave of growth and the
beginnings of opposition. Peter and John, en route to the temple, stop to heal
a lame man (3:1–9). Peter uses the occasion to speak about the life, death and
resurrection of Jesus as fulfilment of the Old Testament messianic promises,
and exhorts his listeners to repent that times of refreshing may come.[185] In
Acts 3:22 Peter quotes the words of Moses from Deuteronomy 18:15–19 – Jesus
is the prophet like Moses to whom the people must listen. Peter concludes
his speech in verse 25 by reminding his Jewish audience that they are 'heirs of
the prophets and of the covenant God made with your fathers', and cites the
Abrahamic promise 'Through your offspring all peoples on earth will be
blessed.'[186] The mention of the 'servant' in 3:26 (cf. also 3:13) may allude to
Isaiah's Servant Songs; in particular Isaiah 49:1–6, which depicts the Servant as
bringing light to the Gentiles.[187] Peter's speech, as in Acts 2, theologically
interprets the miraculous event in terms of promise and fulfilment. In this
instance the promise includes a nation that will bless nations, led by the
Deuteronomic prophet like Moses. Once again, Luke brings mission and ethics
together.

As a consequence of Peter's action and speech opposition begins to grow,
as does the believing community (to five thousand men, Acts 4:4). The subsequent interrogation by the authorities results in the command not to speak
any longer in the name of Jesus, a command Peter and John refuse to obey

---

184. Bock, *Acts*, pp. 154–155.

185. Johnson notes again the prophecy–fulfilment motif as a favourite rhetorical device
of Luke's. *Acts*, p. 68.

186. There are four such promises to Abraham in the Genesis narrative, with minor
variations in wording: Gen. 12:3; 18:18; 22:18; and 26:4. Witherington notes
with reference to Luke's citation of the Abraham promise vis-à-vis the nations,
'Luke is masterfully preparing for later developments in his narrative'. *Acts*,
p. 188.

187. Peterson, *Acts*, p. 185. Keener states, 'To offer blessing to Israel *first* (of the families
of the earth) probably implies Gentile mission, which follows it, fleshed out in the
rest of Acts.' Craig S. Keener, *Acts: An Exegetical Commentary*, 4 vols. (Grand Rapids:
Baker Academic, 2012), vol. 2, p. 1121. Emphasis original.

(Acts 4:5–22). Luke again notes that 'all the people were praising God for what had happened' (4:21). Upon their release Peter and John report back to the believers who, in response, pray and receive further empowerment from the Spirit to continue to speak for God with boldness (4:23–31).

In similar terms to Acts 2:42–47 Luke begins his second summary passage by describing the community as being one in heart and mind, and sharing everything they possessed (Acts 4:32; cf. 2:44).[188] The sharing of goods draws not only on the Graeco-Roman friendship ideal noted previously, but also on the teachings of the Old Testament and Jesus.[189] The description of being one in heart and mind (*kardia kai psychē mia*) is distinctively Jewish – in particular alluding to the Shema in Deuteronomy 6:5.[190] As a consequence, in verse 33 there is another reference to *charis* (grace) upon the believers that may be another reference to the favour of the people, or it may refer to divine favour upon them.[191] Seccombe rightly observes that the life of the community is 'congruent with God's work in it. It has a reality and beauty which mark it out, even to Gentiles, as the sphere of God's activity.'[192] Luke adds in verse 34 that 'there was no needy person among them', an echo of Deuteronomy 15:4. The word *endeēs* (need) is comparatively rare, occurring only twenty-two times in the literature of the Old Testament (LXX) and New Testament. Notably it appears four times in Deuteronomy (15:4, 7, 11; 24:14) and twice in the Major Prophets (Isa. 41:17; Ezek. 4:17). It appears to carry connotations of impoverishment, thereby stressing an ethical overtone in response. Deuteronomy 15:5 makes this clear, as the divine blessing is connected to ethical obedience with respect to the poor.[193] That which the Deuteronomist anticipates, Luke celebrates. Gerhardsson plausibly suggests that the allusion to Deuteronomy 6:5 in verse 32, followed by the neighbour love displayed in the sharing of possessions, demonstrates the early community to be living in fulfilment of the great commandment, as

---

188. Witherington suggests that the iterative imperfects function both descriptively and prescriptively, perhaps alluding to practices his reading community had neglected. *Acts*, p. 205.

189. Although, as Peterson notes, Graeco-Roman friendship ideals were founded on an ethic of reciprocity, Luke's portrayal of the community is one of the rich sharing their wealth with the poor. *Acts*, p. 204.

190. There may also be an allusion to the one heart and way of Jer. 32:39, and to the new heart and spirit of Ezek. 36:26. Peterson, *Acts*, p. 204.

191. Johnson views the phrase as referring to God's favour upon them. *Acts*, p. 86.

192. Seccombe, *Possessions and the Poor*, p. 218.

193. Johnson, *Acts*, p. 86.

given by Jesus in Luke 10:25–37.[194] As observed when considering Luke 10, the context is missional, as the twelve, then seventy, are sent out, followed immediately by Jesus' parable of the good Samaritan. Luke is skilfully weaving together his narrative with backward allusions so as to present this community of believers as living out the missio-ethical ideal of love for God and love for neighbour. In the early chapters of Acts, Luke uses the Old Testament background (the restored Israel, anticipated by the Prophets, living out the Deuteronomic vision of a missional ethic) to depict the community of believers as the restored Israel – loving God, loving neighbour and attracting outsiders.[195]

As with Acts 2:42–47 a combination of Hellenistic and Jewish ideals lie in the background.[196] The echo of Deuteronomy 6:5 and 15:4, along with the various citations of the Old Testament throughout Acts 3 – 4, suggest that it is the ideals of the Old Testament that are more prominent in Lukan summaries.[197] Luke's summary forms a transition to his next episode in the narrative as he recounts the practice of selling property and entrusting a portion of the proceeds for apostolic distribution.

Acts 5 – 6

Luke presents both the real and the ideal. The story of Ananias and Sapphira demonstrates that while the kingdom of God is inaugurated it is not yet consummated. As Parker notes, Acts 4:23–37 leads into Acts 5 in a similar fashion to the way Genesis 1 – 2 leads into Genesis 3.[198]

The culpable sin of Ananias and Sapphira is deceit, not the retention of part of the price received for the land (vv. 3–4). The severity and immediacy of their

---

194. Birger Gerhardsson, 'Einige Bemerkungen zu Apg 4,32', *ST* 24 (1970), pp. 142–149.

195. At this stage those outsiders are Jewish as, in Luke's terms, the light for the nations is ignited by the restoration of Israel.

196. Mealand, 'Community of Goods', pp. 96–99; Van der Horst, 'Hellenistic Parallels', pp. 49–60; Dupont, 'Community of Goods', pp. 85–102.

197. Lüdemann evaluates the Hellenistic and Jewish backgrounds to the materials and while acknowledging the presence of both, for different audiences, suggests that the themes are more Jewish than Greek. Gerd Lüdemann, *Early Christianity According to the Traditions in Acts: A Commentary* (London: SCM, 1989), p. 61.

198. Andrew Parker, 'The Shame We Don't Want to Face: Acts 4:32–5:11', in *Acts in Practice* (Poole: Deo, 2012), pp. 107–108. Similarly Marguerat notes the analogy with Gen. 3: a husband and wife, the presence of Satan, and death as the punishment. Daniel Marguerat, 'La Mort d'Ananias et Saphira (Ac 5.1–11) dans la Stratégie Narrative de Luc', *NTS* 39 (1993), p. 224.

punishment illustrates the importance of the community's holiness and fellowship.[199] Wright notes that the powerful presence of God by his Holy Spirit, evidenced by the miracles, marks out the community as, in some sense, a living temple.[200] As such their holiness is critical to the life of the community. In the Old Testament the accounts of Leviticus 10 or Joshua 7 demonstrate the necessity of holiness among the people, especially where the things devoted to YHWH are concerned. The effect is that all who heard about the events were seized with great fear.

Acts 5:12 introduces a third summary statement, which repeats the earlier themes of the regard of the people (5:13), the numerical growth of the community (5:14), and the miracles of the apostles (5:15–16). The second half of Acts 5 introduces a second narrative of trial and persecution. The intensity is increased as the apostles are not simply warned, as in Acts 4, but are now beaten. The escalation of persecution is set to continue into Acts 7, but only after Luke has first interwoven another portrait of the life of the community and its effect on the surrounding populace.

Acts 6 introduces a new problem facing the community. In the preceding chapters opposition has come from the Jewish religious leaders (Acts 4 – 5) and from Satan filling the hearts of Ananias and Sapphira (Acts 5); now the threat comes from within as a dispute arises between the Hellenistic and Hebraic widows. Community tension has led to 'grumbling' (*gongysmos*), an unusual word with an Old Testament background that serves as an alarm for the reader.[201] Two things are worthy of note at the beginning of this new episode. First, the problem arises because the community is growing. It is a community on mission and Luke has repeatedly noted the increase in numbers. Luke's explanation is the resurrection of Christ and the empowerment of the Spirit enabling this community to be missionally effective. Second, this community is concerned for the care of widows – a repeated Old Testament ethical command.[202] The

---

199. Witherington, *Acts*, p. 215.

200. N. T. Wright, *Acts for Everyone: Part 1: Chapter 1–12* (London: SPCK, 2008), p. 81.

201. The word *gongysmos* occurs only seventeen times in the Bible, five of which occur in Exod. 16:7–12, which recounts God's judgment on Israel for grumbling against him in a quarrel over food provision.

202. Cf. Deut. 10:18; 14:29; 24:17–21; 26:12–13; Isa. 1:17; 10:2; Jer. 7:6; 22:3; Ezek. 22:7. This is also an interest expressed in Luke's Gospel. See Luke 2:36–38; 4:24–26; 7:12; 18:1–8; 21:2–3; and later, in Acts 9:39–41. Charity to the poor is to be read in the light of OT ideals in contrast to the Graeco-Roman view that equated poverty with iniquity and criminality. Witherington, *Acts*, p. 249.

community does not see itself as a new and different cult or movement, but rather as part of the Jewish people, who have been impacted by the Messiah: they still meet in the temple courts to worship and pray; they appeal to Old Testament Scriptures to demonstrate themselves to be in continuity with the larger narrative of YHWH's people; and they seek to care for the needy, with widows the particular focus of Acts 6.[203] Again Luke is portraying this believing community as the fulfilment of the Deuteronomic and prophetic vision.[204]

The essence of the problem presented in Acts 6:1 is that the Hellenistic Jews feel their widows are being overlooked in the daily distribution of food. The apostles' solution is to appoint seven men 'full of the Spirit and wisdom' (v. 3) and to entrust the responsibility to them, in order that the apostles might focus their attention on the ministry of the word and prayer. The proposal is warmly received and Luke's summary in verse 7 indicates success: 'So the word of God spread. The number of disciples in Jerusalem increased rapidly, and a large number of priests became obedient to the faith.'[205] Luke connects the effective care for widows with the large-scale conversion of not just Jews, but priests also. The narrative has not yet described a large-scale conversion of Gentiles, yet Luke does describe the influx of new disciples who were, in some sense, outside the believing community. Again, mission and ethics belong together, with Acts 6:1–7 giving the reader a concrete and powerful example of missional ethics.[206]

---

203. Penner argues that Luke is casting Jesus and his disciples in the mode of Moses: 'the prophet and his people take the same proactive stance toward the outcast (especially widows, orphans and aliens) that prominently defines the righteous individual/ community throughout Deuteronomy'. Todd Penner, *In Praise of Christian Origins: Stephen and the Hellenists in Lukan Apologetic Historiography*, Emory Studies in Early Christianity 10 (New York: T&T Clark, 2004), p. 265.

204. Hence the reference to the 'Twelve' in Acts 6:2 as a picture of Israel restored and renewed.

205. Wright suggests OT roots for the word Luke uses to describe the 'increase' (*auxanō*) of the word in Acts 6:7. The imagery of the word bearing fruit echoes Isa. 55:10–13, and the word *auxanō* is used in Isa. 61:11 to speak of the 'increase' of righteousness and praise before all nations. *Auxanō* appears again with reference to the progress of the word in Acts 12:24. Wright, *Acts 1–12*, p. 100; Jerome Kodell, '"The Word of God Grew": The Ecclesial Tendency of Λόγος in Acts 1,7; 12,24; 19,20', *Bib* 55 (1974), p. 510.

206. Schnabel suggests that the growth is the result of the apostles' renewed commitment to the ministry of word and prayer, which is likely part of the

This raises an important question concerning the object of the community's care. Twelftree argues that 'so-called social justice or social action is not part of Luke's theology and practice of mission. Rather, social action is directed to the Christian community.'[207] In Twelftree's view, social care is important, but it is primarily directed towards those *inside* the church, rather than being a component part of mission towards those outside the church. In response, two things should be noted. First, the impact of the community's mission (as seen e.g. in Acts 6:1–6) does reach those outside the community, who as a consequence come inside to join the community. Second, Twelftree's argument assumes that the lines between insider and outsider were neat or obvious. In reality this is unlikely to have been the case. In a community of over 5,000 believers the vast majority of whom (if not all) appear to have been Jewish (though note the cultural differences implied by the differentiation of Hellenistic and Hebraic), who happen to be moving around in Jerusalem, among Jewish people, still practising their religion in Jewish ways and Jewish contexts, the boundary lines between the communities would be somewhat blurred.[208] It is highly likely that a large number of people would have positioned themselves on the fringe of the community, enjoying a measure of fellowship and friendship, without having committed themselves fully to the values or beliefs of the apostolic leadership of the community (cf. 5:13).[209] Would Twelftree regard these people as insiders or outsiders? Would their widows benefit in any way, or at any time, from the generosity and care of the believing community? From Luke's portrayal it seems plausible that one of the significant ways the community drew people in was

---

answer, but ignores the missional effect of the care itself. *Acts*, p. 335. Given the narrative focus on the care for widows, it seems more plausible to see this care as the primary catalyst for growth. Peterson captures the nuance well: 'Church growth continued because the word of God had free course among the believers, and outsiders were able to witness its practical effect in a loving, united community.' Peterson, *Acts*, p. 236.

207. Graham H. Twelftree, *People of the Spirit: Exploring Luke's View of the Church* (London: SPCK, 2009), p. 197.

208. Marshall, 'Luke's "Social" Gospel', p. 125.

209. Schnabel notes that the term *kollaō* in 5:13 is used in the LXX to denote physical proximity without necessarily implying full conversion (e.g. Deut. 28:60; 29:20). *Acts*, p. 291. Similarly Schwartz argues that the *loipōn* named in 5:13 are 'non-joining sympathizers', who 'were hesitant to take the most extreme step, [though] many did associate themselves with the Christian community'. Daniel R. Schwartz, 'Non-Joining Sympathizers (Acts 5, 13–14)', *Bib* 64 (1983), p. 554.

through their widespread care and kindness. Luke is presenting this new *ekklēsia* in Deuteronomic terms.[210] Wise men are appointed to a task (Deut. 1:13; Acts 6:3), widows are cared for (Deut. 10:18; Acts 6:5–6) and outsiders are drawn in (Deut. 4:6–8; Acts 6:7).

The second half of Acts 6, and into Acts 7, sees a further escalation in persecution, culminating in the first martyrdom. As a result, much of the community is scattered through Judea and Samaria, in fulfilment of Acts 1:8.[211] Acts 1 – 7 has set the paradigm for the community. They are to be a people on mission who demonstrate their love for God and love for neighbour in ways patterned on the formative revelation of the Old Testament Scriptures, and Jesus' own teachings. It remains for us to consider briefly the extent to which missional ethics features in the remainder of Luke's narrative.

Acts 9 – 28

As Luke's narrative unfolds it is worth considering the extent to which missional ethics continues to be present and effective. A superficial reading of the text suggests that the theme becomes less important to Luke as the believing community spreads out beyond Jerusalem. It is also evident that the early 'favour' experienced by the believers (Acts 2:47) quickly becomes persecution in Jerusalem and further afield. The question is how one accounts for the apparent shift in emphasis, and the persecution experienced.

The first possible answer is to suggest that there is no real change in emphasis – it is simply the case that Luke is unconcerned with the superimposed theme of missional ethics.[212] However, the earlier parts of this chapter and work suggest that Luke does have a real concern for the community's ethic and its missional impact on those around them.[213]

A second answer would be to suggest that after the early years of zeal, as the persecution grew and the believers spread, they failed to live up to the high ideals

---

210. Note *ekklēsia* occurs in the LXX first in Deut. 4:10 and then subsequently in Deut. 9:10; 18:16; 23:2, 3, 4, 9; 31:30. In Acts the term first occurs at 5:11.

211. Johnson, *Acts*, p. 141.

212. Haenchen, for example, suggests that there was no deliberate missionary effort before the apostle Paul. Ernst Haenchen, *The Acts of the Apostles* (Westminster: Philadelphia, 1971), p. 144.

213. Goheen, along with many others, notes that mission is central to Luke's endeavour, and in particular that mission is characterized by the lives of the believing community. Michael W. Goheen, *A Light to the Nations: The Missional Church and the Biblical Story* (Grand Rapids: Baker Academic, 2011), p. 127.

portrayed at the start of Luke's narrative.[214] Yet there are repeated glimmers of a distinctive ethic that run through Acts, to which we shall return below.

A third possibility is that Luke emphasizes Old Testament Jewish ideals in Jerusalem, but is less interested in the repetition of such ideals in the wider Hellenistic contexts of the church's expansion. Like 'signs and wonders' the concentration of the material is presented in the context in which it carries greatest significance. The paradigm is set in Acts 1 – 7 and continuity is assumed; therefore further repetition would be redundant.[215]

A fourth answer may be to see Luke's primary interest, post-Jerusalem, as being in the spread of the gospel message across the Roman Empire; therefore his narratival focus is on growth, with relatively little interest in the lives of the early communities.[216]

The text itself gives evidence to suggest that the first two answers seem untenable, whereas the third and fourth answers (with some supplementary argument) have more to commend them. The portrayal of the Jerusalem church in the summary passages functions, to some degree, as paradigmatic and exemplary for the subsequent communities. Marshall suggests:

> Luke makes it clear enough that the ideal was intended to be upheld and practised elsewhere, though not necessarily in the same precise manner. Having emphasized what happened in Jerusalem, Luke had no need to repeat himself later; he expects his readers to take certain things 'as read.'[217]

They are the blueprint, type or pattern for every community that stands in the line of Jesus and his apostles.

---

214. Bosch, for example, describes Luke's portrait as idealized. This may indeed be the case, but it is nonetheless designed, within Luke's narrative rhetoric, to be inspirational for his readership. David J. Bosch, *Transforming Mission: Paradigm Shifts in Theology of Mission* (Maryknoll: Orbis, 1991), p. 121.

215. Martin C. Salter, *The Power of Pentecost: An Examination of Acts 2:17–21* (Eugene: Resource, 2012), pp. 52–56.

216. Witherington talks about the spread of the gospel in the vertical (social) and horizontal (geographical) axes, with Luke's first volume taking more interest in the former, and his second volume emphasizing the latter. However, this does not mean Luke is uninterested in the social dimensions of missional growth. In many ways that pattern is already established in the life and ministry of Jesus. Witherington, *Acts*, pp. 68–74.

217. Marshall, 'Luke's "Social" Gospel', p. 118.

While a significant interest of Luke is in the growth of Christianity he regularly intersperses miniature portraits of the idealized ethic into his account of growth to demonstrate his continued concern, and the missional import, of the believers' ethic. We see such examples in Acts 9, where Tabitha is characterized as 'always doing good and helping the poor' (Acts 9:36). A few verses later we meet Cornelius, whose devotion and gifts to the poor come up as a memorial offering before God (Acts 10:4). In Acts 11 Barnabas re-enters the narrative and is described as a 'good man, full of the Holy Spirit and faith', and, presumably linked to his goodness, the next phrase reads, 'and a great number of people were brought to the Lord' (v. 24).[218] In Acts 15 the Jerusalem council adjudicates on an ethical issue emerging in the churches containing Jews and Gentiles together – an issue that required distinctive witness in communities where pagan worship was the norm.[219] In Acts 16 Paul liberates a slave girl being abused for economic gain (Acts 16:16–19), and in Acts 19 the public renunciation of idolatry resulted in the spread of the word (Acts 19:18–20). The ending of Luke's narrative is deliberately open ended, inviting Luke's readership to become his third volume.[220]

Throughout the narrative persecution walks hand in hand with growth, as it did in Jesus' own ministry. Luke's message is not that missional ethics has failed, but rather that there is no guarantee that the righteous life will always yield a positive response. Missional ethics is a thread running through Luke's entire two-volume project. Inevitably it receives more attention in some parts than others, but it pervades the whole, insisting that the life of the believing community – a life of love for God, and love for neighbour – has a missional impact on the people who witness and experience Jesus' disciples in action.

---

218. Peterson, *Acts*, p. 355.

219. The distinctive witness of the community is emphasized in the apostolic decree, which, in Witherington's terms, is more about the venue than the menu. The new Christian communities are to be a contrast community in a context of pagan worship and temples. See Witherington, *Acts*, pp. 460–466.

220. See Daniel Marguerat, 'The Enigma of the Silent Closing of Acts', in *Jesus and the Heritage of Israel* (Harrisburg: Trinity, 1999), pp. 284–304; G. W. Trompf, 'On Why Luke Declined to Recount the Death of Paul: Acts 27–28 and Beyond', in *Luke–Acts: New Perspectives from the SBL Seminar* (New York: Crossroad, 1984), pp. 225–239.

Conclusion

In the introduction to this chapter I suggested three Lukan distinctives, noted by Hays in his work *Reading Backwards*. These were a focus on the fulfilment of God's plan as revealed in the Old Testament, a focus on universal mission and a focus on social ethics. Luke weaves these themes together in his two-volume narrative, demonstrating that Jesus and the early church are the fulfilment of the plan of God revealed in the Old Testament: to call out a distinctive people who would be a light to the nations. The means by which they fulfil their mission includes, as an integral part, their life as a community. Furnish suggests that Luke's missional emphasis is much more on 'the practical moral imperative inherent in the kerygma', particularly towards the poor and the outcast: 'What Jesus in fact does in this Gospel, he commands others to do as well. Jesus' *servant* role . . . is given a very particular and practical context in Luke.'[221] The 'mission of the early church in the first chapters of Acts stands parallel to the mission of Jesus in the early chapters of Luke's Gospel . . . the mission of Jesus continues through his people'.[222]

The community's love for God and love for neighbour witness to the nations in fulfilment of the vision set out in Deuteronomy and the Major Prophets. In Luke's Gospel Jesus repeatedly addresses the issues of true and false right-eousness, wealth, generosity, sharing, provision and hospitality, all with an eye towards the outsider or the 'lost'. These themes are picked up and continued in the book of Acts, where the community is repeatedly characterized, in the early chapters, as winning 'favour' through their social care. The people become the hermeneutic of the good news.[223] As Marshall states, 'The faithful proclamation of the gospel . . . includes the expression of God's compassion in care for the sick and disabled and the calling to account of the rulers and "the mighty" to practise righteousness.'[224] Additionally much of the action in the opening chapters of Luke and Acts, and the closing chapters of Luke, occurs in Jerusalem in and around the temple. True worship, or reform of worship, goes hand in hand with social relief and reform. As Goheen observes, 'Witness defines the people of God in the entirety of their lives – all of life is

---

221. Furnish, *Love Command*, p. 86. Emphasis original.

222. Goheen, *Light to the Nations*, p. 123.

223. Newbigin describes the congregation as the 'hermeneutic of the gospel', p. 222. Lesslie Newbigin, *The Gospel in a Pluralist Society* (London: SPCK, 1989), pp. 222–233.

224. Marshall, 'Luke's "Social" Gospel', pp. 126–127.

witness!'[225] Love for God and love for neighbour are the shape of the new Israel's ethic, and the result is a people, centred around a person, who become a 'light to the nations'. Luke has painted a picture of Israel redeemed and restored, equipped to live out their God-given vocation. The result is the communal expression of missional ethics.

Having completed the exegetical chapters we now move to consider the application of this research to contemporary missiological discussion, before moving to offer an exegetical definition of missional ethics.

---

225. Goheen, *Light to the Nations*, p. 128.

5. MISSIONAL ETHICS: TOWARDS A DEFINITION

Introduction

In the introduction to this book we noted that the concept of missional ethics pre-dates the terminology. Developments in missiological thought throughout the twentieth century, in particular through the ecumenical and evangelical movements, have served to bring greater integration between proclamation and social action. Additionally, missiologists such as Newbigin, Bosch and Wright have further demonstrated the biblical and theological underpinnings of integrated mission. However, thus far a definition of the term 'missional ethics' has not been forthcoming. This book has attempted to elicit a more focused exegetical definition of missional ethics to aid further research in this area. In the pursuit of such a definition the methodology employed has utilized a canonical, narratival, missional and performative hermeneutic in the exegesis of sections of Deuteronomy, the Major Prophets and Luke–Acts. The methodology adopted has elicited a number of beneficial results. The canonical approach has provided a reading position from which to examine the texts that is sensitive to their function and relationships. The narratival hermeneutic has highlighted not just the presence of the theme but its narrative development. Appreciating the wider narrative arc of the canon enables the interpreter to understand the place of each contribution in the flow of the biblical story. The missional hermeneutic has offered a particular sensitivity to the missional dimension and intention of the texts. The performative approach enables the interpreter to remain aware, not just of illocution, but of the perlocution of the text.

The exegesis of the texts yields the following four conclusions, which will be developed below, and upon which a definition of missional ethics will be proposed. First, missional ethics, rather than imposing itself upon the text, arises as a significant concern of the texts themselves. Second, the texts present missional ethics as a holistic and integral enterprise. Third, the texts' presentation of missional ethics takes account of both the individual and the communal, with the latter to the fore. Missional ethics is an inherently communal practice. Fourth, although missional ethics is a broad category, there is a particular emphasis on the themes of justice, charity and worship. These conclusions will now be more fully developed, before proposing a definition of missional ethics.

The missio-ethical author: a divine proposal

The first thing to note in coming towards some conclusions is that missional ethics is not superimposed on the biblical text, but rather emerges from the text itself as an important theme. In our exegesis we noted the foundational nature of Deuteronomy 4:5–8, and the promise that if the people were to live out Torah-shaped lives the nations would come to recognize something of the greatness of YHWH. Wright, commenting on these verses, states:

> The ethical quality of life of the people of God (their obedience to the law, in this context) is a vital factor in the attraction of the nations to the living God . . . There is a vital link between the religious claims of the people of God (that God is near them) and their practical social ethic.[1]

Moses' commission to the people is to obey Torah, for it is *through* the keeping of the commandments that God may be known by the surrounding nations.[2] With Genesis 12 and Exodus 19 in the background, Deuteronomy 4:5–8 gives a more specific application of the command to bless the nations, and be a kingdom of priests and a holy nation.[3] We also noted the ending of the section

---

1. Christopher J. H. Wright, *Deuteronomy*, NIBC 4 (Peabody: Hendrickson, 1996), p. 49.
2. Patrick D. Miller, *Deuteronomy*, Int (Louisville: John Knox, 1990), p. 57.
3. Israel's call to be a blessing to the nations was 'in their "genetic code" from the very loins of Abraham'. Wright, *Deuteronomy*, pp. 48–49.

covering the legal material, Deuteronomy 26:18–19. YHWH's declaration in
verses 18–19 is that Israel is a treasured possession and a holy people, phrases
reminiscent of Exodus 19:5–6. The purpose is that Israel's holiness will result
in the praise of the nations.[4]

Missional ethics is a theme equally pervasive through the Major Prophets.
Isaiah 1 – 2 and 65 – 66 frame the book in terms of YHWH's plan to gather the
nations to worship him through his elect community. Recall Tull's comments
on Isaiah 2:1–4:

> [It] cuts right through oppositions between nationalism and universalism, emphasizing
> that Jerusalem's unique calling comes from God not for her sake alone, but so that in
> her all the nations of the earth will be blessed.[5]

Brueggemann added that Israel was to be 'like a magnet, drawing all the nations
of the world toward its peculiar authority'.[6] The conclusion of Isaiah's vision of
restoration proclaims that the purified people will bring the nations to Jerusalem
(Isa. 66:17–21). We noted the theme of missional ethics was more implicit in
Jeremiah, but Wright summarized well the missio-ethical thrust of Jeremiah's
book:

> The missional purpose of the text of Jeremiah, then, was to bring Israel back to their
> covenant shape. But the longer-distant purpose of *that* was to enable them to fulfil
> their mission of bringing blessing to the nations . . . there is a fundamental,
> inextricable connection between the ethical quality of life of the people of God
> and their mission to the nations.[7]

Ezekiel too devotes significant attention to Israel's failure in their vocation to
witness to YHWH among the nations. Israel's centrality among the nations was
noted in Ezekiel 5:

> Israel's centrality is not merely geographical but theological and, in a sense,
> missiological . . . It was a shorthand way of expressing all the universality of

---

4. Miller, *Deuteronomy*, p. 188.

5. Patricia K. Tull, *Isaiah 1–39*, SHBC (Macon: Smyth & Helwys, 2010), p. 85.

6. Walter Brueggemann, *Isaiah 1–39*, WBC (Louisville: Westminster John Knox, 1998), p. 24.

7. Christopher J. H. Wright, '"Prophet to the Nations": Missional Reflections on the Book
of Jeremiah', in *A God of Faithfulness: Essays in Honour of J. Gordon McConville on His 60th
Birthday*, LHB/OTS 538 (London: T&T Clark, 2011), p. 124. Emphasis original.

God's purposes among the nations that was bound up in the particularity
of Israel's election.[8]

Ezekiel, like Isaiah and Jeremiah, depicts the restoration of Israel and the
blessings it will bring to the nations. We noted Launderville's conclusion:

> In Ezekiel's view, the primary way to understand the character of sovereign power
> in the cosmos was to observe living symbols of the personal reality that ruled the
> cosmos . . . Yhwh's Spirit in the Israelites would enable them to be obedient
> and thus to send a true picture of what Yhwh is like through their collective
> existence.[9]

Lukan distinctives included the overarching plan of God, salvation beyond
the borders of Israel, and the social concern for the poor, oppressed and
marginalized, thus bringing together the various components of the narratival
and missional hermeneutics here employed.[10] Ethics and mission are interwoven
through Jesus' instruction to his disciples in the Sermon on the Plain (Luke 6),
his sending out of the seventy (Luke 10), his travel discourse in Luke 11 – 19
and his final commission in Luke 24. The early chapters of Acts portray a community in continuity with the teachings of their leader. Their distinctive, even
Deuteronomic (cf. Acts 4:34 and Deut. 15:4), way of life wins the favour of
outsiders and a great number are added (Acts 2:47). This brief summary of the
exegesis undertaken demonstrates the centrality of the theme of missional
ethics arising from the texts themselves, and running throughout the canonical
narrative. Davy's comments regarding missional hermeneutics, cited in the
methodology, are worth reiterating: a missional hermeneutic considers that
mission is 'not simply one of many themes the Bible touches upon but, rather,
is constitutive of the very nature of the Bible'.[11] Additionally '"Missional", it
could be suggested, characterises the emergence, content, and purpose of the

---

8. Christopher J. H. Wright, *The Message of Ezekiel*, BST (Leicester: Inter-Varsity Press,
    2001), pp. 87–88.

9. Dale F. Launderville, *Spirit and Reason: The Embodied Character of Ezekiel's Symbolic
    Thinking* (Waco: Baylor University Press, 2007), p. 381.

10. Richard B. Hays, *Reading Backwards: Figural Christology and the Fourfold Gospel Witness*
    (London: SPCK, 2015), p. 59.

11. Timothy James Davy, 'The Book of Job and the Mission of God: An Application
    of a Missional Hermeneutic to the Book of Job', PhD diss., University of
    Gloucestershire, 2014, p. 30.

biblical writings.'[12] A missional hermeneutic considers Scripture on its own terms. It is not the only approach to understanding the text, but is central to the Bible's professed self-identity. Missiologists, therefore, have not superimposed particular missiological interests onto the texts or eisegeted their desired outcomes. Rather, the methodology here employed – the canonical, narratival, missional and performative hermeneutic – has elicited positive evidence that missional ethics is a consistent, pervasive and central theme of the biblical text.

The missio-ethical performance: the integration of words and deeds

Since the early twentieth century there has been an ongoing debate concerning the relationship between words and deeds in mission, which invites further reflection regarding the nature and scope of missional ethics.[13]

Some view deeds or actions as important, but separate from 'mission'.[14] Others see deeds as preparatory or confirmatory of evangelism.[15] A number

---

12. Ibid.

13. In the modern history of missiology this debate can be seen in the World Missionary Conferences (1910, 1928, 1938), the International Missionary Councils (1947, 1952), the World Council of Churches gatherings (1948, 1961) and, more recently, through the Lausanne Movement (1974, 1989, 2010) and the Micah Declaration of 2001. Significant figures in those movements have included Hendrick Kraemer, Lesslie Newbigin, John Stott, René Padilla and Christopher Wright. A good summary of the historical debate can be found in Michael W. Goheen, *Introducing Christian Mission Today: Scripture, History and Issues* (Downers Grove: InterVarsity Press, 2014), pp. 152–186; and Scott W. Sunquist, *Understanding Christian Mission: Participation in Suffering and Glory* (Grand Rapids: Baker Academic, 2013), pp. 116–168. Recent publications also address this debate. See for example Kevin DeYoung and Greg Gilbert, *What Is the Mission of the Church?* (Wheaton: Crossway, 2011), and Dean Flemming, *Recovering the Full Mission of God: A Biblical Perspective on Being, Doing, and Telling* (Downers Grove: IVP Academic, 2013).

14. For example, DeYoung and Gilbert, *What Is the Mission?*, p. 26; Eckhard J. Schnabel, *Early Christian Mission*, 2 vols. (Downers Grove: InterVarsity Press, 2005), vol. 1, pp. 11, 83–84.

15. For example, Bosch states, 'The witness of life of the believing community prepares the way for the gospel.' David J. Bosch, *Transforming Mission: Paradigm Shifts in Theology of Mission* (Maryknoll: Orbis, 1991), p. 424.

of writers argue for the centrality, ultimacy or primacy of proclamation evangelism.[16] Additionally there are some who see ethical action as the heart of the gospel and a salvific work in and of itself, particularly those who advocate liberation theologies.[17] The range of opinion demonstrates a lack of clarity as to the part ethics plays in mission, particularly in relationship to verbal proclamation.

The exegetical chapters of this book have argued that missional ethics is an integral part of the overall witness of the covenant community. The ethical life of the covenant community is neither merely preparatory, nor the sum total of the covenant community's witness. Missional ethics is not secondary to the primary act of verbal proclamation, and missional ethics should not be limited to sociopolitical involvement. The exegesis undertaken has demonstrated that witness is an organic whole, where ethics and proclamation are a systemic unity. The discussion is less 'mission and ethics' and more appropriately 'missional ethics'.[18]

Deuteronomy 4:6–8 demonstrated that the Torah-shaped life of the covenant community itself communicated something of God's goodness to the surrounding nations. The missional efficacy is explicitly linked with the ethical distinctiveness of the covenant community. It is when YHWH's Spirit empowers the restored and redeemed community to maintain justice and righteousness (Isa. 56:1–4; 59:21) that the nations will be attracted to Israel's 'light' (Isa. 51:4; 58:8–10; 60:1–3). It is the purified people who are sent with the task of proclamation (Isa. 66:17–20). It is when YHWH restores and renews his people, putting his Spirit within them, and writing his law on their hearts, that his name will be held in renown, praise and honour before all nations, as a consequence of his work in the people (Jer. 31–33). It is when YHWH has cleansed his people, put his Spirit within them, and moved them to follow his laws and keep his decrees that YHWH's name will be esteemed in the eyes of the nations (Ezek. 36:22–28; 37:15–28). In the life of Christ we observed the personification of integration, 'overflowing with the kenotic, self-emptying love of God in speech and action'.[19] In Acts 2:42–47 it is the holistic witness of the community that

---

16. For example, John Stott and Christopher J. H. Wright, *Christian Mission in the Modern World* (Nottingham: Inter-Varsity Press, 2015), pp. 58–59, 80–81.

17. For example, Gustavo Gutiérrez, *A Theology of Liberation: History, Politics and Salvation* (Maryknoll: Orbis, 1973), pp. 71–72.

18. See Darrell L. Guder, *Called to Witness: Doing Missional Theology* (Grand Rapids: Eerdmans, 2015), p. xiii.

19. Sunquist, *Understanding Christian Mission*, p. 320.

wins the favour of the people and causes them to praise God. God's grace is at work through both proclamation and the charity of the early believers (Acts 4:32–34). It is the charity of the community that leads to the continued spread of the word, and the rapid increase in disciples in Acts 6:1–7. Luke does not separate the message and the lives of the believers – they belong together as the integrated witness to the gospel. The texts, as presented in the methodology, invite performance, and performance leads to reflection.[20] The consistent witness of the canonical narrative as examined demonstrates the holistic and integral nature of word and deed.

Many of the debates surrounding the relationship between word and deed since the 1950s had already been addressed by two significant theologians and missiologists writing in the first half of the twentieth century – Karl Barth and J. H. Bavinck. Both men noted the error in attempts to separate speech and action. Karl Barth, though not always prominent in modern missiological discussion, has been described as 'the decisive Protestant missiologist' of his generation.[21] Barth, in his *Church Dogmatics*, defines the mission of the church as a 'witness' to the revelation of the gospel received from Christ.[22] In discussing the form of the community witness he notes twelve characteristics, which include service, care and fellowship.[23] Barth argues that where mission is concerned speech and action must 'always move along these two lines: not merely along either the one or the other, but along both; and no less along the one than the other'.[24] He continues, 'It is not as though it were concerned with something different in the two, but wholly with the same thing though in different ways . . . For its speech is also action and its action speech.'[25] Later, Barth reaffirms, 'If all is well, the speech of the community in all its forms must also be action.

---

20. Stephen B. Bevans, *Models of Contextual Theology* (Maryknoll: Orbis, 2002).
    In Bevans' outline of the various models of contextual theology missional ethics would combine elements of a number of models, and may be described as synthetic, with a bias towards the counter-cultural.
21. Johannes Aagaard. 'Some Main Trends in Modern Protestant Missiology', *ST* 19.238 (1965), p. 238. Online: <www.tandfonline.com/doi/abs/10.1080/00393386508599878>, accessed 25 March 2013.
22. Karl Barth, *Church Dogmatics* IV/3.2: *The Doctrine of Reconciliation*, ed. Geoffrey W. Bromiley and T. F. Torrance (London: T&T Clark International, 2010), p. 148.
23. Ibid., pp. 178–214.
24. Ibid., p. 177.
25. Ibid.

Similarly, action will also necessarily be both implicitly and indeed explicitly speech.'[26] Barth states, 'the voice of the community ... is very largely that of individuals impressing their life and witness on their own time and place and beyond'.[27] Barth concludes, 'the community owes to the world a witness, not to the equality, but to the mutual fellowship of men, which in its final and decisive foundation only the community can give'.[28] In a later work Barth notes, 'the community does not speak with words alone. It speaks by the very fact of its existence in the world.'[29] The exegesis of this work would support Barth's contention. Repeatedly we have noted the way in which the canonical texts hold ethics and speech together, as an integrated holistic missionary paradigm. The biblical text prescribes the performance of the believing community, and the script requires speech and action – both are necessary aspects of the participation in, and communication of, the *missio Dei*. Any attempt to subordinate speech to action or action to speech flies in the face of the exegetical evidence presented.

In a similar vein J. H. Bavinck sought to bring both clarity and nuance to some of the early statements regarding proclamation and action. He criticized approaches that sought to set action and proclamation side by side, often with action preparing the way for speech.[30] Bavinck viewed such approaches as opportunistic and pragmatic, and argued instead for a theological basis for the 'comprehensive' approach. He deemed such an approach unavoidable since 'our entire life is presented as a fundamental unity'.[31] The problem, he suggested, lay in too narrow a view of preaching. He said, 'people think too narrowly and one-sidedly of preaching as speaking, and understand too little of the fact that a person very frequently can speak much more clearly and more directly through deeds'.[32] Bavinck argues:

> The Scriptures view word and deed much more as an indivisible whole. Any
> act wrought in obedience to the will of Christ which takes seriously the person
> with whom we are dealing, and which is not carelessly performed in terms of

---

26. Ibid., p. 196.

27. Ibid., p. 201.

28. Ibid., p. 213.

29. Karl Barth, *Evangelical Theology* (London: Weidenfeld, 1963), p. 38.

30. J. H. Bavinck, *An Introduction to the Science of Missions*, tr. David H. Freeman (Phillipsburg: P&R, 1960), pp. 108–109.

31. Ibid., p. 112.

32. Ibid., p. 113.

our own power and knowledge, is a form of preaching, even though the opportunity is momentarily lacking to further express this preaching in words.[33]

He continues that such good works 'must be so performed that even the pagans who do not understand the deep background of these works inadvertently feel behind them something of the compassion which is not born from man but from God'.[34] Bavinck's use of terminology is open to confusion. The common usage of 'proclamation' does speak of oral address, and therefore Barth's concept of witness is more helpful as it permissibly encompasses not only the verbal but the practical. Both men, however, note that actions have power to witness.

St Francis of Assisi is often quoted as saying, 'Preach the gospel at all times; if necessary use words.'[35] Such an approach is contrary to the exegetical evidence of the texts presented. Life and lip belong together, as the early chapters of Acts demonstrate. The Major Prophets highlight and condemn the anti-missional ethic of words without deeds. The ethical life of the community is not superior to, separate from or merely preparatory for witness – it *is* witness. It is not by itself a sufficient witness since faith comes by hearing (Rom. 10:17), but it is part of an integral whole that is mutually revelatory. The ethical life of the community is intended to communicate in a way analogous to natural revelation. The life of the community is evidence of the creative grace of God and ought to be observable to outsiders, even if they struggle to fully understand or articulate, or even suppress, such revelation. The mission for which God's people are sent is witness, but that witness is both verbal and ethical, and both are necessary to faithful witness. Such an account of the revelatory power of missional ethics would result in the contemporary church taking missional ethics more seriously and putting more thought and resource into this important aspect of the ecclesial vocation.

---

33. Ibid., p. 114.
34. Ibid.
35. Cited in Mike Pilavachi, *When Necessary Use Words: Changing Lives Through Worship, Justice, and Evangelism* (Ventura, Calif.: Regal, 2006). In fact this quote is doubtfully attributed to St Francis, and his emphasis on preaching is evident. See St Francis, *Regula non bullata* (1221); Sunquist, *Understanding Christian Mission*, p. 39.

The missio-ethical cast: the *ekklēsia*

There is also work to be done on the relationship between missional ethics and the church as both organism and institution. This distinction is posited by Abraham Kuyper in his 1870 sermon *Rooted and Grounded*, and has proved useful in subsequent ecclesiological discussion.[36] Kuyper argues that the organism is the living miracle birthed by God's grace: 'A church cannot be manufactured; a polity no matter how tidy, and a confession no matter how spotless, are powerless to form a church if the living organism is absent.'[37] However, 'the church cannot lack the institution, for the very reason that all life among human beings needs analysis and arrangement'.[38] The institution is still divinely mandated as 'a means supplied by God for feeding and expanding that organism . . . From the organism the institution is born, but also through the institution the organism is fed.'[39]

Many of the discussions use the term 'church' interchangeably to refer to both church as organism and church as institution.[40] Yet there are differences in the ways missional ethics should be conceived of in relationship to those two entities. More work is necessary to tease apart the constituent parts of missional ethics in relationship to both individual believers and to the church *qua* church. The exegetical evidence presented in previous chapters has given more weight to the ways in which the covenant community as a whole bears witness to a watching world. That is not to downplay the importance of individuals and their ethical witness in their various spheres of life. Indeed the whole only functions when the individuals perform their necessary parts; yet the emphasis of the texts has been on the community as a whole rather than the isolated individual.

Deuteronomy begins and ends with Moses speaking to 'all Israel' (Deut. 1:1; 32:45). The phrase 'all Israel' appears repeatedly through the book at strategic points to emphasize the corporate call upon and responsibility of the covenant community.[41] We have also noted the repeated theme of the centralization of

---

36. Abraham Kuyper, *Rooted and Grounded*, tr. Nelson D. Kloosterman (Grand Rapids: Christian's Library, 2013; Kindle edn).

37. Ibid., loc. 440.

38. Ibid., loc. 451.

39. Ibid., loc. 484.

40. Further systematic divisions include the church as visible and invisible, and local and universal. For the purposes of the following discussion it is the local, visible community that is being considered.

41. See Deut. 5:1; 13:11; 21:21; 27:9; 31:1, 7, 11; 34:12.

worship, for I have argued that the purpose of centralization was the purity and unity of the corporate gathering (Deut. 12:7–8). Purity is pursued through unity, and the community as a whole bears witness to the outsiders who are invited to participate in the communal act (Deut. 16:11, 14; 26:11). Israel's worship was to be unified and exclusive, wholehearted and joyful, corporate and inclusive.[42] Similarly, the laws addressing justice and charity are addressed to the whole, and are only efficacious if the entire community embraces them. For example, the laws requiring tithes (Deut. 14:28–29) or the cancellation of debts (Deut. 15:1–11) can function as intended only if obeyed by the collective. Justice is administered locally but also centrally (Deut. 17:8), and its work and effect is by and for the benefit of the whole, not just the individual (Deut. 13:11; 19:20; 23:1–14). The whole community is to be concerned with righteousness and holiness (Deut. 16:20; 23:14). The goal of this instruction is not so much a righteous individual as a righteous community.[43] Deuteronomy is a 'social charter' for 'theocentric humanism'.[44] Individuals find their vocation in community.

In the Major Prophets the portrayal of the people's anti-missional ethic is often delivered via the graphic personification of the whole people.[45] The prophetic indictment is delivered against the whole community, or against the leaders who represent the community. Ezekiel 18 is unusual in envisaging a day in which people will die for their own sins. The common vision is of the covenant community as a collective. Other collective imagery includes that of a vineyard (Isa. 5), a bride (Isa. 62:5), a linen belt (Jer. 13), a clay pot (Jer. 18), a tree (Ezek. 17), a lion (Ezek. 19) and a flock (Ezek. 34). It is the community who have failed, and it is the community who will be restored. It is the righteous 'nation' who inhabit YHWH's renewed city (Isa. 26:2). The blossom, bud and fruit will come not from the individual but from 'Israel' and will fill all the world (Isa. 27:6). Even Isaiah's vision of the 'servant' blurs individual and corporate identities.[46] The nations will stream to the brightness and light of a redeemed people (Isa. 60:1–3).

The covenant preaching of Jeremiah (chs. 7, 11) calls the whole community back to the terms of the covenant, with the threat of covenant curses hanging

---

42. Wright, *Deuteronomy*, pp. 167–168.

43. J. G. McConville, *Deuteronomy*, AOTC 5 (Leicester: Apollos, 2002), p. 43.

44. S. Dean McBride Jr, 'Polity of the Covenant People: The Book of Deuteronomy', *Int* 41.3 (1987), pp. 229–244.

45. For example, Israel as the prostitute or adulteress in Isa. 1:21; Jer. 2:20; Ezek. 16; 23.

46. See the earlier discussion on the servant in Deutero-Isaiah in ch. 3 above.

over the community – the thriving olive tree is about to be set on fire (Jer. 11:16). Jeremiah's vision of restoration in his Little Book of Consolation (Jer. 30 – 33) emphasizes the universality of true knowledge of YHWH with his focus on the 'least to the greatest', and they shall 'all know me'. Each individual in the new-covenant community will possess personal knowledge of YHWH and it is this that ensures the future efficacy of the communal vocation.[47]

Ezekiel 5:5 describes the theological purpose of the election of Israel as a nation, at the centre of the nations, as 'the locus of God's salvation'.[48] Israel as a 'bride' has forsaken her bridegroom (Ezek. 16; 23). Ezekiel's vision of restoration is again focused on the people as a whole, coming through YHWH's gift of his Spirit.[49] The singular new heart and new spirit will be given to 'you' plural (Ezek. 36:26).

In Jesus' Sermon on the Plain there is clearly teaching focused on the individual – Jesus' use of a tree metaphor to speak of an individual person, for example (Luke 6:43–45). Additionally Jesus' sending of the seventy-two is evidence that part of the disciples' mission included individual proclamation. However, in the subsequent chapters of Luke's account we begin to see Jesus speak in terms of a kingdom community. The sharing of wealth (14:12), giving to the poor (12:32–34), hospitality (14:1–14) and service (19:1–27) are all designed to be in contrast to the community of the Pharisees and scribes who have hindered and harmed (Luke 11:52).

In Acts the life of the new community of believers is a central factor in the advancement of Luke's narrative. Keener, commenting on Acts 2:42–47, notes that we meet in those verses 'a community modelling the ideal, proleptically eschatological lifestyle of the kingdom'.[50] Bock similarly observes, 'A vibrant community extends itself in two directions: toward God and toward neighbour . . . Their life as a community was a visible part of their testimony.'[51] Luke offers a similar summary statement regarding the missional efficacy of the community's existence in Acts 4:32–35. The life of the community is 'congruent with God's work in it. It has a reality and beauty which mark it out, even to

---

47. Walter Brueggemann, *A Commentary on Jeremiah: Exile & Homecoming* (Grand Rapids: Eerdmans, 1998), p. 294.

48. Horace D. Hummel, *Ezekiel 1–20*, Concordia (St. Louis: Concordia, 2005), p. 180.

49. James Robson, *Word and Spirit in Ezekiel*, LHB/OTS 447 (London: T&T Clark, 2006), p. 262.

50. Craig S. Keener, *Acts 1:1–2:47* (Grand Rapids: Baker, 2012), p. 991.

51. Darrell L. Bock, *Acts*, BECNT (Grand Rapids: Baker Academic, 2007), pp. 154–155.

Gentiles, as the sphere of God's activity.'[52] In Acts 6 we again observe an organized group finding a communal solution to a social problem, which in turn leads to greater growth.

This summary of the exegesis does not deny or preclude the importance of the individual in missional ethics. As argued above, the community is the product of the aggregate. However, the evidence of the exegesis would suggest that missional ethics is primarily concerned with the role of the community as a community.

Guder outlines the contemporary tension between individualism and the corporate Christian calling, claiming it is a 'truism to define our society as profoundly individualistic'.[53] He continues, 'the net effect of the complex individualism we have been discussing constitutes one of the great challenges for the biblical formation of the missional community'.[54] He urges the Christian community to return to its sense of corporate vocation. Citing Acts 1:8, 'you shall be my witnesses', he says, 'This is a profoundly holistic definition of who and what we are as Christian persons and as the Christian community. It is always dealt with as a plural concept.'[55] Goheen, commenting on Acts 1:8, says, 'we err if we limit these words to the witness of individual Christians . . . these words were originally given *to a community* and as such define *its communal identity*'.[56] Lohfink adds, the 'primary issue is not the private holiness of the individual Christian. The point is that *an entire people give witness* to God's plan for the world.'[57] There is something evidently potent about the collective witness of the covenant community. The church exists as an apostle of God's reign, founded on apostolic *kerygma* and undertaking the apostolic vocation in re-presenting Christ.[58]

The dialogue between ecclesiology and missiology is critical. For some, mission is conducted almost entirely outside the institutional structures,

---

52. David P. Seccombe, *Possessions and the Poor in Luke–Acts*, SNTU 6 (Linz: Fuchs, 1982), p. 218.

53. Guder, *Called to Witness*, p. 105.

54. Ibid., p. 109.

55. Ibid., p. 115.

56. Michael W. Goheen, *A Light to the Nations: The Missional Church and the Biblical Story* (Grand Rapids: Baker Academic, 2011), p. 128. Emphases original.

57. Gerhard Lohfink, *Jesus and Community: The Social Dimension of the Christian Faith*, tr. John P. Galvin (Philadelphia: Fortress, 1982), pp. 131–132. Emphasis original.

58. Darrell L. Guder (ed.), *Missional Church: A Vision for the Sending of the Church in North America* (Grand Rapids: Eerdmans, 1998), p. 83; Jürgen Moltmann, *The Church in the Power of the Spirit* (London: SCM, 1977), p. 358.

programmes or gatherings of the *ekklēsia*.[59] Modality plays second fiddle to sodalities; organism trumps institution.[60] At the other end of the spectrum, some consider the church to be 'the universal sacrament of salvation'.[61] The 'bounded-set' churches create obstacles, appear uncaring and may confuse moral restraint with supernatural change.[62] By contrast 'centred-set' churches may confuse belonging with believing, and consequently dilute their distinctive witness.[63]

The exegesis of this work would suggest that while modality and sodality are both important, sodalities are subservient to modality. Additionally, discussion surrounding bounded- and centred-sets misunderstands the dynamic of a communal missional ethic. The church needs to be both bounded and centred. The mission requires the extension of invitation to a journey, but that journey has a terminus in the values and beliefs of the covenant community.[64] Arrival at those convictions turns the community outward: 'the "bounded set" knows it faces and exists in part for the "centred set"'.[65] As Kraus notes, 'The life of the

---

59. The work of LICC veers this way in the understanding of mission articulated in Neil Hudson, *Imagine Church: Releasing Whole Life Disciples* (Nottingham: Inter-Varsity Press, 2012); and Mark Greene, *Fruitfulness on the Frontline: Making a Difference Where You Are* (Nottingham: Inter-Varsity Press, 2014).

60. Modality refers to the institutional church with its structures and governance, while sodality refers to para-church organizations that may report to the church, but would not necessarily consider themselves answerable to the church. See R. D. Winter, 'The Two Structures of God's Redemptive Mission', *Missiology* 2.1 (1974), pp. 121–139.

61. Pope John Paul II, *Redemptoris missio* 9, <http://w2.vatican.va/content/john-paul-ii/en/encyclicals/documents/hf_jp-ii_enc_07121990_redemptoris-missio.html>, accessed 5 January 2017.

62. Bounded-sets have boundaries establishing the parameters of belonging. Demarcation normally exists around confessions, creeds and formal membership. Belief precedes belonging. Centred-sets 'do not define membership and identity at the entrance points or boundaries . . . [but rather] invite people to enter on a journey toward a set of values and commitments'. Belonging precedes believing. See Guder, *Missional Church*, pp. 205–206.

63. Ibid., pp. 206–207. Some seeker-driven methodologies would be a good example of a centred-set approach.

64. Ibid., p. 207.

65. Michael McCoy, '"Community": A Postmodern Mission Paradigm?', *JAS* 1.1 (2003), p. 42.

church *is* its witness. The witness of the church *is* its life. The question of authentic witness is the question of authentic community.'[66] As Newbigin noted, the congregation is the hermeneutic of the gospel.[67]

Further research should give significant attention to the nature of the missio-ethical vocation of the community *qua* community. The exegetical work of this book would suggest that the Bible's own testimony gives more weight to the covenant community than the individual (or the para-church) where missional ethics is concerned. Of course the community is made up of individuals, but those individuals are part of a wider body and it is that wider body to which the biblical text provides the majority of its instruction.[68] The worship of the community and the life of the community in its attempt to seek justice and demonstrate compassion on widows, orphans and aliens is the primary interest of the texts, and the area where the contemporary church needs to continue to consider its vocation *qua* church. An important area for further research could include the ways in which the corporate church might be effective in missional ethics in terms of its organized expressions of worship, charity and the pursuit of justice. This seems all the more important in societies that seek to marginalize the church. In these contexts missional ethics for the institutional church (which would include local and para-church) could bear witness through a powerful and compelling counter-culture.

The missio-ethical script: justice, charity and worship

This work has argued for a broad holistic definition of missional ethics. For some missiologists a broad definition has sometimes led to an unwillingness to attempt greater definitional precision.[69] The argument presented here suggests that greater precision is both desirable and possible, while still acknowledging the breadth in scope of missional ethics. In particular three themes have emerged as prominent across the canonical narrative in this exegetical

---

66. C. Norman Kraus, *The Authentic Witness: Credibility and Authenticity* (Grand Rapids: Eerdmans, 1978), p. 156. Emphases original.

67. Lesslie Newbigin, *The Gospel in a Pluralist Society* (London: SPCK, 1989), p. 222.

68. An obvious exception would be the household codes of the epistles.

69. Bosch, for example, is representative of missiologists who embrace a holistic view. He states, 'Ultimately, mission remains undefinable . . . The most we can hope for is to formulate some *approximations* of what mission is all about.' *Transforming Mission*, p. 9. Emphasis original.

exploration of missional ethics: justice, charity and worship. In this section each will be considered in turn, beginning with the theme of justice.

Justice

In Deuteronomy there are two common word roots for justice – *špṭ* and *ṣdq* – referring to right order and right relationships.[70] The instructions concerning justice are framed by the assertion that YHWH himself executes justice (Deut. 10:18), and that all his ways are just (Deut. 32:4). The Israelite justice ethic is another example of the *imitatio Dei*. The people are repeatedly instructed to judge justly, particularly with reference to the alien, orphan or widow (Deut. 16:18–19; 24:17; 27:19). The principle of justice can be seen in the *lex talionis* (Deut. 19:15–21), which, while often viewed as barbaric, demonstrates the requirement of due process, the equality of all before the law and the limits on retribution.[71] The whole people are to 'pursue justice, justice alone' (*ṣedeq ṣedeq tirdōp*, Deut. 16:20). The proper administration of 'justice' was to be a central plank in the missio-ethical vocation of Israel among the nations.[72]

The opening chapter of Isaiah rebukes the people for their failure to defend the oppressed, take up the orphan's cause and plead the case of the widow (Isa. 1:17, 23). The city of justice and righteousness has become a harlot (Isa. 1:21). The promise is that Israel will one day be restored to once again be the 'City of Righteousness' (*'îr haṣṣedeq*, Isa. 1:26). Repeatedly, in Isaiah 1 – 39 the nation is condemned for its failure to exercise justice and righteousness (Isa. 1:17; 5:7, 23; 10:1–2; 26:10). In Deutero-Isaiah YHWH's servant will be the one who embodies and enacts justice and righteousness (Isa. 42:1–4; 53:11). In Isaiah 56 the opening call is for the people to 'keep justice and do righteousness' (*šimrû mišpāṭ wa'ăśû ṣĕdāqâ*, v. 1). The restored people will live out a righteousness that will go before them and be seen by the nations (Isa. 58:8; 61:11; 62:1–2). Jeremiah also rebukes his audience for their failure to seek justice, promote the case of the orphan or defend the just cause of the poor (Jer. 5:28). Jeremiah commends Josiah as one who defends the cause of the poor and needy, and rebukes Josiah's son, Shallum, for his failure in this regard (Jer. 22:16). Jeremiah, like Deuteronomy, explicitly connects the practice of justice with the alien, orphan and widow

---

70. Christopher J. H. Wright, *Old Testament Ethics for the People of God* (Leicester: Inter-Varsity Press, 2004), pp. 255–257.

71. McConville, *Deuteronomy*, pp. 313–314.

72. David L. Baker, 'Protecting the Vulnerable: The Law and Social Care', in *Transforming the World? The Gospel and Social Responsibility* (Nottingham: Apollos, 2009), pp. 17–34.

(Jer. 7:5–6; 22:3). Twice Jeremiah prophesies a Davidic Branch who will restore justice and righteousness (Jer. 23:5; 33:15), and the promise is given to the people that if they confess YHWH in truth, justice and righteousness the nations will invoke blessings by YHWH (Jer. 4:2). Justice and righteousness are crucial to the blessing of the nations.[73] In Ezekiel the sin of Sodom was neglect of the poor (Ezek. 16:49), and the people are rebuked for denying the foreigner justice (Ezek. 22:7, 29). The catalogue of sins presented in Ezekiel 18 is centred on justice and righteousness, with an emphasis on the need for a new heart and new spirit if the people are not to return to unrighteousness (Ezek. 18:25–31).[74]

The transition from Old to New Testament sees a shift in emphasis from justice to charity. This is not to say that the theme of justice is entirely absent. For example, in Luke 11:42 Jesus rebukes the Pharisees for neglecting justice. However, as the community of Jesus' followers find themselves a marginalized minority without political jurisdiction the primary portrait of their missional ethic is seen in their charitable actions. Contemporary missiologists sometimes speak of the need to pursue justice but often without the necessary canonical and narratival nuance required.[75] The simple appeal to Old Testament texts, in an effort to demonstrate the necessity of the pursuit of justice, fails to recognize the narratival shift that occurs across the Testaments.[76] The church is not a nation state and as such does not provide or administer statutes to which all citizens in a particular locale are subject. Church leaders perform a different function from civic rulers. That is not to say, however, that the New Testament covenant community are to have no interest in justice. As Wright states:

> It is true that we must take into account the radical newness of the era of salvation history inaugurated in the New Testament. We are not Old Testament Israelites living within a theocratic covenant bound by Old Testament law . . . we do need to recognize the typological-prophetic hermeneutic by which the New Testament sees the

---

73. Christopher J. H. Wright, *The Message of Jeremiah*, BST (Nottingham: Inter-Varsity Press, 2014), p. 88.

74. Daniel I. Block, *The Book of Ezekiel: Chapters 1–24*, NICOT (Grand Rapids: Eerdmans, 1998), pp. 588–589.

75. Bosch arguably falls into this in his discussion of mission as the quest for justice in *Transforming Mission*, pp. 410–417. So too C. René Padilla, 'The Biblical Basis for Social Ethics', in *Transforming the World? The Gospel and Social Responsibility* (Nottingham: Apollos, 2009), pp. 187–204.

76. Christopher J. H. Wright, *The Mission of God: Unlocking the Bible's Grand Narrative* (Downers Grove: InterVarsity Press, 2006), p. 304.

fulfilment of all it signified for Israel as now fulfilled for Christians being in Christ . . .
Nevertheless . . . the paradigmatic force of the *socioeconomic* legislation that governed
Israel's life in the land still has ethical and missional relevance for Christians.[77]

The role of the New Testament church may not be in creating or administering
legislature, but it may still promote the cause and plead the case of society's
oppressed, to paraphrase Isaiah 1:17, 23 and Jeremiah 5:28. The missio-ethical
application of the theme of justice should recognize that the church, before a
watching world, should be at the forefront of justice advocacy.[78] Concern for
justice is a significant facet of contemporary missiology and proposals involve
the national and local, and the redistributive and restorative. Langmead suggests
that at its heart justice is connected to shalom and the right ordering of goods
and relationships.[79] Justice is concerned with the right course of action towards
another, or our responsibility to make good on their due. This understanding of
justice can then be applied at the various levels outlined. At the level of national
redistribution, Christians may be involved in advocacy or campaign for reform.[80]
Keller suggests that humble cooperation and respectful provocation may both
be used by individual Christians and Christian organizations and churches to
promote virtue, the common good, and individual rights.[81] National restorative
justice may use similar means with a particular concern – reconciliation, for
example. [82] Reconciliation efforts may also occur at the local level where particular
community groups are mistreated. Keller, building on the work of J. M. Perkins,
suggests that the developmental aspect of justice may occur locally with what

---

77. Ibid., pp. 304–305. Emphasis original.

78. Keller outlines a number of practical ways in which the church may be involved
    with justice advocacy. See Timothy Keller, *Generous Justice* (London: Hodder &
    Stoughton, 2010), pp. 112–169.

79. Ross Langmead, 'Transformed Relationships: Reconciliation as the Central Model
    for Mission', *Mission Studies* 25 (2008), pp. 8–9.

80. For example, a letter from a local church (or churches) to a Member of Parliament,
    signing petitions or involvement with a para-church organization like The
    International Justice Mission.

81. Keller notes the normative, existential and situational aspects to the pursuit
    of these three ends. *Generous Justice*, pp. 158–159.

82. A number of missiologists discuss reconciliation as a central component of
    contemporary mission. See Langmead, 'Transformed Relationships'; Robert
    J. Schreiter, 'Reconciliation and Healing as a Paradigm for Mission', *IRM* 94.372
    (2005), pp. 74–83; Keller, *Generous Justice*.

he calls 're-neighbouring' and 're-weaving'. Keller states that 'most government programs provide help to the poor, but service providers do not live in the community and therefore have no firsthand knowledge of the needs of the neighbourhood, or any real accountability to the residents'.[83] In other words, those best placed to bring genuine help are the people who reside within a particular community. By 're-weaving' Keller suggests that social and economic capital be returned to communities. Typically financial capital flows away from needy neighbourhoods. Businesses and employment opportunities that remain local can enable neighbourhoods to flourish. Similarly, with regard to social capital, school teachers and business owners tend not to live in the needy areas in which their school or business is located. Keller argues that the redistribution and restoration need to happen locally with the reverse-flow of financial, social and spiritual capital.[84] Local churches are best placed to lead the way and cast the vision for such endeavour. Given what has been argued above regarding the missio-ethical cast (the local church) we could argue that while national advocacy is important, it may be more fruitful to give greater consideration to local developmental models of redistributive and restorative justice.

Charity

The theme of charity also emerged from the exegesis of the texts. Charity goes beyond the legal prescription of minimum requirement, and includes an ethic of generosity towards those in need. For example, in the laws regarding the cancellation of debt (Deut. 15) the Israelite is commanded not to be tight-fisted, but rather open-handed and generous towards the poor (Deut. 15:7–8, 10–11). Specific amounts are not prescribed; rather the ethic is to be one of unstipulated generosity. The same may be seen in the laws regarding manumission (Deut. 15:12–13). Freed servants are to be liberally supplied as they are sent on their way. In Deuteronomy 24:19–22 the harvesters are instructed not to go over the crop a second time, but to leave what remains for the foreigner.[85] Further acts of generosity can be seen in the instructions concerning Israel's feasts, festivals and tithes (Deut. 14:22–28; 16:9–17; 26:1–15). Israel were to be marked out, not simply for a strict adherence to the principles of 'justice', but also for their liberal generosity and charity to those in need.[86]

---

83. Keller, *Generous Justice*, p. 117.

84. Ibid., pp. 117–119.

85. The supreme act of such charity is observed in the actions of Boaz (Ruth 2:15).

86. Such instruction is unique within the ANE law-codes, as demonstrated by Baker, 'Protecting the Vulnerable', pp. 25–31.

While we observed the emphasis in the Major Prophets on injustice, there is also evidence of the importance of charity. In Isaiah 58 justice and charity are held together as the initial call for justice (Isa. 58:6) develops into the call to share with the hungry, to provide for the poor and to clothe the naked (Isa. 58:7). The missional value of a charitable ethic is evident a few verses later:

> if you spend yourselves on behalf of the hungry
>   and satisfy the needs of the oppressed,
> then your light will rise in the darkness.
> (Isa. 58:10)

In Ezekiel 18 we noted the sins for which a man shall die: idolatry, adultery and, significantly, failure to return a pledge and lending at interest (Ezek. 18:10–13). By way of contrast Ezekiel instructs his readers that such a man's son shall live if he gives food to the hungry and clothing to the naked (Ezek. 18:16–17).

In Luke–Acts we see the fulfilment of the Deuteronomic and prophetic ideal of charity exercised towards the needy. In the Sermon on the Plain Jesus calls his followers to 'Give to everyone who asks' withholding nothing, and requiring nothing in return (Luke 6:30–31). The story of the good Samaritan is neighbour love taken to controversial heights (Luke 10:25–37). Jesus' teaching throughout the travel narrative emphasizes the need for generosity with money (Luke 12:33; 14:33; 19:1–10) and practising hospitality (Luke 14:1–14). The post-Pentecost community sold possessions and gave to the needy (Acts 2:45; 4:34–35). As a result they won the favour of all the people (Acts 2:47) and there were no needy persons among them (Acts 4:34), a phrase reminiscent of Deuteronomy 15:4. In Acts 6 we see the community committed to ongoing care for widows, which results in the further growth of the faith (Acts 6:1–7).[87] As the narrative progresses we also find the positive characterization of Tabitha and Cornelius, who both have a reputation for their generosity towards the poor and needy (Acts 9:36; 10:2). Repeatedly in the narrative of Acts the charity of the community is one of the means by which the faith advances. Garland's conclusion regarding charity is worth quoting:

> According to Jesus, the wise use of money is to get rid of it through almsgiving ([Luke] 11:40–41; 12:33–34; 19:1–10), cancelling debts, and loaning without expecting

---

87. Todd Penner, *In Praise of Christian Origins: Stephen and the Hellenists in Lukan Apologetic Historiography*, Emory Studies in Early Christianity 10 (New York: T&T Clark, 2004), p. 265.

to get anything back (6:34–35). This generosity with one's possessions is what Luke tells us characterized the early Christian community (Acts 2:44–45; 4:32, 34; 6:1–6; 11:27–30). The foolish use of money is exemplified by the parables of the rich fool (12:13–21) and the rich man and Lazarus (16:19–31), and, in Acts, the stories of Judas (Acts 1:16–20) and Ananias and Sapphira (5:1–11).[88]

The early Christian community was distinctive in its radical generosity and charity to those in need in fulfilment of the Deuteronomic ideal. Rodney Stark notes that a key factor in the growth of the church in the first three centuries was its selfless acts of mercy and charity.[89] Emperor Julian, in his attempt to revive paganism, lamented that 'while the impious Galileans [Christians] support both their own poor and ours as well, all men see that our people lack aid from us'.[90] The missiological debates continue regarding the nature of charitable work in the church. Should it be considered mission? Is it a 'social gospel'? Is it the church's mission at all? As my exegesis has demonstrated, charity was clearly a significant part of all that the covenant community was called to perform, and in the community's performance outsiders were attracted. Charity is neither the means towards, nor the end itself of, mission or missional ethics. Charity is one significant part of a wider holistic vision of missional ethics that the church is called to embody.[91] Catholic missiology in the twentieth century emphasized the importance of charity: 'whenever we have an opportunity to perform a work of mercy, we should rejoice',[92] and works of charity 'reveal the soul of all missionary activity'.[93] Keller notes the historical precedent for

---

88. David E. Garland, *Luke*, ECNT 3 (Grand Rapids: Zondervan, 2011), p. 655.

89. Rodney Stark, *The Rise of Christianity: How the Obscure, Marginal Jesus Movement Became the Dominant Religious Force in the Western World in a Few Centuries* (San Francisco: Harper, 1997), pp. 87–88.

90. Julian, *Letter to Arsacius*. Cited in Timothy J. Keller, *Ministries of Mercy: The Call of the Jericho Road*, 2nd edn (Phillipsburg: P&R, 1997), p. 87.

91. Melvin Tinker, 'The Servant Solution: The Coordination of Evangelism and Social Action', in *Transforming the World? The Gospel and Social Responsibility* (Nottingham: Apollos, 2009), p. 161. See also Keller, *Ministries of Mercy*, pp. 15–57. As Chester notes, such charity must include welfare and development. Tim Chester, *Good News to the Poor* (Leicester: Inter-Varsity Press, 2004), pp. 138–139.

92. Pope Francis, *Evangelii gaudium* 193, <http://w2.vatican.va/content/francesco/en/apost_exhortations/documents/papa-francesco_esortazione-ap_20131124_evangelii-gaudium.html>, accessed 5 January 2017.

93. John Paul II, *Redemptoris missio* 9.

works of mercy, describing the mercy ministry established by Thomas Chalmers in Glasgow in the nineteenth century:

> The entire area was divided into 'quarters,' each with a deacon over it. Each deacon's job was to keep the Session informed about the economic conditions in his quarter . . . When a family was found in need, he was to seek out resources within the neighbourhood. If there were no other options the family was admitted to the poor roll.[94]

The deacon's role was not just confined to emergency provision, but would include efforts to find work for the unemployed and education for unschooled children. As well as enlisting the help of the congregation, a Sunday school teacher and a lay evangelist would assist each deacon, thus holding together word and deed. Keller notes that

> at one point, his ministry was criticized as being in competition with the government welfare system. Chalmers readily agreed! He went on to say that the church could do what the government could not. He saw that it could deal with the moral and spiritual roots of poverty.[95]

Chalmers's approach is compatible with the systems of mercy observed in Acts 6. Charity, it has been observed, is a central element in a missional ethic, and the local church is well placed to participate. If, as argued above, the local church is the principal actor, Chalmers's approach of local charity by local churches should be given fresh consideration in contemporary missiological discussion. National and international charity is legitimate and important, particularly in the case of crises, but there is a principle of moral proximity that demands charity begins in a local community. A missional ethic must have charity as a key component, and for the charitable ethic to be missional it must be relationally and personally embodied and experienced. Further work into reviving something akin to Chalmers's system could prove fruitful in contemporary missional ethics.

Worship

The category of worship has been an unexpected result of this exegetical exploration and warrants some further reflection. Many instinctively categorize

---

94. Keller, *Ministries of Mercy*, p. 88.
95. Ibid., pp. 88–89.

justice and charity as key ingredients within missional ethics, yet missio-ethical thinkers often instinctively consider worship as something else – an insider practice that has little or no relationship to mission.[96] However, a more explicit description and definition requires us to consider the evidence of the Bible's own testimony.

Deuteronomy's legal section (chs. 12–26) opens and closes with instructions regarding corporate worship (chs. 12, 26), and there are further extended instructions in Deuteronomy 14 and 16. We noted in the exegesis of those sections that narrative placement and content were both significant. Worship forms an inclusio for Israel's social ethic.[97] Israel was 'a sacral community first and foremost'.[98] Their worship was to inform their entire existence such that worship must be considered a part of missional ethics. We also noted the presence of outsiders at all of the major celebrations. Deuteronomy 16:14 connects the presence of the whole community (including the *gēr*) with the joyful celebration of the community. The implication is that Israel's joy was incomplete in the absence of the vulnerable and the outsider.[99] The cost of providing for the increased number of dependants heightens the importance accrued by their presence. The 'sabbatical themes of rest, remembrance, and concern for the poor are all woven into Deuteronomy's summary of the three major annual festivals', and outsiders are present at the major feasts and festivals.[100] Their worship was formative for their identity, as their 'deepest convictions are to be found, not in systematic doctrinal or ethical formulations, but in doxology, the language of worship'.[101] In examining Deuteronomy 12 – 26

---

96. Goheen, for example, in discussing Newbigin's distinction between missional intention and dimension states, 'Worship does not have a missional intention . . . It may well witness to the unbeliever (see 1 Cor 14:23–25) and so possesses a missional dimension . . . But its intention is to bring praise to God.' *Introducing Christian Mission*, p. 83. This work has suggested that the biblical text does suggest a missional *intention* in the worship of the covenant community. Worship is a part of the structure given to the covenant community to bear witness to God.

97. Daniel I. Block, *Deuteronomy*, NIVAC (Grand Rapids: Zondervan, 2012), p. 301.

98. Gerhard von Rad, *Old Testament Theology*, 2 vols., tr. D. M. G. Stalker, repr. (London: SCM, 1975), vol. 1, p. 228.

99. Timothy James Davy, 'Looking for Orphans: Approaches for Understanding the Place of Vulnerable Children in the Old Testament', lecture delivered at the Tyndale Fellowship Quadrennial Conference, July 2016.

100. Wright, *Deuteronomy*, p. 198.

101. Wright, *Old Testament Ethics*, p. 45.

we saw that in an ANE culture the corporate and celebratory aspects of Israel's worship would have been strikingly distinctive to those outside the covenant community. As Block notes, 'care for the marginalized is not merely a noble humanitarian issue; it is expressive of one's covenant relationship with Yahweh'.[102] The intended purpose of Israel's cultic life was to bring fame and honour to YHWH in the sight of the nations (Deut. 26:18–29). Their liturgical life served to shape the people for faithfulness and became in itself a 'testimony for conversion'.[103] The performative nature of the text invites each subsequent generation to participate in the divine drama, and to seek both to be transformed and to transform the outsider in the process.[104]

In the same vein the Major Prophets all give extended treatments of the importance of the people's worship in their calling to be a light to the nations.[105] Isaiah's opening chapter describes Israel's worship as 'meaningless' and an 'abomination' due to injustice and idolatry (Isa. 1:13–17). Isaiah's opening chapters also provide a glimmer of hope in the depiction of Mount Zion – a centre of renewed worship and justice to which the nations will stream (Isa. 2:1–4). The theme reappears in Isaiah 12, which presents a hymn of praise that is to make known YHWH's salvation among the nations (v. 4). This song is to be known to the entire world. The cult epitomizes Israel's relationship to YHWH, which in turn should serve to shape Israel's relationship with their neighbours. One of the most dramatic instances we observed in Isaiah of this international worship was in Isaiah 19:23–25, where Assyria, Egypt and Israel would worship together (v. 23), resulting in the blessing of the earth. The opening of Trito-Isaiah incorporates the cultic within the ethical, calling the people to observe the Sabbath (56:2).[106] Isaiah 56:3 extends the invitation to the 'foreigner', promising that if they too observe the Sabbath, choose what pleases YHWH and hold fast to his covenant, then they will be welcomed. Worship thus becomes an 'instrument of mission'.[107] YHWH's 'holy mountain' reappears, tying Isaiah 2

---

102. Block, *Deuteronomy*, p. 605.

103. Patrick D. Miller, '"Enthroned on the Praises of Israel": The Praise of God in the Old Testament Theology', *Int* 39.1 (1985), p. 9.

104. Kevin J. Vanhoozer, *The Drama of Doctrine: A Canonical Linguistic Approach to Christian Theology* (Louisville: Westminster John Knox, 2005), pp. 15–18.

105. Isa. 2; 27; 56; Jer. 4; 7; 11; 17; 30 – 33; Ezek. 10; 37; 40 – 48.

106. Hrobon argues that the Sabbath contains both cultic and ethical dimensions appealing to Deut. 5:15; 10:19; 24:18–22. Bohdan Hrobon, *Ethical Dimension of Cult in the Book of Isaiah*, BZAW 418 (Berlin: de Gruyter, 2010), pp. 163–165.

107. George A. F. Knight, *Isaiah 56–66*, ITC (Grand Rapids: Eerdmans, 1985), p. 4.

and 25 with Isaiah 56. The mountain-sanctuary (56:7), as in Isaiah 2 and 25, has an international draw and will become a 'house of prayer for all nations'. In Isaiah 58 the light that breaks forth from Israel (58:8) is bracketed by commands regarding cultic activity (58:1–5, 13–14), such that Hrobon states, 'ethics, and cult in Isaiah 58 are two sides of the same coin'.[108] In Isaiah, as in Deuteronomy, worship is central to the vocation of the covenant community as a medium of blessing to the nations, both in its transformative and attractive potencies.

In Jeremiah the well-known 'Temple Sermon' in 7:1–8 presents the reader with what Brueggemann termed 'the clearest and most formidable statement we have of the basic themes of the Jeremiah tradition'.[109] With Deuteronomy in the background, the covenantal formula serves to summon the people to face their transgression. In Jeremiah 7:1–8 the prophet is instructed to stand at the gates of the temple and proclaim a message to the worshippers there. The message itself picks up on a number of Deuteronomic themes, including worship and ethics.[110] As in Isaiah 1, cultic failure is linked to the failure of social justice (Jer. 7:4–7). The religious life of the people is inextricably linked to the social, political, economic and judicial.[111] In Jeremiah 11 the nature of covenant breach is again idolatry (11:9–13), where the people are said to have 'as many gods as you have towns' and 'the altars you have set up to burn incense to that shameful god Baal are as many as the streets of Jerusalem' (v. 13). Israel, rather than being a light to the nations, have learned the ways of the nations (Jer. 10:2) in following their idolatrous practices, and therefore the nations have not learnt of the one true God (Jer. 10:10). Wright concludes, 'recalling Israel to their covenant monotheism was thus profoundly missional in its *shaping* function'.[112] In Jeremiah 17 cultic themes were again observed to be to the fore, with mention of both sanctuary and Sabbath (Jer. 17:12–27). Worship must be practised as the outward manifestation of the heart's intent. As in Isaiah, and Jeremiah's prior preaching in 7:3–7 and 11:3–5, the themes of covenant and temple are prominent in 17:19–26. Jeremiah is to announce at the city gates YHWH's command that the Sabbath is to be appropriately observed. It is to be kept 'holy', as was commanded to their forefathers (v. 22). If the people keep

---

108. Hrobon, *Ethical Dimension*, p. 216.

109. Brueggemann, *Commentary on Jeremiah*, p. 77.

110. Holladay notes the Deuteronomistic style. William L. Holladay, *Jeremiah 1*, Hermeneia (Philadelphia: Fortress, 1986), p. 241.

111. Wright, *Message of Jeremiah*, p. 110.

112. Wright, 'Prophet to the Nations', p. 122. Emphasis original.

the Sabbath holy, then the Davidic kings will enter the gates of the city and dwell on the throne. Their followers will accompany them and the city will be inhabited perpetually. Further, people will come from the surrounding regions to bring offerings to the temple (v. 26). Brueggemann also discerns the pivotal nature of the Sabbath for the existence of the covenant community:

> It is the dramatic act whereby this people asserts to itself and announces to the watching world that this is Israel, a different people with a different way in the world . . . the effectiveness of worship (v. 26) depends on Sabbath, an act that hands life back to God in trusting obedience.[113]

The well-being of the people depends upon right worship. As in Deuteronomy, right worship (love for God) and love for neighbour secure a perpetual inheritance. Restoration and renewal are the necessary preconditions for the ingathering of the nations envisaged in Jeremiah 16:19–21. Jeremiah's Book of Consolation (chs. 30–33) offers a vision of a renewed community worshipping YHWH in the sight of the nations. In Jeremiah 30 the community is re-established before YHWH, which likely refers to a restored worshipping community within a restored cultic setting (30:19–20). The result of YHWH's restorative work will be the joyful celebration of the people, which will itself result in the people's praise of YHWH among the surrounding nations (31:7; 33:8–9).[114] The cultic aspect of Israel's life has a missio-ethical aspect. The false assurance in 'the temple of the LORD' (Jer. 7:4) becomes true worship that reaches the nations (Jer. 30:18–21; 33:9, 17–22).

For Ezekiel, as in the other Major Prophets, idolatry is the fundamental problem (Ezek. 5:9). The cultic connection is further seen in Ezekiel 10 as YHWH's throne-chariot leaves the temple, and the promise of Ezekiel 11:18–21 explicitly connects the restoration of the people with true worship.[115] Ezekiel 20 recounts the historical failure of the covenant people, concluding with YHWH's promise to transform the community into one that brings acceptable offerings, gifts and sacrifices (Ezek. 20:40). As a consequence YHWH will be proved holy, through Israel's true worship, in the sight of the nations (Ezek. 20:41).[116] Ezekiel 36 – 37 also presents the importance of worship in its

---

113. Brueggemann, *Commentary on Jeremiah*, p. 166.
114. Walter Brueggemann, *The Theology of the Book of Jeremiah*, OTT (Cambridge: Cambridge University Press, 2007), p. 131.
115. Iain M. Duguid, *Ezekiel*, NIVAC (Grand Rapids: Zondervan, 1999), p. 151.
116. Wright, *Ezekiel*, p. 163.

depiction of a renewed Israel. Once cleansed the people will no longer worship idols (Ezek. 37:23), but will worship in truth with YHWH's sanctuary perpetually in their midst (37:26–28). As a result the nations will come to know the holiness of YHWH (37:28).[117] Ezekiel's final chapters present a picture of a restored and expanded cultic setting with imagery suggestive of international blessing (Ezek. 47:1–12).[118] The departed glory returns (Ezek. 10; 43), the sanctuary is renewed and YHWH's fame is acknowledged by the nations (Ezek. 37:26–28). The Major Prophets present the renewal and reformation of worship as a key component in the covenant community's renewed witness to the nations.

Moving into Luke–Acts, we noted Luke uniquely opens and closes his Gospel in the temple courts, with Zechariah and Elizabeth portrayed as model worshippers (Luke 1:6–10), and the disciples categorized as continually in the temple, praising God (24:53). The early narrative continues in and around the temple with more examples of righteous and devout worshippers (2:25, 37). Jesus himself appears in the temple, at an early age, as someone with understanding, growing in favour with God and man (2:46–51).[119] By contrast the religious leaders are singled out as those whose worship is displeasing to God due to their hypocrisy (11:42; 19:9–14; 20:45–47). In Acts a notable aspect of the early church's life is their worship in the temple courts and from house to house (Acts 2:46). Daily they met in the temple courts, and in Acts 2:42 Luke reports their devotion to the apostolic teaching, the fellowship, the breaking of bread and prayers. As a consequence of their worship Luke informs the reader they enjoyed the 'favour of all the people. And the Lord added to their number daily those who were being saved' (Acts 2:47). The temple courts remain the context for the early narrative, and Luke reiterates in 5:12–14 the presence of the believers in the temple courts and their numerical growth. Though the later chapters in Acts narrate the spread of the gospel, the early chapters set the tone for the means by which the mission is accomplished, and the worship of the community is a significant factor in their missional success.

The exegetical chapters of this work demonstrated that worship serves missional ethics in two ways – indirectly, as worship shapes and forms the

---

117. Walther Eichrodt, *Ezekiel: A Commentary*, tr. Cosslett Quin, OTL (London: SCM, 1970), p. 515.

118. Wright, *Ezekiel*, pp. 355–359.

119. Coleridge notes the narrative ark moves from Jewish piety to Jewish piety, and from temple to temple, with the Spirit's driving the narrative forward. Mark Coleridge, *The Birth of the Lukan Narrative: Narrative as Christology in Luke 1–2*, JSNTSup 88 (Sheffield: JSOT Press, 1993), p. 185.

people, and directly, as those outside the covenant community observe and participate in the liturgical life of the people. Worship is a part of a missional ethic, and can have both missionary dimensions and intentions.[120] Sunquist has noted that there should be 'no sharp distinctions between worship and mission'.[121] Worship and the *missio ecclesiae* have been a subject of debate since the 1960s. Schattauer outlines three approaches to the relationship between worship and mission as follows: inside and out, outside-in and inside-out.[122] The first approach, 'inside and out', views mission and worship as distinct but related activities. Worship serves to equip believers, who in turn go and reach out to others. Worship is an insider-only practice. The second approach, 'outside-in', views worship as a means of mission. This approach can be seen in various attractional models of church gathering.[123] The third approach, 'inside-out', has liturgy as the locus of mission. The act and forms of worship enact the gospel and signify mission. The performance of praise, confession, supplication, peace, gospel address, sacraments, benediction and fellowship are all ways in which the gospel is offered and received.[124] All are welcome and all are invited. The *leitourgia* functions as a public service that communicates the apostolic message. As Goheen states, 'liturgy is a witness to the *real* world and the *true* story'.[125] It is this third approach, what Schattauer terms 'inside-out', that best captures the evidence of the exegesis. Worship functions simultaneously to shape the

---

120. Tormod Engelsviken, 'Three Missiological Perspectives: What Testimony?', *IRM* 95.378–379 (2009), p. 332.

121. Sunquist, *Understanding Christian Mission*, p. 282.

122. Thomas H. Schattauer, 'Liturgical Assembly as the Locus of Mission', in Thomas H. Schattauer (ed.), *Inside Out: Worship in an Age of Mission* (Minneapolis: Fortress, 1999), pp. 1–3.

123. For example, the seeker-driven models popular in the USA since the 1970s, or the homogeneous unity principle espoused by C. Peter Wagner and Donald MacGavran. See Peter Wagner, *Our Kind of People: The Ethical Dimension of Church Growth in America* (Atlanta: John Knox, 1978); Donald A. MacGavran, *Understanding Church Growth* (Grand Rapids: Eerdmans, 1970).

124. Ruth A. Myers, 'Unlocking the Power of Worship', *ATR* 92.1 (2010), pp. 55–70; K. C. Miyamoto, 'Mission, Liturgy, and the Transformation of Identity', *Mission Studies* 27 (2010), pp. 56–70.

125. Michael W. Goheen, 'Nourishing Our Missional Identity: Worship and the Mission of God's People', in David J. Cohen and Mikael C. Parsons (eds.), *In Praise of Worship: An Exploration of Text and Practice* (Eugene: Wipf & Stock, 2010), p. 48. Emphases original.

insider and draw the outsider. Further research on the intersection between liturgy, ecclesiology and missiology would be potentially beneficial in theory and practice. Through our use of a canonical, narratival, missional and performative approach we have observed that worship is a central part of a biblical definition of missional ethics, and more work needs to be done in exploring the relationship between mission, ethics and worship.

These three elements – justice, charity and worship – ought to be major ingredients in any contemporary definition of missional ethics. Kraemer defined mission as including *koinōnia*, *diakonia* and *martyria*.[126] Missiologists understood that such a definition was not exhaustive but representative of the Bible's own emphases. In a similar vein the evidence of my exegesis leads me to propose that missio-ethical emphases include justice, charity and worship. This is not exhaustive but representative, and therefore helpful, as the church seeks to embody its missio-ethical vocation.

Conclusion

In moving towards a proposed definition of missional ethics this chapter has sought to utilize the insights of the exegetical chapters in order to bring some clarity and shape to the discussion. We have seen that the theme of missional ethics is not superimposed upon the text, but arises from the text's own witness. We have also noted that word and deed are an integrated whole – a 'comprehensive proclamation', to paraphrase Bavinck. We have seen how the *ekklēsia* as institution is prominent in the Bible's own account of the community's missional ethic. Finally, we have observed the centrality of justice, charity and worship as components of the missio-ethical script. All that remains is to attempt to draw together these threads to offer a working definition of missional ethics.

---

126. Hendrick Kraemer, *The Christian Message in a Non-Christian World* (London: Edinburgh House, 1938), p. 433.

CONCLUSION

Towards a definition of missional ethics

This book began by acknowledging the lack of a clear definition of the theme of missional ethics. Missional ethics is a relatively new concept, and this book has been working towards a definition of missional ethics by exegeting biblical texts pertinent to the theme.

In chapter 1 I outlined the methodological approach, arguing that a canonical approach – with sensitivity to narrative, performative and missional hermeneutics – was well suited to the presenting question. I also argued that Deuteronomy, the Major Prophets and Luke–Acts were key texts in the exploration of the theme.

In chapter 2 we examined Deuteronomy and noted that Deuteronomy 1 – 11 revealed the fundamental form of Israel's missio-ethical vocation as love for God and love for neighbour. Deuteronomy 12 – 26 revealed worship, justice and charity to be the principal expressions of love for God and love for neighbour. Both Israel's corporate worship and their care for the alien would have been distinctive within their ANE context.

In chapter 3 we saw how the Major Prophets charted the failure of Israel to live out their missio-ethical vocation. The twin foci of the prophetic rebuke are idolatry and injustice – failure to love both God and neighbour. As a consequence YHWH's name is blasphemed among the nations rather than glorified.

Yet the prophets look forward to a day of restoration in a new exodus. In that day Israel will be given a new heart, a new covenant and a new spirit. They will be empowered and enabled to fulfil their missio-ethical calling.

In chapter 4 we saw that Luke–Acts presents the narrative fulfilment of the missio-ethical trajectory. In Jesus, God has come to liberate his people and lead them in fulfilling their missio-ethical calling to the nations. Jesus embodies and instructs his followers, and in Acts the church embodies its missio-ethical vocation in fulfilment of the Deuteronomic ideal. As a consequence it gains the favour of all the people, and many are added to its number.

In chapter 5, drawing together the threads of the argument, we noted the prevalence of missional ethics throughout the biblical texts considered. We observed the integration of words and deeds. We proposed the threefold form of justice, charity and worship. We saw that the *ekklēsia* are the cast of the divine drama of missional ethics.

As noted in the introduction, there is an evident, and at times deliberate, unwillingness to attempt a closer definition and description of missional ethics. For some authors this is a deliberate position based on a broad understanding of mission. The problem is the definition of 'mission' becomes increasingly (and deliberately) unclear and subjective.[1] Some attempt to give a more focused definition of mission. DeYoung and Gilbert have suggested that the definition of mission in contemporary missiology has become unhelpfully broad.[2] For them mission is proclamation, as outlined in the Great Commission (Matt. 28:19–20):

> *The mission of the church is to go into the world and make disciples by declaring the gospel of Jesus Christ in the power of the Spirit and gathering these disciples into churches, that they might worship the Lord and obey his commands now and in eternity to the glory of God the Father.*[3]

Yet, as already argued, such a narrow definition of mission is contrary to the evidence of the biblical text presented. If the whole Bible is to be read missiologically as well as messianically (Luke 24:46–47), then the witness of the whole is clear that it is the holistic integrated witness of the individual and the community that constitutes the *missio ecclesiae* in the service of *the missio Dei*. Missiology as a discipline, therefore, is confronted with a difficulty: either

---

1. Keith Ferdinando, 'Mission: A Problem of Definition', *Them* 33.1 (2008), pp. 46–59.
2. Kevin DeYoung and Greg Gilbert, *What Is the Mission of the Church?* (Wheaton: Crossway, 2011), p. 17.
3. Ibid., p. 62. Emphasis original.

mission is defined so broadly as to be practically meaningless, or too narrowly, and fails to represent accurately the text from which it deduces its evidence. The proposal here offered is that a working definition is a useful tool for ongoing dialogue and research. Such a definition does not claim to be the final word, but rather offers itself for further refinement and critique. Such an approach seeks greater focus for the ongoing discussion and practice of missional ethics, while recognizing the definition is subject to continual refinement.

In the pursuit of a definition of missional ethics the Lausanne Movement offers a helpful starting point in proposing the following definition of mission: 'the whole church, taking the whole gospel, to the whole world'.[4] This definition helpfully encapsulates the individual and corporate, word and deed, and local and global. This book however seeks to develop a definition of missional ethics, not mission. The difficulty with definition is as follows. To define words too narrowly necessarily excludes some of the data. To define words too broadly fails to capture actual usage properly. This difficulty is magnified when attempting to define a word by referencing a text that never uses the word in question. The meanings of words are ordinarily understood according to their usage.[5] However, in the case of theological terms definitions are related to the texts perceived to be most relevant.[6] This is true also of missiological definition, where there is a commonly accepted understanding that mission refers to sending activity where God is the subject and his people are the object of his sending to further his purposes.[7] Therefore, as with other theological themes, it is uncontroversial to

---

4. Paragraph 6. 'The Lausanne Covenant', 1974, <www.lausanne.org/content/covenant/lausanne-covenant>, accessed 4 July 2016. See also James A. Scherer, 'Missiology', in *The Encyclopedia of Christianity*, 5 vols. (Grand Rapids: Eerdmans, 2003), vol. 3, p. 556.

5. A popular example of this can be seen in the use of the word 'wicked', which can be taken in two mutually incompatible senses.

6. Silva discusses this more fully with reference to theological themes, noting that discussion of themes or ideas relies on much more than simple word studies. See Moises Silva, *Biblical Words and Their Meaning: An Introduction to Lexical Semantics*, 2nd edn (Grand Rapids: Zondervan, 1994), pp. 22–28.

7. See for example the following definition of mission: 'Mission is the divine activity of sending intermediaries, whether supernatural or human, to speak or do God's will so that his purposes for judgment or redemption are furthered.' William J. Larkin Jr, 'Mission', *Baker Evangelical Dictionary of Biblical Theology*, <www.biblestudytools.com/dictionaries/bakers-evangelical-dictionary/mission.html>, accessed 18 April 2016.

attempt a definition of missional ethics that arises from the relevant biblical texts. The broad consensus of the missiological community is that mission is concerned with the sending of God's covenant community for a purpose. From this the enquiry can begin as to the nature and scope of this sending activity. The term 'ethics' faces similar challenges as a word not used in the biblical text. Yet it is broadly agreed that ethics is concerned with right being and behaviour, which naturally leads to the exploration of what such being and behaviour look like.[8]

This book affirms that a definition of missional ethics arising from analysis of the biblical text is indeed broad. If mission is participation in the *missio Dei*, then mission is more than verbal proclamation of a select group of gospel truths. Additionally it is conceded that any attempt to define *extra*biblical terminology is difficult. Nevertheless concerted effort and reflection should enable the enquirer to begin to offer a definition that reflects the biblical texts' own points of emphasis. This book, in examining Deuteronomy, the Major Prophets and Luke–Acts, has suggested that love for God and love for neighbour is a good starting point in a biblical definition of missional ethics. In addition I have argued that the biblical texts examined have a particular interest in and emphasis on worship, justice, charity and community. Those categories do not exhaust the content and scope of missional ethics, but begin to bring some shape to a concept that is, so far, somewhat amorphous.

In conclusion, the following working definition of missional ethics is proposed: *Missional ethics refers to the ways in which the believing community's behaviour – in particular their love for God and neighbour, expressed in the exercise of justice, charity and worship – bears witness, in the* imitatio Dei, *to the nature and character of God before a watching world.*

This definition contains all the elements presented in this chapter as a summary of the exegetical argument of the book. Missional ethics arises from the texts themselves. Missional ethics is a broad, holistic integration of word and deed, yet it is focused particularly on the themes of justice, charity and worship. Missional ethics is the preserve of the *ekklēsia* both as an institution and an organism, with emphasis on the former. This definition offers a starting place for further theological, missiological and ecclesiological research.

---

8. For example, ethics is 'The inquiry into man's moral nature so as to discover what are his responsibilities and the means by which he may fulfil them. Ethics shares with certain other human enterprises the quest for truth, but is distinct in its concern for what one ought to do in the light of the truth uncovered. It is not simply descriptive, but prescriptive in character.' M. A. Inch, 'Ethics', in *Evangelical Dictionary of Theology* (Basingstoke: Marshall, Morgan & Scott, 1984), p. 375.

It is hoped that this work will enable the furtherance of the missiological conversation regarding the nature, form and practice of missional ethics. As noted in the introduction, mission is at the heart of many Christian self-understandings. Therefore this important theme is worthy of greater exploration, understanding and application in the twenty-first-century church.

BIBLIOGRAPHY

Aagaard, Johannes, 'Some Main Trends in Modern Protestant Missiology', *ST* 19.238 (1965), pp. 238–259. Online: <www.tandfonline.com/doi/abs/10.1080/00393386508599878>, accessed 25 March 2013.

Adams, Jim W., *The Performative Nature and Function of Isaiah 40–55* (New York: T&T Clark, 2006).

Ahroni, Reuben, 'The Gog Prophecy and the Book of Ezekiel', *HAR* 1 (1977), pp. 1–27.

Albright, William Foxwell, *Archaeology and the Religion of Israel*, 3rd edn (Baltimore: Johns Hopkins, 1953).

———, *From the Stone Age to Christianity*, 2nd edn (New York: Doubleday, 1957).

Alden, Robert L. 'עזב', in *NIDOTTE*, vol. 3, pp. 364–365.

Alexander, Ralph H., 'Ezekiel', in EBC, vol. 7 (Grand Rapids: Zondervan, 2010), pp. 641–924.

Allen, Leslie C., *Jeremiah: A Commentary*, OTL (Louisville: Westminster John Knox, 2008).

———, 'The Structuring of Ezekiel's Revisionist History Lesson', *CBQ* 54 (1992), pp. 448–462.

Altmann, Peter, 'Feast, Famine, and History: The Festival Meal Topos and Deuteronomy 26, 1–15', *ZAW* 124 (2012), pp. 555–567.

Andersen, T. David, 'The Meaning of ECHONTES CHARIN PROS in Acts 2:47', *NTS* 34 (1988), pp. 604–610.

Anderson, Bernard W., 'Exodus and Covenant in Second Isaiah and Prophetic Tradition', in *Magnalia Dei: The Mighty Acts of God* (New York: Doubleday, 1976), pp. 339–360.

———, 'Exodus Typology in Second Isaiah', in *Israel's Prophetic Heritage: Essays in Honor of James Muilenburg* (London: SCM, 1962), pp. 177–195.

————, '"The Lord Has Created Something New": A Stylistic Study of Jer 31:15–22',
   in *Prophet to the Nations: Essays in Jeremiah Studies* (Winona Lake: Eisenbrauns, 1984),
   pp. 367–380.

Aristotle, *The Nichomachean Ethics*, ed. D. Ross, repr. (Oxford: Oxford University Press,
   1998).

Arnold, Bill T., 'The Love–Fear Antimony in Deuteronomy 5–11', *VT* 61.4 (2011),
   pp. 551–569.

Ashmore, James Phillip, *The Social Setting of the Law in Deuteronomy* (Detroit: UMI, 1997).

Assmann, Jan, *Of God and Gods: Egypt, Israel, and the Rise of Monotheism* (Madison:
   University of Wisconsin Press, 2008).

Austin, J. L., *How to Do Things with Words* (Oxford: Clarendon, 1962).

Awabdy, Mark A., *Immigrants and Innovative Law: Deuteronomy's Theological and Social Vision
   for the* גֵר, FZAT 267 (Tübingen: Mohr Siebeck, 2014).

Baker, David L., 'Protecting the Vulnerable: The Law and Social Care', in *Transforming
   the World? The Gospel and Social Responsibility* (Nottingham: Apollos, 2009),
   pp. 17–34.

————, *Tight Fists or Open Hands? Wealth and Poverty in Old Testament Law* (Grand Rapids:
   Eerdmans, 2009).

Baldwin, Joyce G., '*Ṣemaḥ* as a Technical Term in the Prophets', *VT* 14 (1964),
   pp. 93–97.

Balz, Horst, 'τεσσεράκοντα', in *TDNT*, vol. 8, p. 136.

Barr, James, *Holy Scripture: Canon, Authority, Criticism* (Oxford: Oxford University Press,
   1983).

————, *The Semantics of Biblical Language* (Oxford: Oxford University Press, 1961).

Barram, Michael, 'The Bible, Mission, and Social Location: Toward a Missional
   Hermeneutic', *Int* 61.1 (2007), pp. 42–58.

Barrett, C. K., *Acts 1–14*, ICC (London: T&T Clark, 1994).

————, 'The House of Prayer and the Den of Thieves', in *Jesus und Paulus: Festschrift
   für Werner Georg Kummel* (Göttingen: Vandenhoeck & Ruprecht, 1975), pp. 13–20.

Barth, Karl, *Church Dogmatics* IV/3.2: *The Doctrine of Reconciliation*, ed. Geoffrey
   W. Bromiley and T. F. Torrance (London: T&T Clark International, 2010).

————, *Evangelical Theology* (London: Weidenfeld, 1963).

Barton, John, *Oracles of God: Perceptions of Ancient Prophecy in Israel After the Exile* (London:
   Darton, Longman & Todd, 1986).

————, *Reading the Old Testament: Method in Biblical Study*, 2nd edn (London: Darton,
   Longman & Todd, 1996).

Bauckham, Richard, *Bible and Mission: Christian Witness in a Postmodern World* (Carlisle:
   Paternoster, 2003).

————, 'The Parable of the Vine: Rediscovering a Lost Parable of Jesus', *NTS* 33 (1987),
   pp. 84–101.

————, 'The Rich Man and Lazarus: The Parable and the Parallels', *NTS* 37 (1991), pp. 225–246.

Bavinck, J. H., *An Introduction to the Science of Missions*, tr. David H. Freeman (Phillipsburg: P&R, 1960).

Beavis, Mary Ann, 'Expecting Nothing in Return', *Int* 48 (1994), pp. 357–368.

Beck, Brian E., *Christian Character in the Gospel of Luke* (London: Epworth, 1989).

Beeby, Harry Daniel, 'A Missional Approach to Renewed Interpretation', in *Renewing Biblical Interpretation*, Scripture and Hermeneutics 1 (Carlisle: Paternoster, 2000), pp. 268–284.

Beentjes, Panc C., 'What a Lioness Was Your Mother: Reflections on Ezekiel 19', in *On Reading Prophetic Texts: Gender-Specific and Related Studies in Memory of Fokkelien van Dijk-Hemmes*, BIS 18 (Leiden: Brill, 1996), pp. 21–35.

Bellis, Alice Ogden, 'Jeremiah 31:22B: An Intentionally Ambiguous, Multivalent Riddle-Text', in *Uprooting and Planting: Essays on Jeremiah for Leslie Allen*, LHB/OTS 459 (New York: T&T Clark International, 2007), pp. 5–13.

Bennett, Harold V., *Injustice Made Legal: Deuteronomic Law and the Plight of Widows, Strangers, and Orphans in Ancient Israel* (Grand Rapids: Eerdmans, 2002).

Berges, Ulrich F., *The Book of Isaiah: Its Composition and Final Form*, tr. Millard C. Lind, Hebrew Bible Monographs 46 (Sheffield: Sheffield Phoenix, 2012).

Betz, O., 'φωνή', in *TDNT*, vol. 9, p. 296.

Beuken, Willem A. M., *Jesaja 1–12*, HTKAT (Freiburg: Herder, 2003).

Bevans, Stephen B., *Models of Contextual Theology* (Maryknoll: Orbis, 2002).

Biddle, Mark E., *Deuteronomy*, SHBC (Macon: Smyth & Helwys, 2003).

Birch, Bruce C., 'Moral Agency, Community, and the Character of God in the Hebrew Bible', *Semeia* 66 (1995), pp. 23–41.

Bird, Michael F., *Crossing Over Sea and Land: Jewish Missionary Activity in the Second Temple Period* (Peabody: Hendrickson, 2010).

————, *Jesus and the Origins of the Gentile Mission*, LNTS 331 (London: T&T Clark, 2006).

————, 'The Unity of Luke-Acts in Recent Discussion', *JSNT* 29.4 (2007), pp. 425–448.

Blauw, Johannes, *The Missionary Nature of the Church: A Survey of the Biblical Theology of Mission* (London: Lutterworth, 1974).

Blenkinsopp, Joseph, *Ezekiel*, Int (Louisville: John Knox, 1990).

————, *A History of Prophecy in Israel* (Louisville: John Knox, 1996).

————, *Isaiah 1–39*, AB 19 (New York: Doubleday, 2000).

————, *Isaiah 40–55: A New Translation with Introduction and Commentary*, AB 19 (New York: Doubleday, 2002).

————, *Isaiah 56–66*, AB 19B (New York: Doubleday, 2003).

Block, Daniel I., *The Book of Ezekiel: Chapters 1–24*, NICOT (Grand Rapids: Eerdmans, 1998).

————, *The Book of Ezekiel: Chapters 25–48*, NICOT (Grand Rapids: Eerdmans, 1998).

————, *Deuteronomy*, NIVAC (Grand Rapids: Zondervan, 2012).

————, 'How Many Is God? An Investigation into the Meaning of Deuteronomy 6:4–5', *JETS* 47.2 (2004), pp. 193–212.

————, 'The Joy of Worship: The Mosaic Invitation to the Presence of God (Deut 12:1–14)', *BSac* 162.646 (2005), pp. 131–149.

————, 'Marriage and Family in Ancient Israel', in *Marriage and Family in the Biblical World* (Downers Grove: InterVarsity Press, 2003), pp. 33–102.

————, 'The Privilege of Calling: The Mosaic Paradigm for Missions (Deut 26:16–19)', in *How I Love Your Torah, O Lord* (Eugene: Wipf & Stock, 2011), pp. 140–161.

Boadt, Lawrence, 'Do Jeremiah and Ezekiel Share a Common View of the Exile?', in *Uprooting and Planting: Essays on Jeremiah for Leslie Allen*, LHB/OTS 459 (New York: T&T Clark, 2007), pp. 14–31.

Bock, Darrell L., *Acts*, BECNT (Grand Rapids: Baker Academic, 2007).

————, *Luke 1:1–9:50*, BECNT (Grand Rapids: Baker, 1994).

————, *Luke 9:51–24:53*, BECNT (Grand Rapids: Baker, 1996).

————, *Proclamation from Prophecy and Pattern: Lucan Old Testament Christology*, JSNTSup 12 (Sheffield: Sheffield Academic Press, 1987).

————, *A Theology of Luke and Acts* (Grand Rapids: Zondervan, 2012).

Bosch, David J., *Transforming Mission: Paradigm Shifts in Theology of Mission* (Maryknoll: Orbis, 1991).

Botha, P. J., 'The Socio-Cultural Background of Ezekiel 19', *OTE* 12.2 (1999), pp. 249–265.

Bottéro, Jean, *Religion in Ancient Mesopotamia*, tr. Teresa Lavender Fagan (Chicago: University of Chicago Press, 2001).

Botterweck, G. Johannes, Helmer Ringgren and Heinz-Josef Fabry (eds.), *Theological Dictionary of the Old Testament*, tr. David E. Green, 15 vols. (Grand Rapids: Eerdmans, 2006).

Bovon, Francois, *Das Evangelium nach Lukas*, 4 vols., EKK 3 (Zurich: Benziger Verlag, 1989), vol. 1.

Bozak, Barbara A., *Life 'Anew': A Literary-Theological Study of Jer 30–31*, AnBib 122 (Rome: Editrice Pontificio Istituto Biblico, 1991).

Braulik, Georg, 'Law as Gospel: Justification and Pardon According to the Deuteronomic Torah', *Int* 38 (1984), pp. 5–14.

————, *Studien zur Theologie des Deuteronomiums*, SBAB 2 (Stuttgart: Katholisches Bibelwerk, 1988).

————, *The Theology of Deuteronomy: Collected Essays of Georg Braulik, O.S.B*, tr. Ulrika Lindblad (Richland Hills, Tex.: BIBAL, 1994).

Brawley, Robert L., 'Social Identity and the Aim of Accomplished Life in Acts 2', in *Acts and Ethics*, NTM 9 (Sheffield: Sheffield Phoenix, 2005), pp. 16–33.

Briggs, Richard S., 'Speech–Act Theory', in *Words and the Word: Explorations in Biblical Interpretation and Literary Theory* (Nottingham: Apollos, 2008), pp. 75–110.

Brin, Gershon, *Studies in Biblical Law: From the Hebrew Bible to the Dead Sea Scrolls*, JSOTSup 176 (Sheffield: Sheffield Academic Press, 1994).

Brodie, Thomas L., 'Luke–Acts as an Imitation and Emulation of the Elijah–Elisha Narrative', in *New Views on Luke–Acts* (Collegeville: Liturgical Press, 1990), pp. 78–85.

Brosend II, Wm. F., 'The Means of Absent Ends', in *History, Literature and Society in the Book of Acts* (Cambridge: Cambridge University Press, 1996), pp. 348–362.

Brown, Michael L., 'Jewish Interpretations of Isaiah 53', in *The Gospel According to Isaiah 53: Encountering the Suffering Servant in Jewish and Christian Theology* (Grand Rapids: Kregel, 2012), pp. 61–83.

Brown, Rick, 'Contextualization without Syncretism', *IJFM* 23.3 (2006), pp. 127–133.

Brownson, James V., *Speaking the Truth in Love* (Harrisburg: Trinity, 1998).

Brueggemann, Walter, *1 and 2 Kings*, SHBC (Macon: Smyth & Helwys, 2000).

———, *A Commentary on Jeremiah: Exile & Homecoming* (Grand Rapids: Eerdmans, 1998).

———, *Deuteronomy*, AOTC (Nashville: Abingdon, 2001).

———, *Hopeful Imagination: Prophetic Voices in Exile* (Philadelphia: Fortress, 1986).

———, *Isaiah 1–39*, WBC (Louisville: Westminster John Knox, 1998).

———, *Isaiah 40–66*, WBC (Louisville: Westminster John Knox, 1998).

———, *Old Testament Theology: An Introduction*, LBT (Nashville: Abingdon, 2008).

———, *The Theology of the Book of Jeremiah*, OTT (Cambridge: Cambridge University Press, 2007).

———, *Theology of the Old Testament* (Minneapolis: Fortress, 1997).

Byrne, Brendan, *The Hospitality of God: A Reading of Luke's Gospel* (Collegeville: Liturgical Press, 2000).

Cairns, Ian, *Deuteronomy: Word and Presence*, ITC (Grand Rapids: Eerdmans, 1992).

Calvin, John, *Calvin's Commentaries*, tr. John Owen, 22 vols. (Grand Rapids: Baker, 1999), vol. 10.

'The Cape Town Commitment', 2010, <www.lausanne.org/content/ctc/ctcommitment>, accessed 4 July 2016.

Carmichael, Calum, 'The Three Laws on the Release of Slaves', *ZAW* 112 (2000), pp. 507–525.

Carroll, Robert P., *Jeremiah*, OTL (London: SCM, 1986).

Carson, D. A., 'Matthew', in *EBC*, vol. 8 (Grand Rapids: Zondervan, 1984).

Carson, D. A., and Douglas J. Moo, *An Introduction to the New Testament* (Leicester: Apollos, 2005).

Carvalho, Corrine, 'Putting the Mother Back in the Center: Metaphor and Multivalence in Ezekiel 19', in *Thus Says the Lord: Essays on the Former and Latter Prophets in Honor of Robert R. Wilson*, LHB/OTS 502 (New York: T&T Clark, 2009), pp. 208–221.

Cazelles, Henri, 'Jeremiah and Deuteronomy', in *A Prophet to the Nations: Essays in Jeremiah Studies*, tr. Leo G. Perdue (Winona Lake: Eisenbrauns, 1984), pp. 89–111.

Chance, J. Bradley, *Acts*, SHBC (Macon: Smyth & Helwys, 2007).

Charlesworth, James H., *The Old Testament Pseudepigrapha: Vol. 1 & 2*, ed. James H. Charlesworth (Peabody: Hendrickson, 2010).

Chester, Tim, *Good News to the Poor* (Leicester: Inter-Varsity Press, 2004).

Childs, Brevard S., *Biblical Theology: A Proposal* (Minneapolis: Fortress, 2002).

———, *Biblical Theology in Crisis* (Philadelphia: Westminster, 1970).

———, 'The Canon in Recent Biblical Studies: Reflections on an Era', in *Canon and Biblical Interpretation*, Scripture and Hermeneutics 7 (Milton Keynes: Paternoster, 2006), pp. 33–57.

———, 'The Canonical Shape of the Prophetic Literature', in *The Place Is too Small for Us*, Sources for Biblical and Theological Study 5 (Winona Lake: Eisenbrauns, 1995), pp. 513–522.

———, *Introduction to the Old Testament as Scripture* (London: SCM, 1979).

———, *Isaiah*, OTL (Louisville: Westminster John Knox, 2001).

———, *Old Testament Theology in a Canonical Context* (London: SCM, 1985).

Chirichigno, Gregory C., *Debt-Slavery in Israel and the Ancient Near East*, JSOTSup 141 (Sheffield: Sheffield Academic Press, 1993).

Cho, Paul Kang-Kul, and Janling Fu, 'Death and Feasting in the Isaiah Apocalypse (Isaiah 25:6–8)', in *Formation and Intertextuality in Isaiah 24–27* (Atlanta: SBL, 2013), pp. 117–142.

Christensen, Duane L., *Deuteronomy 1:1–21:9*, WBC 6A (Nashville: Thomas Nelson, 2001).

Clements, R. E., *The Book of Deuteronomy: Introduction, Commentary, and Reflections*, NIB 2 (Nashville: Abingdon, 1998).

———, *God's Chosen People: A Theological Interpretation of the Book of Deuteronomy* (London: SCM, 1968).

———, *Jeremiah*, Int (Atlanta: John Knox, 1988).

———, *Prophecy and Covenant* (London: SCM, 1965).

Clines, David J. A., *I, He, We and They: A Literary Approach to Isaiah 53*, JSOTSup 1 (Sheffield: JSOT Press, 1976).

——— (ed.), *The Dictionary of Classical Hebrew*, 8 vols. (Sheffield: Sheffield Academic Press, 1995).

Cohn, Robert L., *The Shape of Sacred Space: Four Biblical Studies*, AARSR 23 (Chico, Calif.: Scholars Press, 1981).

Coleridge, Mark, *The Birth of the Lukan Narrative: Narrative as Christology in Luke 1–2*, JSNTSup 88 (Sheffield: JSOT Press, 1993).

Conn, Harvie M., *Eternal Word and Changing Worlds: Theology, Anthropology, and Mission in Trialogue* (Phillipsburg: P&R, 1984).

Conzelmann, Hans, *An Outline of the Theology of the New Testament*, NTL (London: SCM, 1969).

Cook, Stanley A., *The Laws of Moses and the Code of Hammurabi* (London: Adam and Charles, 1903).

Cook, Stephen L., *Prophecy and Apocalypticism: The Postexilic Social Setting* (Minneapolis: Fortress, 1995).

Cooper, Lamar Eugene, *Ezekiel*, NAC 17 (Nashville: Broadman & Holman, 1994).

Corcoran, Jenny, 'The Alien in Deuteronomy 29 and Today', in *Interpreting Deuteronomy: Issues and Approaches* (Nottingham: Apollos, 2012), pp. 229–239.

Cortez, Marc, 'The Law on Violent Intervention: Deuteronomy 25:11–12 Revisited', *JSOT* 30.3 (2006), pp. 431–447.

Craigie, Peter C., *The Problem of War in the Old Testament* (Grand Rapids: Eerdmans, 1978).

Creach, Jerome F. D., 'Like a Tree Planted by the Temple Stream: The Portrait of the Righteous in Psalm 1:3', *CBQ* 61 (1999), pp. 34–46.

Dahl, Nils A., 'The Story of Abraham in Luke-Acts', in *Studies in Luke-Acts* (Nashville: Abingdon, 1966), pp. 139–158.

Davis, Ellen F., *Swallowing the Scroll: Textuality and the Dynamics of Discourse in Ezekiel's Prophecy*, BLS 21 (Sheffield: Sheffield Academic Press, 1989).

Davy, Timothy James, 'The Book of Job and the Mission of God: An Application of a Missional Hermeneutic to the Book of Job', PhD diss., University of Gloucestershire, 2014.

———, 'Looking for Orphans: Approaches for Understanding the Place of Vulnerable Children in the Old Testament', lecture delivered at the Tyndale Fellowship Quadrennial Conference, July 2016.

Dempsey, Carol J., 'Words of Woe, Visions of Grandeur: A Literary and Hermeneutical Study of Isaiah 24–27', in *Formation and Intertextuality in Isaiah 24–27* (Atlanta: SBL, 2013), pp. 209–225.

Derrett, J. Duncan M., *Law in the New Testament* (London: Darton, Longman & Todd, 1970).

DeYoung, Kevin, and Greg Gilbert, *What Is the Mission of the Church?* (Wheaton: Crossway, 2011).

Dickson, John P., *Mission-Commitment in Ancient Judaism and in the Pauline Communities: The Shape, Extent and Background of Early Christian Mission* (Tübingen: Mohr Siebeck, 2003).

Dillon, Richard J., *From Eye-Witnesses to Ministers of the Word*, AnBib 82 (Rome: Biblical Institute, 1978).

Dim, Emmanuel Uchenna, *The Eschatological Implications of Isa 65 and 66 as the Conclusion of the Book of Isaiah*, Bible in History 3 (Bern: Peter Lang, 2004).

Downey, Glanville, 'Who Is My Neighbour? The Greek and Roman Answer', *ATR* 47 (1965), pp. 3–15.

Draycott, Andy, and Jonathan Rowe (eds.), *Living Witness: Explorations in Missional Ethics* (Nottingham: Apollos, 2012).

Drury, John, *The Parables in the Gospels* (London: SPCK, 1985).

Duguid, Iain M., *Ezekiel*, NIVAC (Grand Rapids: Zondervan, 1999).

———, *Ezekiel and the Leaders of Israel*, VTSup 56 (Leiden: Brill, 1994).

Dumbrell, William J., *The Faith of Israel: A Theological Survey of the Old Testament*, 2nd edn
(Grand Rapids: Baker Academic, 2002).

Dupont, J., 'Ascension du Christ et don de l'Esprit d'après Actes 2:33', in *Christ and Spirit
in the New Testament: Studies in Honour of Charles Francis Digby Moule* (Cambridge:
Cambridge University Press, 1973), pp. 219–228.

———, 'Community of Goods in the Early Church', in *The Salvation of the Gentiles: Studies
in the Acts of the Apostles* (New York: Paulist Press, 1979), pp. 85–102.

Eichrodt, Walther, *Ezekiel: A Commentary*, tr. Cosslett Quin, OTL (London: SCM, 1970).

Ellens, Deborah L., *Women in the Sex Texts of Leviticus and Deuteronomy: A Comparative
Conceptual Analysis* (London: T&T Clark, 2007).

Engelsviken, Tormod, 'Three Missiological Perspectives: What Testimony?',
IRM 95.378–379 (2009), pp. 329–333.

Enns, Peter, *Exodus*, NIVAC (Grand Rapids: Zondervan, 2000).

Enslin, Morton S., 'The Samaritan Ministry and Mission', *HUCA* 51 (1980), pp. 29–38.

Epsztein, Leon, *Social Justice in the Ancient Near East and the People of the Bible*, tr. John
Bowden (London: SCM, 1986).

Escobar, Samuel, *A Time for Mission: The Challenge for Global Christianity* (Leicester:
Inter-Varsity Press, 2003).

Esler, Philip Francis, *Community and Gospel in Luke–Acts: The Social and Political Motivations
of Lucan Theology* (Cambridge: Cambridge University Press, 1987).

Eslinger, Lyle, 'Ezekiel 20 and the Metaphor of Historical Teleology: Concepts of
Biblical History', *JSOT* 81 (1998), pp. 93–125.

Espinoza, Hector, 'The Biblical Mission of the Church in Worship, Witness, and Service',
in *Let the Earth Hear His Voice: International Congress on World Evangelization, Lausanne,
Switzerland* (Minneapolis: World Wide, 1975), pp. 1093–1102.

Evans, Craig A., *Luke*, NIBC 3 (Peabody: Hendrickson, 1990).

———, 'Luke's Use of the Elijah/Elisha Narratives and the Ethic of Election',
JBL 106.1 (1987), pp. 75–83.

Evans, C. F., 'The Central Section of St. Luke's Gospel', in *Studies in the Gospels: Essays
in Memory of R. H. Lightfoot* (Oxford: Blackwell, 1955), pp. 37–53.

Eynde, Sabine van den, 'Interpreting "Can These Bones Come Back to Life?" in Ezekiel
37:3: The Technique of Hiding Knowledge', *OTE* 14.1 (2001), pp. 153–165.

Fabry, H. J., and N. van Meeteren, 'שָׁרְרוּת', in *TDOT*, vol. 4, p. 487.

Fagothey, Austin, *Right and Reason: Ethics in Theory and Practice*, 6th edn (St. Louis: Mosby,
1975).

Falk, Daniel K., 'Jewish Prayer Literature and the Jerusalem Church in Acts', in *The Book
of Acts in Its First Century Setting*, 5 vols. (Grand Rapids: Eerdmans, 1995), vol. 4,
pp. 267–301.

Farris, Stephen, *The Hymns of Luke's Infancy Narratives: Their Origin, Meaning and Significance*, JSNTSup 9 (Sheffield: JSOT Press, 1985).

Feldman, Louis H., *Jew and Gentile in the Ancient World: Attitudes and Interactions from Alexander to Justinian* (Princeton: Princeton University Press, 1993).

Fensham, F. Charles, 'The Curse of the Dry Bones in Ezekiel 37:1–14 Changed to a Blessing of Resurrection', *JNSL* 13 (1987), pp. 59–60.

———, 'Widow, Orphan, and the Poor in Ancient Near Eastern Legal and Wisdom Literature', *JNES* 21.1 (1962), pp. 129–139.

Ferdinando, Keith, 'Mission: A Problem of Definition', *Them* 33.1 (2008), pp. 46–59.

Fewell, Danna Nolan, 'Introduction', in *Reading Between Texts: Intertextuality and the Hebrew Bible*, LCBI (Louisville: Westminster John Knox, 1992), pp. 11–20.

Firth, David G., and H. G. M. Williamson, 'Introduction', in *Interpreting Isaiah: Issues and Approaches* (Nottingham: Apollos, 2009), pp. 15–17.

Fischer, Georg, *Jeremia 1–25*, HTKAT (Freiburg: Herder, 2005).

———, *Jeremia 26–52*, HTKAT (Freiburg: Herder, 2005).

Fishbane, Michael, *Biblical Interpretation in Ancient Israel* (Oxford: Oxford University Press, 1985).

Fitzmyer, Joseph A., *The Acts of the Apostles*, AB 31 (New York: Doubleday, 1998).

———, *The Gospel According to Luke I–IX*, AB 28 (New York: Doubleday, 1981).

———, *The Gospel According to Luke X–XXIV*, AB 28A (New York: Doubleday, 1985).

Flemming, Dean, *Recovering the Full Mission of God: A Biblical Perspective on Being, Doing, and Telling* (Downers Grove: IVP Academic, 2013).

Foster, Benjamin R., 'Social Reform in Ancient Mesopotamia', in *Social Justice in the Ancient World* (Westport, Conn.: Greenwood, 1995), pp. 165–177.

Fox, Michael V., 'The Rhetoric of Ezekiel's Vision of the Valley of the Bones', *HUCA* 51 (1980), pp. 1–15.

Frame, John M., *The Doctrine of the Christian Life* (Phillipsburg: P&R, 2008).

Francis, Pope, *Evangelii gaudium* 193, <http://w2.vatican.va/content/francesco/en/apost_exhortations/documents/papa-francesco_esortazione-ap_20131124_evangelii-gaudium.html>, accessed 5 January 2017.

Fretheim, Terence E., *Jeremiah*, SHBC (Macon: Smyth & Helwys, 2002).

Fuhrmann, Justin M., 'Deuteronomy 6–8 and the History of Interpretation: An Exposition on the First Two Commandments', *JETS* 53.1 (2010), pp. 37–63.

Furnish, Victor Paul, *The Love Command in the New Testament*, NTL (London: SCM, 1973).

Gadamer, Hans-Georg, *Philosophical Hermeneutics* (Berkeley: University of California Press, 1977).

———, *Truth and Method* (London: Sheed & Ward, 1975).

Gaffin, Richard B., 'The Redemptive-Historical View', in *Biblical Hermeneutics: Five Views* (Downers Grove: InterVarsity Press, 2012), pp. 89–110.

Galambush, Julie, *Jerusalem in the Book of Ezekiel: The City as Yahweh's Wife*, SBLDS 130
      (Atlanta: Scholars Press, 1992).
Garland, David E., *Luke*, ECNT 3 (Grand Rapids: Zondervan, 2011).
Garner, David B., 'High Stakes: Insider Movement Hermeneutics and the Gospel',
      Them 37.2 (2012), pp. 249–274.
Garr, W. Randall, *In His Own Image: Humanity, Divinity, and Monotheism*, Culture and
      History of the Ancient Near East 15 (Leiden: Brill, 2003).
Gaventa, Beverly Roberts, *Acts*, ANTC (Nashville: Abingdon, 2003).
Gehring, Roger, *House Church and Mission* (Peabody: Hendrickson, 2004).
Gentry, Peter J., and Stephen J. Wellum, *Kingdom Through Covenant* (Wheaton: Crossway,
      2012).
Gerhardsson, Birger, 'Einige Bemerkungen zu Apg 4,32', *ST* 24 (1970), pp. 142–149.
Gilbert, Gary, 'From Eschatology to Imperialism: Mapping the Territory of
      Acts 2', in *The Gospels According to Michael Goulder* (Harrisburg: Trinity, 2002),
      pp. 84–110.
Gile, Jason, 'Ezekiel 16 and the Song of Moses: A Prophetic Transformation?',
      JBL 130.1 (2011), pp. 87–108.
Gladson, Jerry A., 'Jeremiah 17:19–27: A Rewriting of the Sinaitic Code?', *CBQ* 62
      (2000), pp. 33–40.
Glanville, Mark, 'A Missional Reading of Deuteronomy', in *Reading the Bible Missionally*
      (Grand Rapids: Eerdmans, 2016), pp. 124–150.
Gnuse, Robert Karl, *No Other Gods: Emergent Monotheism in Israel*, JSOTSup 241 (Sheffield:
      Sheffield Academic Press, 1997).
Goheen, Michael W., 'Continuing Steps Toward a Missional Hermeneutic', *Fideles* 3
      (2008), pp. 49–99.
———, *Introducing Christian Mission Today: Scripture, History and Issues* (Downers Grove:
      InterVarsity Press, 2014).
———, *A Light to the Nations: The Missional Church and the Biblical Story* (Grand Rapids:
      Baker Academic, 2011).
———, 'Nourishing Our Missional Identity: Worship and the Mission of God's People',
      in David J. Cohen and Mikael C. Parsons (eds.), *In Praise of Worship: An Exploration
      of Text and Practice* (Eugene: Wipf & Stock, 2010), pp. 32–53.
Goldingay, John, *Old Testament Theology*, 3 vols. (Downers Grove: InterVarsity Press
      Academic, 2003), vol. 3.
Gooding, David, *According to Luke: A New Expostion of the Third Gospel* (Leicester: Inter-
      Varsity Press, 1987).
———, *True to the Faith: A Fresh Approach to the Acts of the Apostles* (London: Hodder &
      Stoughton, 1990).
Goodman, Martin, *Mission and Conversion: Proselytizing in the Religious History of the Roman
      Empire*, new edition (Oxford: Clarendon, 1995).

Gossai, Hemchand, *Justice, Righteousness and the Social Critique of the Eighth-Century Prophets*, AUS 7.141 (New York: Peter Lang, 1993).

Gottwald, Norman K., 'Two Models for the Origins of Ancient Israel: Social Revolution or Frontier Development', in H. B. Huffmon, F. A. Spina and A. R. W. Green (eds.), *The Quest for the Kingdom of God: Studies in Honor of George E. Mendenhall* (Winona Lake: Eisenbrauns, 1983), pp. 5–24.

Goulder, Michael D., *Psalms of Asaph and the Pentateuch*, Studies in the Psalter 3 (Sheffield: Sheffield Academic Press, 1996).

Graham, Billy, 'Why Lausanne', in *Let the Earth Hear His Voice: International Congress on World Evangelization, Lausanne, Switzerland* (Minneapolis: World Wide, 1975), pp. 22–36.

Green, Chris, *The Word of His Grace: A Guide to Teaching and Preaching from Acts* (Leicester: Inter-Varsity Press, 2005).

Green, Joel B., '"In Our Own Languages": Pentecost, Babel, and the Shaping of Christian Community in Acts 2:1–13', in *The Word Leaps the Gap: Essays on Scripture and Theology in Honor of Richard B. Hays* (Grand Rapids: Eerdmans, 2008), pp. 198–213.

———, *The Theology of the Gospel of Luke*, New Testament Theology (Cambridge: Cambridge University Press, 1995).

Greenberg, Moshe, *Ezekiel 1–20*, AB 22 (New York: Doubleday, 1983).

———, *Ezekiel 21–37*, AB 23 (New Haven: Yale University Press, 2007).

———, 'Some Postulates of Biblical Criminal Law', in *A Song of Power and the Power of Song: Essays on the Book of Deuteronomy*, Sources for Biblical and Theological Study 3 (Winona Lake: Eisenbrauns, 1993), pp. 283–300.

Greene, Mark, *Fruitfulness on the Frontline: Making a Difference Where You Are* (Nottingham: Inter-Varsity Press, 2014).

Gregory, Andrew, 'The Reception of Luke and Acts and the Unity of Luke-Acts', *JSNT* 29.4 (2007), pp. 459–472.

Grimme, H., *The Law of Hammurabi and Moses*, tr. W. T. Pilter (London: SPCK, 1907).

Guder, Darrell L., *Called to Witness: Doing Missional Theology* (Grand Rapids: Eerdmans, 2015).

———, 'Missional Hermeneutics: The Missional Authority of Scripture – Interpreting Scripture as Missional Formation', *Mission Focus: Annual Review* 15 (2007), pp. 106–121.

——— (ed.), *Missional Church: A Vision for the Sending of the Church in North America* (Grand Rapids: Eerdmans, 1998).

Gutiérrez, Gustavo, *A Theology of Liberation: History, Politics and Salvation* (Maryknoll: Orbis, 1973).

Haenchen, Ernst, *The Acts of the Apostles* (Westminster: Philadelphia, 1971).

Hägglund, Fredrik, *Isaiah 53 in the Light of Homecoming After Exile*, FZAT 2.31 (Tübingen: Mohr Siebeck, 2008).

Hahn, Scott W., 'Canon, Cult and Covenant: The Promise of Liturgical Hermeneutics', in *Canon and Biblical Interpretation*, Scripture and Hermeneutics 7 (Milton Keynes: Paternoster, 2006), pp. 207–235.

Hahn, Scott W., and John Sietze Bergsma, 'What Laws Were "Not Good"? A Canonical Approach to the Theological Problem of Ezekiel 20:25–26', *JBL* 123.2 (2004), pp. 201–218.

Hallo, William W. (ed.), *The Context of Scripture*, 3 vols. (Leiden: Brill, 2003), vol. 2.

Hamilton, Jeffries M., *Social Justice and Deuteronomy: The Case of Deuteronomy 15*, SBLDS 136 (Atlanta: Scholars Press, 1992).

Harnack, Adolf, *The Mission and Expansion of Christianity*, 2 vols. (London: Williams and Norgate, 1908).

Harris, R. Laird, Bruce K. Waltke and Gleason L. Archer Jr, *Theological Wordbook of the Old Testament*, 2 vols. (Chicago: Moody, 1980).

Hartstock, Chad, *Sight and Blindness in Luke–Acts: The Use of Physical Features in Characterization*, BIS 94 (Leiden: Brill, 2008).

Hasel, Michael G., *Military Practice and Polemic: Israel's Laws of Warfare in Near Eastern Perspective* (Berrien Springs: Andrews University Press, 2005).

Hauerwas, Stanley, *Character and the Christian Life: A Study in Theological Ethics* (San Antonio: Trinity University Press, 1975).

Hayes, Christine E., 'Golden Calf Stories: The Relationship of Exodus 32 and Deuteronomy 9–10', in *The Idea of Biblical Interpretation: Essays in Honor of James L. Kugel* (Leiden: Brill, 2004), pp. 45–93.

Hayman, Peter, 'Monotheism – A Misused Word in Jewish Studies', *JJS* 42 (1991), pp. 1–15.

Hays, Christopher M., *Luke's Wealth Ethics*, WUNT 275 (Tübingen: Mohr Siebeck, 2010).

Hays, Richard B., *Reading Backwards: Figural Christology and the Fourfold Gospel Witness* (London: SPCK, 2015).

Heiser, Michael S., 'Monotheism, Polytheism, Monolatry, or Henotheism? Toward an Assessment of Divine Plurality in the Hebrew Bible', *BBR* 18.1 (2008), pp. 1–30.

Hengel, Martin, *Between Jesus and Paul: Studies in the Earliest History of Christianity* (London: SCM, 1983).

———, *Judaism and Hellenism*, 2 vols. (London: SCM, 1974).

Hesselgrave, David J., 'Will We Correct the Edinburgh Error? Future Mission in Historical Perspective', *SWJT* 49.2 (2007), pp. 121–149.

Hezser, Catherine, *Jewish Slavery in Antiquity* (Oxford: Oxford University Press, 2005).

Hibbard, J. Todd, and Hyun Chul Paul Kim, *Formation and Intertextuality in Isaiah 24–27* (Atlanta: SBL, 2013).

Hiebert, Paul G., 'Conversion, Culture, and Cognitive Categories', *Gospel in Context* 1.4 (1978), pp. 24–29.

Hiers, Richard H., 'Purification of the Temple: Preparation for the Kingdom of God', *JBL* 90 (1971), pp. 82–90.

Hobbs, T. R., 'Hospitality in the First Testament and the "Teleological Fallacy"', *JSOT* 95 (2001), pp. 3–30.

Hoffman, George, 'The Social Responsibilities of Evangelization', in *Let the Earth Hear His Voice: International Congress on World Evangelization, Lausanne, Switzerland* (Minneapolis: World Wide, 1975), pp. 698–709.

Hoffman, Yair, 'The Deuteronomistic Concept of the Herem', *ZAW* 111 (1999), pp. 196–210.

Holladay, William L., *Jeremiah 1*, Hermeneia (Philadelphia: Fortress, 1986).

Hǒlmas, Geir Otto, '"My House Shall Be a House of Prayer": Regarding the Temple as a Place of Prayer in Acts Within the Context of Luke's Apologetical Objective', *JSNT* 27.4 (2005), pp. 393–416.

Horst, Pieter W. van der, 'Hellenistic Parallels to the Acts of the Apostles', *JSNT* 25 (1985), pp. 49–60.

Horton, Michael S., *Covenant and Eschatology: The Divine Drama* (Louisville: Westminster John Knox, 2002).

Hrobon, Bohdan, *Ethical Dimension of Cult in the Book of Isaiah*, BZAW 418 (Berlin: de Gruyter, 2010).

Hudson, Neil, *Imagine Church: Releasing Whole Life Disciples* (Nottingham: Inter-Varsity Press, 2012).

Hummel, Horace D., *Ezekiel 1–20*, Concordia (St. Louis: Concordia, 2005).

———, *Ezekiel 21–48*, Concordia (St. Louis: Concordia , 2007).

Hunsberger, George R., 'Mapping the Missional Hermeneutics Conversation', in Michael W. Goheen (ed.), *Reading the Bible Missionally* (Grand Rapids: Eerdmans, 2016), pp. 45–67.

———, 'Proposals for a Missional Hermeneutic: Mapping a Conversation', *Missiology* 39.3 (2011), pp. 309–321.

Hurtado, Larry W., *One God, One Lord: Early Christian Devotion and Ancient Jewish Monotheism* (London: SCM, 1988).

Hvalvik, Reidar, 'In Word and Deed: The Expansion of the Church in the Pre-Constantinian Era', in *The Mission of the Early Church to Jews and Gentiles*, WUNT 127 (Tübingen: Mohr Siebeck, 2000), pp. 265–287.

Hwang, Jerry, *The Rhetoric of Remembrance: An Investigation of the 'Fathers' in Deuteronomy*, Siphrut 8 (Winona Lake: Eisenbrauns, 2012).

Hyatt, J. Philip, 'Jeremiah and Deuteronomy', in *Prophet to the Nations: Essays in Jeremiah Studies* (Winona Lake: Eisenbrauns, 1984), pp. 113–127.

Inch, M. A., 'Ethics', in *Evangelical Dictionary of Theology* (Basingstoke: Marshall, Morgan & Scott, 1984), p. 375.

Jackson, Bernard S., *Essays in Jewish and Comparative Legal History*, SJLA 10 (Leiden: Brill, 1975).

————, 'Revolution in Biblical Law: Some Reflections on the Role of Theory in
    Methodology', *JSS* 50.1 (2005), pp. 83–115.

Janzen, David, *The Necessary King: A Postcolonial Reading of the Deuteronomistic Portrait
    of the Monarchy*, HBM 57 (Sheffield: Sheffield Phoenix, 2013).

Janzen, J. Gerald, 'On the Most Important Word in the Shema (Deuteronomy VI 4–5)',
    VT 37.3 (1987), pp. 280–300.

Jervell, Jacob, *Luke and the People of God: A New Look at Luke-Acts* (Minneapolis:
    Augsburg, 1972).

John Paul II, Pope, *Redemptoris missio* 9, <http://w2.vatican.va/content/john-paul-ii/en/
    encyclicals/documents/hf_jp-ii_enc_07121990_redemptoris-missio.html>, accessed
    5 January 2017.

Johnson, Luke Timothy, *The Acts of the Apostles*, SP 5 (Collegeville: Liturgical Press, 1992).

Josephus, *The Works of Josephus: Complete and Unabridged*, tr. William Whiston (Peabody:
    Hendrickson, 1987).

Jouon, Paul, and T. Muraoka, *A Grammar of Biblical Hebrew*, SubBi 27 (Rome: Editrice
    Pontificio Istituto Biblico, 2006).

Joyce, Paul M., *Divine Initiative and Human Response in Ezekiel*, JSOTSup 51 (Sheffield:
    Sheffield Academic Press, 1989).

————, *Ezekiel: A Commentary*, LHB/OTS 482 (New York: T&T Clark, 2007).

Kaiser Jr, Walter C., 'The Identity and Mission of the "Servant of the Lord"', in *The
    Gospel According to Isaiah 53: Encountering the Suffering Servant in Jewish and Christian
    Theology* (Grand Rapids: Kregel, 2012).

————, *Mission in the Old Testament: Israel as a Light to the Nations* (Grand Rapids: Baker,
    2000).

Kamionkowski, S. Tamar, '"In Your Blood Live" (Ezekiel 16:6)', in *Bringing the Hidden
    to Light: Studies in Honor of Stephen A. Geller* (Winona Lake: Eisenbrauns, 2007),
    pp. 103–113.

Kautzsch, E. (ed.), *Gesenius' Hebrew Grammar*, tr. R. E. Cowley (Mineola, N.Y.: Dover,
    2006).

Keener, Craig S., *Acts 1:1–2:47* (Grand Rapids: Baker, 2012).

————, *Acts: An Exegetical Commentary*, 4 vols. (Grand Rapids: Baker, 2012).

————, *Commentary on the Gospel of Matthew* (Grand Rapids: Eerdmans, 1999).

Keil, C. F., *Biblical Commentary on the Prophecies of Ezekiel*, tr. James Martin, 2 vols.
    (Edinburgh: T&T Clark, 1876), vol. 1.

Keil, C. F., and Delitzsch F., *Biblical Commentary on the Old Testament* (Edinburgh:
    T&T Clark, 1865).

Keller, Timothy, 'Evangelistic Worship', n.p., <http://download.redeemer.com/pdf/
    learn/resources/Evangelistic_Worship-Keller.pdf>, accessed 5 January 2017.

————, *Generous Justice* (London: Hodder & Stoughton, 2010).

————, *Ministries of Mercy: The Call of the Jericho Road*, 2nd edn (Phillipsburg: P&R, 1997).

Kidner, Derek, *Jeremiah* (Downers Grove: IVP Academic, 1987).

Kiel, Micah, 'Did Paul Get Whacked? The Endings of the Sopranos and the Acts of the Apostles', n.p., 2007, <www.sbl-site.org/publications/article.aspx?ArticleId=695>, accessed 7 November 2016.

Kim, Hyun Chul Paul, 'City, Earth, and Empire in Isaiah 24–27', in *Formation and Intertextuality in Isaiah 24–27* (Atlanta: SBL, 2013), pp. 25–48.

Kimball, Charles, 'Jesus' Exposition of Scripture in Luke 4:16–30: An Inquiry in Light of Jewish Hermeneutics', *PRSt* 21 (1994), pp. 179–202.

Kitchen, Kenneth A., *Ancient Orient and Old Testament* (London: Tyndale, 1966).

Kitchen, Kenneth A., and Paul J. N. Lawrence, *Treaty, Law and Covenant in the Ancient Near East*, 3 vols. (Wiesbaden: Harrassowitz, 2012), vol. 3.

Klein, George L., *Zechariah*, NAC 21B (Nashville: B&H, 2008).

Klein, Ralph W., *Ezekiel: The Prophet and His Message* (South Carolina: University of South Carolina Press, 1988).

Kline, Meredith G., *Treaty of the Great King: The Covenant Structure of Deuteronomy* (Grand Rapids: Eerdmans, 1963).

Klingbeil, Gerald A., *Bridging the Gap: Ritual and Ritual Texts in the Bible*, BBRSup 1 (Winona Lake: Eisenbrauns, 2007).

Knight, George A. F., *Isaiah 56–66*, ITC (Grand Rapids: Eerdmans, 1985).

Koch, Klaus, *The Prophets: The Assyrian Period*, 2 vols. (London: SCM, 1982), vol. 1.

———, *The Prophets: The Babylonian and Persian Periods*, 2 vols. (London: SCM, 1983), vol. 2.

Kodell, Jerome, '"The Word of God Grew": The Ecclesial Tendency of Λόγος in Acts 1,7; 12,24; 19,20', *Bib* 55 (1974), pp. 505–519.

Koenig, John, *New Testament Hospitality: Partnership with Strangers As Promise and Mission*, OBT (Philadelphia: Fortress, 1985).

Kohn, Risa Levitt, *A New Heart and a New Soul: Ezekiel, the Exile and the Torah*, JSOTSup 358 (Sheffield: Sheffield Academic Press, 2002).

Kollman, Paul, 'At the Origins of Mission and Missiology: A Study in the Dynamics of Religious Language', *JAAR* 81.1 (2013), pp. 425–458.

Köstenberger, Andreas J., *John*, BECNT (Grand Rapids: Baker, 2004).

Köstenberger, Andreas J., and Peter T. O'Brien, *Salvation to the Ends of the Earth: A Biblical Theology of Mission*, NSBT 11 (Leicester: Apollos, 2001).

Kraemer, Hendrick, *The Christian Message in a Non-Christian World* (London: Edinburgh House, 1938).

Kraus, C. Norman, *The Authentic Witness: Credibility and Authenticity* (Grand Rapids: Eerdmans, 1978).

Kraut, Judah, 'Deciphering the Shema: Staircase Parallelism and the Syntax of Deuteronomy 6:4', *VT* 61.4 (2011), pp. 582–602.

Kutsko, John F., *Between Heaven and Earth: Divine Presence and Absence in the Book of Ezekiel*, Biblical and Judaic Studies 7 (Winona Lake: Eisenbrauns, 2000).

Kuyper, Abraham, *Rooted and Grounded*, tr. Nelson D. Kloosterman (Grand Rapids: Christian's Library, 2013; Kindle edn).

Laato, Antti, *The Servant of YHWH and Cyrus: A Reinterpretation of the Exilic Messianic Programme in Isaiah 40–55*, CBOTS 35 (Stockholm: Almqvist & Wiksell, 1992).

Lalleman, Hetty, *Jeremiah and Lamentations*, TOTC 21 (Nottingham: Inter-Varsity Press; Downers Grove: IVP Academic, 2013).

Langmead, Ross, 'Transformed Relationships: Reconciliation as the Central Model for Mission', *Mission Studies* 25 (2008), pp. 5–20.

Lapsley, Jacqueline E., *Can These Bones Live? The Problem of the Moral Self in the Book of Ezekiel*, BZAW 301 (Berlin: de Gruyter, 2000).

Larkin Jr, William J., 'Mission', *Baker Evangelical Dictionary of Biblical Theology*, <www.biblestudytools.com/dictionaries/bakers-evangelical-dictionary/mission.html>, accessed 18 April 2016.

Launderville, Dale F., *Piety and Politics: The Dynamics of Royal Authority in Homeric Greece, Biblical Israel, and Old Babylonian Mesopotamia* (Grand Rapids: Eerdmans, 2003).

———, *Spirit and Reason: The Embodied Character of Ezekiel's Symbolic Thinking* (Waco: Baylor University Press, 2007).

'The Lausanne Covenant', 1974, <www.lausanne.org/content/covenant/lausanne-covenant>, accessed 4 July 2016.

Leclerc, Thomas L., *Yahweh Is Exalted in Justice: Solidarity and Conflict in Isaiah* (Minneapolis: Fortress, 2001).

Lee, Mark, 'An Evangelical Dialogue on Luke, Salvation and Spirit Baptism', *The Journal of the Society for Pentecostal Studies* 26.1 (2004).

Lee, Stephen, *Creation and Redemption in Isaiah 40–55*, JDDS 2 (Hong Kong: Alliance Bible Seminary, 1995).

Leeuwen, Raymond C. Van, 'What Comes Out of God's Mouth: Theological Wordplay in Deuteronomy 8', *CBQ* 47.1 (1985), pp. 55–57.

Lemaire, Andre, *The Birth of Monotheism: The Rise and Disappearance of Yahwism* (Washington, D.C.: Biblical Archaeological Society, 2007).

Lemke, Werner E., 'Circumcision of the Heart: The Journey of a Biblical Metaphor', in Brent A. Strawn and Nancy R. Bowen (eds.), *A God So Near: Essays on Old Testament Theology in Honor of Patrick D. Miller* (Winona Lake: Eisenbrauns, 2003), pp. 299–319.

Levenson, Jon D., *Theology of the Program of Restoration of Ezekiel 40–48*, HSMS 10 (Missoula: Scholars Press, 1976).

———, 'Zion Traditions', *ABD*, vol. 6 , pp. 1098–1102.

Levinson, Bernard M., 'The Reconceptualization of Kingship in Deuteronomy and the Deuteronomistic History's Transformation of Torah', *VT* 51.4 (2001), pp. 511–534.

Lightfoot, J. B., and J. R. Harmer (tr.), *The Apostolic Fathers*, 2nd edn, repr. (Grand Rapids: Baker, 1989).

Lilley, J. P. U., 'Understanding the Herem', *TynB* 44.1 (1993), pp. 169–177.

Lincicum, David, *Paul and the Early Jewish Encounter with Deuteronomy*, WUNT 284 (Tübingen: Mohr Siebeck, 2010).

Lind, Millard C., 'Monotheism, Power, and Justice: A Study in Isaiah 40–55', *CBQ* 46 (1984), pp. 432–446.

Lindblom, J., *Prophecy in Ancient Israel* (Oxford: Blackwell, 1963).

———, *The Servant Songs in Deutero-Isaiah* (Lund: Gleerup, 1951).

Lindenberger, James M., 'How Much for A Hebrew Slave?', *JBL* 110.3 (1991), pp. 479–498.

Lipka, Hilary B., *Sexual Transgression in the Hebrew Bible*, HBM 7 (Sheffield: Phoenix, 2006).

Loewenberg, Frank M., *From Charity to Social Justice: The Emergence of Communal Institutions for the Support of the Poor in Ancient Judaism* (New Brunswick: Transaction, 2001).

Lohfink, Gerhard, *Jesus and Community: The Social Dimension of the Christian Faith*, tr. John P. Galvin (Philadelphia: Fortress, 1982).

Lohfink, Norbert, 'Distribution of the Functions of Power: The Laws Concerning Public Offices in Deuteronomy 16:18–18:22', in *A Song of Power and the Power of Song: Essays on the Book of Deuteronomy* (Winona Lake: Eisenbrauns, 1993), pp. 336–352.

———, 'Reading Deuteronomy 5 as Narrative', in *A God So Near* (Winona Lake: Eisenbrauns, 2003), pp. 261–281.

———, *Studien zum Deuteronomium und zur deuteronomistischen Literatur I*, SBAB 8 (Stuttgart: Katholisches Bibelwerk, 1990).

———, 'Tora und Gewaltenteilung in den Ämtergesetzen', in *Studien zum Deuteronomium und zur deuteronomistischen Literatur I*, SBAB 8 (Stuttgart: Katholisches Bibelwerk, 1990), pp. 305–323.

Lucas, Ernest, *Ezekiel*, The People's Bible Commentary (Oxford: Bible Reading Fellowship, 2002).

Lüdemann, Gerd, *Early Christianity According to the Traditions in Acts: A Commentary* (London: SCM, 1989).

Lundbom, Jack R., *Deuteronomy: A Commentary* (Grand Rapids: Eerdmans, 2013).

———, *The Hebrew Prophets: An Introduction* (Minneapolis: Fortress, 2010).

———, *Jeremiah 1–20*, AB 21A (New York: Doubleday, 1999).

———, *Jeremiah 21–36*, AB 21B (New York: Doubleday, 2004).

Lust, Johan, 'Ezekiel Salutes Isaiah: Ezekiel 20, 32–44', in *Studies in the Book of Isaiah: Festschrift Willem A. M. Beuken*, BETL 132 (Leuven: Leuven University Press, 1997), pp. 367–382.

———, 'The Sour Grapes: Ezekiel 18', in *Scripture in Transition: Essays on Septuagint, Hebrew Bible, and Dead Sea Scrolls in Honour of Raija Sollamo*, JSJSup 126 (Leiden: Brill, 2008), pp. 223–237.

Luz, Ulrich, *Matthew 1–7: A Commentary*, ed. Helmut Koester, tr. James E. Crouch, Hermeneia (Philadelphia: Augsburg Fortress, 2007).

McBride Jr, S. Dean, 'Polity of the Covenant People: The Book of Deuteronomy',
    Int 41.3 (1987), pp. 229–244.

———, 'The Yoke of the Kingdom: An Exposition of Deuteronomy 6:4–5', *Int* 27
    (1973), pp. 273–306.

McConville, Gordon, *Deuteronomy*, AOTC 5 (Leicester: Apollos, 2002).

———, *Law and Theology in Deuteronomy*, JSOTSup 33 (Sheffield: JSOT Press, 1984).

———, 'Old Testament Laws and Canonical Intentionality', in *Canon and Biblical
    Interpretation*, Scripture and Hermeneutics 7 (Milton Keynes: Paternoster, 2006),
    pp. 259–281.

McCoy, Michael, '"Community": A Postmodern Mission Paradigm?', *JAS* 1.1 (2003),
    pp. 31–45.

MacDonald, Nathan, *Deuteronomy and the Meaning of 'Monotheism'* (Tübingen: Mohr Siebeck,
    2012).

———, *Not Bread Alone: The Uses of Food in the Old Testament* (Oxford: Oxford University
    Press, 2008).

McDonald, Lee M., *The Formation of the Christian Biblical Canon* (Peabody: Hendrickson,
    1995).

MacGavran, Donald A., *Understanding Church Growth* (Grand Rapids: Eerdmans,
    1970).

McKnight, Scot, *A Light Among the Gentiles: Jewish Missionary Activity in the Second Temple
    Period* (Philadelphia: Augsburg Fortress, 1991).

Maddox, Robert, *The Purpose of Luke-Acts* (Edinburgh: T&T Clark, 1982).

Maile, John F., 'The Ascension in Luke–Acts', *TynB* 37 (1986), pp. 29–59.

Malchow, Bruce V., *Social Justice in the Hebrew Bible* (Collegeville: Liturgical Press, 1996).

Malherbe, Abraham J., *Social Aspects of Early Christianity* (Philadelphia: Fortress, 1983).

Malul, Meir, 'Adoption of Foundlings in the Bible and Mesopotamian Documents:
    A Study of Some Legal Metaphors in Ezekiel 16:1–7', *JSOT* 46.1 (1990), pp. 97–126.

———, *The Comparative Method in Ancient Near Eastern and Biblical Studies*, AOAT 227
    (Neukirchen-Vluyn: Neukirchener Verlag, 1990).

'The Manila Manifesto', 1989, <www.lausanne.org/content/manifesto/the-manila-
    manifesto>, accessed 4 July 2016.

Mann, Thomas W., *Deuteronomy*, WBC (Louisville: Westminster John Knox, 1995).

Manning, Gary T., 'Shepherd, Vine, and Bones: The Use of Ezekiel in the Gospel
    of John', in *After Ezekiel: Essays on the Reception of a Difficult Prophet*, LHB/OTS 535
    (New York: T&T Clark International, 2011), pp. 25–44.

March, W. E., 'Laken: Its Functions and Meanings', in J. Jackson and A. Kessler (eds.),
    Rhetorical Criticism: Essays in Honor of J. Muilenburg (Pittsburgh: Pickwick, 1974),
    pp. 256–286.

Marguerat, Daniel, 'The Enigma of the Silent Closing of Acts', in *Jesus and the Heritage
    of Israel* (Harrisburg: Trinity, 1999), pp. 284–304.

————, 'La Mort d'Ananias et Saphira (Ac 5.1–11) dans la Stratégie Narrative de Luc', *NTS* 39 (1993), pp. 209–226.

Marshall, I. Howard, *Luke: Historian and Theologian* (Grand Rapids: Zondervan, 1971).

————, 'Luke's "Social" Gospel: The Social Theology of Luke-Acts', in *Transforming the World? The Gospel and Social Responsibility* (Nottingham: Apollos, 2009), pp. 112–128.

Marshall, Paul A., Sander Griffioen and Richard J. Mouw (eds.), *Stained Glass: Worldviews and Social Science* (Lanham: University of America Press, 1989).

Martin-Achard, Robert, *A Light to the Nations* (London: Oliver & Boyd, 1962).

Massyngbaerde Ford, J., *My Enemy Is My Guest: Jesus and Violence in Luke* (Maryknoll: Orbis, 1984).

Matthews, Victor H., *The Hebrew Prophets and Their Social World* (Grand Rapids: Baker Academic, 2012).

Matthies, Gordon H., *Ezekiel 18 and the Rhetoric of Moral Discourse*, SBLDS 126 (Atlanta: Scholars Press, 1990).

Mayes, A. D. H., *Deuteronomy*, NCB (London: Oliphants, 1979).

————, 'Deuteronomy 4 and the Literary Criticism of Deuteronomy', *JBL* 100.1 (1981), pp. 23–51.

————, 'Exposition of Deuteronomy 4:25–31', *IBS* 2.2 (1980), pp. 67–83.

Meadors, Edward P., *Idolatry and the Hardening of the Heart: A Study in Biblical Theology* (New York: T&T Clark, 2006).

Mealand, David L., 'Community of Goods and Utopian Allusions in Acts II–IV', *JTS* 28 (1977), pp. 96–99.

Meeks, M. Douglas, 'Being Human in the Market Society', *QR* 21.3 (2001), pp. 254–265.

Mein, Andrew, *Ezekiel and the Ethics of Exile*, OTM (Oxford: Oxford University Press, 2001).

Mendenhall, George E., 'The Suzerainty Treaty Structure: Thirty Years Later', in *Religion and Law: Biblical-Judaic and Islamic Perspectives* (Winona Lake: Eisenbrauns, 1990), pp. 85–100.

Menoud, Philippe H., 'The Acts of the Apostles and the Eucharist', in *Jesus Christ and the Faith: A Collection of Studies by Philippe H. Menoud*, tr. Eunice M. Paul (Pittsburgh: Pickwick, 1978), pp. 84–106.

Menzies, Robert P., *The Development of Early Christian Pneumatology*, JSNTSup 54 (Sheffield: Sheffield Academic Press, 1991).

————, *Empowered for Witness: The Spirit in Luke-Acts* (London: T&T Clark, 2004).

Merrill, Eugene H., *Deuteronomy*, NAC 4 (Nashville: Broadman & Holman, 1992).

————, *Haggai, Zechariah, Malachi – An Exegetical Commentary* (Chicago: Moody, 1994).

Metzger, Bruce M., 'Ancient Astrological Geography and Acts 2:9–11', in *Apostolic History and the Gospel: Biblical and Historical Essays Presented to F. F. Bruce* (Exeter: Paternoster, 1970), pp. 123–133.

Meyers, Carol, *Discovering Eve: Ancient Israelite Women in Context* (Oxford: Oxford University Press, 1988).

'Micah Declaration', 2001, <www.micahnetwork.org/sites/default/files/doc/page/
    mn_integral_mission_declaration_en.pdf>, accessed 4 July 2016.

Miles, Gary B., and Gary Trompf, 'Luke and Antiphon: The Theology of Acts 27–28
    in the Light of Pagan Beliefs About Divine Retribution, Pollution and Shipwreck',
    HTR 69 (1976), pp. 259–267.

Milgrom, Jacob, *Cult and Conscience: The Asham and the Priestly Doctrine of Repentance*, SJLA
    (Leiden: Brill, 1976).

Millar, J. Gary, *Now Choose Life: Theology and Ethics in Deuteronomy*, NSBT 6 (Leicester:
    Apollos, 1998).

Millar, William R., *Isaiah 24–27 and the Origin of Apocalyptic*, HSMS 11 (Missoula: Scholars
    Press, 1976).

Miller, Patrick D., *Deuteronomy*, Int (Louisville: John Knox, 1990).

———, '"Enthroned on the Praises of Israel": The Praise of God in the Old Testament
    Theology', *Int* 39.1 (1985), pp. 5–19.

———, 'God and the Gods: History of Religion as an Approach and Context for Bible
    and Theology', in *Israelite Religion and Biblical Theology: Collected Essays*, JSOTSup 267
    (Sheffield: Sheffield Academic Press, 2000), pp. 365–396.

———, 'Luke 4:16–21', *Int* 29 (1975), pp. 417–421.

———, 'The Way of Torah', in *Israelite Religion and Biblical Theology: Collected Essays*,
    JSOTSup 267 (Sheffield: Sheffield Academic Press, 2000), pp. 497–507.

Minear, Paul S., 'Luke's Use of the Birth Stories', in *Studies in Luke–Acts* (Nashville:
    Abingdon, 1966), pp. 111–130.

Miscall, Peter D., 'Isaiah: New Heavens, New Earth, New Book', in *Reading Between Texts:
    Intertextuality and the Hebrew Bible*, LCBI (Louisville: Westminster John Knox, 1992),
    pp. 41–56.

Miura, Yuzuru, *David in Luke-Acts*, WUNT 232 (Tübingen: Mohr Siebeck, 2007).

Miyamoto, K. C., 'Mission, Liturgy, and the Transformation of Identity', *Mission Studies* 27
    (2010), pp. 56–70.

Moberly, R. W. L., '"Yahweh Is One": The Translation of the Shema', in J. A. Emerton
    (ed.), *Studies in the Pentateuch*, VTSup 41 (Leiden: Brill, 1990), pp. 209–215.

Moltmann, Jürgen, *The Church in the Power of the Spirit* (London: SCM, 1977).

Moon, Joshua N., *Jeremiah's New Covenant: An Augustinian Reading*, JTISup 3 (Winona
    Lake: Eisenbrauns, 2011).

Moor, Johannes C. de, *The Rise of Yahwism: The Roots of Israelite Monotheism*, rev. and
    enlarged edn, BETL 41 (Leuven: Leuven University Press, 1997).

Moore, Thomas S., 'Luke's Use of Isaiah for the Gentile Mission and Jewish
    Rejection Theme in the Third Gospel', PhD diss., Dallas Theological Seminary,
    1995.

Moran, W. L., 'The End of the Unholy War and the Anti-Exodus', *Bib* 44 (1963),
    pp. 333–342.

Moyise, Steve, and Maarten J. J. Menken, 'Introduction', in *Isaiah in the New Testament* (London: T&T Clark, 2005), pp. 1–5.

Myers, Ruth A., 'Unlocking the Power of Worship', *ATR* 92.1 (2010), pp. 55–70.

Nardoni, Enrique, *Rise up, O Judge: A Study of Justice in the Biblical World*, tr. Sean Charles Martin (Peabody: Hendrickson, 2004).

Nasrallah, Laura, 'The Acts of the Apostles, Greek Cities, and Hadrian's Panhellenion', *JBL* 127.3 (2008), pp. 533–566.

Naugle, David K., *Worldview: The History of a Concept* (Grand Rapids: Eerdmans, 2002).

Neill, Stephen, *Creative Tension* (London: Edinburgh House, 1959).

———, *A History of Christian Missions*, rev. edn (Harmondsworth: Penguin, 1986).

Nelson, Richard D., *Deuteronomy*, OTL (Louisville: Westminster John Knox, 2002).

———, 'Ḥerem and the Deuteronomy Social Conscience', in *Deuteronomy and Deuteronomic Literature: Festschrift C. H. W. Brekelmans* (Leuven: Leuven University Press, 1997), pp. 39–54.

Neufeld, E., *The Hittite Laws* (London: Luzac, 1951).

Newbigin, Lesslie, *Foolishness to the Greeks: The Gospel and Western Culture* (London: SPCK, 1986).

———, *The Gospel in a Pluralist Society* (London: SPCK, 1989).

———, *One Body, One Gospel, One World: The Christian Mission Today* (London: IMC, 1958).

———, *The Open Secret: Introduction to the Theology of Mission*, 2nd rev. edn (London: SPCK, 1995).

———, *Trinitarian Doctrine for Today's Mission*, repr. (Edinburgh: Paternoster, 1998).

———, *Truth to Tell: The Gospel as Public Truth* (Grand Rapids: Eerdmans, 1991).

Niditch, Susan, *The Symbolic Vision in Biblical Tradition*, HSMS (Chico, Calif.: Scholars Press, 1983).

———, *War in the Hebrew Bible: A Study in the Ethics of Violence* (Oxford: Oxford University Press, 1993).

Nielsen, Kirsten, *There Is Hope for a Tree: The Tree as Metaphor in Isaiah*, JSOTSup 65 (Sheffield: JSOT Press, 1989).

Niemandt, C. J. P., 'Trends in Missional Ecclesiology', *HTS Theological Studies/Teologiese Studies* 68.1 (2012), n.p., <www.hts.org.za/index.php/HTS/article/viewFile/1198/2353>, accessed 10 December 2012.

Nolland, John, *Luke 1–9:20*, WBC 35a (Dallas: Word, 1989).

———, *Luke 9:21–18:34*, WBC 35b (Dallas: Word, 1993).

North, Christopher R., *The Suffering Servant in Deutero-Isaiah: An Historical and Critical Study* (London: Oxford University Press, 1948).

North, Robert, 'Yahweh's Asherah', in *To Touch the Text: Biblical and Related Studies in Honor of Joseph A. Fitzmyer* (New York: Crossroad, 1989), pp. 118–137.

Noth, Martin, *The History of Israel*, tr. P. M. Ackroyd, 2nd edn (London: Adam and Charles, 1959).

Nouwen, Henri J. M., *Reaching Out: The Three Movements of the Spiritual Life* (London: Collins, 1976).

O'Connell, Robert H., 'Deuteronomy VII 1–26: Asymmetrical Concentricity and the Rhetoric of Conquest', *VT* 42.2 (1992), pp. 248–265.

Odell, Margaret S., *Ezekiel*, SHBC (Macon: Smyth & Helwys, 2005).

O'Dowd, Ryan, *The Wisdom of Torah: Epistemology in Deuteronomy and the Wisdom Literature*, FRLANT 225 (Göttingen: Vandenhoeck & Ruprecht, 2009).

O'Hanlon, John, 'The Story of Zacchaeus and the Lukan Narrative', *JSNT* 12 (1981), pp. 2–26.

Olson, Dennis T., *Deuteronomy and the Death of Moses* (Minneapolis: Fortress, 1994).

Oosthuizen, Martin J., 'Deuteronomy 15:1–18 in Socio-rhetorical Perspective', *ZAR* 3 (1997), pp. 64–91.

Orlinsky, Harry M., *Studies on the Second Part of the Book of Isaiah: The So-Called 'Servant of the Lord' and 'Suffering Servant' in Second Isaiah*, VTSup 14 (Leiden: Brill, 1977).

Oswalt, John N., *The Book of Isaiah: Chapters 1–39*, NICOT (Grand Rapids: Eerdmans, 1986).

————, *Isaiah*, NIVAC (Grand Rapids: Zondervan, 2003).

Otto, Eckhart, 'False Weights in the Scales of Biblical Justice? Different Views of Women from Patriarchal Hierarchy to Religious Equality in the Book of Deuteronomy', in *Gender and Law in the Hebrew Bible and the Ancient Near East*, JSOTSup 262 (Sheffield: Sheffield Academic Press, 1998), pp. 128–146.

Padilla, C. René, 'The Biblical Basis for Social Ethics', in *Transforming the World? The Gospel and Social Responsibility* (Nottingham: Apollos, 2009), pp. 187–204.

————, *How Evangelicals Endorsed Social Responsibility* (Nottingham: Grove, 1985).

————, *Mission Between the Times* (Grand Rapids: Eerdmans, 1985).

Pao, David W., *Acts and the Isaianic New Exodus* (Grand Rapids: Baker Academic, 2000).

Parker, Andrew, 'The Shame We Don't Want to Face: Acts 4:32–5:11', in *Acts in Practice*, Practice Interpretation 2 (Poole: Deo, 2012), pp. 107–112.

Parsons, Mikael C., *Acts*, Paideia Commentaries on the New Testament (Grand Rapids: Baker Academic, 2008).

————, 'The Place of Jerusalem on the Lukan Landscape: An Exercise in Symbolic Cartography', in *Literary Studies in Luke–Acts* (Macon: Mercer University Press, 1998), pp. 155–171.

Patton, Corrine, '"I Myself Gave Them Laws That Were Not Good": Ezekiel 20 and the Exodus Traditions', *JSOT* 69 (1996), pp. 73–90.

Paul, Shalom, *Studies in the Book of the Covenant in the Light of Cuneiform and Biblical Law*, VTSup 18 (Leiden: Brill, 1970).

Pelikan, Jaroslav, *Acts*, BTCB (Grand Rapids: Brazos, 2005).

Penner, Todd, *In Praise of Christian Origins: Stephen and the Hellenists in Lukan Apologetic Historiography*, Emory Studies in Early Christianity 10 (New York: T&T Clark, 2004).

Pervo, Richard I., *Acts*, Hermeneia (Minneapolis: Fortress, 2009).

Peterson, David G., *The Acts of the Apostles*, PNTC (Nottingham: Apollos, 2009).

Peterson, David L., *The Prophetic Literature* (Louisville: Westminster John Knox, 2002).

Phillips, Thomas E. (ed.), *Acts and Ethics*, NTM 9 (Sheffield: Sheffield Phoenix, 2005).

Pilavachi, Mike, *When Necessary Use Words: Changing Lives Through Worship, Justice, and Evangelism* (Ventura, Calif.: Regal, 2006).

Pilgrim, Walter E., *Good News to the Poor: Wealth and Poverty in Luke–Acts* (Minneapolis: Augsburg, 1981).

Plato, *Timaeus and Critias*, tr. Desmond Lee, rev. edn (London: Penguin Classics, 2008).

Pleins, J. David, *The Social Visions of the Hebrew Bible: A Theological Introduction* (Louisville: Westminster John Knox, 2001).

Polan, Gregory J., *In the Ways of Justice Toward Salvation*, AUS 13 (New York: Peter Lang, 1986).

Polaski, Donald C., *Authorizing an End: The Isaiah Apocalypse and Intertextuality* (Leiden: Brill, 2001).

Poulsen, Frederik, *God, His Servant, and the Nations in Isaiah 42:1–9*, FZAT 2.73 (Tübingen: Mohr Siebeck, 2014).

Poythress, Vern S., *Symphonic Theology: The Validity of Multiple Perspectives in Theology* (Grand Rapids: Academie, 1987).

Pressler, Carolyn, 'Sexual Violence and Deuteronomic Law', in *A Feminist Companion to Exodus to Deuteronomy* (Sheffield: Sheffield Academic Press, 1994), pp. 102–112.

———, *The View of Women Found in the Deuteronomic Family Laws*, BZAW 216 (Berlin: de Gruyter, 1993).

Preuss, H. D., 'תּוֹעֵבָה', in *TDOT*, vol. 15, pp. 595–604.

Prinsloo, G. T. M., 'Lions and Vines: The Imagery of Ezekiel 19 in the Light of Ancient Near-Eastern Descriptions and Depictions', *OTE* 12.2 (1999), pp. 339–359.

Pritchard, James B. (ed.), *Ancient Near Eastern Texts Relating to the Old Testament* (Princeton: Princeton University Press, 1950).

Pruitt, Brad A., 'The Sabbatical Year of Release: The Social Location and Practice of Shemittah in Deuteronomy 15:1–18', *RQ* 52.2 (2010), pp. 81–92.

Rad, Gerhard von, 'Grundprobleme einer biblischen Theologie des Alten Testaments', *ThLZ* 68.9/10 (1943), pp. 225–234.

———, *Old Testament Theology*, 2 vols., tr. D. M. G. Stalker, repr. (London: SCM, 1975).

———, *The Problem of the Hexateuch and Other Essays*, tr. E. W. Trueman Dicken (Edinburgh: Oliver & Boyd, 1966).

———, *Studies in Deuteronomy*, trans. D. M. G. Stalker (London: SCM, 1953).

Räisänen, Heikki, *Challenges to Biblical Interpretation: Collected Essays 1991–2001*, BIS (Leiden: Brill, 2001).

Ramsey, George W., *The Quest for the Historical Israel: Reconstructing Israel's Early History* (London: SCM, 1981).

Ravens, David, *Luke and the Restoration of Israel*, JSNTSup 119 (Sheffield: Sheffield Academic Press, 1995).

Rindge, Matthew S., *Jesus' Parable of the Rich Fool: Luke 12:13–34 Among Ancient Conversations on Death and Possessions*, ECL 6 (Atlanta: SBL, 2011).

Robinson, Anthony B., and Robert W. Wall, *Called to Be Church: The Book of Acts for a New Day* (Grand Rapids: Eerdmans, 2006).

Robson, James, *Honey from the Rock: Deuteronomy for the People of God* (Nottingham: Apollos, 2013).

———, *Word and Spirit in Ezekiel*, LHB/OTS 447 (London: T&T Clark, 2006).

Ross, Kenneth R., and David A. Kerr, 'The Commissions After a Century', in *Edinburgh 2010: Missions Then and Now* (Oxford: Regnum, 2009), pp. 307–318.

Roth, S. John, *The Blind, the Lame, and the Poor: Character Types in Luke–Acts*, JSNTSup 144 (Sheffield: Sheffield Academic Press, 1997).

Rowe, C. Kavin, *Early Narrative Christology: The Lord in the Gospel of Luke*, BZNW 139 (Berlin: de Gruyter, 2006).

Rowe, Jonathan, 'What Is Missional Ethics?', in *Living Witness: Explorations in Missional Ethics* (Nottingham: Apollos, 2012), pp. 13–31.

Ruthven, Jon, 'This Is My Covenant with Them: Isaiah 59:19–21 as the Programmatic Prophecy of the New Covenant in the Acts of the Apostles (Part II)', *JPT* 17.2 (2008), pp. 219–237.

Ryken, Leland, James C. Wilhoit and Tremper Longman III, *Dictionary of Biblical Imagery* (Downers Grove: IVP Academic, 1998).

Saggs, H. W. F., *The Encounter with the Divine in Mesopotamia and Israel* (London: Athlone, 1978).

Sailhamer, John H., *The Pentateuch as Narrative* (Grand Rapids: Zondervan, 1992).

Sakenfeld, Katharine Doob, 'Ezekiel 18:25–32', *Int* 32.3 (1978), pp. 295–300.

Salo, Kalervo, *Luke's Treatment of the Law: A Redaction-Critical Investigation*, AASFDHL 57 (Helsinki: Suomalainen Tiedeakatemia, 1991).

Salter, Martin C., *The Power of Pentecost: An Examination of Acts 2:17–21* (Eugene: Resource, 2012).

Sanders, James A., *Canon and Community: A Guide to Canonical Criticism*, repr. (Eugene: Wipf & Stock, 2000).

———, 'The Ethic of Election in Luke's Great Banquet Parable', in *Essays in Old Testament Ethics* (New York: Ktav, 1974), pp. 245–271.

———, *From Sacred Story to Sacred Text* (Philadelphia: Fortress, 1987).

———, *Torah and Canon* (Philadelphia: Fortress, 1972).

Scalise, Charles J., *Hermeneutics as Theological Prolegomena: A Canonical Approach*, SABH 8 (Macon: Mercer University Press, 1994).

Schattauer, Thomas H., 'Liturgical Assembly as the Locus of Mission', in Thomas H. Schattauer (ed.), *Inside Out: Worship in an Age of Mission* (Minneapolis: Fortress, 1999), pp. 1–21.

Scherer, James A., 'Missiology', in *The Encyclopedia of Christianity*, 5 vols. (Grand Rapids: Eerdmans, 2003), vol. 3, pp. 553–557.

Schnabel, Eckhard J., *Acts*, ECNT 5 (Grand Rapids: Zondervan, 2012).

———, *Early Christian Mission*, 2 vols. (Downers Grove: InterVarsity Press, 2005).

Schramm, Brooks, *The Opponents of Third Isaiah: Reconstructing the Cultic History of the Restoration*, JSOTSup 193 (Sheffield: Sheffield Academic Press, 1995).

Schreck, C. J., 'The Nazareth Pericope: Luke 4, 16–30 in Recent Study', in *L'Evangile de Luc* (Leuven: Leuven University Press, 1989), pp. 399–471.

Schreiter, Robert J., 'Reconciliation and Healing as a Paradigm for Mission', in *IRM* 94.372 (2005), pp. 74–83.

Schröter, Jens, *From Jesus to the New Testament: Early Christian Theology and the Origin of the New Testament Canon*, tr. Wayne Coppins, BMSEC (Waco: Baylor University Press, 2013).

Schultz, Richard L., 'Nationalism and Universalism in Isaiah', in *Interpreting Isaiah: Issues and Approaches* (Nottingham: Apollos, 2009), pp. 122–144.

Schwartz, Daniel R., 'Non-Joining Sympathizers (Acts 5,13–14)', *Bib* 64 (1983), pp. 550–555.

Schweizer, Eduard, *The Good News According to Luke* (Atlanta: John Knox, 1984).

Scott, James M., 'Luke's Geographical Horizon', in *The Book of Acts in Its First Century Setting*, 5 vols. (Grand Rapids: Eerdmans, 1994), vol. 2, pp. 483–544.

Seccombe, David P., 'Luke's Vision for the Church', in *A Vision for the Church: Studies in Early Christian Ecclesiology in Honour of J. P. M. Sweet* (Edinburgh: T&T Clark, 1997), pp. 45–63.

———, *Possessions and the Poor in Luke–Acts*, SNTU 6 (Linz: Fuchs, 1982).

Seitz, Christopher R., 'The Canonical Approach and Theological Interpretation', in *Canon and Biblical Interpretation*, Scripture and Hermeneutics 7 (Milton Keynes: Paternoster, 2006), pp. 58–110.

———, 'Ezekiel 37:1–14', *Int* 46 (1992), pp. 53–56.

———, *Isaiah 1–39*, Int (Louisville: John Knox, 1993).

Shead, Andrew G., *A Mouth Full of Fire: The Word of God in the Words of Jeremiah*, NSBT 29 (Downers Grove: Apollos, 2012).

Shields, Mary E., *Circumscribing the Prostitute: The Rhetorics of Intertextuality, Metaphor and Gender in Jeremiah 3.1–4.4*, JSOTSup 387 (London: T&T Clark, 2004).

Silva, Moises, *Biblical Words and Their Meaning: An Introduction to Lexical Semantics*, 2nd edn (Grand Rapids: Zondervan, 1994).

Sire, James, *The Universe Next Door* (Leicester: Inter-Varsity Press, 1988).

Slater, Susan, 'Imagining Arrival: Rhetoric, Reader, and Word of God in Deuteronomy 1–3', in *The Labour of Reading: Desire, Alienation, and Biblical Interpretation*, SBLSS (Atlanta: SBL, 1999), pp. 107–122.

Smith, Gary V., *Isaiah 1–39*, NAC 15A (Nashville: B&H, 2007).

———, *Isaiah 40–66*, NAC 15b (Nashville: B&H, 2009).

Smith, James K. A., *Desiring the Kingdom: Worship, Worldview, and Cultural Formation*, Cultural Liturgies 1 (Grand Rapids: Baker Academic, 2009).

———, *Imagining the Kingdom: How Worship Works*, Cultural Liturgies 2 (Grand Rapids: Baker Academic, 2013).

Smith, Mark S., *The Origins of Biblical Monotheism: Israel's Polytheistic Background and the Ugaritic Texts* (Oxford: Oxford University Press, 2001).

Sneed, Mark, 'Israelite Concern for the Alien, Orphan, and Widow: Altruism or Ideology?', *ZAW* 111 (1999), pp. 498–507.

Sonsino, Rifat, *Motive Clauses in Hebrew Law: Biblical Forms and Near Eastern Parallels*, SBLDS 45 (Chico, Calif.: Scholars Press, 1980).

Spencer, F. Scott, *Journeying Through Acts* (Peabody: Hendrickson, 1994).

Stark, Rodney, *The Rise of Christianity: How the Obscure, Marginal Jesus Movement Became the Dominant Religious Force in the Western World in a Few Centuries* (San Francisco: Harper, 1997).

Stec, David M., *The Targum of Psalms*, 16 vols., ArBib (London: T&T Clark, 2004).

Steele, Francis R., *The Code of Lipit-Ishtar* (Philadelphia: University of Pennsylvania, 1948).

Steiner, Beth, 'Food of the Gods: Canaanite Myths of Divine Banquets and Gardens in Connection with Isaiah 25:6', in *Formation and Intertextuality in Isaiah 24–27* (Atlanta: SBL, 2013), pp. 99–115.

Stern, Philip D., *The Biblical Ḥerem: A Window on Israel's Religious Experience*, BJS 211 (Atlanta: Scholars Press, 1991).

Stiebert, Johanna, 'The Woman Metaphor of Ezekiel 16 and 23', *OTE* 15.1 (2002), pp. 200–208.

Stott, John, and Christopher J. H. Wright, *Christian Mission in the Modern World* (Nottingham: Inter-Varsity Press, 2015).

Strange, Daniel, *'For Their Rock Is Not as Our Rock': An Evangelical Theology of Religions* (Nottingham: Apollos, 2014).

Strauss, Mark L., *The Davidic Messiah in Luke-Acts: The Promise and Its Fulfillment in Lukan Christology*, JSNTSup 110 (Sheffield: Sheffield Academic Press, 1995).

Stuhlmueller, Carroll, *Creative Redemption in Deutero-Isaiah*, AnBib 43 (Rome: Biblical Institute, 1970).

———, 'The Theology of Creation in Second Isaias', *CBQ* 21 (1959), pp. 429–467.

Stulman, Louis, *Jeremiah*, AOTC (Nashville: Abingdon, 2005).

Sunquist, Scott W., *Understanding Christian Mission: Participation in Suffering and Glory* (Grand Rapids: Baker Academic, 2013).

Sweeney, Marvin A., 'Jeremiah's Reflection on the Isaian Royal Promise: Jeremiah 23:1–8 in Context', in *Uprooting and Planting: Essays on Jeremiah for Leslie Allen*, LHB/OTS 459 (New York: T&T Clark, 2007), pp. 308–321.

———, 'The Royal Oracle in Ezekiel 37:15–28: Ezekiel's Reflection on Josiah's Reform', in *Israel's Prophets and Israel's Past: Essays on the Relationship of Prophetic Texts and Israelite*

History in Honor of John H. Hayes, LHB/OTS 446 (New York: T&T Clark, 2006), pp. 239–253.

Talbert, Charles H., *Reading Acts: A Literary and Theological Commentary* (New York: Crossroad, 1997).

———, *Reading Luke: A Literary and Theological Commentary on the Third Gospel* (Macon: Smyth & Helwys, 2002).

Tannehill, Robert C., *The Narrative Unity of Luke–Acts: A Literary Interpretation*, 2 vols. (Minneapolis: Fortress, 1994), vol. 2.

Thiselton, Anthony C., 'Canon, Community and Theological Construction', in *Canon and Biblical Interpretation*, Scripture and Hermeneutics 7 (Milton Keynes: Paternoster, 2006), pp. 1–30.

———, *New Horizons in Hermeneutics* (London: HarperCollins, 1992).

Thompson, J. A., *The Book of Jeremiah*, NICOT (Grand Rapids: Eerdmans, 1980).

———, *Deuteronomy*, TOTC 5 (Leicester: Inter-Varsity Press, 1974).

Tigay, Jeffrey H., *Deuteronomy*, JPS Torah Commentary (Philadelphia: Jewish Publication Society, 1996).

———, 'A Talmudic Parallel to the Petition from Yavneh-Ham', in *Minḥah le-Naḥum*, JSOTSup 154 (Sheffield: Sheffield Academic Press, 1993), pp. 328–333.

Tinker, Melvin, 'The Servant Solution: The Coordination of Evangelism and Social Action', in *Transforming the World? The Gospel and Social Responsibility* (Nottingham: Apollos, 2009), pp. 147–167.

Tomasino, Anthony J., 'Isaiah 1.1–2.4 and 63–66, and the Composition of the Isaianic Corpus', *JSOT* 57 (1993), pp. 81–98.

Toorn, Karel van der, 'Echoes of Judean Necromancy in Isaiah 28,7–22', *ZAW* 100 (1988), pp. 199–217.

———, *Family Religion in Babylonia, Syria and Israel: Continuity and Change in the Forms of Religious Life*, Studies in the History and Culture of the Ancient Near East 7 (Leiden: Brill, 1996).

Topel, L. John, *Children of a Compassionate God: A Theological Exegesis of Luke 6:20–49* (Collegeville: Liturgical Press, 2001).

Trompf, G. W., 'On Why Luke Declined to Recount the Death of Paul: Acts 27–28 and Beyond', in *Luke–Acts: New Perspectives from the SBL Seminar* (New York: Crossroad, 1984), pp. 225–239.

Tsevat, Matitiahu, 'The Basic Meaning of the Biblical Sabbath', in *The Meaning of the Book of Job and Other Biblical Studies: Essays on the Literature and Religion of the Hebrew Bible* (New York: Ktav, 1980), pp. 39–52.

———, 'The Hebrew Slave According to Deuteronomy 15:12–18', *JBL* 113.4 (1994), pp. 587–595.

Tuckett, Christopher M., 'The Parable of the Mustard Seed and the Book of Ezekiel', in *The Book of Ezekiel and Its Influence* (Aldershot: Ashgate, 2007), pp. 87–101.

Tull, Patricia K., *Isaiah 1–39*, SHBC (Macon: Smyth & Helwys, 2010).

Turner, M. M. B., *Power from on High: The Spirit in Israel's Restoration and Witness in Luke–Acts*, JPTSup 9 (Sheffield: Sheffield Academic Press, 1996).

Twelftree, Graham H., *People of the Spirit: Exploring Luke's View of the Church* (London: SPCK, 2009).

Van Houten, Christiana, *The Alien in Israelite Law*, JSOTSup 107 (Sheffield: JSOT Press, 1991).

VanderKam, James, 'Covenant and Pentecost', *CTJ* 37 (2002), pp. 239–254.

VanGemeren, Willem A., *Interpreting the Prophetic Word: An Introduction to the Prophetic Literature of the Old Testament* (Grand Rapids: Zondervan, 1990).

Vanhoozer, Kevin J., *Biblical Narrative in the Philosophy of Paul Ricoeur: A Study in Hermeneutics and Theology* (Cambridge: Cambridge University Press, 1990).

———, *The Drama of Doctrine: A Canonical Linguistic Approach to Christian Theology* (Louisville: Westminster John Knox, 2005).

———, *Is There a Meaning in This Text?* (Leicester: Apollos, 1998).

Varughese, Alex, *Jeremiah 1–25: A Commentary in the Wesleyan Tradition*, NBBC (Kansas: Beacon Hill, 2008).

Verhoef, Pieter A., 'חדשׁ', in *NIDOTTE*, vol. 2, p. 35.

Vermes, Geza, *The Dead Sea Scrolls: Qumran in Perspective* (London: Collins, 1977).

Visser t'Hooft, Willem Adolf, 'The Genesis of the World Council of Churches', in *A History of the Ecumenical Movement 1517–1968* (London: SPCK, 1993), vol. 1, pp. 695–724.

Vos, Geerhardus, 'The Idea of Biblical Theology as a Science and as a Theological Discipline', in *Redemptive History and Biblical Interpretation* (Phillipsburg: P&R, 1980), pp. 3–24.

Vries, S. J. de, 'The Development of the Deuteronomic Promulgation Formula', *Bib* 55 (1974), pp. 301–316.

Wagner, Peter, *Our Kind of People: The Ethical Dimension of Church Growth in America* (Atlanta: John Knox, 1978).

Wall, Robert W., *Acts*, NIB 10 (Nashville: Abingdon, 2002).

———, 'The Canonical View', in *Biblical Hermeneutics: Five Views* (Downers Grove: InterVarsity Press, 2012), pp. 111–130.

———, 'Martha and Mary (Luke 10:38–42) in the Context of a Christian Deuteronomy', *JSNT* 35 (1989), pp. 19–35.

Walls, Andrew, 'The Mission of the Church Today in the Light of Global History', *WW* 20.1 (2000), pp. 17–21.

Walls, Andrew F., 'Proselytes or Converts', <www.earticle.net/FileArticle/200707/633192053164218750.pdf>, accessed 15 September 2014.

Walsh, Brian J., and J. Richard Middleton, *The Transforming Vision: Shaping a Christian World View* (Downers Grove: InterVarsity Press, 1984).

Walton, John H., *Ancient Near Eastern Thought and the Old Testament* (Nottingham: Apollos, 2007).

Walton, Steve, 'Where Does the Beginning of Acts End?', in *The Unity of Luke-Acts* (Leuven: Leuven University Press, 1999), pp. 447–467.

Ward, Timothy, *Word and Supplement: Speech Acts, Biblical Texts, and the Sufficiency of Scripture* (Oxford: Oxford University Press, 2002).

Washington, Harold, 'Lest He Die in Battle and Another Man Take Her: Violence and the Construction of Gender in the Laws of Deuteronomy 20–22', in *Gender and Law in the Hebrew Bible and the Ancient Near East*, JSOTSup 262 (Sheffield: Sheffield Academic Press, 1998), pp. 185–213.

Watson, Francis, *Text and Truth: Redefining Biblical Theology* (Grand Rapids: Eerdmans, 1997).

Watts, John D. W., *Isaiah 1–33*, WBC 24 (Waco: Word, 1985).

———, *Isaiah 34–66*, WBC 25 (Waco: Thomas Nelson, 2005).

Weatherly, Jon A., *Jewish Responsibility for the Death of Jesus in Luke–Acts*, JSNTSup 106 (Sheffield: Sheffield Academic Press, 1994).

Webb, Barry, *The Message of Isaiah*, BST (Leicester: Inter-Varsity Press, 1996).

Weinfeld, Moshe, 'The Ban on the Canaanites in the Biblical Codes and Its Historical Development', in *History and Traditions of Early Israel: Studies Presented to Eduard Nielsen*, VTSup 50 (Leiden: Brill, 1993), pp. 142–160.

———, *Deuteronomy 1–11*, AB 5 (New York: Doubleday, 1991).

———, 'The Origin of the Humanism in Deuteronomy', *JBL* 80 (1961), pp. 241–247.

Wells, Bruce G., 'Sex, Lies, and Virginal Rape: The Slandered Bride and False Accusation in Deuteronomy', *JBL* 124 (2005), pp. 41–72.

Wells, J. B., *God's Holy People: A Theme in Biblical Theology*, JSOTSup 305 (Sheffield: Sheffield Academic Press, 2000).

Wells, Roy D., 'Isaiah as an Exponent of Torah: Isaiah 56:1–8', in *New Visions of Isaiah*, JSOTSup 214 (Sheffield: Sheffield Academic Press, 1996), pp. 140–155.

Wenham, Gordon J., 'Deuteronomy and the Central Sanctuary', *TynB* 22 (1971), pp. 103–118.

Wenk, Matthias, *Community Forming Power: The Socio-Ethical Role of the Spirit in Luke–Acts*, JPTSup 19 (Sheffield: Sheffield Academic Press, 2000).

Wessels, W. J., 'The Fallibility and Future of Leadership According to Jeremiah 23:1–4', *OTE* 6 (1993), pp. 330–338.

Westbrook, Raymond, 'Biblical and Cuneiform Law Codes', *RB* 92.2 (1985), pp. 247–264.

———, 'The Character of Ancient Near Eastern Law', in *A History of Ancient Near Eastern Law*, Handbook of Oriental Studies 72 (Leiden: Brill, 2003), vol. 1, pp. 1–90.

———, 'The Laws of Biblical Israel', in *Law from the Tigris to the Tiber: The Writings of Raymond Westbrook*, 2 vols. (Winona Lake: Eisenbrauns, 2009), vol. 2, pp. 317–340.

———, 'Social Justice in the Ancient Near East', in *Social Justice in the Ancient World* (Westport, Conn.: Greenwood, 1995), pp. 149–163.

Westermann, Claus, *Isaiah 40–66*, OTL (London: SCM, 1969).

Whybray, R. N., *Thanksgiving for a Liberated Prophet: An Interpretation of Isaiah Chapter 53*, JSOTSup 4 (Sheffield: JSOT Press, 1978).

Wildberger, Hans, *Isaiah 1–12: A Commentary*, tr. Thomas H. Trapp (Minneapolis: Fortress, 1991).

———, *Isaiah 13–27: A Continental Commentary*, tr. Thomas H. Trapp (Minneapolis: Fortress, 1997).

———, *Isaiah 28–39: A Continental Commentary*, tr. Thomas H. Trapp (Minneapolis: Fortress, 2002).

Williamson, H. G. M., *He Has Shown You What Is Good: Old Testament Justice* (Cambridge: Lutterworth, 2012).

———, 'Promises, Promises! Some Exegetical Reflections on Isaiah 58', *WW* 19.2 (1999), pp. 153–160.

Willis, John T., 'Yahweh Regenerates His Vineyard: Isaiah 27', in *Formation and Intertextuality in Isaiah 24–27* (Atlanta: SBL, 2013), pp. 201–207.

Willis, Timothy M., '"Eat and Rejoice Before the Lord": The Optimism of Worship in the Deuteronomic Code', in *Worship and the Hebrew Bible: Essays in Honor of John T. Willis*, JSOTSup 284 (Sheffield: Sheffield Academic Press, 1999), pp. 276–294.

Wilson, Stephen G., *The Gentiles and the Gentile Mission in Luke-Acts*, SNTSMS 23 (Cambridge: Cambridge University Press, 1973).

Winter, R. D., 'The Two Structures of God's Redemptive Mission', *Missiology* 2.1 (1974), pp. 121–139.

Witherington III, Ben, *The Acts of the Apostles* (Grand Rapids: Eerdmans, 1998).

Wolff, Hans Walter, *Anthropology of the Old Testament* (London: SCM, 1974).

Wolterstorff, Nicholas, *Reason Within the Bounds of Religion* (Grand Rapids: Eerdmans, 1976).

Woods, Edward J., *Deuteronomy*, TOTC 5 (Nottingham: Inter-Varsity Press, 2011).

Wright, Christopher J. H. *Deuteronomy*, NIBC 4 (Peabody: Hendrickson, 1996).

———, *The Message of Ezekiel*, BST (Leicester: Inter-Varsity Press, 2001).

———, *The Message of Jeremiah*, BST (Nottingham: Inter-Varsity Press, 2014).

———, *The Mission of God: Unlocking the Bible's Grand Narrative* (Downers Grove: InterVarsity Press, 2006).

———, *The Mission of God's People: A Biblical Theology of the Church's Mission* (Grand Rapids: Zondervan, 2010).

———, *Old Testament Ethics for the People of God* (Leicester: Inter-Varsity Press, 2004).

———, '"Prophet to the Nations": Missional Reflections on the Book of Jeremiah', in *A God of Faithfulness: Essays in Honour of J. Gordon McConville on His 60th Birthday*, LHB/OTS 538 (London: T&T Clark, 2011), pp. 112–129.

Wright, David P., *Inventing God's Law: How the Covenant Code of the Bible Used and Revised the Laws of Hammurabi* (Oxford: Oxford University Press, 2009).

Wright, N. T., *Acts for Everyone: Part 1: Chapter 1–12* (London: SPCK, 2008).

————, 'Narrative Theology: The Evangelists' Use of the Old Testament as an Implicit Overarching Narrative', in *Biblical Interpretation and Method: Essays in Honour of John Barton* (Oxford: Oxford University Press, 2013), pp. 189–200.

————, *The New Testament and the People of God*, COQG 1 (London: SPCK, 1992).

————, *Virtue Reborn* (London: SPCK, 2010).

Wright, T. John, 'The Concept of Ruach in Ezekiel 37', in *Seeing Signals, Reading Signs*, JSOTSup 415 (London: T&T Clark, 2004), pp. 142–158.

Yaron, Reuven, *The Laws of Eshnunna*, 2nd edn (Jerusalem: Magnes, 1988).

Zimmerli, Walther, *Ezekiel 1*, Hermeneia (Philadelphia: Fortress, 1979).

————, *Ezekiel 2*, Hermeneia (Philadelphia: Fortress, 1979).

Zwiep, Arie, *The Ascension of the Messiah in Lukan Christology*, NovTSup 87 (Leiden: Brill, 1997).

————, *Judas and the Choice of Matthias* (Tübingen: Mohr Siebeck, 2004).

INDEX OF AUTHORS